The Treaty of Waitangi

The treaty of Waitangi was
signed in 1840 by William Hobson,
representing the British Crown,
and over 500 Maori chiefs.
The British considered that they
had acquired sovereignty over
New Zealand, but to Maori
people the treaty had a very
different significance. Claudia
Orange offers new interpretations
of the treaty in New Zealand
history from 1840 to the present
day.

The Treaty of
WAITANGI

Claudia Orange

Allen & Unwin
Port Nicholson Press
with assistance from the
Historical Publications Branch
Department of Internal Affairs, Wellington

First published in 1987 by Allen & Unwin New Zealand Limited
in association with the Port Nicholson Press, 60 Cambridge Terrace,
Wellington, New Zealand.
Reprinted 1987, 1988 (April, July, August, September)

Allen & Unwin Australia Pty Ltd, NCR House, 8 Napier Street, North
Sydney, NSW 2060, Australia

Unwin Hyman Limited, 40 Museum Street, London WC1, England

Allen & Unwin Inc, 8 Winchester Place, Winchester, Mass., USA

ISBN 086861 634 6 hardback
ISBN 0 86861 427 0 paperback

Cover material reprinted by kind permission of National Archives, Wellington.
Cover: Signatures on the Treaty of Waitangi, from the copy taken to the
East Coast of the North Island.
Designed by Missen & Geard
Typeset in Bembo by Graphicraft Typesetters Ltd, Hong Kong
Printed by Wright and Carman Ltd

CONTENTS

LIST OF MAPS

LIST OF APPENDICES

LIST OF ABBREVIATIONS

AJHR	Appendices to the Journals of the House of Representatives
AJLC	Appendices to the Journals of the Legislative Council
AML	Auckland Institute and Museum Library
APL	Auckland Public Library
APS	Aborigines Protection Society
ATL	Alexander Turnbull Library
AUL	Auckland University Library
AULR	*Auckland University Law Review*
CMS	Church Missionary Society
CO	Colonial Office Papers
GBPD	Great Britain Parliamentary Debates
GBPP	Great Britain Parliamentary Papers
JHR	Journals of the House of Representatives
JLC	Journals of the Legislative Council
JPS	*Journal of the Polynesian Society*
NA	National Archives
NZJH	*New Zealand Journal of History*
NZLJ	*New Zealand Law Journal*
NZLR	*New Zealand Law Reports*
NZPD	New Zealand Parliamentary Debates
NZULR	*New Zealand University Law Review*
VUWLR	*Victoria University of Wellington Law Review*

PREFACE

When I began this study in 1977, Maori and Pakeha opinion on the treaty was clearly divided. There was a substantial gap in understanding and experience between the two races, one that was not explicable in simple terms, nor clarified by any easily accessible publication. As debate on the treaty continued, lack of academic studies on the subject became increasingly irritating. A collection of seminar papers given at Victoria University in 1972 was virtually the only reference to which students or the curious could turn. Peter Adams's 1977 work on British intervention in New Zealand provided some background, but the study concluded in 1847 and the book's orientation precluded an assessment of Maori opinion. Students still looked to Buick's *The Treaty of Waitangi*, published first in 1914. Essentially a compilation of official documents, it had little analysis and a good deal of error. What was needed was a comprehensive history of the treaty's making and subsequent fortunes – the treaty 'on the ground' in New Zealand.

This book is the result. It moves from first contacts between British Crown and Maori people, through the treaty-making and the colonial period, to the colony's fiftieth anniversary in 1890. A final chapter traces events from 1890 to 1987. It is not an analysis of law cases and legislation relating to the treaty, though some of these are discussed briefly where appropriate; nor is it a history of deeply felt tribal experience, of the minutiae of events and institutions involved in the treaty. These histories have yet to be written by Maori and Pakeha scholars. This study is presented as an overview – a springboard for further searching into the treaty's history. Above all, it tries to establish a basis for understanding the divergence of Maori and Pakeha attitudes to Waitangi.

Over the past ten years I have built up many debts. My husband and family have indulged my treaty work beyond the limits of endurance, and I will always be grateful to them. I have been very fortunate in having the perceptive and challenging comment of many fellow historians and specialists who have generously given their time to aid my research and to read either the original PhD thesis or the revised text, and in some cases both. My warmest thanks to Keith Sorrenson, Keith Sinclair, Alan Ward, Judith Binney, John Owens, Mary Boyd, David McIntyre, and especially to Bill Oliver and colleagues at the Dictionary of New Zealand Biography, Wellington. Staff and students of the Auckland University History Department have encouraged and helped in many ways. Ranginui Walker, Pat Hohepa and the staff of the Maori Studies Department at Auckland gave me a grounding in Maori language and studies and to them I am deeply indebted, as I am to my late father, M.V. Bell, who became fluent in Maori before I was born. Numerous friends and colleagues, Maori and Pakeha, have contributed to this work by offering thoughtful advice, shrewd insight and precious pieces of information. To them all, my warmest thanks. As always, libraries and research institutions in New Zealand and in England have been unfailingly supportive. Shelley Carlyle typed the final manuscript, deciphering the text with utmost care and endearing patience. To all who have made this work possible my deepest appreciation.

Claudia Orange
Wellington, 1987

INTRODUCTION

Treaties with indigenous peoples were not unusual in the history of British imperial expansion. Most have been shelved or forgotten, however, whereas the treaty of Waitangi, signed in 1840 by a Crown representative and over 500 chiefs, remains a central issue in New Zealand. This puzzles many New Zealanders; there is as much division over the treaty now as there was in the 1840s, when Governor Robert FitzRoy wrote that 'some persons still affect to deride it; some say it was a deception; and some would unhesitatingly set it aside; while others esteem it highly as a well considered and judicious work, of the utmost importance'.[1]

Confusion surrounded the treaty from the first. The treaty in English ceded to Britain the sovereignty of New Zealand and gave the Crown an exclusive right of pre-emption of such lands as the Maori people wished to sell. In return, the Maori were guaranteed full rights of ownership of their lands, forests, fisheries and other prized possessions. The treaty also promised them the rights and privileges of British subjects, together with assurances of Crown protection. Only thirty-nine chiefs signed this treaty in the English language, however. Most signed a treaty in the Maori language. The text failed to convey the meaning of the English version, and the treaty negotiations did not clarify the difference. Each party to the treaty was left with expectations about the power they would exercise.

Difficulties of interpretation and implementation dogged the colony's early years and were to continue. Questions were raised. What rights did the treaty confer or confirm? What responsibilities did it imply for both contracting parties? Did it apply to all Maori or only to the tribal groups committed by their chief's agreement? The problems were not easy to solve. In the following years it became clear that the treaty contained the seeds of continuing conflict, particularly over land, power and authority.

This study is concerned first with official dealings relating to the treaty, initially with the role of the British government in 1840 but thereafter largely with New Zealand's colonial administration. This concentration on central government is not a comment on the unimportance of provincial, and later local, government; nor does it indicate any lack of awareness of local, group or individual influences. These are all part of the treaty story, but they tend to be subordinate to central government. And it is upon government at the national level that the Maori people have appropriately placed responsibility for working out the treaty.

The second purpose of the book is to show in broad outline the effect of the treaty on the Maori people, particularly in relation to their search for its 'real meaning'. For years Maori have struggled to secure public recognition of rights based on their understanding of the treaty – rights to land, fisheries, and taonga or prized possessions – as well as a degree of genuine autonomy within the mainstream of New Zealand life. But there has seldom been a meeting of minds and hearts between Maori and non-Maori. This is revealed in the treaty's effects on various tribes, in legislation that Maori perceived as seriously infringing treaty rights, in the fortunes of Maori movements that have taken their stand on the treaty, and in the interplay of all these factors.

A great deal of confusion over the treaty arises from the way it has been used to further what the different parties have each considered legitimate interests and to validate certain assumed rights. Europeans, in particular, have shifted their position on the treaty to suit their purposes.

Initially, the treaty cleared away a legal impediment to the assertion of British sovereignty. Crown law experts were aware that, on at least three occasions, British statutes had recorded New Zealand as outside British dominion. In 1835 Britain had also recognised a Maori Declaration of Independence. James Stephen at the Colonial Office considered it wise to make a treaty rather than rely on Cook's 'discovery' or on the contemporary view of native rights at international law, which could have relieved Britain from the necessity of treaty-making.

The treaty was also an answer to contemporary humanitarian interests. At the peak of its activities in the 1830s, the humanitarian movement succeeded in emancipating slaves, in establishing the Aborigines Protection Society and in producing the House of Commons Committee's Report on Aborigines in British settlements. Humanitarians shared a conviction that trusteeship of native races should be complementary to the expanding British Empire. This was expressed in concern to 'protect' native races from the worst effects of uncontrolled European contact – disease, loss of land, degradation, depopulation and ultimately racial extinction. In New Zealand, they hoped to avert this 'fatal impact' to redeem the British record. This 'salvation', however, was not intended to preserve traditional Maori society but ultimately to destroy it and to amalgamate Maori with the settler community. The treaty laid the basis for this amalgamation.

There was a need, too, to secure Maori co-operation as a basis for peaceful European settlement. For some twenty years after the signing in 1840, official commitment to the agreement ensured the reasonably safe existence of a largely unarmed European minority amidst a well-armed Maori majority. Officials found it expedient to reiterate the benefits of the treaty to Maori people and to play down corresponding responsibilities. Europeans generally, however, were not unanimous in accepting the treaty. Some no doubt believed sincerely that justice and the good faith of the Crown required the keeping of treaty promises, but colonists arriving in the country well after 1840 were unlikely to have the same commitment to an agreement in which they had played no part.

Matters came to a head towards the end of the 1850s with the formation of the Maori King movement and the outbreak of fighting in Taranaki. The issues were land, authority and sovereignty. The treaty had given Britain a nominal sovereignty only; it was to the assertion of substantive sovereignty, or absolute supremacy, that the colonial government bent its energies in the 1860s.

Throughout that decade a war of sovereignty was fought on two fronts – on the battlefield and on the floor of the colonial parliament. In the long term the latter was more telling. The sword of war touched only some areas, but the pen of the legislature reached out to all Maori. Twelve thousand miles away, imperial halls of government reverberated with the echoes of this struggle, but the humanitarian impulse that had modified government policy in 1840 was no longer influential. Government thinking now favoured self-government for British colonies.

At the end of the 1860s, as the colonial government assumed full responsibility for Maori affairs, a new translation of the treaty spelt out the official understanding of the agreement: Maori had signed away sovereignty of the country in 1840. There was no cause for them to seek separate institutions and no basis for alleging that their rights under the treaty had been ignored or imperfectly implemented. They had virtually the same rights as Europeans, and in some instances additional rights.

As the structure of a new colonial society emerged rapidly after 1870, the treaty dropped from settler consciousness. It could easily have been ignored by the government too, but difficulties in dealing with the Maori people, especially regarding Maori-owned land, kept it alive. In the 1880s Maori protest based on the treaty forced the government to make a public stand. William Fox, veteran colonial politician, wrote a lengthy exposition on the treaty, refuting the argument that it had been a valid basis for the 1840 assertion of sovereignty and maintaining that the British claim rested on the grounds of Cook's discovery just as surely as did British claims in Australia where no treaty had been made. The statement was indicative of official and public dismissal of the treaty, although it would be 'rediscovered' and again given official prominence as New Zealand moved towards centenary celebrations in 1940.

For Maori, the story of the treaty is different. It is scarcely possible to speak of a single Maori understanding; there was a variety of understandings. In treaty negotiations and in subsequent statements, officials asserted that the treaty was a binding agreement guaranteeing Maori rights. Thus encouraged, Maori in the 1840s began to call upon the treaty to justify claims. There was, however, still a good deal of confusion. A major conference of chiefs, held under government auspices near Auckland in 1860, clarified the treaty's clauses and in a sense served as a Maori 'ratification' of the 1840 agreement. But officials, as in 1840, presented the treaty in a most benevolent light. Maori leaders left the conference believing that their mana was upheld, and that the partnership of races, begun in 1840, might still flourish. They took away other ideas, too, that have survived to the present. One was that the treaty was a covenant in the religious sense, forged between the Crown and the Maori people on the basis of a close personal relationship begun before 1840. This idea, incorporating the 1835 Declaration of Independence and most closely associated with Ngapuhi, gained more widespread acceptance and supported Maori expectations of the treaty as primarily protective.

In the 1870s the treaty became a much debated issue with most tribes. Despite government policies and legal decisions hostile to their rights, Maori continued to believe that some effect could be given to treaty promises. In the 1880s they directed hundreds of petitions at the government and sent two deputations to England. Although the British government made it clear that decision-making rested with the New Zealand government failure to move the latter body turned Maori protest to England and the monarchy again in the twentieth century. Continuing failure has not halted appeals; nor has a lack of success in seeking legal redress stemmed such efforts.

Through the treaty, however, Maori found a union of purpose. In the 1890s the kotahitanga or Maori parliaments were established to complement the Wellington parliament. As they began to falter, however, Young Maori Party leaders fought to secure Maori aspirations by working within the government, a trend followed by Ratana-Labour MPs and other Maori in the twentieth century. Their fight continues for a degree of autonomy, for a fairer share in the nation's decision-making, for land, fishery and other rights under the treaty.

This Maori protest has kept the treaty alive more than any other single factor. It has challenged the long-standing assumption that the treaty forged 'one people' and that New Zealand was a special experiment in relationships between a European and an indigenous people. The treaty has had a modifying influence on official dealings with Maori people, and more generally on public attitudes, but the European record in the last century and a half has shown a determination to dominate. In many respects New Zealand, in spite of the treaty, has been merely a variation in the pattern of colonial domination of indigenous races.

The gap between Maori and European expectations of the treaty remains unbridged.

Chapter One

THE BRITISH CROWN AND THE MAORI PEOPLE

When a representative of the British Crown arrived in New Zealand in 1840 to negotiate with the Maori for the cession of the country, British and Maori were no strangers to each other. Some seventy years of contact preceded the formal climax of treaty-making. After Cook's three exploratory voyages and the establishment of the British penal colony in New South Wales, British frontiers of trade and Christianity advanced to the New Zealand coast. British naval and commercial vessels began to exploit the country's resources, at first occasionally, but more regularly after 1800. While Sydney and Hobart gangs engaged in sealing in the south, British and American sperm whalers frequented the northern harbours to refresh and refit. From the mid-1820s commercial activity turned to timber, flax, shore-whaling, ship-building and general trading.

By the mid-1830s the coast was dotted with semi-permanent trader-settlers. They were a varied set – the adventurers who frequent most frontier societies, a sprinkling of escaped convicts and some Pakeha-Maori (Europeans who had 'gone native'). There were also several missionaries and their families. The Church Missionary Society (CMS) established its first station in the Bay of Islands in 1814, the Wesleyan Missionary Society (WMS) at Whangaroa in 1822, and both expanded north and south in the 1830s. Although 'transients' in thousands had spent short periods on shore, there were only 2,000 'permanent' settlers by 1839, about 1,400 in the North Island and 600 in the South.[1] The hinterland remained virtually unknown to them. The exploitative nature of early commercial activity had left the land relatively untouched; a few traders and missionaries had purchased land to supply essential needs but the acreage was rarely extensive. In the late 1830s, however, several farming ventures suggested the pattern that Europeans would ultimately impose on the land. At the same time, there was a rush of speculative purchases by New South Wales buyers, most of them not taken up and most of dubious legality. These trends gave some forewarning of the impending European struggle to wrest the land from the Maori.

Through written and published accounts, as well as by personal experience, the British knew a good deal about the Maori people by 1840.[2] Observations were limited and often biased, but they formed a basis for understanding a complex people who had lived in New Zealand for more than 1,000 years. Maori society was both homogeneous, with a shared belief system, culture and language, and varied, with strong tribal identity based on kinship. There was a recognised chiefly leadership, partly hereditary, partly ascribed by prowess in battle and ability to support kin. Mana and tapu, central points of Maori belief and behaviour, had to be respected by Europeans to avoid conflict. Ceremonies like the hui, the tangi, the haere mai of welcome, the hongi and the haka were often recognised by newcomers to the country. Just before 1840, Europeans hazarded guesses about the size of the Maori population and differed wildly in their estimates from 90,000 to 200,000.[3]

From the beginning, Maori–European contact was mutually advantageous. Maori wanted trade goods that Europeans could supply: initially substitutes for traditional implements and weapons, then muskets, and later blankets, clothing, tools and luxuries. Europeans needed Maori co-operation to obtain services and provisions and to extract the country's products. By the early 1830s chiefs competed to secure resident Europeans because they brought trade, skills and knowledge to the tribes. For the European trader or missionary, a chief's protection was essential. It was an uneasy balance of interests not always free from violence, but generally it worked.

Maori society underwent substantial change in the seventy years before 1840. Once subsistence cultivators and food-gatherers, the Maori adjusted their living habits, organised their labour resources and cultivated suitable crops to accommodate trade needs. Many learnt to read and write in the Maori language, committed to written form by the missionaries. Some adopted Christianity and many more blended Christian practices into the traditional Maori ritenga or custom. The change was remarkable but in the long term it proved not so much a revolutionary overturning of old ways as selective development by a resilient, adaptable culture.[4]

Change was most evident amongst coastal Maori, especially in the north. For years, they had visited ships, engaged in searching discussions and entertained crews. Some had travelled abroad, serving on ships for up to four years. On their return, they often became intermediaries in the European trade, having acquired some fluency in English (as had other Maori in regular contact with Europeans).[5] Inland tribes, on the other hand, were not much affected by European influence until the 1830s, and some were

7

barely touched even then. For all tribes, the fact that when contact came it involved mainly two peoples – Maori and British – greatly eased communication.

Official British policy towards New Zealand up to the late 1830s exhibited one consistent and fundamental attitude – a reluctance to intervene formally.[6] The Colonial Office preferred to see British interests advanced through non-governmental agents of empire – the traders, missionaries, explorers and adventurers who moved beyond imperial frontiers at their own risk. Yet the Crown admitted a certain responsibility for them, both in supporting their legitimate pursuits and in restraining their excesses; and they felt entitled to call on Crown support for the promotion of honest enterprise. As the New South Wales frontier expanded, Britain was drawn inevitably into New Zealand affairs.

Early New South Wales governors were given a vague jurisdiction over New Zealand, which was seen as potentially useful for resources to support the penal colony. Some took an active interest in developing trade and influence, and in mitigating problems of lawlessness. Phillip King issued orders in 1805 to curb the ill-treatment of Maori on ships operating out of Sydney; five years later, Lachlan Macquarie endeavoured to apply more stringent regulations governing recruitment, wages and maltreatment. These rules were repeated in 1814 when the missionary Thomas Kendall was appointed Justice of the Peace; three Bay of Islands chiefs – Ruatara, Hongi and Korokoro – were vested with authority to implement the orders.[7]

The legality of these orders was doubtful because the country was technically outside British dominion. Moreover, it was virtually impossible to make British subjects answerable under law in Sydney or London for crimes committed in New Zealand. At best, the moves were gestures of goodwill, an indication that the Crown took some responsibility for the actions of British subjects. Since problems of law and order continued, the British government attempted to provide legal remedy with three statutes, passed in 1817, 1823 and 1828. The Acts were no more successful in bringing serious criminals to trial than the previous moves, but they did clarify one matter: they defined New Zealand as 'not within His Majesty's dominions'.[8] This legal recognition of the country as independent territory was to be taken into account by the Colonial Office when it decided to negotiate for a cession of sovereignty in 1840.

Paradoxically, from the time that statutory definition placed New Zealand outside the limits of British dominion, the country was confirmed as a British economic interest. Trade dealings with Pacific-bound shipping out of Australian ports increased steadily and a thriving trans-Tasman trade soon engaged some seventeen ships on a regular basis. The value of New Zealand's exports to New South Wales and Tasmania was never less than £20,000 in the 1830s and reached a high point of £83,470 in 1839. New Zealand's imports were substantial too; valued at over £23,000 in the fifteen months beginning 1 January 1830, they continued to grow.[9] It was not unusual for the Bay of Islands to have some thirty ships at anchor with a complement of about 1,000 men. Several hundred seamen might be ashore at any one time, their carousing and associations with local women leading to regular bouts of fighting, sometimes involving Maori. As shipping increased, the attendant problems grew.[10]

While British interests continued to be predominant, American and French activity increased in the 1830s. The United States, prompted by their whaling and trading interests, began treaty-making in the Pacific in 1826, and in 1839 appointed James Clendon as American consul in New Zealand. In the same year, eighty American whalers frequented New Zealand waters, most of them calling at the Bay of Islands.[11] That year too, Kororareka became the headquarters for the French Catholic mission begun under Bishop Jean Baptiste François Pompallier in the Hokianga in 1838. Unlike the United States, France supported its traders and missionaries by regular naval visits. This increase in French and American activity worried local British traders and missionaries; Britain's earlier freedom of action, based on commercial and maritime supremacy, was contracting. While it was not a decisive factor leading to intervention, French and American expansion could not be ignored.[12]

Maori accepted Americans as first cousins to the British but they had a deep distrust of the French, based on the 1772 massacre of 250 northern Maori when the French retaliated for the slaying of Marion du Fresne and some of his crew. Moreover, Maori had long been encouraged to look to the British Crown for 'protection'. Early New South Wales governors had worked at this. King had invited Maori to confer about the early shipping problems, promising redress for maltreatment,[13] and had sent gifts to the influential northern chief, Te Pahi, who had twice visited New South Wales. King had even taken one of Te Pahi's sons back to England. British traders and travellers likewise hoped that good treatment of the Maori people by officialdom would oblige them to reciprocate. Over the years, lessons in the value of good relationships had been learnt from bitter experience; it paid to be conciliatory. The Crown, therefore, turned a benevolent face to the Maori people.

Crucial in shaping Maori attitudes to the Crown was the missionary activity of New South Wales chaplain Samuel Marsden. On his seven visits to New Zealand, from 1814 to 1839, Marsden promoted the belief that the Crown had a paternal interest in Maori welfare. The 1814 regulations and the 1817 Act were drawn to Maori attention,[14] while the 1823 Act was translated into Maori, facilitating the explanation that Australian courts were empowered to deal with crimes committed by British subjects against Maori people, either within New Zealand or overseas.[15] Resting their confidence in such assurances, Thames Maori in 1820 requested that Britain afford them protection.[16]

Marsden also encouraged Maori to move out of New Zealand. Many chiefs visited him in Sydney, their sons remaining to be educated. A permanent Maori settlement was proposed, but the plan was shelved for lack of suitable coastal land. More importantly, Marsden gave Maori an introduction to government circles in Sydney and in England. Thus the notion of a personal approach to the Crown was established from the earliest years.[17] To see the British monarch became a not unnatural aim, though few Maori succeeded. The most notable to make the journey were Hongi and Waikato, Ngapuhi chiefs who accompanied Kendall to England in 1820. Favoured with an audience by George IV, Hongi returned equipped to initiate a ten-year period of tribal warfare, more violent and destructive than the traditional battles.[18] He also carried back the idea that he had come to some agreement with the King. It was based on no more than the exchange of pleasantries by the two men, but in northern Maori tradition it was understood as a special bond.

Major chiefs near northern harbours were drawn into direct, personal relationships with the Crown through visiting British naval vessels. Te Horeta of Thames, Te Taonui, Nene and Patuone of Hokianga – later all strong government supporters – were involved. Maori believed that their assistance furthered the power and might of Britain. Titore, referring to Britain's past conflict with France, offered to place a tapu on certain forests from which spars could be cut for any future Anglo-French engagement, a commitment which was acknowledged by a letter from the King and the gift of a suit of armour.[19] The reciprocal nature of the naval trade was usually officially recognised by gift-giving. Patuone, for example, received a suit of plate armour from King William IV and a sword from William Hobson, a visiting naval captain.[20]

Maori derived a good deal of prestige from an association of any kind with the British Crown, and Europeans sometimes used this to advantage. Joel Polack, a Bay of Islands trader, claimed that his rank rose 'full five hundred percent' when it was known that he was from London, the kainga (village) of King George, because Maori concluded that he must somehow be related to the monarch 'by blood and marriage' to live in such close proximity. The very personal interest taken in the Crown was also demonstrated in Maori curiosity about the monarch. Was the King a believer? What was the extent of his power?[21]

In oral tradition, too, Maori recalled that the British were the first Europeans to come to New Zealand. Details of Cook's visits were known in the north, at Thames, the Bay of Plenty, Tolaga Bay and in the South Island, information that possibly received wider dispersion through Maori society by ships carrying the published accounts of Cook's voyages, which Maori were sometimes shown.[22] As increasing numbers of Maori travelled outside New Zealand they were impressed by the fact that Britain was the major maritime power.[23] British might had proved itself in defeating France, and Britain had a stable Crown that had not tumbled, as France's had, through several revolutions. From distant shores, as far apart as India, Capetown, North America and, later, Singapore and the East, Maori travellers took home tales of British power.[24] It is hardly surprising, then, that Maori looked to Britain for assistance when circumstances seemed to demand this in the early 1830s.

Two events sparked off Maori appeals to the Crown. The first was a visit from a French naval vessel, *La Favorite*, to the Bay of Islands on 3 October 1831. Two weeks earlier, CMS missionary William Yate and local chief Rewa had returned from Sydney with the rumour that the warship intended to annex New Zealand to France and to avenge the killing of Marion du Fresne and his men in 1772.[25] Several chiefs had discussed a possible 'letter to the King', and when *La Favorite* arrived, local tension was high. Rawiri Taiwhanga, a Christian chief of the Paihia mission, urgently sought permission to hoist a British flag on the mission flagstaff, reasoning that if the French tore it down, the missionaries would be able to appeal to England 'to fight for us'.[26]

The French 'threat' turned out to be harmless, but in the uncertainty thirteen major northern chiefs gathered at Kerikeri to sign a petition to the King. They acknowledged the special trade and missionary contacts with Britain, and requested that the King become a 'friend and the guardian of these islands', preserving them from foreign threat, from the 'teazing of the other tribes', and from the misconduct of British subjects.[27] Immediately after the signing, it became clear to the missionaries that *La Favorite* had no designs on New Zealand, but the petition was allowed to go forward to the authorities. Later, officials found it a useful diplomatic tool, claiming that British intervention was at Maori request, an assertion often repeated and difficult to deny.

A second appeal to the Crown was prompted by the participation of British subjects in the *Elizabeth* affair of 1830. The ship's English captain and crew conspired with Ngati Toa of Kapiti to raid Ngai Tahu of the South Island. Tamaiharanui, the most senior southern chief, was tortured and killed, along with other members of his family. The culprits avoided punishment, partly because of legal uncertainties regarding New South Wales jurisdiction over British subjects in New Zealand. Governor Ralph Darling, appalled at the grisly case and urged on by Marsden, recommended the appointment of a British Resident in New Zealand, preferably supported with a warship.

Marsden predicted an end to New Zealand commerce if the Colonial Office did not act on the recommendation. Two Maori, Ahu, a close relative of Tamaiharanui's, and Whare [Wharepoaka?] from the Bay of Islands had travelled to Sydney to lodge a protest with the governor. Whereas Ahu sought compensation from the British for the murders, Whare was concerned about the wider implications. Northern Maori were disturbed by the alliance of Maori and British force in the *Elizabeth* affair, fearing that it would set a precedent for their enemies seeking to avenge Hongi's raids; already, East Coast tribes were deliberately giving offence by selling to visitors recognisable preserved Ngapuhi heads. Whare reminded officials of the meeting in 1820 when George IV was reputed to have told Hongi and Waikato that Maori and British subjects were not to kill each other. This 'agreement', according to northern Maori, had been violated in the *Elizabeth* affair. Marsden shrewdly picked up this point and, with some exaggeration, claimed that the Maori people at large were looking 'for redress and protection to the British government according to His late Majesty's promise'.[28]

Memorials from merchants, missionaries and individuals, citing the *Elizabeth* affair and seeking British intervention in New Zealand for a variety of reasons, were placed before the British government. In 1832, the decision was finally taken to appoint James Busby as Resident. Humanitarian reasons influenced the timing, but protection of British trade was the decisive factor for the Colonial Office.[29]

When Busby arrived at the Bay of Islands on 5 May 1833, he carried with him the official reply to the 1831 Maori petition. Although the Resident's appointment had not been made in response to that appeal, the New South Wales governor, now Richard Bourke, wanted Busby to use it to maximum effect on his arrival. This was orchestrated with some care. The twenty-two chiefs who gathered at the Paihia mission on 17 May might well have seen the event as indicating British recognition of the Maori people as their equals.[30] Busby landed to a seven-gun salute, made a progress the length of the Paihia settlement, and was finally accorded a traditional Maori welcome. Near the Paihia church a meeting was held. Europeans stood with heads respectfully uncovered as Busby read the 'King's letter' which was then translated into Maori by missionary William Williams. The chiefs were told that the King was pleased that the danger threatening them had passed away (only the Maori version referred to the French 'scare' of 1831), and that he hoped that their trade relationship with Britain would not be disturbed in future. To ensure their protection and the better control of British subjects, Busby, the 'King's man', was sent to be a 'kaiwhakarite', an intermediary between the races. In an accompanying address, Busby supported these sentiments. He pointed out that the King was honouring them (whakarangatiratanga – literally, increasing their chiefly mana) by his appointment, just as similar appointments were made to European states and to America. There was more than a suggestion of ambassadorial representation to an independent country.

Busby concluded his speech with a homily on British history with the intended moral that Maori progress depended on their first listening to the word of God. From this, their land would flourish, and 'ships ... shall bring clothing, and all other things which you desire'.[31] Some of this beneficence made its appearance at the end of the meeting when each of the twenty-two senior chiefs received a blanket and six pounds of tobacco; a feast was held for the 600 or more Maori present, while fifty of the Europeans were entertained by William Williams.[32] On missionary recommendation, the two addresses of the day were printed in Sydney and distributed among northern chiefs, presumably to reinforce the words of the Crown and to disseminate them among a wider audience.[33] Nothing quite like this had happened before, and the attempt to impress the Maori probably had some effect.

At the suggestion of the chiefs, the Resident and his family selected land at Waitangi where building began on a residency. From the beginning, Busby's position was circumscribed. The

Colonial Office had directed that he operate under orders from the governor of New South Wales and be paid from that colony's funds. A somewhat pernickety and troublesome character when his personal interests were affected, Busby clashed with Bourke who was not disposed to work co-operatively with the new Resident. The two men also differed on colonial politics. Busby came from a Tory, free-settler family, whereas Bourke was a Whig and pro-emancipist. There was resentment too in New South Wales that New Zealand had become a tax on that colony's treasury when the country should have been a charge on the British treasury.

Busby's requests for assistance were treated with uncompromising parsimony. The British government declined to support him with a warship stationed permanently in New Zealand, and, as a civilian appointee, Busby was not entitled to troops. Bourke even quibbled about payment for constables. So Busby lacked naval, military and civil backing. His appointment to an independent territory precluded his holding magisterial office; he had no powers of arrest and was unable to take sworn testimony. His role was reduced to that of a mediator and peacemaker in matters affecting British subjects alone, and a kind of race relations conciliator in affairs between Maori and Pakeha.[34]

To achieve his objectives, Busby was directed by Bourke to utilise chiefly authority. He was also to encourage a more settled form of orderly rule and law so that the chiefs might eventually accept responsibility for controlling European behaviour. Missionary support was officially requested to assist the Resident.[35] Other than this, the only backing Busby could hope for was the occasional naval visit. It is not surprising that he failed to meet the needs outlined in missionary and merchant appeals; the Crown, reluctant to be drawn too deeply into New Zealand affairs, had made an appointment that would satisfy no one.

Busby himself was fully aware of the inadequacies of his position. He knew that Bourke disliked him and had been dissatisfied with Britain's limited commitment. Within Busby's first year, Bourke took a strong line. He acted independently by authorising HMS *Alligator* to rescue survivors from the barque, *Harriet*, driven ashore at Cape Egmont in April 1834. Some of the ship's crew had been killed by local Maori and others were being held to ransom, including the wife and two children of a well-known whaler, John Guard. The *Alligator* bombarded several pa, destroyed canoes and killed a number of Maori. Bourke subsequently used the *Harriet* affair to exemplify the deficiencies of the Residency. He reported that Busby was 'ineffectual', which was hardly surprising when the Resident had not been consulted and had no force to hand.[36]

The Secretary of State for Colonies, Lord Glenelg, was unable to determine whether the fault in the *Alligator* affair lay with Busby or in the terms of his appointment, but because neither New Zealand's needs nor Britain's policy had changed, he decided to continue the Residency position. Bourke was given the discretion to replace Busby, but he took no action. He wanted more than just a replacement. He believed that unless a British appointee to New Zealand held judicial authority or was supported by a warship, British law and order would be held in contempt.[37]

The British in New Zealand, were quick to see the shortcomings of the Resident's appointment. Their expectations, raised by the presence of a Crown representative, were soon disappointed by his incapacity to deal with their problems. Faced with brawling, maltreatment of crew or misappropriation of cargo on the ships, and boundary disputes, stock trespass, theft, assault and murder on land, Busby could do little more than arbitrate, sometimes on his own initiative, sometimes with missionary advice or co-operation from local chiefs. The majority of cases were beyond his mandate.[38]

Bourke and his successor, George Gipps, realised the limitations of Busby's jurisdiction, yet they were remarkably unsympathetic to his dilemma. On the rare occasions when justice was done, or seen to be done, Busby was cautioned for acting beyond the limits of his responsibility and was left to stand the costs of his initiatives. For Busby, a 'man of war without guns', it was a thankless position. Although Robert FitzRoy, calling at the Bay of Islands in 1835, sympathised with Busby in his predicament, a later visitor assessed the Resident's ill-defined and unsupported appointment with brief, shrewd insight. Busby simply was not 'devil enough' for a situation which called for a man of some 'nous'.[39]

British subjects became increasingly exasperated. The CMS missionary Thomas Chapman noted that Busby's arrival had greatly encouraged British trade activity because it was 'tantamount ... to a promise of protection to life and property, to such as might become residents in New Zealand'. But, as Chapman lamented, echoing local British opinion: 'where is the increase of protection or rather where is the protection at all?'[40] British subjects at the Bay of Islands petitioned for more effective official support in 1834, 1836 and 1838. Attention was also drawn to the

absence of effective law and order agencies when the 'respectable'
Bay of Islands settlers twice organised themselves into citizen
vigilante groups.[41]

If Europeans had expectations of Busby, Maori, too, anticipated
something from the appointment of a Crown representative. Busby's introduction to Maori society by the English missionaries
was crucial. The missionaries had offered Busby their hospitality,
their network of contacts among northern Maori and, most importantly, their mana, which had been boosted by the beginnings
of Maori conversion in the early 1830s. Busby was also able to
build upon Maori expectations that the Crown, closely associated
by Maori with the English church, took a special interest in the
Maori people. Busby stressed that he would be a facilitator of
European–Maori contacts, a kaiwhakarite, a role for which mission efforts had partially established a precedent. While Busby
moved into a negotiating role at first with missionary help, Maori
seem to have appreciated that the Resident had an identity independent of missionary mana. This was essential, because many
chiefs were neither Christian nor very well disposed to the missionaries; and, from 1838 on, some adopted the Roman Catholic
faith.

Busby's six-year term of office prepared Maori to accept further
British intervention. In small ways Busby appeared helpful.
Northern Maori appealed directly to him on a number of occa-
sions to provide redress, especially when problems involved
Europeans.[42] In a case of theft in the Kawakawa area, for instance,
the chief Mauparama called on Busby to settle the dispute as the
King's 'Kaiwhakarite'. In the Hokianga, the chiefs Nene, Taonui,
Pi, Moetara and Haimona Pita pledged their co-operation with the
King's 'Rite'. Nene approached Busby with a complaint of European intimidation, and Taonui, refraining from the customary utu
or compensation for cattle trespass, sought Busby's advice and
finally requested documentary authority to enforce his point with
the offending Europeans. In the Kaipara, Busby established connections with Tirarau and Mate, in the central hinterland with
Hau and a group that had close mission associations at Waimate,
and in the northern Bay of Islands with Hemi Kepa Tupe and
others. In the vital Bay of Islands area itself, Titore proved most
co-operative in Busby's first years. After his death, Busby dealt
with Tareha, Rewa and Hakiro. Pomare had adopted a fairly
neutral stance towards the Resident from the beginning, possibly
because of Busby's relationship with Titore, to whom Pomare
had lost Kororareka in 1830 inter-hapu fighting. Nevertheless,
Pomare also called on Busby to negotiate, in a case of theft by a

European, referring to the Resident as the 'Tahuhu'. The tahuhu was the ridge-pole that held the Maori house together; this was a subtle metaphor which would gain significance in the crises of the late 1850s.[43] Its use in the 1830s suggests a Maori acceptance of Busby's role as a middle-man, a conciliator in relationships between the races. And if his record in controlling British nationals was not as satisfactory as some Maori wished, this would later be persuasive in their acceptance of more formal methods of political control.

While northern Maori were mainly concerned in Busby's early years to settle disputes with Europeans, by 1838 there were new problems. Papahia and other northern Hokianga Maori had become involved with the newly arrived Roman Catholic Bishop Pompallier. The chief and his tribe were subjected to a kind of sectarian harassment by tribes associated with the Protestant missions. Papahia appealed to Busby, who assured him that affiliation with the newcomers in no way affected his relationship with the Crown.[44] Land speculators from New South Wales also began to exert pressure on northern Maori, and just before 1840 Busby received a number of appeals from chiefs who were anxious to secure their land title. Hau was concerned that tribal land had been sold by an individual Maori; Tupe and others requested that land between Matauri and Whangaroa would be left untouched; and in the Mahurangi area, where Ngapuhi and Hauraki Gulf Maori interests overlapped, Herua expressed his fears that Pomare might use his powerful position in the Bay of Islands to effect a sale.[45]

Although such appeals might have been encouraged by local missionaries, Maori themselves seemed to be increasingly aware that the Crown alone possessed the kind of authority capable of controlling new and essentially temporal difficulties. Maori concern about land in 1838 and 1839, for example, seemed to indicate a predisposition to accept a greater regulation of Maori–European affairs. One chief, Wakena Rukaruka, put this explicitly to Busby: chiefly rank was not always an advantage in negotiations, since in certain situations a chief would be lowering his prestige if he initiated discussions with another tribe. Such circumstances, in Wakena's opinion, were ideally suited for the intermediary role of the Resident.[46] It was a pointer to the future.

Busby's official reports created two somewhat erroneous impressions. The first was that Busby was a weak character; his own admission of helplessness left him open to this attack. The second was that New Zealand affairs were out of control, that there was a 'state of anarchy' in the 1830s. If Busby meant a lack of strong, central government, this was true, but contemporaries in England construed it as a widespread breakdown of law and order. Despite settler memorials to the British government and formation of protection societies, it is the more remarkable that, without any regular form of government, general business and European–Maori relationships fared as well as they did. This surprised the naval-trained FitzRoy during his stay in 1835, and it impressed Anglican Bishop William Broughton of New South Wales on his visit in 1839. As on any imperial frontier, the possibility of violence was never entirely absent, but Busby's position at Waitangi was only twice threatened, once in 1834 when burglary was attempted and again in 1836 when two Maori groups forsook negotiation to brawl on the Residency lawn. Busby used both occasions to seek stronger backing, but privately confessed that he considered New Zealand the 'safest country in the world', certainly more secure than the Australian bush.[47]

The most certain indicators of European confidence in New Zealand in the late 1830s are provided by the shipping numbers for the Bay of Islands and the trade statistics for the whole country. These show a steady growth and diversification of activity.[48] Together with increasing investment by New South Wales speculators in Maori land, they indicate a situation in which Europeans could operate with reasonable safety. As contacts between the races multiplied in the 1830s, Europeans and Maori were forced into a workable accord to further mutual interests. Petitions publicising the lack of government and Busby's 'failure' should be recognised less as an indictment of the Resident's performance than as pressure on the British government for further commitment. Likewise, Busby's reports should be judged as the efforts of a man who had a vested interest in encouraging more decisive moves by the Crown. Had Busby seemed too successful at his job there would have been little cause to justify further British intervention; it was the very weakness of the Resident's position that opened the way for the next intrusion. But before that happened, Busby tried an alternative – the creation of an independent Maori government.

Chapter Two

MAORI SOVEREIGNTY AND ITS DEMISE

When Busby took up his appointment, Governor Bourke instructed him to direct Maori people, if possible, 'towards a settled form of government and ... some system of jurisprudence'. It would be a 'more efficient' means of achieving law and order for all persons in the country than anything else he could suggest', added Bourke.[1] Busby himself was convinced that only the exercise of a 'collective' Maori sovereignty could put a stop to inter-tribal warfare: 'I am resolved to lend the whole strength of my mind to effect this object ... and it is probable that the surest method of commanding success is if possible to discover a case in which such a union would prove to their [Maori] advantage, and to give it the appearance of originating with themselves.' Busby found such a case in the need for a national flag.[2]

From 1829, ships built in New Zealand had sailed without a register. They did not qualify to fly the British ensign, nor carry a British register, because New Zealand was technically independent territory; in the absence of an acknowledged national flag the ships became liable to seizure. With an increase in the number of New Zealand-built ships and in trans-Tasman trade, some arrangement was needed. This had been emphasised at Sydney, in November 1830, by the seizure of the Hokianga-built *Sir George Murray* and the impounding of her cargo. The fact that the ship carried two leading chiefs, almost certainly Patuone and Taonui, had angered Maori, who interpreted the incident as an insult to their mana. When Busby arrived in New Zealand, two other Hokianga ships were awaiting registration.[3]

Busby shrewdly perceived that settlement of the registration question might also provide an opportunity to create an embryonic Maori government. He proposed that the acknowledged chiefs of the district where a ship was built should provide it with a register which the Resident would certify. He would grant his certification, however, only if two-thirds of the chiefs at his inaugural meeting agreed on a flag, and petitioned the King that their flag be respected. On this basis, he hoped subsequently to persuade the chiefs into acting in a 'collective capacity' as a 'tribunal', thereby establishing a government of confederated chiefs. There was also talk of a Parliament House, and a passport system that included deportation of undesirable Europeans, but Bourke favoured neither.[4] Ten months after Busby's arrival only the suggestion of the flag had been implemented.

On 20 March 1834, at Busby's invitation, some twenty-five northern chiefs assembled with their followers in a large tent specially erected on the Waitangi lawn in front of the newly completed Residency. Out of a choice of three flags, brought from Sydney by HMS *Alligator* and displayed on short poles, the chiefs voted for a national flag of white with a red Saint George's cross and, in the upper corner on the left side, a blue field with a red cross and four white stars. The flag was immediately hoisted with the British flag alongside it, cheered by some fifty invited Europeans, and honoured with a twenty-one-gun salute by the man of war. It was later gazetted in Sydney, and the Admiralty directed its naval vessels to acknowledge the flag and respect the Maori registers.[5] A number of ships subsequently flew under the flag, although in lieu of the proposed registers they carried a 'certificate of registration' from Busby.[6] At Australian ports they were accorded the same duty-free entry as British and colonial vessels.[7]

Busby, the missionaries and the *Alligator*'s crew had taken considerable trouble to make the presentation of the flag an impressive event.[8] But the Maori present – a wider selection of northern chiefs than the handful who had signed the 1831 petition – may have been somewhat disappointed at the way proceedings were handled. Busby, determined to press the business to a successful conclusion, lectured the chiefs on the 'advantages' of the flag, and gave them no chance to discuss the matter before voting.[9] The final vote was split. Two abstained because they were 'apprehensive lest under this ceremony lay hid some sinister design'. Others, excluded from voting because Busby considered their rank too inferior, expressed 'no small discontent'; one group remained after the voting to engage in 'warlike' and 'wordy' debate, preferring to abstain from Busby's celebration feast. This was served apart from the 'collation' for Europeans, despite Busby's inaugural speech the previous May which had stressed Maori equality.[10] Only one chief, Pomare, succeeded in drawing attention to the inconsistencies of European attitudes: he deliberately arrived late and waited to be fittingly received in the traditional manner. He also objected to his followers being disarmed: carrying weapons was customary, akin to the right of the *Alligator*'s officers ('rangatira') to wear swords.[11]

Although the flag was given a somewhat mixed reception, its long-term significance lay in Maori understanding of the event: the belief that the mana of New Zealand, closely associated with the mana of chiefs, had been recognised by the British Crown. New Zealand-built ships, carrying the national flag, were tangible evidence of this; so, too, was duty-free entry of produce and cargo at Australian ports, a point that trade-seasoned northern Maori would hardly overlook. The significance of the flag was also increased by its use on shore. In 1835 Robert FitzRoy (a visiting naval captain and later governor) saw it flying at the Bay of Islands, probably before the trading depot of Gilbert Mair at Te Wahapu. A year or so later, traveller John Bright noted that it flew on a 'rocky outcrop', not far from Waitangi.[12] The flag identified New Zealand as a separate country, yet associated it with Britain, known by Maori to be the world's most powerful nation. Northern Maori absorbed the flag into their oral tradition, possibly regarding it as a special rahui or protection of their identity. As New Zealand ships developed a thriving coastal trade in the 1830s, the flag probably became familiar in other areas.

Busby's hopes that his conference of chiefs might lead to a government of confederated chiefs came to nothing. But another opportunity arose when it became known that a Frenchman, Baron de Thierry, was planning to establish a 'sovereign and independent state' on some Hokianga land which he claimed to have purchased. Busby thought that de Thierry was probably a madman, but could not entirely dismiss the possibility that the Frenchman, supported by a bodyguard of Maori trained in Tahiti, might establish a power base in New Zealand in co-operation with one or other tribal groups. This would lead to tribal unrest or even inter-tribal war.[13] He quickly alerted British subjects to the potential danger, and called a meeting of thirty-four chiefs on 28 October 1835. He persuaded them to sign a Declaration of Independence (He whakaputanga o te Rangatiratanga o Nu Tirene), asking King William IV 'to be the parent of their infant state ... its protector from all attempts upon its independence'. The signatories designated themselves the United Tribes of New Zealand, and pledged to assemble at an annual Waitangi congress where they could frame laws for the promotion of peace, justice and trade.[14]

This Declaration was acknowledged by the Colonial Office with the assurance that the King would protect the Maori people as long as it was 'consistent with a due regard to the just rights of others and to the interests of His Majesty's subjects'.[15] The reply was given apparently without much thought for the legal consequences. If Britain chose to intervene formally, the independent status of the country would have to be either qualified or nullified. Like Busby, the Colonial Office may have reasoned that, rather than compromising Britain's position, these moves gave her a prior advantage: 'the establishment of the independence of the country under the protection of the British Government would be the most effectual mode of making the country a dependency of the British Empire in everything but the name'. With the backing of a military force, Britain could control Maori government and law-making, and a British Protectorate would evolve.[16] Busby privately enthused about the 1835 moves; the Declaration was the 'Magna Charta of New Zealand'.[17] Bourke and his council commended Busby for his initiative in creating an 'approach' to a regular form of government; the action was exactly what Bourke had suggested originally.

De Thierry did not arrive in New Zealand until late October 1837, and concern about him ebbed. Ever present inter-hapu and inter-tribal tensions took precedence over political co-operation. Busby decided to abandon his original plan of seeking a country-wide adherence of chiefs; the winter of 1836 made travel difficult and no permission had been received from Bourke. By the time Glenelg's acceptance of the Declaration arrived, the north was disturbed again by tribal warfare. To call a meeting of chiefs would immediately demonstrate the Confederation's weakness; well-disposed chiefs would not attend for fear of fighting, and those who did attend would possibly resort to force if discussion did not resolve business to their liking. Busby finally proposed an alternative of sending the 'King's message' to each of the chiefs by circular letter, to which Bourke agreed.[18] While it was a more effective way of spreading knowledge about the Confederation and British recognition, it took Busby no closer to implementing the Confederation proposal. Timber set aside for a Parliament House lay unused.[19]

Yet the Confederation was not completely abandoned. On the odd occasion, Busby called together a small committee of Confederation chiefs.[20] He also continued to collect signatures right up to July 1839 when the total stood at fifty-two. Southern tribes were invited to join but most who did were chiefs from north of Thames; the exceptions were Te Hapuku from Hawke's Bay and Te Wherowhero from the Waikato.[21] The Declaration was twice printed, presumably to encourage its circulation, and there is some evidence of a 'constitution' being drawn up.[22]

The Confederation was similar to tactics being used with other indigenous peoples in the Pacific where foreign powers were vying with each other to further their interests.[23] Busby remained wary of the increasing French and United States activity in New Zealand waters; by adding new adherents to the Confederation he hoped to inhibit the intrusion of any political power other than Britain.[24] Similar motives had no doubt prompted local Europeans (including Thomas McDonnell, Additional British Resident at odds with Busby)[25] to secure signatures to the Confederation.

Chiefs, however, were shrewd enough to see the advantages to be gained by forming some alliance. Indigenous societies in Tahiti, Hawaii and Tonga were adjusting to accommodate the challenges accompanying European intrusion. Law codes and port regulations being promulgated in Polynesian kingdoms were a matter for discussion in New Zealand. The 1831 petition had shown that Maori appreciated the need to look to their interests; it had set a precedent for acting as a body. In 1835 Busby secured the accession of not only most 1831 petitioners[26] but also of most major northern chiefs, including Pomare, Kawiti, Panakareao and Tirarau.[27] Christian and non-Christian, friend and enemy, were brought together in one cause. This was no mean achievement.

Contemporary observers, however, were pessimistic about the immediate chances of any centralised Confederation government working.[28] New Zealand lacked an indigenous political foundation for such a structure; the country was too large and tribal divisions were still too strong. At most, a territorial concept called Nui Tireni had emerged in the 1820s; so too had a sense of 'Maoriness'. Both were stimulated among Maori by a sharing of new experiences and by opportunities to define themselves as different from other races[29] (although the term 'Maori' was not used widely until the mid-nineteenth century).[30] But these developments had not led to the formation of a central polity, recognised in international law as a credential for entry to the family of nations. Nevertheless, by the yardstick of contemporary assessments of native rights, influenced by the writings of European jurists like Emerich de Vattel, the Maori people qualified as being more 'civilised' than almost any other native race.[31] As cultivators rather than wandering herdsmen, Maori had a claim to territorial sovereignty or land ownership superior to most other indigenous peoples. Since this still did not qualify them, in international usage, to exercise full rights as an independent, sovereign nation state, British acknowledgement of the Declaration of Independence left Maori in an anomalous position.

Early in 1837, a serious outbreak of tribal fighting began in the Bay of Islands, involving local European riff-raff;[32] the more law-abiding settlers and traders saw an opportunity to appeal to the Crown. A petition, promoted by the CMS with Wesleyan Missionary Society support, was signed by over 200 British nationals; it sought vaguely for 'that relief which may appear most expedient to your Majesty'.[33] Reference was made to the 'threatened usurpation of power' in New Zealand by de Thierry, but this was merely a calculated bid to secure maximum support from local British. The Frenchman was still a nuisance but no real threat;[34] nor was the tribal warfare a danger to those not implicated. The heart of the matter was that the petitioners wanted more than the half-hearted official commitment represented by Busby.

The missionaries had a vested interest in sponsoring this appeal. To hold the advances they had made, they were convinced that further government action was essential. Larger numbers of unruly settlers and transients made them apprehensive for the steadfastness of their converts and fearful of a detrimental influence on non-Christian Maori. Also unsettling was the first 'adjustment cult' of Papahurihia or Ngakahi (an amalgam of Christian and Maori belief) which had appeared in the early 1830s.[35] There was uncertainty too in 1837 about how a re-alignment of Maori power following the death of Titore might affect British interests.[36] To the south, there were other disappointing signs; the first flush of conversion had been cooled by inter-tribal fighting in the Bay of Plenty and Rotorua districts, and in August 1836 the CMS station at Matamata was forced to close.

No one was more aware of the absence of effective government than Busby himself. He followed up a lengthy review of the dilemma in January 1836 with letters in February and May when he sought leave to put a case personally before the Colonial Office, but Bourke deterred him.[37] As the 1837 fighting boiled up at the Bay of Islands, Busby requested a 'ship of war' or an armed force so that British subjects could receive protection. Bourke dispatched HMS *Rattlesnake* under the command of William Hobson, but local Maori declined Hobson's offers of mediation and the affair was finally settled without British involvement.[38]

The visit was not without result, however. Requested by Bourke, Hobson presented a report, in which he suggested that 'factories' could be set up along the lines of the early British trading factories in India. Initially, two or three sites could be purchased and placed under British jurisdiction; a treaty with the chiefs would confirm this. A factory head would be accredited to the Confederation chiefs as political agent and consul. Hobson reasoned that his plan had several advantages: it was unlikely to arouse Maori or foreign power jealousy, it would restrain frontier lawlessness (prisons were allowed for), provide a 'safe retreat' for Europeans in times of tribal war, and introduce civil government to the country at large. The scheme was quite unsuited to the dispersed nature of British settlement and commercial activity, and Hobson knew this, but he was giving his superiors what they wanted – a proposal that fitted the need for something to be done with minimal cost and intrusion. Bourke recommended the plan to the Colonial Office.[39]

Bourke also requested a report from Busby, which was sent to the Colonial Office. The Resident had long since dismissed a factory-type plan.[40] He proposed a British protectorate with the Crown administering affairs in trust for all inhabitants; precedents existed in the Ionian Islands and in states bordering on British India. Chiefs would assist, while going through a period of tutelage, with the protectorate gradually being extended over the entire country. The greater part of the report went on to describe the 'miserable condition' of the Maori people, especially the high mortality rate which promised 'at no very distant period, to leave the country destitute of a single aboriginal inhabitant'. While Busby admitted various contributing factors such as infanticide, disease and war, he placed some of the blame on the total European impact. The Maori, therefore, had 'some claim of justice upon the protection of the British Government', particularly in view of the 'present humane policy' towards native peoples of British colonies. This was an appeal calculated to draw a humanitarian response.

The missionary-inspired petition of 1837, Hobson's report and Busby's dispatch arrived at the Colonial Office in late 1837 and early 1838. Together, they painted a dismal picture of a deteriorating situation on a remote imperial frontier. For some time officials had been aware of the need to change British policy towards New Zealand, but other imperial problems had priority. Moreover, by the time the gloomy documents arrived, the crises that had sparked them off were over. Any precipitate change was unlikely. At this point, however, another crisis occurred, this time in the metropolis itself where plans for private colonisation were under way.

The New Zealand Association, which held its inaugural meeting in May 1837, aimed to establish a New Zealand colony on the systematic principles of Edward Gibbon Wakefield.[41] Parliamentary approval was sought as a first step to making an agreement with the Maori people, and to this end a Bill was drawn up. The scheme was coolly received at the Colonial Office, the Secretary of State for Colonies, Lord Glenelg, finding fault with the business details. He was also reluctant to admit that colonisation in any form was desirable for New Zealand. As an evangelical humanitarian who had been vice-president of the CMS, he considered that an injustice would certainly be done if any rights in New Zealand were granted by the British government before Maori consent was obtained. As the Association began to publicise and promote its plans in the latter half of 1837, the London headquarters of the CMS and WMS waged a campaign in opposition, through pamphlets and lobbying in official circles.[42] In December 1837, both the Association and the CMS, backed by the WMS, had deputations ready to wait on government, and expected a firm reply.[43]

Glenelg himself would have preferred to see the missions continue their task of civilising the Maori, possibly with increased government support. But the Association had influential connections, and its case was supported by a memorial from forty London ship-owners and merchants engaged in the South Seas trade.[44] Almost simultaneously, Glenelg received Busby's June 1837 report. Glenelg's anti-colonisation, pro-missionary stance was undermined; the government weakened and offered the Association a Crown charter. It was a victory for the colonisers because official policy now accepted colonisation in principle, although the Association finally refused the charter and in mid-1838 lapsed into a period of quiescence.

Glenelg now reverted to his anti-colonisation position. The report of a House of Lords select committee, appointed in 1838 to examine the New Zealand situation, supported him by coming out against interference by private enterprise.[45] His resolve was further strengthened by a House of Commons select committee report on Aborigines in British settlements, which emphasised that European contact for indigenous peoples had generally been calamitous. But the remedy it proposed for New Zealand – that Busby be invested with consular powers and judicial authority, with the backing of periodic naval visits – was outdated.[46] In highlighting the need for increased government responsibility, however, the report did serve a useful function; the principles of trusteeship were influential in official decision-making on New Zealand. Moreover, the Aborigines Protection Society continued to keep a watching brief on native rights, including New Zealand affairs, throughout the nineteenth century.[47]

All parties who expressed an interest in New Zealand in 1838 shared the conviction that British intervention was both necessary and desirable. Opinion differed only on the extent of that intervention and the role that the Maori people should play. It was now a question of whose interests were to come first – Maori or

British? Since British colonisation seemed to be inevitable, some observers hoped that the interests of the two could be reconciled.

Those groups or individuals, mainly missionary, whose interest in New Zealand centred primarily on the Maori, naturally favoured imperial trusteeship. Whereas in London they were still thinking of a small step forward – building up the Resident's position – New Zealand missionaries favoured something akin to Busby's protectorate plan.[48] They were virtually unanimous in their opposition to organised colonisation, in particular to the Association's plans,[49] although they supported government intervention to control the already existing irregular settlement and to restrain a potentially overwhelming settler influx.

Those connected with the New Zealand Association were inevitably more concerned with the part the government would play in colonisation. They were prepared to make some concession to contemporary thinking on indigenous races,[50] but their first commitment was to settler interests, which they expected the government to back.[51] Between these two poles stood groups such as the Aborigines Protection Society which was attempting to reconcile the previously irreconcilable – settler and native rights.[52] While only remedial action was possible in the old empire, a new start could be made in New Zealand. Maori and settlers could ultimately be one people although, considering the North American Indian experience, some were not overly optimistic.[53]

During 1838 there was a marked shift in British attitudes towards New Zealand – a fatalistic or defeatist acceptance of the inevitable. The tide of British colonisation could not be held back forever, the Maori world was changing and the initiative would pass by right to the British. Maori capacity to exercise control over New Zealand affairs was belittled, and it was easy to conclude that an unencumbered Maori sovereignty was no longer worth supporting. Maori innocently contributed to this by periodically expressing a desire for British law. They also seemed to be acquiescing in speculative land dealings in the last year or so before 1840; if evidence were needed to justify the loss of Maori independence, land-sharking provided it.

In December 1838 Glenelg took the first step of seeking the appointment of a consul to New Zealand to obtain jurisdiction over two or three districts before establishing them as a Crown colony under a governor. From February 1839, when Hobson accepted the post of consul, the independent, sovereign status of New Zealand was progressively whittled away. Hobson confessed that his 1837 'factory' plan had constituted only a minimum step, designed so that neither humanitarians nor foreign powers would take fright, and proposed on the understanding that British policy was not to take formal possession of New Zealand but to preserve its independence.[54] In 1837 he had admitted privately to his wife that there was so much British labour and capital invested in fisheries in New Zealand that British intervention was called for to exclude other powers, to protect settlers and to restrain their aggression; and that the Maori race was diminishing so fast that it would not be long before New Zealand would be occupied entirely by Europeans.[55] To the Colonial Office, therefore, he now recommended establishing British sovereignty over the whole country, and 'transplanting to its shores the nucleus of a moral and industrious population'.

Glenelg refused to be moved by Hobson's reasoning; when he relinquished his seals of office to Lord Normanby in February 1839, he still preferred limited government intervention. Normanby was more favourably disposed to colonisation, but determined to seek an arrangement with the Maori regarding their sovereignty first. The government's hand was, however, forced by the colonisers. The Colonial Office was aware that several colonisation schemes were under way, including a revitalised New Zealand Association (now known as the New Zealand Company).[56] The news that the government intended to send Hobson to negotiate a cession of sovereignty from the Maori, to set up a government, and to investigate land titles was most unwelcome to the Company's directors. Their scheme depended on acquiring cheap land for sale at a high price to make a profit for shareholders and to fund colonisation. Even if a charter were given to the Company, it had lost its chance of having a free hand in New Zealand. In the hope of pre-empting government actions, the Company's directors sent off the *Tory* on 12 May 1839 to make the first Company land purchase; the first emigrants followed in September. The success of the venture hung on the Company forcing the British government to accept its land claims as a fait accompli.

From March to July 1839, Colonial Office minutes indicate a degree of vacillation. In March, James Stephen, the Permanent Undersecretary, had drawn up a minute summing up the government's position.[57] Like Glenelg, he was concerned that Britain should maintain a responsibility for both British subjects and Maori, but accepted that the colonisation of the country was, by 1839, an 'inevitable measure'. He noted that two cardinal points were to be kept in view: protection of the Maori people and the introduction of self-government for the settlers.

The news of the *Tory*'s planned May departure prompted Stephen to review the situation.[58] It was recognised that any decisions would have to acknowledge the 'independent national character' of the Maori people, albeit qualified in various ways. Complete annexation was still rejected as both an unnecessary invasion of Maori rights, and an undesirable cost and responsibility. For the present, cession of only part of New Zealand would be sought. A Crown colony would be established, with extra-territorial jurisdiction over British subjects in the rest of the country.

The alternative possibility of a Maori governing body – a Confederation of chiefs legislating for both races under British protection – was briefly considered, but Stephen thought the idea 'impracticable' and 'inadequate'. All authority would really rest in the British governor; the capacity of chiefs was too uncertain. Stephen surmised that on the slightest provocation or caprice chiefs might disown all part in enactments ostensibly clothed with their authority. He did concede that if a Crown colony were established in part of the country, then in areas outside its boundaries a Confederation might serve some useful purpose: it could prevent unauthorised settlement, stop the individual acquisition of land and give preferential treatment to British trade and religion. If Maori ceded some territory and sovereign rights, then recognition could be given to the 'national character' of the Maori race and to their flag.[59]

Stephen continued to stress that limited intervention was directed only partly at protecting settler interests; its chief purpose was to avert the 'calamities' threatening the Maori people and to lead them towards the 'blessings' of a civilised life. No encouragement was to be given to colonisation by British subjects or to sales of Maori land. And no allowance was made for schemes of organised colonisation, although Stephen had been convinced for some months that this was inevitable. By the time final instructions were drawn up for Hobson, however, the Colonial Office had shifted from a 'no-colonisation' stance to one favouring colonisation.[60]

At the end of August 1839, Hobson left for New Zealand as consul. Since this was to be a temporary arrangement, he was to act under Colonial Office supervision. He was armed with instructions from Normanby and a supplementary explanation covering various points of policy.[61] He was left with discretion to acquire sovereignty over either 'the whole or any parts' of New Zealand that the Maori wished to cede. British authority would be immediately assumed by Letters Patent, New Zealand becom-

ing temporarily a dependency of New South Wales. The Lieutenant Governor, with the assistance of a nominated Legislative
Council, would make laws and, since no British troops were
immediately available, Hobson was advised to form a local militia
or armed police. The new government was to handle all land
transactions and to hold all waste lands that might be acquired. By
applying the New South Wales system, a land fund could be set
up to cover costs of administration and development; the surplus
would finance further British emigration. This land fund, supplemented by import duties, would rapidly make the administration financially self-sufficient. In simple terms, these were directions for setting up a British Crown colony.

Incorporated in the instructions were provisions for Maori welfare. A Protector would be appointed to safeguard Maori interests
in land negotiations; mission work would receive the moral and
financial support of government, and schools would be established; with the exception of 'savage practices', such as human
sacrifice and cannibalism (which were to be forcibly suppressed),
Maori custom was to be tolerated until Maori could be 'brought
within the pale of civilized life'. In deference to Maori sensitivities,
the instructions laid down the principle that no convict was ever
to be sent to New Zealand to undergo punishment.

As an introduction, Normanby wrote a lengthy dissertation
which amounted to an apology for British intervention. It reflects
Colonial Office difficulty in reconciling conflicting principles
and in accommodating the interests of opposing pressure groups.
Normanby had to recognise Maori independence, even a sovereignty of sorts, but he also had to negate it; he had to allow for
British colonisation and investment in New Zealand, yet regret its
inevitability; and he had to show that justice was being done the
Maori people by British intervention, even while admitting that
such intervention was nevertheless unjust. As various government
sources had noted, a move to nullify or infringe upon New
Zealand's independence had to make allowance for the feelings of
foreign powers, humanitarians, missionaries, and the Maori
themselves.[62]

Normanby wrote that New Zealand had been officially acknowledged as a 'sovereign and independent state', but only 'so far
at least as it is possible to make that acknowledgement in favour
of a people composed of numerous dispersed, and petty tribes,
who possess few political relations to each other, and are incom-
petent to act, or even deliberate in concert'. But, since the admission of Maori rights had been made, it was 'binding on the faith
of the British Crown'. Consequently, the Crown would make no

claim on New Zealand, 'unless the free and intelligent consent of the Natives, expressed according to their established usages' was first obtained. The decision to intervene was made with 'extreme reluctance', and it did not alter the official attitude, which corresponded with the Aborigines Report, that such a measure was 'essentially unjust, and but too certainly fraught with calamity to a numerous and inoffensive people, whose title to the soil and to the Sovereignty of New Zealand is indisputable'. The inevitability of British colonisation had changed circumstances and justified intervention. Colonisation was a threat to Maori welfare which could best be met by a 'surrender to Her Majesty of a right now so precarious and little more than nominal ... a national independence which they are no longer able to maintain'. In exchange, the Maori would receive British protection and law.

Much of this discussion was exaggeration, giving a distorted impression of an enfeebled Maori race and a secured British ascendancy; in fact, for some years after 1840, New Zealand would be British in name but continue to be largely Maori. Had the Maori people been presented as more capable, however, British intervention could scarcely have been justified. Decisions had been based as much upon the expectation of a rapid growth in British settlement and its effects on the Maori as upon the current situation.

While Normanby's apology tried to argue that a balance was being held in fulfilling Britain's duty towards the Maori as well as to her own subjects, the official insistence on the upholding of Maori rights is deceptive, for along the trail of decision-making those rights had already been severely restricted.

Hobson's instructions did not provide for the incorporation of Maori within the colony's administrative structure nor allow for the development of Maori government of any sort – options which had come before the government earlier. It was as if the perception of Maori capacity in this respect had diminished as the government moved towards accepting that New Zealand was destined to be a British settler colony. No longer were they considering a Maori New Zealand in which a place had to be found for British intruders, but a settler New Zealand in which a place had to be found for the Maori.

Chapter Three

THE TREATY AT WAITANGI

Once the Colonial Office had taken the decision to intervene in New Zealand, Hobson's primary task was to secure sovereignty for Britain, by treaty if possible, but above all in a peaceful manner. Three main factors had to be considered: the legal status of the country, humanitarian concern for Maori welfare, and the need to convince the Maori population that further British intrusion should be accepted. Because these three aspects were inextricably interwoven in the treaty-making, the negotiations were a source of confusion both at the time and subsequently.

Crown recognition of New Zealand's independence, arising from several statutes and from official acknowledgement of the 1835 Declaration of Independence, was Hobson's first concern. Before 1840, Britain had made no official claim on New Zealand. Any right deriving from Cook's 'discovery' in 1769 had not been confirmed by official declaration of intent to exercise exclusive control, nor secured by occupation – factors considered necessary by contemporary international legal experts to validate territorial claims.[1] Moreover, Britain's official recognition of New Zealand's independence had been duly noticed by other nations, as well as by British nationals.[2] From an official viewpoint, therefore, the move to secure recognition, by treaty, of New Zealand's changed status was deemed wise.

Related to the legal aspect but subordinate to it was official acknowledgement of humanitarian concern for Maori interests. It was considered only just for Britain to recognise and confirm certain rights vested in an indigenous people. In addition to this the Waitangi treaty would promise Maori people the status of British subjects – a formal commitment which was unusual in British colonial practice at that time. Such moves were humanitarian, but they also helped to secure Maori and missionary co-operation. Expediency as well as justice are reflected in the measures.

Hobson's third concern was diplomatic: Maori agreement to the treaty would entitle the Crown to proceed with peaceful colonisation. Securing that agreement would depend on the solemnity of a treaty meeting and the significance accorded it by accompanying celebrations, the status as well as the ability of negotiators and, most importantly, the explanations and understanding conveyed to Maori people. The treaty was presented in a manner calculated to secure Maori agreement. The transfer of power to the Crown was thus played down. Maori suspicions were lulled by official recognition of Maori independence, by the confirmation of a degree of that independence under British sovereignty, and by the extension of Crown protection and other rights. Maori were told that the Crown needed their agreement in order to establish effective law and order – primarily for controlling Europeans, or Pakeha as they were called.[3] Finally, the benefits to be gained from the treaty were stressed, rather than the restrictions that would inevitably follow.

Hobson was able to draw on the knowledge of others. Before leaving London, he had talked with Bourke, past governor of New South Wales. More up-to-date information was obtained in Sydney from George Gipps who had held the governorship since 1837. Hobson arrived there on Christmas Eve 1839 in HMS *Druid*, but was delayed for three weeks until HMS *Herald*, under Captain Joseph Nias, was ready to leave for New Zealand. During the Sydney stop-over, he was provided with an ill-chosen assortment of local men who were to form the nucleus of a New Zealand civil service – George Cooper, Treasurer, Felton Mathew, Surveyor-General, Willoughby Shortland, Police Magistrate, and James Freeman, Chief Clerk. A small guard of a sergeant and three troopers of the New South Wales mounted police was added.[4]

Hobson's arrival brought to the fore the question of land purchases in New Zealand. In 1839, some leading Sydney settlers and businessmen were laying claim to purchases which embraced almost all the South Island and parts of the North Island's east coast. In the far north, large land blocks on the east and west coasts were said to have been alienated. In some instances, land had been sold several times over.[5] The New Zealand Company's *Tory*, arriving in New Zealand in August 1839, was known to be seeking land in the Cook Strait area and elsewhere.[6] Within a few days of Hobson's arrival in Sydney, Gipps peremptorily halted a Sydney auction of some 2,000 acres of Bay of Islands land. The ensuing uncertainty of Sydney claimants to New Zealand land was only partially eased by Hobson's pleasant reception of a delegation of their representatives.[7]

Official concern now led to a series of pre-emptive measures which anticipated British sovereignty. Gipps swore Hobson in as Lieutenant Governor of any territory which might be acquired and provided for the necessary extension of New South Wales jurisdiction to cover New Zealand, announcing these moves after Hobson's departure on 18 January. Another proclamation declared that title to New Zealand land would be valid only if derived from or confirmed by the Crown, that commissioners would be appointed to investigate lands purchased, and that any further purchases would be null and void.[8] Across the Tasman at Kororareka, on 30 January, the day after HMS *Herald* had anchored in the Bay of Islands, Hobson announced to a public meeting of Pakeha that he was assuming his duties as Lieutenant Governor; on that authority, he then proclaimed the land restrictions as they had been issued in New South Wales.

Neither Gipps nor Hobson was acting outside the limits of authority. On the contrary, Normanby's instructions to Hobson had directed him to issue such a proclamation 'immediately' on his arrival. At Hobson's request, a draft had been supplied which Gipps and Hobson were at liberty to alter.[9] The extent of New Zealand land-holding by New South Wales settlers made it imperative that Gipps issue the proclamation in Sydney almost simultaneously with its release in New Zealand.

This series of actions placed the British government in the ambiguous position of asserting an authority that would not be formally requested from Maori chiefs until a few days later at the Waitangi meeting. Although Hobson made this first assumption of authority dependent on the Maori cession, the procedures indicated little care for legal niceties. Within two months, William Charles Wentworth and other New South Wales purchasers of New Zealand land were challenging the legality of the situation.[10] Later in the year, Edward Gibbon Wakefield strongly criticised the action before a House of Commons committee hearing on New Zealand.[11] Even on arrival at the Bay of Islands, Captain Nias of HMS *Herald* had jibbed at Hobson's course of action by refusing to accord him the fifteen-gun salute of a lieutenant governor, but only the strictly correct eleven-gun salute of a consul. According to one historian, Busby also advised Hobson to act in his capacity as a British consul until such time as an agreement with the Maori allowed him to assume the position of lieutenant governor.[12]

In retrospect, Busby argued that the urgency of the land situation justified these procedures. Expectation of Hobson's arrival in late 1839 had prompted a noticeable rush of new settlers in the north,[13] and in the south, the New Zealand Company and others had already been making vast 'purchases'. Without an embargo, sales would have escalated, causing even greater confusion of title. These January 1840 measures, setting aside the question of their legality, effectively halted land acquisition. But, not surprisingly, land purchasers in the north turned in anger to provoke local Maori, telling them that the land had 'gone to the Queen', and that the Maori people were now taurekareka (slaves).[14] Even before Hobson had come to terms with the chiefs, therefore, a Maori opposition was created to question the motives and actions of the Crown.

Hobson, having asserted Crown authority over British subjects, now turned to treat with the Maori. His conviction that sovereignty over the whole country was desirable had been strengthened by events in New Zealand in 1839. He had hoped to circumnavigate the coast by the end of February, but priority had to be given to a meeting with northern chiefs, particularly the Confederation chiefs. Plans for a quick trip to Hokianga were shelved; business and visitors (including Bishop Pompallier and two priests) took up his time. Hobson was also showing signs of stress, caused partly by pressure of work but aggravated by disagreements with Nias, which would lead to a stroke a month later.[15]

Busby, now relieved of his official position, pledged his assistance 'as a private individual', to organise a formal assembly of chiefs. On the afternoon of Hobson's arrival, it was decided that this should be held the following week, on 5 February, at Busby's Waitangi home.[16] The site, associated with the British government and with consultation over Maori–Pakeha problems, made an ideal setting. Busby offered to prepare invitations, asking the CMS printer, William Colenso, to print 100 'as soon as possible'. Hobson, too, urged haste.[17] The invitations were ready early on Thursday morning, 30 January. In Busby's name, they asked the recipient, as a chief of the Confederation (whakaminenga) to attend a meeting (huihuinga) with the 'chief of the Queen' who had arrived to be a governor for everyone. On Busby's instruction, Colenso was supposed to have altered 'about twenty' of the invitations so that representatives of Confederation chiefs who had died could be asked. He also took the opportunity, it seems, to tidy up Busby's Maori, which was a rather literal translation.[18]

Hobson evidently favoured negotiation specifically with the Confederation. One obstacle to the free assertion of British sovereignty was the official acknowledgement of New Zealand's independence in 1835, but, as Hobson noted in England, British recognition extended, strictly speaking, only to the northern Confederation. Elsewhere in the country, he argued, the Crown might well exercise, with greater freedom, all the rights 'usually assumed by first discoverers'. He further believed (erroneously, it proved) that the disparity between the Confederation area and the rest of New Zealand would be accentuated by the inability of Maori, especially the 'wild savages' of the South Island, 'to observe even the form of a treaty'. Normanby, however, admitting to an 'inevitable ignorance of the real state of the case', had simply referred Hobson to Gipps for advice and counselled him to use his discretion. [19]

There were other advantages in negotiating with a defined body. A formal transfer of Confederation rights to Britain would strengthen her position before the world as well as with her own subjects in New Zealand. In a practical sense, the body also gave a semblance of unity to a situation where independent Maori leadership might lead to serious disunity. It was also a helpful checklist of major northern chiefs. Initially, invitations were to be extended only to the Confederation chiefs, but a few days before the Waitangi meeting other invitations, possibly handwritten, were sent to 'high chiefs who had not yet signed the declaration'. [20]

Before the assembly on 5 February, Hobson's most urgent task was to draw up terms of agreement to lay before the meeting. While he held Normanby's authority to enter into a treaty, there is no evidence that either the Colonial Office or Gipps provided any draft treaty. Hobson, however, knew well enough what the British government required – a cession of sovereignty, absolute control over all land matters, and authority to impose law and order on both Maori and non-Maori. With the assistance of his secretary, J.S. Freeman, he drafted some preliminary notes as the basis of a treaty. By Busby's account, Hobson then became too unwell to leave the *Herald* and the draft notes were delivered to the ex-Resident by two officers. Busby considered them inadequate 'to accomplish the object'; he would prepare a draft treaty himself. This was submitted to Hobson on 3 February. [21]

The notes that Busby received from Hobson, together with Busby's draft, have survived and are reproduced in the *Facsimiles of the ... Treaty of Waitangi*. Busby received two sets of notes. [22] The first, in Hobson's handwriting, is the draft of a preamble only. In sentiment and phrasing, it owes something to Hobson's instructions from Normanby. Both 'confederated' and 'independent' chiefs are included. This preamble became the introduction to the treaty. The second set of notes, in Freeman's handwriting, consists of a differently worded draft preamble, briefer than Hobson's and referring only to the confederated chiefs. There were also three articles: in the first, the 'united chiefs' cede the sovereignty of an area to be specified in degrees of latitude and longitude; in the second, they yield to the Queen the exclusive right of pre-emption over any waste lands they might wish to alienate; and in the third, the Queen extends her protection to the 'Natives of New Zealand' and imparts to them 'all the rights and privileges of British subjects'.

Busby's draft consisted of three articles and a lengthy postscript.[23] These articles, with no alteration, were accepted for the treaty. Lengthier and more precise than Freeman's, they differed significantly by including a guarantee to the Maori people, collectively and individually, of the 'full exclusive and undisturbed possession of their lands and estates, forests fisheries and other properties' as long as they wished to retain them. Busby's draft postscript also became part of the final treaty but there were two changes. The first was the deletion of a wordy conclusion which made assertions (about Maori weakness and the need for British protection and authority) that Maori may have chosen to debate and which provided for cession by degrees of latitude and longitude, as Freeman's draft had done. The second change was the shifting of a final statement of intent (that the independent chiefs would adhere to the treaty terms) so that the statement applied both to confederated and independent chiefs. This was possibly the alteration that he later referred to as 'a transposition of certain sentences which did not in any degree affect the sense', one involving just two sentences.[24]

In brief then, the treaty in its final English form, comprised Hobson's preamble, the articles developed by Busby from Freeman's skeletal versions, with the most important addition of the guarantee of land and other possessions, and finally, Busby's amended postscript. On this analysis, it becomes clear that the essentials of the English text of the treaty came from Busby and that his claim that he 'drew' the treaty is not altogether an exaggeration.[25] Perhaps he should be forgiven the proprietary pride with which he discussed the treaty in later years.

The drafting alterations, which applied mainly to the extent of sovereignty and the land question, reflect the decisions forced upon Hobson by circumstances in New Zealand. On 3 or 4 February, after Busby had submitted his draft to Hobson, the terms were broadened so that the one treaty would apply to all Maori, whether under the Confederation or not, and wherever they might be resident. As a result, the progressive acquisition of sovereignty, allowed for by specification of degrees of latitude and longitude, was abandoned and tribal or hapu affiliation was substituted. This was probably done to avoid confusion: some chiefs had affiliations with more than one hapu, and/or territorial interests in several districts. Moreover, if areas where chiefs refused to adhere to the treaty were too clearly excluded, those parts of the country would become vulnerable to foreign interests, a danger that the Colonial Office had discussed in 1839.

The final form of the treaty also reveals Hobson's solution to a problem that the Colonial Office had left unanswered: did Maori understand the distinction between proprietary land rights and sovereign rights? In May 1839, it had been suggested at the Colonial Office that Maori might consider that they relinquished 'dominion' along with ownership when they sold land; in this case the British government could simply assert authority over those lands which had passed out of Maori hands. While the suggestion to take advantage of Maori ignorance was set aside as being unjust, the idea appeared once more in Hobson's August draft instructions before being deleted. Hobson was then directed to have the 'most frank and open dealings' with the Maori people although it was still doubted that they would grasp the real meaning of the sovereignty Hobson would seek from them.[26]

In New Zealand, however, Hobson's advisers left him in little doubt about Maori insistence on their rights. Indeed, in 1835, Busby had told his superiors in New South Wales that: 'As far as has been ascertained every acre of land in this country is appropriated among the different tribes; and every individual in the tribe has a distinct interest in the property; although his possession may not always be separately defined.'[27] The land guarantee acknowledged these rights; its insertion by Busby ensured that there would be a differentiation between national sovereignty and territorial rights. Without the land guarantee, the treaty proposal would almost certainly have been rejected (as was a treaty that Gipps tried to press upon some South Island Maori visiting Sydney in early February 1840).[28] In later years, the importance of the land guarantee would be overlooked too easily by settlers, and attacked as unnecessary and an overly generous reaction to the humanitarian conscience of the treaty period. It was a just policy, but it was also an expedient response to the New Zealand situation.

Contemporary accounts of the crucial few days of early February 1840 do not positively identify the participants in the meetings which decided the wording of the treaty. Hobson certainly had the advice of Busby, Freeman and other officials on the *Herald*. Normanby had assured Hobson, too, that he could expect to 'find powerful auxiliaries amongst the missionaries'.[29] Before Hobson arrived the Wesleyans had already been urged by their London-based headquarters to support his mission, and Henry Williams and his CMS colleagues had been asked by Bishop Broughton of Sydney to help influence the Maori people to surrender sovereignty.[30] Hobson, therefore, expected missionary co-operation and received it in full. By the evening of 3 February, when he held several sets of notes from which the final treaty draft had to be selected, he had been visited by a number of missionaries - Henry Williams, Charles Baker, George Clarke, William Colenso and Richard Taylor of the CMS, and the Wesleyan James Buller, who was passing through. Any or all of these men may have influenced the treaty's wording. But it was Williams's presence on the *Herald* that Hobson had first requested, and had he sought advice on the final treaty wording it was to Williams, head of the CMS mission, that he was most likely to refer.[31]

The role that Williams played in final decisions on the English draft will probably never be known precisely. Nor can any trace be found of the final English draft put together on the *Herald*.[32] But Williams has left his own testimony: 'On the 4th of February, about 4 o'clock p.m., Captain Hobson came to me with the Treaty of Waitangi in English, for me to translate into Maori, saying that he would meet me in the morning at the house of the British Resident, Mr Busby, when it must be read to the chiefs assembled at 10 o'clock.' According to Hugh Carleton, Williams's son-in-law and biographer, Williams made the translation with 'the assistance of his son Edward', said to be an expert in the Ngapuhi dialect. This was something of an exaggeration.[33] While the twenty-one-year-old Edward probably had the facility with spoken Maori that one might expect from someone who had spent most of his youth in New Zealand, he was not an experienced translator. Nor was Henry Williams an acknowledged expert in that field. Those who had that skill – William Williams, Robert Maunsell and William Puckey, together with the Wesleyan, John Hobbs – were not available. The young mission printer, Colenso, does not seem to have been asked to help, Taylor was otherwise engaged and there is no evidence of Maori assistance.[34]

The task facing Henry Williams and Edward was no easy one. In a few brief evening hours the English draft of the treaty had to be accurately rendered in the Maori language. This Maori text would become the treaty document signed by almost all chiefs throughout New Zealand. The two men, knowing that their work was of vital importance, were certainly aware of some of the translation problems. As Henry Williams explained: 'In this translation it was necessary to avoid all expressions of the English for which there was no expressive term in the Maori, preserving entire the spirit and tenor of the treaty.'[35] The comment suggests that Williams may have decided to recast the English draft, as translators often do. A comparison of the English and Maori texts tends to confirm this view.

The preamble, drafted by Hobson, was a convoluted expression of the Queen's desire to protect the Maori people from the worst effects of British settlement and to provide for her own subjects, by appointing Hobson to obtain 'sovereign authority', and to establish a 'settled form of Civil Government'. In translation, the whole was simplified and there were certain omissions. To translate both 'sovereign authority' and 'civil government', for example, Williams resorted to the single word, 'kawanatanga'.

In article one, the chiefs of the Confederation and the separate and independent chiefs were said to 'cede to Her Majesty, the Queen of England, absolutely and without reservation all the rights and powers of Sovereignty' which they exercised or possessed over their respective territories. In the Maori, this became 'ka tuku rawa atu ki te Kuini o Ingarani ake tonu atu te Kawanatanga katoa o o ratou wenua'.[36] The emphasis given to an absolute and lasting yielding up seems to be conveyed clearly, but the choice of 'kawanatanga' for 'sovereignty' is not such a happy one. Williams had already used it to render 'sovereign authority' and 'civil government' in the preamble. The concept of sovereignty is sophisticated, involving the right to exercise a jurisdiction at international level as well as within national boundaries. The single word 'kawanatanga' covered significant differences of meaning, and was not likely to convey to Maori a precise definition of sovereignty.

Article two introduced further difficulties: the Queen 'confirms and guarantees to the Chiefs and Tribes of New Zealand and to the respective families and individuals thereof the full exclusive and undisturbed possession of their Lands and Estates, Forests Fisheries and other properties which they may collectively or individually possess so long as it is their wish and desire to retain the same in their possession.' Translated into Maori, the condition of collective and individual possession was omitted altogether, and the guarantee of possession – expressed as 'te tino rangatiratanga o o ratou wenua o ratou kainga me o ratou taonga katoa' – covered only lands, dwelling places and property of all kinds. It has been suggested that the absence of forests and fisheries from the Maori translation can be explained by an accidental omission from the English draft given to Williams. While there might be other explanations, such as Williams's general tendency to simplify the text, this one is quite probable. Indeed, there might have been more than one 'final' draft.[37]

But it was the guarantee of te tino rangatiratanga (chieftainship) that was to lead to confusion, for Maori understood the word to mean far more than 'possession', as in the English text. In fact, it was a better approximation to sovereignty than kawanatanga. Although both words implied an exercise of power, authority and jurisdiction, rangatiratanga was of Maori derivation, with con- notations of chiefly power that were familiar to Maori. Kawana- tanga, on the other hand, derived from kawana (governor) and had associations with Pontius Pilate, Roman governor in the Bible, or with governors of New South Wales. It tended to imply authority in an abstract rather than a concrete sense.

Contemporary use of the words in scripture and liturgy rein- forced this implication. In the decade before 1840, the dispersion of thousands of biblical texts, translated by CMS missionaries and Wesleyans, had familiarised many Maori with the nuances of meaning which they debated exhaustively.[38] Rangatiratanga ex- pressed God's 'kingdom' in translations of the Lord's Prayer, daily evening prayers, in the burial prayers and in the gospels, whereas kawanatanga most often referred to rulership or princi- pality in a vaguer sense.[39] The shades of meaning in the biblical references were not great but they were significant to Maori understanding, or lack of it. Rangatiratanga, moreover, had been used in the 1835 Declaration of Independence to refer to New Zealand's 'independence' which Britain had acknowledged. Maori might well have assumed, therefore, that their sovereign rights were actually being confirmed in return for a limited concession of power in kawanatanga.

The choice of terms by Williams may not have been accidental, of course. It is possible that he chose an obscure and ambiguous wording in order to secure Maori agreement, believing (as did most missionaries at the time) that Maori welfare would be best served under British sovereignty. On the other hand, like many of his contemporaries, he may have believed that Maori could not claim an internationally recognisable sovereignty; even powers of chieftainship were seriously compromised by the rapid changes of the 1830s. In ensuring that rangatiratanga was guaranteed, there- fore, Williams was not only safeguarding Maori land and posses- sions, but reinforcing the authority of the chiefs by building into the treaty a right to exercise some control. Williams could hardly know the extent to which chiefs might retain this under British sovereignty, although Hobson had probably confided to him plans to establish a Protectorate of Aborigines designed to safeguard Maori rights. This could have been the 'spirit and intent' of the treaty which he had expressly wanted to retain in the translation.

Whatever Williams intended, it is clear that the treaty text, in using kawanatanga and rangatiratanga, did not spell out the implications of British annexation. Nor would the translation of 'sovereignty' with the single word 'mana' have been helpful, as some argue;[40] rangatiratanga and kawanatanga each has its own mana. As John Hobbs (a participant in the 1840 events) later pointed out, a chief's mana *was* his rangatiratanga.[41]

In other sections of the treaty there were further translation and interpretation difficulties. By the second section of article two, the chiefs were said to yield to the Queen the 'exclusive right of pre-emption over such lands as the proprietors thereof may be disposed to alienate at such prices as may be agreed upon between the respective proprietors and persons appointed by Her Majesty to treat with them in that behalf'. Whatever the true legal meaning of pre-emption (which was included in the treaty from Freeman's first draft), the intention of Normanby, Gipps and Hobson was to secure to the Crown exclusive control over all transactions in Maori land. This was later confirmed by Busby.[42] When Williams came to translating this section, the word 'pre-emption' was rendered as 'hokonga', a word commonly used for buying and selling, for barter or exchange – a familiar concept to Maori with their long experience of such dealing. Since the British government would be involved in the selling of land once they had purchased it, hokonga seems to be a reasonable choice. But Williams's translation did not stress the absolute and exclusive right granted to the Crown. It is unlikely that he did not understand this point; Hobson's proclamations on 29 January had given clear warning of Crown intention to handle all land transactions. Much depended, then, on the explanation of this section and on Maori comprehension of its full import.

The third article probably presented Williams with the least difficulty. The Queen extended her protection to the Maori people and granted them 'all the rights and privileges of British subjects' ('nga tikanga katoa rite tahi ki ana mea ki nga tangata o Ingarani'), a reasonable equivalent of the English. Elsewhere in the British Empire, native races were supposed to enjoy the status of British subjects, although they were not always treated accordingly. What was remarkable in New Zealand was that this was explicitly stated and the expression of humanitarian idealism thus publicised. However, the implications of accepting the 'rights and privileges' of a British subject (that Maori would be subject to

British law and committed to certain responsibilities) were not emphasised. Once again, as with the pre-emption clause, explanation of the articles would be crucial.

While the final form of the treaty was being decided, other preparations were in progress.[43] On the lawn in front of Busby's house, officers of the *Herald* saw to the erection of a spacious tent. Made of sails, the marquee stretched 120-150 feet in length, its side-ropes and poles decorated with the flags of all nations. Food for the invited chiefs was collected together – a half-ton of flour, five tons of potatoes, thirty pigs and other goods. An air of excitement hung over the bay, with a great deal of shipping lying at anchor and considerable business being transacted. After several days of summer showers, the weather began to clear on Tuesday 4 February as Maori gathered in preparation for the fifth. Wednesday dawned 'particularly fine'.[44] From early in the morning, as groups of Maori moved off towards Waitangi, the bay came alive with canoes paddling from all quarters, each with thirty to forty rowers keeping time to the call and gesture of the kaituki (stroke), who stood to the centre of every canoe. The boats of settlers living round the shores of the bay joined the stream, together with those from vessels at anchor. Most ships were decorated with the flags of their respective nations.

The Waitangi lawn, a vivid green against the surrounding sombre bush, rapidly assumed a gala atmosphere. The Sydney police, in their brilliant uniforms, paraded the lawn where local settlers and traders were 'comfortably walking up and down in different little parties, socially chatting with each other'. Maori, squatting in groups according to their tribes, sat smoking and talking. Many had come from some distance and carried guns. Outside Busby's grounds, vendors plied visitors with refreshments – stout, ale, brandy and rum, pork, cold roast, pies and baskets of bread. It seemed to Colenso, as he arrived for the ceremony, that 'even the cicadae, those little gallant monotonous-toned summer gentlemen, sang livelier than usual. Everything, in fact, wore the appearance of cheerfulness and activity.'[45]

The final touches were still to be added to the treaty. Hobson arrived about 9 a.m. accompanied by Nias, and for the next hour, Hobson, Busby and Henry Williams were closeted in Busby's house with a police guard at the door. According to Colenso, they were 'translating the treaty, and arranging other preliminary matters for the meeting'; but Williams, who had already prepared a translation, later explained that 'on a careful examination of the translation of the treaty, by Mr Busby, he proposed to substitute the word whakaminenga for huihuinga, which was done and approved of'. Whakaminenga was the word used to refer to the Confederation of the United Tribes, whereas huihuinga was any meeting or assembly; since this distinction had been made in the invitations, Busby obviously thought it important to be consistent.[46] The change necessitated five corrections where the word appeared. With the Confederation document to hand, other changes in the translation could have been made to clarify the text, but there is no record of this.[47] Hobson, who did not know the Maori language, was relying on Williams and Busby to check the treaty's accuracy. Presumably, Williams gave an account of his translation, but this is not certain. The treaty, with Busby's amendments, stood as Williams had translated it.

In the meantime, a large crowd was gathering – officers of the *Herald*, Hobson's suite, all the missionaries living in or near the bay, settlers and old residents, new arrivals and visiting sailors. About 10.30 a.m., the French Bishop Pompallier, together with a priest, Father Servant, moved confidently into the Residency. Hobson now held a levee, inviting anyone who wished to be presented to file through. Nias supported Hobson on his right, and to the left stood Williams, Taylor and the French missionaries; Freeman acted as Hobson's aide-de-camp; other members of his suite stood nearby. These formalities quickly over, the group broke up and about 11 a.m. moved off towards the marquee, with the police leading Hobson, Nias and Pompallier, the rest following in an 'irregular procession'. The Union Jack, floating over Busby's lawn since the arrival of the *Herald*, was lowered before proceedings commenced, an indication to the public at large that the transfer of sovereignty had yet to be negotiated.[48]

The scene at the marquee was impressive. A narrow raised platform had been placed at one end, together with a table covered by the Union Jack. Hobson and Nias, both in full uniform, now took central seats on the dais, Busby to the left of Hobson, and Taylor and Williams (appointed as interpreter) immediately to the right. Other missionaries, in their plain black cloth, ranged themselves behind Williams. To Busby's left sat the two Frenchmen, Pompallier especially splendid in his long purple cassock, gold episcopal cross and ruby ring. The Wesleyans, who had arrived late, found a place next to Pompallier. Officers in full dress and Hobson's suite stationed themselves wherever they could, some on the dais, others just in front of it. Willoughby Shortland, Police Magistrate, and later New Zealand's first Colonial Secretary, acted as Master of Ceremonies.

The tent filled rapidly. The Pakeha, mostly 'respectably' dressed, formed an outer circle, standing against the sides of the marquee. The Maori moved into the remaining space and were seated on the ground:

> In front of the platform, in the foreground, were the principal Native chiefs of several tribes, some clothed with dogskin mats made of alternate longitudinal stripes of black and white hair; others habited in splendid-looking new woollen cloaks of foreign manufacture, of crimson, blue, brown, and plaid, and, indeed, of every shade of striking colour ... while some were dressed in plain European and some in common Native dresses ... here and there a ... taiaha, a chief's staff of rank, was seen erected, adorned with the long flowing white hair of the tails of the New Zealand dog and crimson cloth and red feathers.[49]

Among the chiefs, there were many women, 'their ears adorned with white feathers or the entire wing of a bird', a 'striking contrast' against the black gloss of a head.[50] Over the whole, bright sunlight picked out the vivid colours in the flags. To the eye of several observers – Colenso, Taylor and Felton Mathew – the effect was striking ; Mathew thought he would never forget the scene to the day of his death.

The business of the day opened with Hobson very briefly explaining to the Pakeha the purpose of the meeting – to inform the chiefs of the Queen's intentions and to seek their consent to a treaty. Turning to the chiefs, he began (with Williams translating) by explaining that, because of the Queen's concern for the welfare of both Maori and British subjects in New Zealand, he had been sent as governor. But, since the country was outside the Queen's dominion, he lacked the authority that was essential if he were to be of any benefit in controlling British subjects. The chiefs could give Hobson that authority if they signed the treaty laid before them. The treaty was also an offer of Crown protection which Maori had 'often' asked for.[51] In conclusion, Hobson read the English text of the treaty.

Williams now read the Maori text, 'in the midst of profound silence'. By his own account he amplified by way of explanation (presumably following the lead given by Hobson in English): 'I told them all to listen with care, explaining clause by clause to the chiefs, giving them caution not to be in a hurry, but telling them that we, the missionaries, fully approved of the treaty, that it was an act of love towards them on the part of the Queen, who desired to secure to them their property, rights, and privileges. That this treaty was as a fortress for them against any foreign power which might desire to take possession of their country, as the French had taken possession of Otiaiti [Tahiti]', he concluded, anticipating that event by some two years.[52]

When Hobson reported these proceedings to the Colonial Office, he asserted that efforts had been made to explain to the chiefs 'in the fullest manner' the effect that might result from the treaty. It is difficult to see how he could honestly claim this. As presented, the treaty seemed to be confirming the chiefs' authority and directing its effects mainly at Pakeha, aiming specifically at better control of British subjects. Such control might be to the advantage of the Maori people, even though it would mean accepting an increased British authority and sharing the ruling power of the land. Apart from this, however, other predictable changes that would affect Maori life do not appear to have been touched on. Most importantly, there is an absence of any explanation that Maori agreement to kawanatanga ('sovereignty' in the English text) would mean British annexation, a substantial transfer of power that would bring international recognition of New Zealand as a British colony. On the contrary, from the emphasis on protection, Maori might have expected that they were being offered an arrangement akin to a protectorate.

The full import of the loss of sovereignty was also softened by Williams and Hobson representing the Crown through the person of the Queen, who wished to create a close, familiar tie with the Maori people. The impersonal nature of Crown authority and the potentially restrictive effect of British law were thereby diminished and the tradition of personalised Crown-Maori relationships perpetuated. In addition, by a brief reference to Maori encouragement of British settlement and to the earlier Maori appeals to Britain, Hobson subtly implied that the Maori people themselves were not without some responsibility for the situation they now faced. All this put Maori at a grave disadvantage.

The chiefs were now free to question and comment as they pleased. There was a short lull in proceedings as chiefs greeted Hobson by shaking hands, and Busby seized the opportunity to address the gathering on what he knew was the most sensitive issue, the matter of land. He assured the assembly that 'the Governor was not come to take away their land, but to secure them in the possession of what they had not sold; that he (Mr Busby) had often told them that land not duly acquired from them would not be confirmed to the purchaser, but would be returned to the Natives, to whom it of right belonged; that this the Governor would be prepared to do'. When debate on the treaty began,

Hobson repeated this promise, that 'all lands unjustly held would be returned'. These were crucial explanations of article two of the treaty and would later be significant to Maori understanding of promises about land, especially about 'surplus' lands.[53]

In response to a complaint from Moka, a Kororareka chief, Hobson was also pressed to expand on the pre-emption clause of article two. Local British settlers, Gilbert Mair and James Clendon, were allegedly still privately purchasing Maori land, despite the proclamation of 30 January; so Moka doubted Hobson's ability to enforce Crown control. But Hobson insisted that 'all claims to lands, however purchased, after the date of the Proclamation would not be held to be lawful'.[54] While the Crown's exclusive right to future land dealings in the pre-emption clause was still not explicitly stated, Hobson's assurance went some way to clarifying the point. Moka, who had evidently been the only chief present when the land proclamation had been made public,[55] showed by his queries that he grasped the import of Crown control over all land transactions, but whether this was fully understood by other chiefs at the Waitangi meeting remained to be seen.

The chiefs debated the treaty proposal for about five hours. As senior chief and tohunga of the Waitangi locality, the elderly Te Kemara was assigned first right of speech. The customary procedure of Maori debate was followed, each chief rising to speak, sometimes grasping a taiaha or paddle, and usually moving up and down in a cleared space before the dais. To watching Pakeha, some lacking experience of Maori custom, the intensity of the oratory was often disconcerting and alarming, yet at the same time the flow of language and Maori ability to command attention impressed onlookers.

In the first half of the meeting, a number of Maori speakers launched a vociferous attack. This articulate group comprised the Kororareka chiefs, Rewa, Moka, Hakiro and Tareha, Te Kemara of Te Tii (Waitangi), Kawiti from Waiomio on the Kawakawa River, Whai and another chief from the Waikare arm of the Bay of Islands.[56] Most were experienced in trade dealings with Pakeha, some had made extensive land sales in the previous ten years, and these factors clearly influenced their attitudes. Te Kemara, Rewa and Moka, for instance, challenged the purchasers of their lands – Busby, and the missionaries Henry Williams, Richard Davis, George Clarke and Charles Baker – to return the lands to their original owners.[57] Since the challenge was directed in a very personal manner at these men present in the assembly, it created considerable embarrassment. This increased when several Pakeha

(Kororareka traders [John?] Johnson, Jones and an unidentified third man) complained that Williams was not conveying an adequate translation of these speeches, implying that he was protecting himself.[58] Williams and Busby interrupted the Maori speeches so that each could present, in English, a brief defence of their land transactions.

It is difficult to know whether these outspoken chiefs genuinely believed that an injustice had been done in the land transactions, or whether they were simply seizing the opportunity to draw attention to Maori loss of land. On the basis of Te Kemara's evidence, given later to validate land sales, Colenso judged it to be the latter, 'all mere show'.[59] Whatever their motives, the protest was undoubtedly a shrewd debating tactic for it highlighted Pakeha eagerness to grasp the land.

In spite of this apparent resentment over land sales, almost all the main speakers voiced a preference to retain the services of the missionaries and Busby, which they argued were sufficient to Maori needs. In rejecting the alternative – Hobson and his authority – they expressed their fear that it would inevitably lead to a diminishing of chiefly status, a submission to a superior authority and the imposition of restrictive controls. These chiefs were aware that the substantial loss of land each had suffered was leading to weakened control, so a further erosion of authority by sharing power with the British government was unacceptable. Various speakers spoke directly to this point. Rewa, in particular, revealed a good grasp of the difference between sovereign power and territorial possession, an insight which should have forced Hobson and the British government to cast aside previous doubts about Maori capacity to understand this area. The chief asserted that the Maori people did not need a governor for they were neither 'whites nor foreigners'. Although some land had gone, 'this country is ours . . . we are the Governor – we, the chiefs of this our fathers' land'. If the governor were accepted, New Zealand would suffer the fate of other areas (such as New South Wales), taken by the British.[60]

Rewa's clear enunciation of the wish to retain Maori authority was expressed again by Tareha, an immense man with a 'deep sepulchral voice': the governor would be acceptable only if chiefs were given an equal rank. Other arguments in opposition to Hobson were raised by Whai and by a Waikare chief who queried the effectiveness of the proposed new authority to control Pakeha behaviour. Whai objected to the lying, cheating and stealing of Pakeha, and also mentioned the Pakeha habit of cursing which Maori found particularly offensive and threatening. Both chiefs complained about the inequality and injustices of trade deals, especially the practice of Pakeha middle-men who bought up Maori produce cheaply to sell at inflated prices.[61]

Neither Hobson nor any of the official party had ready rejoinders to some of these arguments. To those on the dais it was evident that the force of Maori oratory, set against the Waitangi proposal, was having a marked effect on the whole Maori audience. In addition, Hobson's case had not been helped by the early exchange over land, involving Williams, Busby and certain Pakeha onlookers. The unpleasantness was seen by some as evidence that the 30 January proclamations, coupled with the terms of the treaty just made public, had produced an anti-government faction among disgruntled local traders and settlers. The same group was suspected of inciting Maori opposition. Suspicion of a similar kind fell on Pompallier, because the Kororareka opposition group were neither CMS converts nor close supporters, but inclined to the Catholic faith.

While this tide of opposition was running against Hobson, only four speakers had briefly voiced their support, asking that he stay to be a 'father' to the Maori people, to protect their lands and to keep the peace. The four – Tamati Pukututu, Matiu, Pumuka and Wharerahi – were either mission converts, or old friends of the English missionaries. Their support had been no more than affirmation of Hobson and British authority. In comparison to the speakers in opposition, who had so influenced the crowd, these chiefs had not advanced persuasive arguments in Hobson's favour. Nor did a short, well-disposed effort by Rawiri [Taiwhanga, the CMS's first major convert] assist the British government's cause.

At this critical juncture, Heke, Nene and Patuone, all long-time associates of the English missionaries, rose to speak, one after the other; this swung the mood of the meeting towards Hobson. Heke reasoned that without a governor the Maori people might be subjected to the influence of the French and other unscrupulous Pakeha; that good would derive from Hobson remaining to be 'all as one' with the missionaries; that it would be not unlike the benefit brought by the Word of God – Te Kawenata Hou, the New Covenant or Testament, recently printed in the Maori language and widely circulated. Heke admitted, however, that Maori were uncertain of the future and inexperienced, like children; in the circumstances, they had to rely on the direction of their missionaries, their 'fathers'.[62]

Following this dramatic delivery, Tamati Waka Nene was even more emphatic. Dignified and persuasive, he appealed directly to the assembled Maori, stressing his belief that the situation in northern New Zealand left the Maori people with no option but to accept Hobson and British authority. In support of this, he pointed out that much land had gone already; that it was filled with numerous Pakeha over whom the chiefs had no power; and that the chiefs were losing influence while Pakeha power was expanding. If the traders and grog-sellers had been turned away 'in the old time', Nene reasoned, then the chiefs would have been in a position to reject Hobson's offer unanimously. But the time for that choice had passed, as the chief indicated by pointing to the many articles of foreign apparel being worn by chiefs and to a number of half-caste children, living evidence of the degree to which the two races were mingled. It was fitting, he concluded, that Hobson should remain to be a 'father, a judge, a peacemaker'. The British were not out to enslave the Maori; in Australia, no Maori was a slave and many had European friends.[63] These sentiments were endorsed by Patuone, Nene's elder brother, who also associated Hobson with the benefits brought by the missionaries and with the New Covenant.

The more promising disposition towards Hobson and the treaty caused by these speeches was not dispelled when Te Kemara made another extreme sally against Hobson. A remonstrance by another chief, together with the information that Te Kemara might have Hobson dwelling under his patronage at Busby's Waitangi home,[64] were sufficient to halt the chief's outpouring and turn him to shaking Hobson's hand wildly and greeting him repeatedly in English. General amusement over this incident broke the tension of the gathering and the meeting was brought to a close. Speech-making had been in progress for some five hours with a break only for a rather disruptive and poorly organised distribution of tobacco among the chiefs. Things had not gone too well for the British government and Hobson expressed his fears to Williams that the chiefs might not sign the treaty. Williams, long experienced in negotiating with Maori, 'cautioned' Hobson against showing any anxiety. He advised him to allow the chiefs time to think over the Waitangi proposal, as one of the chiefs had asked. Public notice was given that the meeting would reconvene on Friday, 7 February, and the meeting closed with three cheers for the governor, in which all 'lustily joined'. The official party then withdrew to Busby's house before returning to dine on the *Herald*. Everyone else dispersed.

During the evening of 5 February, the treaty was the subject of serious discussion among Maori who camped on the flat land south of the Waitangi River mouth (present-day Te Tii marae). As Williams recollected:

> There was considerable excitement amongst the people, greatly increased by the irritating language of ill-disposed Europeans, stating to the chiefs, in most insulting language, that their country was gone, and they now were only taurekareka (slaves). Many came to us to speak upon this new state of affairs. We gave them but one version, explaining clause by clause, showing the advantage to them of being taken under the fostering care of the British Government, by which act they would become one people with the English, in the suppression of wars, and of every lawless act; under one Sovereign, and one Law, human and divine.

When many had had their say, Williams urged them to attend the Waitangi meeting when it reconvened, because 'the question was for their own benefit, to preserve them as a people'.[65] He was obviously committed to the persuasive line of argument adopted during that day's meeting, emphasising the beneficial aspects of the treaty and distracting Maori attention from matters to which they might take exception.

By Thursday morning, 6 February, the chiefs had come to the decision that the treaty business should be concluded immediately so that they could return home. Williams was informed accordingly and by mid-morning between 300 and 400 Maori had gathered once more on Busby's lawn. Scattered in small groups, according to their tribes, they waited. On the *Herald*, however, there was no sign of movement. When Shortland, Cooper and Mathew came ashore towards noon to 'see what was going on', they were surprised to find the crowd waiting. On the ship they knew nothing about a meeting. A boat was quickly sent for Hobson who confirmed this fact; he had 'not the least notion' of a meeting being held.[66]

One of the missionaries, Richard Taylor, later explained that on the evening of 5 February he had sent a message to Hobson requesting permission to give notice that the meeting scheduled for Friday would be held on Thursday. Taylor claimed that Hobson had agreed to this, but Hobson denied any knowledge of it. Taylor may have been encouraged in his misapprehension by receiving from Hobson the 'rough copy of the treaty' to be copied afresh. This was on paper and contained the alterations made at Busby's suggestion.[67] According to Taylor, he 'sat up late' on Wednesday, copying the treaty on parchment and keeping the 'original draft' for his pains.[68]

Whatever the cause of the bungling, Taylor was clearly

anxious to hasten the treaty business to a successful conclusion. He feared that the majority of chiefs would return home because of a shortage of food, leaving the treaty unsigned. The several hundred Maori camping in the Waitangi vicinity had brought little or no food with them, and while the quantity of flour, sugar, pigs and potatoes distributed at the conclusion of the Wednesday meeting had seemed to one Pakeha to be 'vast', it was little enough to satisfy the appetites of such a large crowd through to Friday. Other supplies were several miles away at Kororareka where Pakeha influence might adversely affect Maori attitudes to signing the treaty. Taylor, no doubt in consultation with Williams and Busby, deemed any movement of chiefs away from Waitangi to be unwise; the sooner the treaty was signed the better. This was how Colenso read the drift of events. Surprised by news of the early reconvening at Waitangi, he reflected that 'perhaps the old proverb was borne in mind, "strike the iron while it is hot"'.[69] He noticed, for example, that some Maori had already begun to drift away; the assembly was not as large as on the first day. It was not only the lack of food that might have caused this; additional factors were the 'fierce squabble' over the poorly distributed tobacco on Wednesday, and memories of a meeting at Waitangi some four years earlier which had ended in bloodshed.[70]

After some discussion and hesitation among the official party, it was decided to go ahead with the meeting on 6 February, although Hobson 'more than once' expressed his concern that it could not be considered a 'regular public meeting', since proper notice had not been given. In the circumstances, this preference for the correct form was understandable. In fact, Hobson suggested that the Friday meeting, for which notice had been given, should still be held. On the Thursday, only signatures would be accepted; no discussion would be allowed.

Events now moved towards the signing. The official party took their places in the marquee. There was none of the pomp and circumstance of the previous day's meeting. Hobson, taken by surprise, had come ashore in plain clothes except for his hat, and unaccompanied by any of the *Herald*'s officers. Apart from Busby and several English missionaries, only about a dozen other Pakeha were present. Pompallier, accompanied by a priest, arrived just as proceedings were about to begin. The chiefs, who had become 'very impatient' at the morning's delay, were now reluctant to meet and had to be 'prevailed upon to assemble'.[71] At one estimate there were about 500 of them 'all seated on the ground with great decorum and regularity'. Several hundred more were outside the tent.[72]

Hobson opened proceedings by announcing that, since it was not a regular public meeting, he was restricting business to signing. The treaty in the Maori language, copied on parchment, lay on the table before him. It was read aloud once more by Williams. A pause followed before one or two chiefs rose to speak: the previous day they had not fully understood the matter but they had made enquiries and considered the business; they were prepared to sign because they believed it would be to their advantage.[73] Before anyone could move, however, there were two important interruptions, one from Pompallier, the other from Colenso.

Pompallier, fully aware that a British colony was being established, was concerned that religion should not be interfered with, that 'free toleration' would be allowed in 'matters of faith'.[74] He asked that a public guarantee to this effect be given the Maori, to which Hobson agreed. Williams had to interpret that 'all creeds alike' would receive Hobson's protection. Outraged at this concession to the Roman Catholics, and having tried unsuccessfully to dissuade Hobson, he made a calculated attempt to get round the issue. A carefully written statement was read to the assembly: 'The Governor says the several faiths of England, of the Wesleyans, of Rome, and also the Maori custom, shall be alike protected by him.' This last, Maori 'ritenga', was inserted at Colenso's suggestion to act as a 'correlative' to the clause on Rome. The English missionaries hoped that the Roman Catholic faith would suffer by association with ritenga (what Busby termed 'heathen practices')[75] which they quite explicitly attacked as decadent and which they aimed to eliminate from Maori society. The official recognition seemingly given Maori custom should be seen for what it was – an inclusion arising from sectarian jealousy. It ran counter to nineteenth-century Christian sensitivities, and barely accorded with Normanby's instructions to suppress, by force if necessary, the more extreme Maori usages. This promise to protect Maori custom – a verbal commitment given only by chance – amounted to very little.

As Pompallier retired from the meeting, his request granted, Colenso was steeling himself to intervene. From that morning, aware of the haste with which treaty negotiations were being concluded, he had been 'most agitated as to the correctness of the proceeding'. Not only was he disturbed about the failure of negotiators to make Maori fully cognisant of all aspects, he was also aware that some chiefs did not understand the treaty because they had not been present when explanations were given. Chiefs were still arriving during the 5 February meeting, over that evening, and even while the 6 February meeting was in progress. The understanding of these late-comers was based on hearsay. Colenso, wanting to raise the issue with Hobson, hoped that someone else might do so first, but his own brethren did not want the matter mentioned. Time was running out. Chiefs were being invited to come forward and sign, Busby calling them by name from a list (probably of Confederation chiefs). Heke, who was said by Colenso to be the most favourably disposed towards the treaty, was chosen first.[76] As Heke advanced towards the table where the treaty lay, Colenso finally rose and put a question directly to Hobson: did Hobson think that Maori understood the articles of the treaty which they were about to sign?

No query could be more pertinent to the matter in hand and none more significant to the future status of the treaty, but for Hobson and his colleagues it would have been most unwelcome. Hobson responded testily, asserting that he had expended all means in order to achieve full Maori comprehension. But Colenso refused to be so easily dismissed, claiming that some chiefs had 'no idea whatsoever as to the purport of the Treaty', that it was imperative that they should understand it to 'constitute its legality'. Busby now tried to resolve the issue by reasoning that Maori would have to trust the missionaries, as Heke had observed the previous day. Colenso could see the weakness in this argument only too well: unless the treaty was explained 'in all its bearings' so that Maori assent would be 'their own very act and deed', the missionaries would not be free from future reproach. His particular worry, as he confided to his journal that evening, was that Maori had not been made 'fully aware of ... the situation in which they would by their so signing be placed'.[77]

Detailed explanations, however, were probably what Hobson and Williams wanted to avoid. Committed to their task and facing the uncertainties of the future, they could scarcely be expected to act otherwise. Hobson, therefore, expressed the hope that the missionaries would keep their converts and associates 'peaceable enough'; and for the rest, 'we must do the best we can with them'. This impatient response, expedient in the circumstances, brushed aside a serious query raised in good faith and with good reason, thereby deferring the issue of full Maori understanding of the treaty clauses. Hobson had also placed a particular onus on the English missionaries – responsibility for Maori relationships with the Crown – that Colenso had specifically tried to avoid.

The exchange had evidently not perturbed the assembled Maori because the signing now went ahead with Heke again taking the initiative, followed by the other chiefs. Meanwhile, two chiefs,

Ruhe and Marupo, kept up a running challenge in the traditional manner. As each Maori signed, he shook hands with Hobson (and with the other members of the official party), the Lieutenant Governor repeating, 'He iwi tahi tatou' – 'We are now one people.' The ceremony closed with 'three thundering cheers' from the assembled Maori and with Patuone's presentation to Hobson of a mere (club) 'expressly' for Queen Victoria. As Hobson retired to the *Herald*, taking with him Patuone to dine, Colenso was left to attend to the customary distribution of gifts. In this instance, there were two blankets and a small quantity of tobacco for each signatory to the treaty, a detail which Colenso recorded with the wry comment: 'Sic transit gloria Nova Zealandia!'[78]

From an official point of view, the treaty signing had occurred almost by accident on 6 February. That evening, on the *Herald*, there was still some idea of a meeting on 7 February for late arrivals, but the following morning there was a sense of relief that the Waitangi meeting had been concluded early, because bad weather made any gathering, indeed any movement from the ship, quite impossible. It was Saturday, 8 February, therefore, when the *Herald* hoisted a 'profusion of British colours and fired a Royal salute of twenty-one guns'. There was also a 'great display' on shore at Kororareka. The celebration, said Colenso, was 'in honour of the new British Colony of New Zealand'.[79]

It is obvious that Hobson attached great significance to the Waitangi treaty signing, especially to the participation of the Confederation chiefs. In a 6 February dispatch to Gipps he noted that they had numbered twenty-six out of the forty-six 'head chiefs' who had signed.[80] (Later he was able to report that the majority of Confederation chiefs had given their assent.)[81] A technical hindrance to the assertion of British sovereignty had thus been removed. With the acquiescence of other northern chiefs this, he claimed, 'must be deemed a full and clear recognition of the sovereign rights of Her Majesty over the northern parts of this island'.[82] A further comment from Mathew suggests that it was believed officially that the treaty signed at Waitangi held the key to British acquisition of the whole country: 'We now consider', he said, 'that the first and most difficult part of our undertaking is completed, and do not anticipate any further trouble.'[83] The Waitangi signing, though only the first step in a planned series of signings, was regarded officially as virtually conclusive.

A perusal of signatures, however, shows that the Waitangi signing was far from conclusive. It is clear that Hobson had no intention of requiring unanimous Maori assent to the treaty as a prerequisite to his first assertion of British sovereignty. Rather, he was prepared to settle for a counting of heads. The first group of signatories at Waitangi was not widely representative of the north. In Colenso's opinion, the 'greater part of them were from the Bay of Islands and its immediate vicinity', a point repeated by Henry Williams and confirmed by names on the treaty sheet.[84] It seems that the only ones from any distance were Nene from Hokianga, Kauhata, Wharau and Ngere from Whangaruru, and the Hokianga chief Patuone, who had possibly been fetched from Whakatiwai pa in the Hauraki Gulf.[85] Colenso's critical eye also perceived that 'not many chiefs of first rank' had signed. It was a shrewd comment: neither Pomare nor Kawiti, two major Bay of Islands chiefs, had signed on 6 February;[86] other notable absentees were Waikato and Wharepoaka. Hobson was assuming sovereignty over northern New Zealand on the basis of an agreement with a rather selective group.

As for Maori understanding of the treaty, it left much to be desired. As well as those who had not heard or grasped explanations, there were signatories who had not been made fully aware of the nature of the agreement. Williams's Maori text failed to convey the full meaning of the national sovereignty being conceded. Adequate explanations could have overcome this, but failed to do so. Couched in terms designed to convince chiefs to sign, explanations skirted the problem of sovereignty cognisable at international law and presented an ideal picture of the workings of sovereignty within New Zealand. Maori authority might have to be shared, but Hobson would merely be more effective than Busby, and British jurisdiction would apply mainly to controlling troublesome Pakeha; Maori authority might even be enhanced. The oral nature of the Waitangi deliberations was thus of paramount importance, particularly in a Maori tradition in which relationships were customarily sustained and modified through lengthy discussion. Since chiefs at Waitangi did not have the treaty text before them, the oral record was all the more crucial to understanding.

Another significant element in persuading chiefs was the tradition of a personalised, caring Crown, an image long cultivated by the British among northern Maori. Williams, for example, played on this idea by presenting the treaty as the Queen's 'act of love' towards the Maori people. He perceived, too, that for Maori converted to or associated with Christianity there was an additional spiritual dimension – under one Sovereign, Maori and British could be linked as one people with the same law, spiritual and temporal. Hobson, prompted perhaps by Williams, also promoted this concept with his greeting 'He iwi tahi tatou' ('We are now one people').[87] Chiefs had indicated already that they were disposed to think of the treaty in spiritual terms; Heke and Patuone had both likened the agreement to the new covenant. The role of the English missionaries in determining Maori understanding, therefore, was crucial through the way explanations were given. It determined that Ngapuhi, in particular, would understand the treaty as a special kind of covenant with the Queen, a bond with all the spiritual connotations of the biblical covenants; there would be many tribes, including the British, but all would be equal under God.

A few chiefs had reservations to the very end of the Waitangi meeting. Rewa, for instance, still refused when all other chiefs of note had signed, although the persuasion of some of his fellow chiefs, as well as the CMS missionaries, finally weakened his resolve.[88] Hobson, Busby and the English missionaries attributed this Maori opposition to the treaty to the influence of Pompallier. While Hobson treated the Bishop in public with courtesy and consideration, inviting him to attend the meeting and assuring him that religious tolerance would be observed, he later reported to Gipps that Pompallier had encouraged Maori to oppose the agreement.[89] Suspicions of Pompallier were based on comments by Rewa and Te Kemara. The latter claimed that the Bishop had told them not to sign the document for they would become slaves as a result: 'Kei tuhituhi koe ki to pukapuka ki te mea ka [tupono?] taurekarekatia koe.'[90] It was also well known that these and other chiefs in opposition were close associates of the Catholic mission; Rewa had actually arrived from Kororareka in Pompallier's company.[91]

Suspicions of Pompallier were partially correct. Writing about the event some years later, he admitted that the 'Catholic chiefs' (mainly from the Kororareka district), and 'above all' Rewa, had consulted him over the treaty. He had told them: 'It was for them to determine what they might desire to do with their national sovereignty, whether to keep it or to transfer it to a foreign nation; they were therefore at liberty to sign or not to sign the treaty which was going to be put before them.' But whatever their decision it would not affect the French mission administering to Maori spiritual needs, which were his sole concern. From this, the Bishop concluded that he had kept himself 'entirely aloof from politics'.[92]

This was true in a sense only. As a Frenchman and a Catholic, Pompallier was undoubtedly able to adopt a more neutral position than could the Englishmen committed to Crown success in the treaty negotiations. He could, therefore, have more open, honest discussion with the Catholic chiefs concerning the transfer of Maori authority. While not opposing the treaty, he was certainly not promoting it, as were most of the English missionaries. His early departure from the Waitangi meeting of 6 February, before any chiefs had signed the treaty, was probably sufficient to suggest the Bishop's public dissociation from the business in hand. Even allowing for Maori exaggeration and national or sectarian jealousies, there was some justification for suspecting the French Bishop. It is not surprising that the Kororareka chiefs, with Pompallier as their adviser, had demonstrated a more accurate grasp of the nature and effect of the treaty than most.

Yet Maori expectations of benefits from the agreement must in the end have outweighed fears, enabling reluctant chiefs to put aside reservations. The alternative of French intrusion, for example, would scarcely have been attractive to most northern Maori, even to those with Catholic sympathies. Although Pompallier's work had created a good impression in the north, France was still referred to with a 'twinge of bitterness'. Contemporary French pressure on Pacific Islanders was certainly brought to Maori attention by the English missionaries and was possibly confirmed by shipping contacts.[93] Other motives for Maori adherence to the treaty would become apparent later – expectation of increased trade, desire for various material benefits, assistance in handling the changes disturbing Maori life and, not least, the possibility of manipulating British authority in inter-tribal rivalries. Above all, Maori fear that the mana of the land might pass from them if they signed the treaty was eased by the treaty's guarantee of rangatiratanga. It looked as if the treaty was asking little of them but offering much. The promises, moreover, were backed by a document of the kind that northern Maori, long experienced in contact with Pakeha, knew was important to Europeans.[94]

For Maori chiefs, the Waitangi decision required a remarkable degree of trust. They were encouraged by the advice of the English missionaries that Maori interests would be best served by agreeing to the treaty. The missionaries had become convinced in the two or three years before 1840 that a regularisation of English intrusion into the country would be much preferable to the haphazard influx of settlers and transients that was proving increasingly detrimental to Maori welfare. They had also become concerned about the pressure being applied to Maori to sell their land, encouraging northern Maori to retain their most fertile acres and attempting to hold land in trust.[95] Their anxieties had been heightened by news of the New Zealand Company's colonisation plans and confirmed when Henry Williams returned from the south in January 1840 with tales of dubious Company purchases. If New Zealand became a British colony a conjunction of Maori and Pakeha interests might be effected; CMS and Wesleyan missionaries shared this view.[96] They had good reason, then, to suppress any qualms about misleading the Maori people. They were no doubt also able to overcome any twinge of guilt by reference to the point, partially true, that Maori could not possibly appreciate the full implications of what they were doing. Hence the missionaries tended to emphasise the fact that the good faith of the Crown to honour the Waitangi agreement was pledged in a unique way. This came to be accepted as part of the 'spirit' of the treaty which morally bound the Crown to uphold the several guarantees given. Later, when the ambiguities of the agreement became apparent and doubts about its legal status arose, it would be this 'spirit' of the treaty that would sustain a sense of Maori expectation and Pakeha obligation that treaty promises should be kept.

Chapter Four

EXTENDING THE TREATY

With the Waitangi meeting concluded, Hobson set out to obtain more Maori signatures to the treaty. Although the legal aspect of retracting British recognition of Maori independence was less pressing, the agreement of some 1835 signatories had still to be obtained. Normanby's injunction to seek the 'free and intelligent consent' of the Maori people as a whole also had to be fulfilled.[1] The continuing interest of France and the United States provided further impetus, highlighted when a group of French settlers arrived in mid-1840 to establish a colony in the South Island.

For Hobson, the initial signing at Waitangi was the 'de facto' treaty; the later signings he represented as merely acts that 'further ratified and confirmed' it.[2] When he issued a proclamation on 21 May asserting sovereignty over the North Island on the ground of cession by treaty, he stated that 'full sovereignty' was vested in the Crown from the date of the Waitangi signing. In fact, the confident dating of 'full sovereignty' from 6 February owed much to subsequent Maori accession to the treaty.

At the end of the signings Hobson had not secured unanimous Maori agreement. The Colonial Office had not, however, required this, knowing that a dispersed leadership structure would make full coverage difficult.[3] Hobson nevertheless did his best to secure as many signatures as possible, knowing full well that events would be scrutinised by several audiences – international, humanitarian and Maori. In the months following Waitangi, he had to cope with an increasingly complex situation requiring careful diplomatic skills. Essentially, success depended on the degree to which Maori could be persuaded that they would benefit from signing the treaty. Inevitably, this required a continuation of explanations that stressed the advantages of British intrusion and minimised the effects on Maori independence. The pattern established at Waitangi would be repeated around the country.

On 10 February, the official party, accompanied by Maori porters, travelled fifteen miles inland to the CMS mission station at Waimate where an overnight stop was made.[4] The strong missionary affiliation of Maori in this area greatly assisted Hobson in his mission. A group of senior Waimate chiefs had accompanied the missionary, Richard Davis, to Waitangi where Hobson had been invited to visit Waimate. Several had signed at Waitangi – Reweti Atuahaere, Wiremu Hau, Hara and others. Presumably they had acquainted other Waimate men with the terms of the treaty for there is no record of the treaty being read nor any explanation being given. When the official party had rested briefly at Richard Taylor's mission residence, Hobson received six chiefs who signed. This appears to have been the only treaty signing at Waimate.[5]

Early on 11 February, Hobson's party, escorted now by the missionaries Taylor and Clarke, moved on to the Wesleyan mission station at Mangungu on the Hokianga Harbour. Their arrival was expected; a large crowd of Pakeha and Maori had gathered up-river, with a flotilla of gaily decorated boats and canoes, to bear the official group down to the harbour. A meeting with Hokianga chiefs was held the following day at Mangungu, with John Hobbs, a Wesleyan missionary, acting as interpreter at Hobson's request. The mission house was a suitable venue, since several hundred Maori were accustomed to gathering there each Saturday evening to prepare for Sunday services. By 9 a.m. on 12 February between 2,000 and 3,000, the majority associated with the mission, had assembled. According to Hobson, about 500 of these were chiefs 'of different degrees'. When a table and chairs had been placed on the verandah for the official party, the chiefs were invited to come forward and sit on the lawn. A number of local Pakeha were also present. The meeting followed the pattern at Waitangi, with Hobson briefly addressing the Pakeha before explaining his mission and reading the treaty.[6]

When the meeting was thrown open to discussion, it became apparent that the chiefs were very well prepared to debate the treaty; there had been time and opportunity to become informed about its provisions and effects. News of Hobson's arrival and his intentions had reached the area more than a week before, creating 'great excitement'. Reports had been circulating that the 'Queen had sent her officers to take the country as they had taken New Holland [Australia], and that the chiefs would thereby lose both their dignity and their country'.[7] Maori had canvassed missionary opinion and a contingent of Hokianga chiefs, accompanied by the Wesleyan missionaries, Samuel Ironside and John Warren, had attended the Waitangi meeting. Some had decided to sign then, the most notable being Nene, who now supported Hobson's cause at the Hokianga assembly.

As at Waitangi, the first and most articulate speakers were chiefs who opposed the treaty.[8] They were highly suspicious of the real motives behind the British proposal, citing the experience

MAP 1: LOCATIONS OF TREATY SIGNINGS

National Archives (Wellington) hold the treaty sheets which are listed below. In 1877 they were first published in *Facsimiles...of the Treaty of Waitangi*. The sheets are numbered according to the sequence in which they are found in the *Facsimiles*. The names attributed to the sheets here are not part of any official record. The list indicates the place of signing, the dates or date of signing, and gives approximate numbers of signatures. (See also Chapters 3 and 4, and Appendix 2.)

There is a further printed sheet which is not included here because it is not referred to in the 1840 negotiations. It has several signatures and is witnessed by R. Maunsell. It may date from an 1844 printing of the treaty.

Map	Location	Date	Signatures
1.	*Waitangi*		total – over 213
1a	Waitangi	6 February	43
1b	Waimate	10 February	8
1c	Hokianga	12 February	70
	Waitangi [?]	17 February	1
1a	Paihia [?]	13[?] May	4
	Russell	5 August	3
	Bay of Islands	6 February–August	28[?]
1d	Waitemata	4 March	16
1e	Kaitaia	28 April	61
1d	Tamaki	9 July	7
2.	*Bay of Plenty* (Fedarb)		26 total
2a	Opotiki	27 & 28 May	7
2b	Torere	11 June	2
	Torere	14 June	1
2c	Te Kaha	14 June	4
2d	Whakatane	16 June	12
3.	*Herald-Bunbury*		27 total
3a	Coromandel	4 May	4
3b	Mercury Bay (Is.)	7 May	2
3c	Akaroa	30 May	2
3d	Ruapuke	10 June	3
3e	Otago	13 June	2
3f	Cloudy Bay	17 June	9
3g	Mana (off-shore)	19 June	2
3h	Hawke's Bay	24 June	3
4.	*Henry Williams*		132 total
4a	Port Nicholson	29 April	34
4b	Queen Charlotte Sound	4–5 May	27
4c	Rangitoto Island	11 May	13
4d	Kapiti	14 May	4
4e	Waikanae	16 May	20
4f	Otaki	19 May) 21 May)	18
4g	Manawatu	26 May)	
4h	Wanganui	23 May	10
	Wanganui	31 May	4
4i	Motungarara	4 June	2
5.	*Waikato-Manukau*		39 total
5a	Waikato Heads	March [April?]	32
5b	Manukau	26 April	7
6.	*Tauranga*		21 total
6	Tauranga	10 April–23 May	
7.	*East Coast*		41 total
7a	Turanga (Gisborne)	5 May and later	25
7b	Uawa (Tolaga Bay)	16/17 May	2
7c	Waiapu (Whaka-whitira)	25 May)	
	(Rangitukia)	1 June)	10
7d	Tokomaru	9 June	4
8.	*Manukau-Kawhia*		13 total
8a	Manukau	20 March	3
8b	Kawhia	28 April	1
		21 May	3
		25 May	1
		15 June	3
		27 August	1
		3 September	1

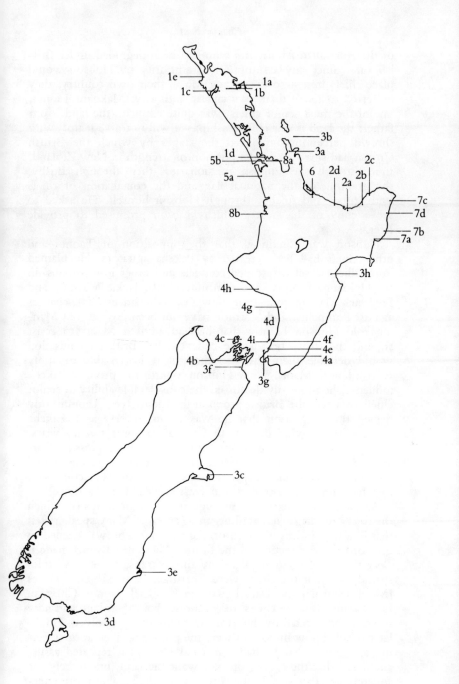

of the Australian Aborigines who had been degraded under British rule. Since any assumption of authority by Hobson would
place chiefs in a subordinate position in their own country, they
preferred to retain their own chiefly authority. Makoare Taonui,
one of the most senior chiefs, was quite explicit: 'the land is our
father; the land is our chieftainship; we will not give it up.' With
shrewd perception he traced the stages by which the British
Crown had slowly gained a position of strength in New Zealand,
first through the English missionaries; then through Busby,
the granting of the national flag and the conciliation of chiefs
with gifts;[9] and finally, through Hobson himself. He asked to
see a copy of the treaty, which Hobson promised to provide
later.

Hobson was convinced that the opposition of Taonui and
other chiefs had been created by Pakeha agitators. He blamed
Pompallier, a 'set of escaped convicts and other low ruffians' in
the Hokianga vicinity, and two individuals, Jackie Marmon and
Frederick Maning, long-time New Zealand residents. The charges
against Pompallier and Marmon have not been proved, but Maning told Hobson bluntly that he had advised Maori to resist
signing the treaty because he believed that British colonisation
would degrade them; he also thought it inadvisable to apply
British law to Maori. While Hobson took this as proof of Pakeha
influence, he too easily dismissed the considerable ability of senior
chiefs to assess the British proposal for themselves. Taonui hotly
denied the suggestion that he was acting merely as a Pakeha
mouthpiece. Having dealt with Pakeha for some twenty years,
visiting Sydney on at least one occasion, he was expressing fears
grounded on personal experience and observation. Others based
their criticisms on local experience, expressing dissatisfaction with
the sharp practice of traders and with past land transactions.

As the meeting extended through the day, the terms on which
the treaty might be accepted began to emerge. Many speakers felt
that it was pointless to dwell on the past; Hobson was needed to
give order and direction to the future. These discussions made it
clear that concern to regulate any future transactions was widespread, whether the chiefs were Christian, such as Nene, Moses
[Mohi Tawhai?] and Daniel [Raniera Kahika?], or non-Christian
like Taonui. But the chiefs' reservations about their land and how
it would be affected by the treaty were not easily resolved. Hobbs
later recalled how important were the promises given at the meeting and noted that he had translated Hobson's 'repeated assurances ... that the Queen did not want the land, but merely the
sovereignty, that she, by her officers, might be able more effec-
tually to govern her subjects who had already settled ... or might

... arrive, and punish those of them who might be guilty of crime'. Hobbs further pledged that land would 'never be forcibly taken' from the Maori, but would always be purchased by the Queen if it were needed, a statement that he reiterated many times. He also interpreted what he considered to be Hobson's '*most solemn assurance*' (the emphasis was Hobbs's) that if the chiefs signed the treaty, 'truth and justice would always characterize the proceedings of the Queen's Government'.[10] Such explanations, which stressed the seriousness of the negotiations, undoubtedly shaped Maori understanding, one chief referring to the treaty that same night as a 'very sacred' deed.[11]

Most chiefs, though cautious, resolved to commit themselves. Hobson claimed that the decisive factor had been his skill in rebutting Maning's influence, but Hobbs attributed success to missionary persuasion, which Hobson subsequently acknowledged.[12] As Hobbs recalled, speech-making had continued without a break from morning to almost six in the evening, with no resolution reached. One of the principal Christian chiefs turned then to Hobbs and the other missionaries, seeking their opinion. When they stated that the treaty would be good for Maori, the signing went ahead. Between six and midnight, 'upwards of 56 signatures were given'. Hobson, in fact, had to restrain the enthusiasm of some who wished to sign but were considered of insufficient rank.[13]

The solemnity of the agreement entered into at Hokianga was reinforced, as at Waitangi, by a degree of pomp and circumstance. At the suggestion of various chiefs, Hobson cancelled arrangements to confirm the cession of sovereignty by raising the Union Jack at Hokianga Heads, some thirty miles from Mangungu, so that a local celebration could be held. On the day after the signing, this took place at Horeke, a well-established timber-milling site, a mile or so up-river from Mangungu. The celebration, staged at official expense, occupied the entire day, beginning with a haka of 1,500 men, which the official party viewed from boats anchored offshore; 3,000 men, women and children then participated in the feast of pork, potatoes, rice and sugar; blankets were distributed and every man received a small portion of tobacco. The significance of the occasion was further recognised by a salute from a small battery of about a dozen guns at Horeke and by a similar volley from the home of local trader George Frederick Russell at Kohukohu across the river, where Hobson stopped briefly.[14]

Support had not been unanimous. Two major chiefs refused to sign, another returned a gift of money and others attempted to withdraw their commitment to the agreement. According to one account, just as Hobson was about to depart from Hokianga, he received a letter signed by a chief and fifty of his tribe, asking that they be dissociated from the treaty and stating that they were not prepared to acknowledge the Queen.[15] (When Hobson reported this matter to Normanby he asserted that two tribes were involved.) Attributing the act to Catholic influence and regretting Maori 'credulity', Hobson bluntly refused to make any alteration. Although the about-face annoyed Hobson at the time, he was evidently more vexed by public embarrassment than by any question of sovereignty. He concluded his Hokianga report by reiterating his earlier statement that he deemed the Waitangi signing to be the essential act of cession which had made British sovereignty over the north 'complete'; the signing of the Hokianga chiefs was merely an 'adherence' which rendered the question 'beyond dispute'.[16] This was to be his attitude to all subsequent treaty signings.

Hobson, returning through Waimate to the Bay of Islands, was keen to hasten treaty signing in other parts of the country. He planned to proclaim sovereignty by degrees, beginning first with a proclamation covering the territory from North Cape to the thirty-sixth degree of latitude (a line just south of Dargaville and Waipu), but this idea was dropped. It might have irritated some chiefs who had not given their assent although they lived within the limits to be claimed. Hobson's plans were also thwarted by Nias falling ill and by adverse winds which delayed the *Herald's* departure for the south.[17]

There was now time to attend to other treaty affairs. At Hobson's request, Colenso printed 200 copies of the Maori text of the treaty on the CMS press at Paihia.[18] About this time, too, the treaty sheet itself received an important additional signature – that of Pomare.[19] Just as this chief had arrived late for the ceremony at which a national flag had been selected, so he now made a late adherence to the treaty. His signature was witnessed by the American Consul, James R. Clendon. When Charles Wilkes, an American naval commander, called at the Bay of Islands a few weeks later, Clendon gave him the impression that he had played a significant role in securing agreement to the treaty. Wilkes, however, was critical of Pomare's understanding. He thought that the chief anticipated some special mark of recognition from the Queen, such as an officer's uniform, to enhance his prestige; he was sure that Pomare had not grasped that he had relinquished any authority or rights in regard to land.[20] Wilkes's attitude may have been soured by resentment that an American representative had served British interests. Nevertheless, it would appear that Pomare, like many other signatories, lacked a full understanding of the nature of the contract.

On 21 February, the wind finally allowed the *Herald* to head south, intending to circumnavigate the North Island. Hobson was especially concerned to call at Port Nicholson where the New Zealand Company settlers had arrived several weeks before, but the first stop was at Waitemata Harbour where he hoped to collect further adherents to the treaty and to see if the area was suitable for a settlement. Mathew, Cooper and Freeman accompanied Hobson in exploring the harbour and its adjacent territory for nearly a week. Henry Williams, who had joined the *Herald* at Hobson's request, had left the ship for Maraetai, a CMS mission station, to arrange a treaty meeting. On 1 March, however, before Williams had reported back, Hobson suddenly suffered a stroke which paralysed his right side and impaired his speech. His condition seemed to be 'very precarious' at first; three days later, still 'much shaken', he had begun to improve.[21]

Hobson's illness seemed to jeopardise the planned series of treaty negotiations; talk of his resignation cast doubt on the likelihood of consolidating British sovereignty by treaty. A Waitemata signing, at least, now appeared very unlikely. An unsigned sheet had been appended to the original parchment signed by northern chiefs, but by 3 March those on the *Herald* had heard nothing from Williams. His silence, coupled with Hobson's condition, produced among the official party a growing uneasiness which was only relieved when word reached the ship that some chiefs were ready to sign. Early on 4 March, Nias, Cooper and Mathew sailed to an appointed 'rendezvous' where the signing was 'soon performed'. Some sixteen chiefs from the western side of the Hauraki Gulf, its hinterland and its islands gave their adherence.[22]

The most likely attraction of the treaty for Maori in this area was its promise of protection. Caught between the major tribal groupings of Waikato to the south and Ngapuhi to the north, Maori from the Hauraki Gulf and from the narrow isthmus between the east and west coasts had been decimated by inter-tribal fighting in the previous twenty years. A peace, negotiated with missionary assistance in 1835–36, was still uncertain.[23] For these Maori, then, as for many tribes elsewhere, the treaty offered a Pax Britannica which would protect them from old foes. This, at least, was the reasoning recollected by a local Maori some years later. After a meeting of morehu (remnants of tribes) held at Okahu, Auckland, seven Waitemata chiefs had travelled to the Bay of Islands in February to invite Hobson to settle among them.[24] Their circumstances made Maori of the Waitemata isthmus receptive to the treaty, while Williams's role as main negotiator had special significance, for he had been the instrument of the peace-making four years earlier.

Some Waitemata chiefs had not signed, but Hobson's condition now forced the *Herald* to return to the Bay of Islands. The ship's surgeon, Alexander Lane, reported that, by 11 March, Hobson was 'rapidly recovering'; 'he could walk without any assistance, could use a stick in his right hand, and could sign his name.' Lane, nevertheless, recommended complete rest and Hobson was moved to Waimate where he remained for several weeks.

While the *Herald* returned to Sydney,[25] Shortland took command and shouldered the task of organising further treaty signatures. Several longhand copies of the text signed at Waitangi were made, and on 13 March Shortland sent one copy, under his own signature, to Captain William C. Symonds to obtain signatures in the Manukau and adjacent districts on the west coast.[26] Symonds, an unattached British army officer, had been active in that area during 1839 on behalf of a proposed Scottish land company settlement. When the *Herald* had visited the Waitemata, he had been a member of the official group, and had remained in the area.[27] He now sought the assistance of James Hamlin, a CMS catechist living on the southern shore of the Manukau Harbour. Symonds and Hamlin immediately assembled 'as many of the Maori chiefs as could be collected in a short notice'. The proposals of the British government were explained, but Maori agreement to the treaty was not forthcoming. Symonds attributed this to the presence of Rewa. A strenuous opponent of the treaty and a reluctant signatory at Waitangi, this Kororareka chief had been dropped off by Pompallier's ship at the Waitemata isthmus after the February meeting. Among Waitemata–Manukau chiefs Rewa 'exerted all his influence' against the treaty, leaving Symonds scope only to correct Rewa's 'misrepresentations'.

On 20 March a second Manukau meeting was held.[28] Many Waikato chiefs were present along with some from Tauranga and Taupo, but none would sign, although some promised to commit themselves later. Symonds believed that the problem was a chiefly 'feeling of pique' that they had not been accorded due recognition by an earlier official approach. Among this group was the paramount chief of Waikato, Te Wherowhero (who was related to Rewa by marriage). It was fortunate for the government that Te Wherowhero did not oppose the British move outright because, had he exercised a chiefly power of veto (as Te Heuheu seems to have done later with his tribe), Waikato chiefs would not have committed themselves; a number did give their adherence at various other meetings. Symonds had some success, however. Three major Ngati Whatua chiefs – Te Kawau, Te Tinana and Te Reweti – agreed to sign, apparently also seeking protection from their enemies.

During March 1840 official attention turned again to Waikato and to other North Island tribes. Hobson had now recovered sufficiently to append his rather shaky signature to a number of treaty copies. Various missionaries were authorised to act as official negotiators. On the west coast at Waikato Heads, Robert Maunsell received a copy in English (the only English copy known to be circulated); at Tauranga in the Bay of Plenty, Alfred Nesbitt Brown received a treaty copy by 1 April; and by that date, Henry Williams, who had volunteered his services, was preparing to leave the Bay of Islands to visit the southern districts of the North Island and perhaps the South Island. In all cases, Hobson's instructions were substantially the same: the missionaries were to explain the treaty's 'principle and object', which Maori were to 'clearly understand' before they would be permitted to sign.[29]

By chance, the copy of the treaty sent to Maunsell arrived as large numbers of Maori were assembling for an important annual mission meeting. Many had travelled from districts four and five days distant. The station, sited near the mouth of the Waikato River, did not have a significant permanent Maori population, but was frequented by Maori from many areas, seeking the stores of shellfish at the river mouth. For several years, Maunsell, with James Hamlin's assistance, had worked in this area, moving between the Heads and the Manukau. His influence was extensive; in June 1840, he reported that three-quarters of the estimated 7,000 Maori in his district had accepted Christianity. At the March 1840 meeting, about 1,500 were present.[30]

Maunsell considered that the thirty-two chiefs who signed the treaty at Waikato Heads comprised most of the leading men of the area over which he had some influence, although he had to admit failure in the case of two Waikato chiefs (one of whom was possibly Te Wherowhero).[31] The tribal affiliations of those who signed represented many Waikato–Ngati Maniapoto groups, as far south as Mokau on the coast and inland to Taupiri, Matamata and Te Awamutu. While there is no record that any explanation of the treaty was given at the meeting, one signatory, Wiremu Neira Te Awaitaia, recalled some four years later that it was on missionary advice that the chiefs had signed; they had been given to understand that any nation other than Britain would have forcibly compelled Maori to give up possession of the country, whereas government by the British could be relied upon to be benevolent.[32]

Symonds had intended to seek treaty signatories down the coast to Taranaki, but since Maunsell's work had made this unnecessary, he bore Maunsell's treaty copy, together with an accompanying report, back to Manukau where seven more Waikato chiefs signed on 26 April. Symonds felt at a disadvantage, for Hamlin's interpreting services were not available. Moreover, Te Wherowhero and 'several others' continued to object to the agreement, although Symonds believed that they showed no ill will to the government itself. He attributed his failure to secure Maori accession, especially that of Te Wherowhero, to the lack of pomp and circumstance which chiefly pride might have expected as a right.[33] Symonds's negotiations, for instance, were in marked contrast to the government efforts made some two months earlier at the Waitangi and Hokianga meetings.

Before Symonds left Waikato Heads, he and Maunsell had scrutinised Maunsell's list of signatories. Since there were four or five chiefs at Kawhia and two at Whaingaroa (Raglan) whose signatures were wanted, Symonds had sent his own treaty copy (with its three Ngati Whatua signatures) down to John Whiteley, the Wesleyan missionary at Kawhia, requesting him to secure their agreement and that of any other chiefs of note in Kawhia and the surrounding area 'stretching as far to the southward as possible among the Maniapoto'. Whiteley, together with his co-worker James Wallis, carried out this task over several months. How agreement was obtained is not known, but Symonds directed Whiteley to explain 'perfectly' the 'nature of the cession of rights' and the missionary later believed that he had done this to the best of his ability. A last signing, on 3 September, made Maori agreement to the treaty almost unanimous on the west coast down to Mokau.[34]

Gathering treaty signatures elsewhere was similarly protracted, the response from different tribes varying considerably. At Tauranga, for example, Brown hesitated even to broach the subject with chiefs of rank. For some months, the whole Bay of Plenty district had been disturbed by inter-tribal fighting. Moreover, Christian influence was not strong among the senior chiefs. Brown, however, decided to try for signatures; on 10 April, CMS personnel, assembled at Tauranga for a committee meeting, spent the day on this task.[35] That day, or in the weeks following, twenty-one Tauranga chiefs signed. But the major Ngai Te Rangi chief, Tupaea, at Otumoetai pa, and other chiefs (mostly associated with Tupaea), would not sign. Probably for this reason Brown then put the treaty copy aside, hoping perhaps that the chiefs would change their minds.

Around the beginning of April, Henry Williams left the Bay of Islands on the schooner *Ariel* to carry out treaty negotiations in the south.[36] On 8 April, he delivered a copy to his brother, William Williams, at Turanga, where a CMS mission had been established earlier in the year. William was charged with securing agreement among Maori from East Cape to Ahuriri (Napier). On 5 May, almost a month after receiving the treaty, he discussed the matter with local chiefs, several of whom agreed to sign that day; the final count of twenty-five, according to William, comprised almost the whole leadership of the Turanga district.[37] In the latter half of May, he travelled up to East Cape, combining treaty business with mission work, and gathering further signatures: two at Uawa (Tolaga Bay), ten at Waiapu, and four at Tokomaru on the return journey to Turanga. William had informed Hobson of his intention to seek treaty adherents among the mixed tribal groupings south of Turanga at the end of July or in August, but this plan was shelved. (By chance, a Wairoa chief signed at Turanga and an Ahuriri chief at Uawa or Waiapu.) William's hope that seventy or eighty signatures would be obtained was not fulfilled, for his treaty sheet shows roughly half that number.

William Williams left no record of his explanations or discussions with chiefs. In his anxiety to thwart wholesale land purchases, he would undoubtedly have stressed the treaty's promise to protect Maori land. Since February he had been trying to impress upon East Coast Maori the seriousness of the land situation. On 10 February, he had told a large meeting of nearly every principal Turanga chief that Pakeha were everywhere, 'buying the whole country' out of the hands of the Maori who would 'soon be left at the mercy of the new proprietors'. Williams managed to secure a trust agreement over Turanga land from local chiefs whose fears were given some substance by news of two vessels seeking land at Wairoa. Two weeks later at Mahia, Williams warned a Maori assembly that 'Europeans being the strongest would give them [Maori] the head of the pig and the feet and take all the flesh and the fat to themselves'.[38] If proof to convince the Maori were wanting, it was provided about this time by Captain William Barnard Rhodes's nominal purchase of some 100 miles of coast between Port Nicholson and Ahuriri. Rumour that seven shiploads of settlers were reputed to be arriving shortly from Cook Strait, added to Maori apprehensions.[39] Their anxiety to protect their land rights was always acute; such circumstances would surely have predisposed them to accept the protective assurances built into the treaty.

Some East Coast Maori were also reassured by the fact that the treaty was carried to them by William Williams. At Waiapu, for instance, where the missionary was 'almost worshipped' for his part in returning some local people from Ngapuhi captivity some four years before, the treaty was well received. Williams failed, however, to persuade the great chief Te Kani a Takirau to sign, although he used the chief's house at Uawa as a place of assembly.[40] William Williams could not claim to have successfully secured the full adherence of his district.

By contrast, Henry Williams was able to report that Port Nicholson (Wellington) chiefs had 'unanimously' signed the treaty for him on 29 April. Yet this was achieved only with patience, for he was obliged to wait for ten days at Port Nicholson before the chiefs were 'disposed to come forward'; he attributed their reluctance to the influence of the New Zealand Company settlers.[41] In the next two weeks, however, further signatures were received, apparently without difficulty, at Queen Charlotte Sound and Rangitoto (d'Urville Island) on the south side of Cook Strait. At Kapiti, the accession of Te Rauparaha was secured.

Te Rauparaha's agreement was most significant because it opened the way to a wider reception of the treaty in this part of the country. In fact, Hobson stated that Henry Williams's 'principal object' in going south was to win his adherence, because this would secure to the Crown the 'undisputed right of sovereignty over all the southern districts'. Williams told Hobson almost immediately after the chief's signing that he had succeeded to his 'utmost satisfaction' and expected to carry his task through to completion.[42] This he did in the following weeks, procuring signatures from chiefs of Otaki, Waikanae and Manawatu, travelling to Wanganui where the senior chiefs signed, and finally securing two last signings at Motungarara, the tiny island off the southern tip of Kapiti. By then, Williams's treaty copy listed approximately 132 chiefs. Most major chiefs in all the areas visited seem to have consented to the treaty.

These west coast negotiations were carried out entirely by Henry Williams. The merchant George Thomas Clayton of the *Ariel* was merely a witness, a role that was taken on the Kapiti coast and at Wanganui by the missionary, Octavius Hadfield, although the latter would have preferred to have had no connection at all with the government.[43] Williams's success must be attributed solely to his own persuasion. That he was a man of considerable mana among the Maori was undoubtedly significant. Only a few months before, he had travelled over this southern territory bringing Hadfield, at Te Rauparaha's request, to establish a mission on the coast opposite Kapiti.

Most of the coast from Port Nicholson to Taranaki had been disturbed for some years by Maori migrations and by continuing struggles among the tribes to adjust their rights. By the end of 1839 the New Zealand Company negotiations to purchase extensive land tracts on both sides of Cook Strait and up the west coast were causing more tension. This had been apparent to Williams late in 1839 when he had visited Port Nicholson where Reihana, a CMS Maori teacher from the north, had already begun mission work. In order to thwart Company designs on Maori land, Williams, returning to the north by way of Wanganui, had managed to secure land in trust for Maori at Putiki-Wharenui pa. When he returned in May 1840 to negotiate the treaty he was certain to emphasise the treaty's ability to protect Maori in their land rights,[44] a factor he had stressed at the initial Waitangi meeting. In the south, however, where tribal migrations were so recent, Crown protection of tribal rights against other Maori claimants was probably as significant as the protection offered to counter unjust Pakeha claims.

Henry Williams had considered seeking signatures at Otago, but on his return from Wanganui to Kapiti at the end of May, he heard that Major Thomas Bunbury had been deputed to promote the treaty in the south. Bunbury, who had arrived at the Bay of Islands on 16 April with a detachment of eighty troops and officers of the 80th Regiment, had been dispatched from New South Wales by Gipps when he heard news of Hobson's illness.[45] Since Gipps had stressed that 'prompt measures' were 'urgently required' to extend Crown authority over the South Island, on 28 April Hobson sent Bunbury in the *Herald* to attend to this, and to complete negotiations in North Island areas that had not been covered. It was also deemed advisable to use the opportunity to make a display of Crown 'dignity and importance'. The interpreter appointed for the trip was Henry Williams's son, Edward, who had assisted with the translation of the Waitangi draft treaty into Maori.[46]

Bunbury's first treaty meeting was held on 4 May at Coromandel Harbour.[47] Edward Williams explained the necessity of the treaty, emphasising that the influx of Pakeha made it desirable; protection of the Maori people in their land rights was also mentioned. According to Edward, the meeting was 'rather a long one' with 'a great deal of discussion', but of the six principal chiefs present only four could be persuaded to sign. One of the signatories was the elderly Te Horeta, long accustomed to European contact, reputed to have seen Cook, and for some years the patron of a nearby trading station run by an American, William Webster. Te Horeta, apparently delighted by Bunbury's visit, had satisfied himself about the treaty and the new governor as soon as the *Herald* had anchored on 30 April. By contrast, Piko (an experienced orator) and an unnamed chief (possibly Taraia) firmly refused to sign. Piko declined to relinquish any authority over his tribe although the British government was free to do as it wished with Pakeha; he also insisted that more time was needed for consultation among the Thames tribes before a decision could be reached.

The following day Williams and Bunbury, disappointed with this result, made another effort to influence the chiefs with the aid of a local CMS missionary James Preece, but still with no success. The negotiators concluded that the chiefs were reluctant to sign for two reasons: first, local Pakeha had used their influence against the agreement, and second, chiefs knew about the assertion of British law against a Maori offender in the Bay of Islands – a practical demonstration of what might follow on the establishment of British authority. Both reasons suggested that the treaty negotiations should be concluded as quickly as possible.

The task of obtaining treaty signatures proved a chancy business for Bunbury. As the *Herald* moved south to pick up William Stewart, who would act as pilot, the ship anchored briefly off one of the Mercury Islands. There she was boarded by two chiefs who signed without hesitation, yet at Mercury Bay itself no signatures were obtained because local chiefs had gone inland on business.[48] Accidents of location or absence might be as important as any other reason for adherence or non-adherence.

Bunbury had been specially charged with securing signatures at Tauranga; Hobson believed little progress had been made there because of local fighting. But, arriving on 11 May, he was surprised to find that most of the chiefs had already signed Alfred Brown's treaty copy.[49] The significant exceptions were Tupaea and several other Otumoetai chiefs with whom Bunbury arranged a meeting on 12 May at Te Papa, the CMS mission station. The usual procedure was followed, with Edward Williams reading the treaty and interpreting.

Bunbury's explanations at Tauranga reveal one line of official argument, possibly used elsewhere, that the treaty was just one more step in an ongoing relationship with the Crown. He acknowledged that the Maori people had been recognised by Britain as an independent nation, but asserted that the 1835 'treaty' had been rendered 'abortive' by Maori fighting and lack of unity; the Queen now sought the 'spontaneous gift' of Maori consent so that a regular government could be established to assist them and to control the growing number of Pakeha in the country. Assurances were also given that Crown pre-emption would protect Maori land.

The Otumoetai chiefs were not easily convinced. They were suspicious of Crown intentions and sceptical about the advantages to be gained from British government. By Edward Williams's account, it was not that they did not favour a British administration (pre-emption, for example, was just); rather, they could see no clear purpose in the treaty itself. On one particular issue, the inter-tribal fighting with Rotorua, the chiefs queried the methods of adjustment that would be used if they ceased fighting: would the government, for instance, be prepared to provide adequate protection for them? Bunbury emphasised that the Crown would play only a mediatory role, although some allowance would be made for compensating any injured party, as Maori custom required.

Neither Bunbury nor Edward Williams was able to secure further signatures at Tauranga. Bunbury blamed Pakeha influence, as at Coromandel, and hinted at opposition from Roman Catholics at Otumoetai. (Pompallier had stayed there in February–March.)[50] It was also suggested that chiefs were waiting until the Queen's gift of blankets was produced, these being in short supply. But these reasons, though contributing to Maori hesitation, avoided the main issue – a chiefly reluctance to relinquish an authority that Bunbury had clearly acknowledged, and a lack of confidence in government ability to deal with tribal conflicts. Such impediments might still have been removed had Bunbury given adequate time for discussion, so necessary in Maori decision-making. But he became impatient at the 'dilatory habits' of Maori and left Williams at Otumoetai, to hurry on to the other Tauranga pa at Maungatapū. There he was assured by Nuka, the senior chief, that all but two absentee chiefs had already signed Brown's treaty copy. Setting aside Nuka's courteous invitation to dine, Bunbury left hurriedly.[51]

Compared with the days spent at Coromandel, the visit to Tauranga reveals an unseemly haste. Bunbury was impatient to push the task ahead. Inter-tribal fighting was used as an excuse to cancel a side trip to Rotorua. This omission lost the adherence of Te Arawa and Ngati Tuwharetoa, tribes which numbered several thousand each.[52] To solicit the signatures of these and other groups, Bunbury authorised CMS missionary James Stack, temporarily in charge of the Tauranga mission, to make another copy of the treaty from the sheet initially sent to Brown; Bunbury told Stack that signatures on the copy would be 'as good as those on the original document'. Stack made two copies, and sent one to the CMS missionaries, Thomas Chapman and John Morgan, asking them to 'use their influence' to obtain signatures in the Arawa-Ngati Tuwharetoa districts near Rotorua and Taupo. He gave the other to James Fedarb, once a CMS worker but now trading-master on the Bay of Islands schooner, *Mercury*, which was putting in at various places on the coast towards East Cape.[53]

Stack's efforts drew mixed results. The copy sent to Chapman and Morgan has disappeared without trace. It was referred to only once, in 1913, by the Ngati Tuwharetoa chief Tureiti Te Heuheu.[54] Tureiti recalled that his grandfather, Mananui Te Heuheu, had attended a treaty meeting held by Chapman and Morgan at Te Papai-o-Uru pa, Ohinemutu, in 1840; Mananui had publicly rejected the mana of the Queen and the need for British 'protection'. Earlier, two Ngati Tuwharetoa chiefs, Iwikau (Mananui's younger brother) and Te Korohiko, had signed the treaty at the Bay of Islands, but they had no authorisation to act on behalf of the tribe and Mananui had refused to accept the customary gift of blankets (though the signatures remained on the treaty). The Arawa, allied in tribal interests, also refused to sign. (Their spokesmen were said to be Te Amohau, Te Haupapa and Te Pukuatua.) In both the Arawa and Ngati Tuwharetoa regions missionary influence was not strong enough to swing the balance and as a result both confederations remained outside the treaty commitment.

Fedarb had more success with his copy. Leaving Tauranga on 22 May, he sailed down a coastline broken by a number of small harbours, each with a population of 600–700.[55] He secured the adherence of twenty-six chiefs in spite of recent visits to the same coastal settlements by Pompallier. In fact, at Opotiki, seven chiefs of both Catholic and CMS affiliation signed on 27–28 May, the CMS chiefs requesting that identification of the Catholic adherents be made on the treaty sheet, which was marked accordingly.[56] Over the next three weeks, while Fedarb pursued his trading interests, he collected nineteen more signatures – two at Torere on 11 June, with a third added later, possibly offshore;

four at Te Kaha on 14 June; and twelve at Whakatane on 16 June. Fedarb, accustomed to moving among the Maori people, was no doubt aware of the need to allow time for consultation and, unlike Bunbury, he was in no hurry. At Opotiki and Te Kaha, at least, he also had the support of the local Maori teachers.

When he returned to the Bay of Islands on 19 June, Fedarb entrusted his copy of the treaty to Colenso to pass on to Hobson, who duly acknowledged the work achieved.[57] No one commented on the fact that Hobson's signature on Fedarb's copy was forged. Stack and Fedarb had advanced the government's treaty mission in the Bay of Plenty-East Coast region and the forgery was not questioned. Indeed, Hobson's officials were so concerned to secure adherents there that Shortland had sent off yet more copies (possibly printed) to Tauranga on 7 May, only a few days after Bunbury had departed for that very place with his copy.[58] When Stack returned the original Brown copy on 23 May, he voiced a hope that Tupaea's agreement might still be obtained, but it was not.[59]

Meanwhile, after his brief hurried call at Tauranga, Bunbury abandoned a proposed visit to Opotiki and continued south to fulfil Hobson's directive that the South and Stewart Islands be secured to the Crown. Neither Hobson nor Bunbury was well informed about southern New Zealand. Bunbury, however, knew that Hobson doubted the ability of South Island Maori to observe 'even the form of a treaty'. Hobson had also drawn his attention to Normanby's view that unless a treaty were entered into 'intelligently' by the Maori it would be a 'mere illusion and pretence which ought to be avoided'. However, if a treaty could not be negotiated, sovereignty would still be asserted on the ground of discovery.[60]

While the *Herald* fought adverse weather for well over a week to reach the South Island, Bunbury had plenty of time to gather information from his pilot, William Stewart, at one time a sealer, whaler and trader in the south. Through the sealing trade of the early nineteenth century and the later growth of shore-whaling, Maori in the south had been associated with Pakeha for longer than those in any area other than the Bay of Islands. By intermarriage and co-habitation, southern Maori had acquired considerable knowledge of Pakeha ways. Contact had brought changes: diseases had decimated southern Maori in the decade or two before 1840, and raids by North Island Maori had taken their toll.[61] The survivors had formed loosely associated, mobile tribal groupings. These factors – limited numbers and a fear of renewed attacks from the north – predisposed southern Maori to agree to the treaty as a means of protecting their interests.

When Bunbury landed at Akaroa on 28 May, he found only a small party of Maori, but they were not 'wild savages', as Hobson had supposed. According to Edward Williams, most of them spoke English 'pretty well'.[62] At first, they feared that the treaty negotiators might be conspiring to repeat the *Elizabeth* affair, but they were reassured when told that the Crown could still look into that case. Williams then read and explained the treaty. At a second meeting on 30 May two chiefs, Iwikau and John Love [Tikao], signed the treaty 'after a little more explanation'. Stewart may have assisted in this; he was known in the south and was familiar with the South Island dialect which caused Williams some difficulties. Stewart's support, the assurances of Crown protection, and a more leisurely and courteous pace of negotiation were probably all significant elements in securing agreement. Bunbury considered that the signatures of the two chiefs were of some 'consequence'; Iwikau was a near relative of the deceased paramount chief, Tamaiharanui, and John Love [Tikao] was an important local chief. The latter, in fact, showed how imperfect British knowledge of the South Island had been, since Bunbury found him to be a 'very intelligent well-dressed native' who spoke English better than any other the major had met.[63]

On leaving Akaroa, Bunbury planned a call at Otago but was prevented by bad weather. At this stage he was probably more concerned to assert British sovereignty in the south than to seek further signatories. The Waitangi agreement was now four months old and it was exactly two months since Gipps, anticipating complications arising from South Island land transactions, had urged that 'prompt measures' were 'urgently required'. Bunbury may also have known of Gipps's failure in February to persuade Tuhawaiki, the acknowledged paramount chief on the South Island's east coast, to sign a treaty of cession in Sydney. He may have feared the chief's continued opposition, for the *Herald* now bypassed Ruapuke Island where Tuhawaiki was living and headed for an uninhabited part of Stewart Island, Port Pegasus, where Stewart had at one time embarked on a ship-building venture. It is impossible to determine whether Bunbury deliberately chose to avoid Maori habitation or whether the weather prevented him reaching Paterson River (or Inlet) where there was a Maori village.[64] In any case, Bunbury and Nias decided to proclaim British sovereignty over Stewart Island, basing Crown rights on Cook's discovery, a course suggested by Normanby, recommended by Gipps, and possibly pressed upon Bunbury by Nias, who was impatient to see the mission accomplished.[65] The Maori of Stewart Island were given no chance to consider the Waitangi agreement.

After a few days at Stewart Island, the *Herald* moved to Ruapuke Island, where Tuhawaiki was expecting the ship. On 10 June, he went on board 'in the full dress staff uniform of a British aide-de-camp, with gold lace trousers, cocked hat and plume' and signed 'without hesitation'. Although Tuhawaiki appeared to understand the 'nature' of the treaty, Bunbury took care to observe correct form by having it read and explained in the presence of a Pakeha witness.[66]

The chief was familiar with Pakeha. He was an accomplished trader and whaler, had his own whaleboats and employed Europeans. He spoke some English, had visited Sydney several times and had engaged in more than one land deal. Once he had signed the treaty, he presented Bunbury with a memorandum concerning the register of a twenty-five to thirty ton vessel being built for him at Moeraki, and sought Bunbury's endorsement of a guarantee, written in English, that Ruapuke belonged to Tuhawaiki and his tribe. The first matter Bunbury forwarded to Hobson, but the latter he dealt with by referring to the land guarantee in the treaty. Tuhawaiki was clearly keen to secure his significant land and trading interests and viewed the treaty as a way of obtaining Crown protection. Bunbury, however, aware that the chief considered himself to be the principal leader on the south coast and might make claims to much of the South Island, was cautious not to commit the Crown to any land claim that had not been officially investigated. With this, Tuhawaiki was apparently satisfied. His request that two other chiefs sign the treaty was allowed.

Bunbury had been anxious to obtain the agreement of Taiaroa, the other chief of consequence in the south. Although a chief by that name had signed at Ruapuke it was evidently not the famous Taiaroa, who could not be found in the Maori village at the Otago harbour entrance; he was said to be at Moeraki. Since Nias refused to hold the ship for Taiaroa's return or to seek out Taiaroa's son further up-harbour, Bunbury had to be content with gaining the adherence of Korako and Karetai.

With the aim of acquiring the sovereignty of the South and Stewart Islands now almost fulfilled, Bunbury made his last South Island call at Cloudy Bay where there were several shore-whaling stations. The Maori population had become largely integrated into these establishments; tribal affiliations related more to the North Island than to the South Island. Cloudy Bay was an area much frequented by overseas ships; seven foreign whalers were in the bay as the *Herald* came in to anchor. Bunbury and his party, landing at Guard's Cove on the evening of 16 June, were well received by the elderly chief Nohorua (a close relative of Te Rauparaha), but the chief and his three nephews adamantly refused to sign. The following day, a second approach to Nohorua was successful, but his nephews first temporised and then again refused to sign. Chiefs from adjoining coves, however, came to the *Herald* in three separate groups, all readily giving their assent to the treaty.

At Cloudy Bay retention of the land rather than cession of sovereignty was uppermost in the chiefs' minds. In the preceding months the New Zealand Company had tried to force land sales, and, as one young chief, Maui Pu, explained in broken English, all the chiefs were fearful that if they signed the treaty the Queen would seize their territory. When Maui Pu read the Maori text of the treaty, however, he rapidly grasped the significance of the land guarantee which he then concisely explained to the other chiefs. Nohorua was finally persuaded to agree to the treaty. He retained such suspicion of British intentions, however, that his signature had to be witnessed by his English son-in-law, the whaler Joseph Thoms, 'in order, as Nohorua said, should his grandchildren lose their land, their father might share the blame'.[67] Fears over land loss were so great that initially even the customary gift of a blanket was turned down for fear that it might be construed as an admission of a land sale.

Bunbury now decided to proclaim the Queen's sovereignty over the South Island, on the basis of cession. Nias supported the idea, possibly encouraged by news that Maori in Queen Charlotte Sound had also consented to Henry Williams's treaty overtures. Later, Bunbury justified the proclamation of sovereignty to Hobson: 'It may appear like cutting the Gordian knot, where so many and such intricate interests are interwoven; yet the further delaying this step could only tend to create further difficulties.' More specifically, he saw the need to assert British sovereignty as the 'most effectual means of preventing further dissension amongst the natives and Europeans'. And the time was opportune, for 'the presence of so many foreign vessels contributed to render the declaration of Her Majesty's sovereignty more solemn and imposing'. On 17 June, therefore, having informed the chiefs of his intentions, Bunbury landed the marines and hoisted the Union Jack at 'Horikaka' Pa on little Horahorakakahu Island, Port Underwood; the *Herald* gave a twenty-one-gun salute with the ship's yard arm manned. This public proclamation brought Bunbury's South Island mission to an end.

Before he returned to the Bay of Islands, Bunbury dealt with two further pieces of business. First, he visited Te Rauparaha at Kapiti on 19 June. Bunbury was assured by Te Rauparaha that his assent to the treaty had already been given to Henry Williams. Since Bunbury had no means of confirming this, he asked for Te Rauparaha's adherence a second time – an indication of the significance attached to that chief's agreement. From nearby Mana Island, Rangihaeata was also brought to sign, with Te Rauparaha's assistance, but Bunbury missed Te Hiko, son of Te Pehi, once paramount chief of the tribe, who was on the mainland.[68]

Bunbury also approached Te Hapuku of Hawke's Bay, who had been a signatory to the 1835 Declaration of Independence and was regarded as the undisputed principal chief of the Ahuriri coastal district, although for some years he had lived at Mahia. That William Williams did not intend to seek treaty adherents on this coast until late July or even August may have come to Bunbury's notice during a brief stopover at Port Nicholson. There he had also heard that Hobson had proclaimed sovereignty over all New Zealand on 21 May.[69] The *Herald* tried to make contact with Te Hapuku on 24 June as the ship, working its way back north, put into shore near the mouth of the Tukituki River. Bunbury's expectations that the chief would be evasive proved correct. Te Hapuku had been so troublesome with whalers that Busby had once threatened him with the visitation of a warship,[70] and only when Bunbury clarified the nature of his mission through a Maori messenger did Te Hapuku appear. But he refused to sign at first, alleging that Ngapuhi were now slaves through the treaty, a claim that he illustrated by way of a diagram on a piece of board showing the Queen above the chiefs, as they were over their tribes. Subsequently, he appended his agreement on 24 June, two other chiefs also signing.[71]

Bunbury's detailed record gives an interesting insight into the means used to secure Te Hapuku's adherence. He countered Te Hapuku's assertions of Crown supremacy by insisting that the British government would not 'lower the chiefs in the estimation of their tribes'; rather, Te Hapuku's assent to the treaty 'could only tend to increase his consequence'. Bunbury also reasoned that good government would apply 'equally' to Maori and Pakeha, opening the way to mediation in inter-tribal fighting. Confident now in the assertion of British sovereignty, he also warned Te Hapuku that, whether he signed or not, British authority was a fait accompli, a point that Bunbury threatened to demonstrate with the *Herald's* guns unless local Maori returned a whaleboat stolen from a Pakeha. Finally, he turned for support to Hara, a

Ngapuhi treaty signatory accompanying Te Hapuku; Hara advised signing, which Te Hapuku did. Bunbury had used flattery, promises, threats and chiefly support in order to achieve his objective.

With the southern treaty now as complete as he could make it, Bunbury returned to the Bay of Islands, arriving at Russell on 2 July. His mission, which had taken just over two months to complete, had succeeded in securing twenty-seven signatories – a modest figure in comparison with some other treaty sheets but representative of a wider geographical area than any other copy.

In Bunbury's absence, Hobson had completed further business relating to the treaty and British sovereignty. At Kaitaia on 28 April the signing by sixty chiefs of Te Rarawa and Te Aupouri constituted a unanimous decision in favour of the treaty.[72] On this occasion there was no dissension, although the format of the meeting had been the same as other major northern gatherings. As usual, the chiefs were assured that the government would control Pakeha better, that it would protect Maori interests and that this new British intrusion was a response to earlier Maori approaches to the Crown. For their part, Kaitaia Maori expressed a desire to have land sales and trade regulated, and for misdemeanours to be controlled. They expected improved chiefly status and increased material benefits to result from agreement to the treaty.

According to the official negotiators, the decisive factor at this meeting was the attitude of the paramount chief, Nopera Pana-kareao. A man of supreme influence in the far north, Nopera had enhanced his mana by association with Christianity, proselytising among his own tribe from 1837 on. By the end of 1839, the principal Te Rarawa chiefs were Christian, or at least nominal believers. For them, Nopera combined old and new leadership qualities, and this influence meant that he could give a more complete agreement than was possible through the more dispersed leadership of the Ngapuhi federation.[73]

Nopera, who had signed the earlier Declaration of Independence, believed that he had prepared carefully for the treaty meeting. On the previous evening he had questioned both the resident CMS missionary, William Puckey, and government officials about the treaty, in particualr the word sovereignty. An attempt had been made to make it 'intelligible' to him. It became clear, however, that Nopera had failed to grasp the transfer of power and authority implied in the treaty. When other chiefs had finished speaking, Nopera, 'in a very impressive and commanding manner', asserted his right as paramount chief. Drawing on the precedent set by his ancestor, he reminded the assembly that Te Rarawa had welcomed Pakeha; he reasoned that the Maori people needed a helmsman such as Hobson, and that the governor did not intend to deprive Maori of payment either for land or for produce. 'Ko te atakau o te whenua i riro i a te Kuini, ko te tinana o te whenua i waiho ki nga Maori,' he concluded – only 'the shadow of the land is to the Queen, but the substance remains to us'.[74] (It was a statement that he reversed a year later.) He urged the chiefs, for these reasons, to agree unanimously to the treaty, a direction that was immediately obeyed.

Hobson also obtained further signatures at the Bay of Islands while Bunbury was away. Among these was Kawiti, an adherent to the Declaration of Independence who had not signed at Waitangi. A rumour that Kawiti was behind a conspiracy to kill Hobson and to oust Pakeha from New Zealand was given substance at the Kaitaia meeting; Nopera had talked about overtures to draw him into the plot which involved Hokianga, Whangaroa and Taiamai (near Paihia) tribes.[75] This had spurred Hobson to action. Pomare, who had already been asked to persuade Kawiti, promised to bring not only Kawiti but also Tirarau of Uriohau at Kaipara and other chiefs over whom he had influence.[76] Tirarau and other Uriohau chiefs, all signatories to the 1835 Declaration, had received official invitations to the Bay of Islands, yet had made no move.[77] In the second week of May, Pomare accompanied Kawiti, Tirarau and two other chiefs [Tirarau's son and brother?] to a meeting with Hobson.

Tirarau, influenced by Christianity though not a convert, was the acknowledged senior chief of his district and carried with him the assent of other chiefs who had not yet signed the treaty; he and the two chiefs with him gave their agreement 'willingly', expressing their pleasure that 'the Queen had sent them a governor'. Kawiti, on the other hand, became 'exceedingly violent and intractible [*sic*]' as the signing commenced. He attributed his antagonism to the offence given by the improper distribution of tobacco at the 5 February meeting. He was reluctant to 'sign away his land' which, he believed, the Pakeha would get in any case, as the Maori population was declining fast. Yet, having said his piece, he inscribed his moko beside his name at the head of the lengthening list of chiefs on the Waitangi parchment. The real reason for his original antagonism and his subsequent about-face is not clear. He gave his assent to the treaty with reservations – a position that would lead him, within a few years, to take up arms against the government. In May 1840, however, it was sufficient for Hobson that Kawiti had finally acceded.

With the outstanding success at Kaitaia, the securing of the territory south of Ngapuhi through Tirarau's signature, and the additional signings of Kawiti and other chiefs, Hobson had received virtually an entire cession from northern New Zealand. Only some few chiefs of the Waitemata isthmus had still to be persuaded. Hobson was in that area when Bunbury arrived back at the Bay of Islands at the beginning of July. Since Waikato and Manukau chiefs had been invited to this second Waitemata meeting on 9 July, Hobson was possibly making a final bid to obtain Te Wherowhero's signature, but the Waikato chief was not to be moved. The seven chiefs who did sign at Karaka Bay, Auckland, were from the western shores of the Hauraki Gulf, among them Kupenga, the major chief of Whakatiwai pa and a brother-in-law to Patuone.[78] This seems to have been the last formal treaty meeting held by Hobson.

At this point, both Hobson and Bunbury had issued proclamations of sovereignty, each unaware of the other's actions. Bunbury had made two proclamations, one on 5 June at Stewart Island which had been claimed by right of Cook's discovery, and the other on 17 June at Cloudy Bay by right of cession of the South Island by 'several independent native chiefs', not knowing that Hobson had already proclaimed sovereignty over the whole country.

Hobson argued that his decision to proclaim sovereignty had been forced upon him by the actions of the New Zealand Company settlers who had arrived at Port Nicholson in January 1840. He concluded that they were illegally assuming powers of government that were the prerogative of the Crown. The settlers, realising that Hobson's negotiations to that date could be interpreted as not applying to their district, had introduced on 2 March a form of government which claimed to derive its legality from authority granted by local chiefs. The flag of an independent New Zealand, made on the *Tory*, flew above Port Nicholson. Such proceedings seemed to Hobson to smack of 'high treason', and he had immediately issued two proclamations: the first proclaimed sovereignty over the North Island by right of cession, the second over the South and Stewart Islands on the ground of discovery. In addition he swiftly dispatched Shortland, invested with the powers of a Justice of the Peace, with troops and mounted police, to deal with the situation. Shortland hauled down the flag of the United Tribes, read Hobson's proclamations of sovereignty and issued a proclamation demanding allegiance to the Crown.[79]

Hobson's actions were those of a man who believed he was facing an emergency, but he justified his decision by false argument. The British government was assured that cession of the North Island had been secured by the 'universal adherence' of the chiefs. Yet at this stage, apart from the original Waitangi sheet which Hobson still held, only the Maunsell copy, signed at Waikato Heads and the Manukau, had been returned. No more than encouraging reports had come in from Symonds, from Henry and William Williams and from Bunbury at Coromandel. In no region (with the exception of Kaitaia and possibly the Wellington to Wanganui area) could adherence to the treaty be said to be 'universal'. Hobson was also in error in justifying the assertion of sovereignty over the South Island on the ground of discovery. He claimed a 'perfect knowledge of the uncivilized state of the natives', although he had no grounds whatsoever for this statement. Aware perhaps of the weakness of his argument, he informed the Colonial Office that Gipps supported his action.[80]

The Colonial Office would also have been unaware from his reports that there might be a substantial difference in meaning between the English treaty text and the Maori text, the one that had been usually signed. Hobson, indeed, might not have realised it. Henry Williams, best placed to know this, only created confusion. Hobson sent his superiors several English copies, each with slight variations. On one copy Williams appended a certification that the English text was 'as literal a translation of the Treaty of Waitangi as the idiom of the language will admit of'. This was not so. There was no translation of the Maori text, nor was the Maori text an accurate translation of any one of the English versions. To add to the confusion, when Hobson finally sent both Maori and English texts to London on 15 October, both were headed 'Treaty', were said to be 'certified' and to have received 512 signatures. But when the same copies were printed for publication, the Maori text was headed 'Treaty' and the English '(Translation)'.[81]

On the basis of Hobson's inaccurate reporting, the Colonial Office approved the May proclamations which were officially published in the *London Gazette* on 2 October 1840. This sanction of the Crown was the only condition or ratification required under British government usage; British sovereignty over New Zealand was thereby confirmed.[82] There were no second thoughts in 1841 when the Colonial Office received reports that revealed some of the shortcomings in treaty negotiations. Officials were rather impressed by the long list of chiefs' names with moko, signs or signatures, and by the Maori oratory reported by treaty negotiators, Nopera's reference to losing only the shadow of the land particularly appealed, though one official feared that the Maori would discover that 'the subjects of Queen Victoria have something more than the shadow'.[83] The whole exercise of gaining possession of New Zealand had cost the government £3,635 18s for general expenses, with gifts for the Maori valued at £562 1s 5d.[84] The Colonial Office was not going to quibble over the fact that large areas of the North Island had not given assent, for the government had never asked for unanimity.

Hobson, though aware of humanitarian concern for Maori rights, had been forced by events to be pragmatic from the outset, even anticipating a successful Waitangi treaty signing by proclaiming, with Gipps's co-operation, Crown authority over British subjects in New Zealand. Similarly, the strategy of making the agreement of 6 February definitive, and seeking only 'adherents' thereafter, was designed to cope with a dispersed and fragmented Maori society. The 21 May proclamations of sovereignty also sprang from decisions forced on Hobson rather than from the reasonable fulfilment of Normanby's instructions not to seize the country but to seek a 'free and intelligent' Maori consent. The New Zealand case was unusual, however, there were several needs to be served at the same time and, together with the pressure of events, this was bound to lead to confusion. France and the United States, both with economic interests in New Zealand fisheries, might take exception to outright British denial of the country's independent status. There was also the question of how much sovereignty was to be gained. If Maori groups were left outside a British colony, they would be vulnerable to foreign powers. Only with Maori co-operation could Britain hope to hold the country against any foreign challenge. Complete sovereignty, voluntarily ceded, was politically and diplomatically desirable, and it gave Britain an unquestionable right to exercise authority.

The treaty was to serve other needs. The British government wanted to have complete control over all land transactions. Because this could only be achieved with Maori agreement, the treaty's second article including pre-emption was as vital to government interests as the land guarantee was to Maori interests. The third article, conferring Crown protection and the status of British subjects on Maori, also served a dual purpose: it placed the Maori people under British law, and at the same time extended rights that could be construed as privileges of some significance for an indigenous race.

In negotiating the treaty, the language of persuasive diplomacy was critical to success. The element of protection was much emphasised at all treaty meetings, though officials hoped that protection against foreign powers would never have to be undertaken. Negotiators took advantage of Maori antagonism to the French by drawing comparisons between the British, who had peacefully entered into the country, and the French who, it was alleged, would have forcibly acquired New Zealand, given the chance. They were also concerned that Britain's military power might seem a threat and they carefully played it down in the treaty-making. It was significant that no signatures were gathered from tribes against whom British force had been used; no attempt was made in South Taranaki where the *Alligator's* 1834 reprisal had made such an impact, and Ngati Tamatera in the Thames, where similar gun-boat tactics had been used in the late 1830s, refused to have anything to do with the treaty.[85]

In England and New Zealand the treaty was deemed officially to be a measure of justice that acknowledged the rights held by an indigenous people. It was a declaration of good intent on the part of Britain, a commitment which missionary negotiators felt obliged to draw to official attention when aspects of the treaty were later questioned and when there were threats not to implement its terms. The treaty's legal status in 1840, however, is not so clear. Normanby's instructions recognised New Zealand as a 'sovereign and independent state' but at the same time expressed grave doubts about Maori capacity to govern. Yet Normanby, like his predecessor Glenelg and his successor Lord John Russell, admitted that British sovereignty was to be established by cession. All three Secretaries of State for Colonies in 1840, then, appear to have regarded the treaty as a valid treaty of cession (despite later arguments to the contrary which continue to the present).

Contemporary viewpoints in New Zealand varied. The American naval commander, Charles Wilkes, visiting the Bay of Islands in March 1840, viewed the treaty as 'nothing more or less than a cession of their [Maori] lands, authority, and persons to Queen Victoria'. He attributed British intervention to a desire to thwart land speculation and to pre-empt French plans for the country.[86] Pompallier shared this view. The English missionaries working in New Zealand, however, stressed the potential benefit of British protection for the Maori and muted the fact of cession. The missionary Robert Maunsell returned his signed copy to Hobson with a reminder that the good faith of the British Crown should hold the government to the terms of the agreement.[87] He was anticipating the 'different ground' that would be taken by settlers, which Octavius Hadfield at Otaki noticed some two years later. It was being 'broadly hinted' by then that the treaty had been 'a mere blind to deceive foreign powers'.[88] Among the missionaries, only John Wilson totally refused to be a 'servant of the government'; he predicted the shortfall between theory and practice in implementing the treaty.[89]

Variations in Maori understanding of the agreement arose from the great diversity of situations in which the treaty was signed. In the negotiations at Waitangi, Hokianga and Kaitaia, the significance of the treaty meetings was given due recognition by Hobson and his associates. Each of these assemblies was numerously attended and generally progressed in an organised fashion. An impression of formality was created by the presence of the brilliantly uniformed police (at Waitangi and Kaitaia) and in each case the gathering was followed by suitable feasting and gift-giving. These were important factors from a Maori point of view – fitting recognition of chiefly mana.

The northern signings contrasted markedly with other areas. Elsewhere, much depended on the individual negotiators and their ability to convey the import of the treaty document; generally, meetings seem to have been brief and the subject not explored at great length in discussion. In some instances, there were problems with gift-giving (a custom established before 1840), which Maori might well have construed as British failure to give chiefs due respect. The blankets given at Waitangi were not good quality, and Bunbury noted that blankets were such common items in the Coromandel district that they were barely adequate as tokens of official esteem. Further down the coast, Fedarb resorted to giving clothing, pipes and tobacco, to the cost of £5 4s, in lieu of blankets. There is no evidence that Maori signed the treaty merely to obtain gifts. On the contrary, Maunsell gave gifts some time after the signing; and in the Cook Strait signings some Maori were reluctant to accept gifts for fear that they might be interpreted as payment.[90]

Overall, the organisation of treaty signings was a haphazard affair in most areas other than the north, and it is not surprising that the treaty was seen later by many Maori as a specifically northern matter, even though it had been circulated around much of the country. When Maori were moved later to complain about the non-implementation of the treaty, it was to Ngapuhi that other tribes pointed, for that tribe was considered to have taken the initiative in 'pulling ashore the Pakeha canoe' – traders, missionaries, and the British government. The task of fighting for treaty rights would be seen primarily as a Ngapuhi responsibility; for them, the treaty was a special cause (take).

The explanations given at treaty signings support the conclusion that, though Maori expected the treaty to initiate a new relationship, it would be one in which Maori and Pakeha would share authority. The intervention of Britain would still be limited. At Kaitaia at least, chiefs were assured that Maori customs and law would not be interfered with,[91] and Maori were encouraged to believe that their rangatiratanga would be enhanced. While they might have reasoned, as Heke did, that they could not be certain of the effect of the treaty, they might reasonably have believed that they were ceding only limited rights to Britain – perhaps a relinquishment of responsibility for external affairs – and that Maori control over tribal matters would remain.

Maori reaction to the treaty also depended on local experience. Areas where missionary activity was greatest were usually those where a protectorate-type relationship with Britain was greeted most favourably. Long association with Pakeha, however, as at Kororareka, might deter Maori from signing. The promised benefits of land protection also had a mixed reception. They were pertinent to the districts where the New Zealand Company was operating and they could also be made to appear vital even where land pressure was possibly not so serious, as on the East Coast where William Williams deliberately conveyed to local Maori his own anxieties over land loss. In untouched areas, such as the central North Island, the treaty was seen as neither necessary nor desirable in order to protect land, at least from Pakeha.

The furthering of rival tribal interests in land, however, was a determining factor both with Maori who signed and those who did not. This was apparent in the Bay of Plenty where some Maori would not sign, and in the accession of Wiremu Kingi Te Rangitake of Waikanae. When Kingi went to the Bay of Islands with Henry Williams in June 1840, he was already sounding official support for his tribe's return to Taranaki lands from which they had been displaced by the Waikato.[92] Some Maori certainly perceived the possibilities of using the treaty and the government's promises of mediation and protection to further traditional tribal interests.

Apart from local factors, Maori agreement to the treaty depended a good deal on the tact and patience of the treaty negotiators. It was crucial to allow adequate time for consultation with chiefs. Hobson had cautioned Bunbury about this, but the major showed impatience at Coromandel and Tauranga where Maori assent was not readily forthcoming. Missionary negotiators took more time to obtain Maori adherence. In comparison with Bunbury (and possibly Symonds), they also took greater pains in collecting signatures, and were more conscious of the need to make concessions to Maori sensitivities. Their knowledge of Maori custom was invaluable.

An instance of this was the signing by Maori women. A precedent was established at Waitangi when Ana Hamu, the widow of Te Koki, original patron of the Paihia mission, had been allowed to sign.[93] Henry Williams, knowing that women of high rank in Maori society could be given fitting acknowledgement, acted accordingly elsewhere. At Port Nicholson, the accession of Te Rau o te Rangi (Kahe) was allowed; at Kapiti the chieftainess Rangi Topeora signed. Williams also drew Hobson's attention to a situation at Kapiti where 'the ladies have expressed some disapprobation in not having a more prominent part in the Treaty with Her Majesty' in as much as the agreement was with a woman.[94] Subsequently, Williams appears to have allowed a Wanganui woman of rank, Rere o Maki, to sign.[95] And in the north, at Kaitaia, the missionaries Taylor and Puckey had allowed the signing of Ereonora, high-born wife of Nopera, chief of Te Rarawa.

Bunbury, however, refused to allow the signing of the daughter of Te Pehi, the celebrated Ngati Toa chief who had been of paramount importance in Cloudy Bay and further south before his death some years earlier. The woman was naturally angered by the insult. Her husband, one of Nohorua's three nephews and possibly inferior to her in rank, would not sign, probably as a consequence.[96]

More generally, missionary influence was significant simply because many Maori trusted the missionaries' good intentions. This appears to have added a religious aspect to Maori understanding of the agreement. At Waitangi, Henry Williams was responsible for developing the idea that Maori and Pakeha could be one people in both a spiritual and a temporal sense. The treaty could therefore be construed as a covenant between the Maori people and the Queen as head of the English Church and state (a concept that had its parallel in Maori society where a chief might also hold the rank of tohunga).

Other aspects of the covenant analogy might have encouraged its use. Heke, for example, spoke of the treaty as the New Covenant. As Christ was the New Covenant and as the old Mosaic Law was put aside on conversion to Christianity, so the treaty, with its promise of a new relationship between the Crown and the Maori chiefs, could be likened to the New Covenant. The idea had been echoed at Kaitaia when one young chief expressed the hope that 'if your [British] thoughts are towards Christ as ours are, we shall be one'.[97]

For British officials the religious understanding, like the humanitarian element, was merely part of the business of securing sovereignty. Certainly there was a desire to deal more fairly with the Maori, to improve on the record of British settlement, but tact, flattery, guile, bluff and a dash of subterfuge were all part of the diplomatic equipment. The *Bay of Islands Observer*, reflecting the opinion of Pakeha smarting under the restrictions of the new British administration, wrote grimly: 'For the good people at home, the affair was made to assume the appearance of one of the purest pieces of philanthropy on the part of England in favour of the Natives to protect them against European aggression; but the simple truth is, disguise it as we may, that under this cloak of benevolence, has been practised the greatest hypocrisy, to obtain possession of the country honestly, if possible, but, nevertheless to obtain it.'[98] This, of course, was sour grapes, but there was more than a grain of truth in the comment.

After the Waitangi signing, certainly after the northern signings, it was inconsequential whether Maori signed the treaty or not. Hobson's intention, of which Maori were unaware, was to assume British sovereignty anyway. The freedom of choice for those Maori involved in the treaty negotiations through 1840 was more apparent than real. For Hobson, however, there was also little choice. Against a threatened flow of British settlement, the treaty at least laid down some guidelines. How adequate these would be Hobson could not tell.

Chapter Five

EARLY YEARS OF DOUBT AND DEBATE

The Waitangi treaty gave Britain only a partial entitlement to the country. This is evident from official moves to consolidate sovereignty. The first was to secure the country against the potential claims of other nations; the second was to assert effective power and authority within New Zealand.

International recognition of British sovereignty was achieved during 1840, partly through official publicity given the treaty, which the Colonial Office saw as important in justifying claims, and partly through other government actions to establish a British colony. Early in 1840 the jurisdiction of New South Wales had been extended to New Zealand in anticipation of the success of Hobson's mission,[1] but Hobson remained anxious to secure Britain's position in New Zealand by excluding other claimants. Despite the proclamation of sovereignty over the whole country on 21 May, in July, fearing a French conspiracy to annex the South Island, he swiftly dispatched government officers to Akaroa, where they made a show of authority and occupation just before the arrival of French settlers intent on forming a small colony.[2] With greater confidence, then, he was able to assume the title of Lieutenant Governor, having initially signed as 'Lieutenant-Governor of the British Settlements in progress in New Zealand'.[3] Late in 1840, the imperial government separated New Zealand from the temporary jurisdiction of New South Wales. By Royal Charter, the country became a fully fledged British colony; Hobson was commissioned as Governor and instructed to establish the machinery of state, a small Executive Council and a Legislative Council. The instructions came into operation in New Zealand in May 1841.

Asserting effective power and authority within New Zealand was more difficult. Because of Colonial Office frugality, Hobson's initial group of officials was small, and lacked ability or dedication. Young men recruited mostly from missionary families provided immediate assistance, but only when Hobson urgently requested adequate 'judicial and legal functionaries' did the Colonial Office send William Swainson as Attorney-General and William Martin as Judge of the Supreme Court, two able men who reached New Zealand in September 1841. The arrival of Bunbury and his troops in April 1840 had strengthened the government, but Hobson remained acutely aware of the weakness of British authority.[4] In dealing with the Maori, he had been forced to rely on the assistance of the missionaries from the very first, but there was a limit to their willingness to be associated with government. While missionary mediation between Maori and non-Maori was to continue informally for some time, it was given formal status in April 1840 when Hobson appointed George Clarke, a missionary with twenty-three years' experience in New Zealand, as Protector of Aborigines.[5]

The Protector's appointment, fulfilling a recommendation of the Aborigines Report, was an admirable, humanitarian shift in colonial policy, but Clarke soon became aware of the ambiguity of his position. The government expected him to be not only an impartial guardian of Maori welfare, but also the government's main negotiator for purchases of land, even initiating moves for lands not voluntarily offered by Maori owners. Clarke repeatedly drew government attention to his anomalous position, but the dual responsibility remained until the Protectorate Department was abolished in 1846. The Protector, as a government agent, could not be truly neutral in supporting Maori interests. Moreover, the treaty's promise to treat Maori as British subjects, with the goal of amalgamation implicitly understood, was contradicted by the creation of a separate institution for Maori business outside the central machinery of state.[6]

Some Maori were uneasy from the outset. Many Pakeha provocatively flaunted Britain's newly acquired status; they used 'such ... infamous language' at Whangaroa that local Maori threatened to 'knock them on the head'.[7] In early April 1840, several chiefs from the Kaikohe, Waimate and Waitangi districts laid complaints with Hobson: 'Our hearts are dark and gloomy from what the Pakeha have told us, they say that the missionaries first came to pave the way for the English who have sent the Governor here, that soldiers will follow and then he will take away our lands.' Nene, confirming that similar remarks had been made to him, sketched a circle on the ground to demonstrate how Pakeha would encircle the Maori and finally sweep them away. Deputations from Kaikohe and Hokianga told Hobson that they knew of the extermination of natives by the English in every other country, particularly in Australia. Faced with allegations that he could not deny, Hobson assured the Maori that in New Zealand British might would be used to protect, not to destroy or dispossess, them.[8] Since rumours were widespread, an official circular in Maori was sent to chiefs at the end of April, rebutting the charge that the government intended to seize any Maori land and blaming ill-disposed Pakeha for such notions.[9]

Clarke's knowledge of the Maori people proved useful. By the latter half of 1840, he was reporting to Hobson the extent of Maori unease over the treaty and the establishment of a British administration. Maori, signatories to the treaty or not, were anxiously weighing the advantages and disadvantages of their relationship with the new administration. At Orere, on the Hauraki Gulf, the Ngati Paoa chief, Kahukoti, related the tales told by local Pakeha that within a few years Maori would be no better than slaves if they had signed the treaty, whereas those who had refused to sign would maintain their independence and keep their land. Matamata Maori were similarly confused and uncertain; few had signed for fear that they would be 'enslaved', but they were becoming convinced that the course of government was inevitably going to operate against Maori interests. They already had some understanding of the restrictions of pre-emption in the treaty's second clause (which gave the Crown sole right to deal with Maori land); and they concluded that regulations would multiply and one governor succeed another until Maori were 'ensnared'. There was strong language also at Pukitea (downstream from Ngaruawahia) where Robert Maunsell had conducted treaty negotiations. Local Maori claimed that they had been 'betrayed', that if the government wanted the land, it would be better to take it openly, for then they would 'know how to act'.[10]

By mid-1840, Maori were becoming uneasy about New Zealand being a dependency of New South Wales, a colony which had so 'degraded' the Aborigines. Their fears were heightened by news that the New South Wales legislature was debating Gipps's New Zealand Land Claims Bill, introduced on 28 May 1840.[11] The main purpose of the Bill was to set up an investigation of all land purchases made before 1840. While many purchases had been carefully negotiated and paid for, others were outrageous in the extent of land claimed, in the inadequate amount paid, and in the dubious validity of the contract. Under the legislation, two commissioners would be appointed to hear claims that had to be lodged within a given period. If the commissioners determined that land had been equitably purchased, then the claim would be allowed; but if claims exceeded 2,560 acres (or 4 square miles), land in excess of this amount would become the property of the Crown and would be commonly known as 'surplus lands'.[12]

The Bill raised important issues. It called into question the competence of Maori to enter into contracts and, by implication, challenged the independent sovereign status of New Zealand before the treaty. These points were thoroughly aired in the New South Wales Assembly, together with the general status of indigenous races in international law and under British practice. Gipps argued that in the absence of a formal law of nations, the law had to be deduced from practice; he reasoned that New Zealand did not depart from the accepted British North American experience and supported his arguments by citing American legal decisions and definitions.[13] According to Gipps, sovereignty had been acquired by Cook's discovery, the treaty merely confirming this and securing, as customary in such situations, the Crown right of pre-emption; this left the Maori people only a restricted right of occupancy and use.

Gipps insisted that his main aim was to establish Crown prerogative, not to debate the methods by which sovereignty had been acquired, nor to assess the status of the Maori before 1840. He nevertheless expressed opinions on these two latter points: Britain had not acknowledged New Zealand's independence 'expressly', only 'tacitly'; and Normanby had gone further than was necessary with regard to the Maori.

Several petitions were brought against the Bill, the well-known Sydney lawyer-politician and claimant of Maori land, William Charles Wentworth, appearing before the Council to challenge the Bill's legality.[14] He attacked the historical foundation upon which the Crown right regarding land title was said to have evolved. He maintained that, although Britain's experience had been derived from North America, pre-emption had developed there primarily as a convenient means of regulating affairs between European powers in their negotiations with native peoples; it did not affect the actual rights of natives to their lands. There was no justification for adopting the British North American precedent in New Zealand; Maori, unlike Indians, were a civilised race with a long history of independent contact with the British. Their title should be considered valid. Wentworth also pointed out that, according to the definition of jurist Emerich de Vattel, the Crown had let its right of discovery lapse by failing to follow it up with occupation within a reasonable period of time – the very conclusion that had persuaded the Colonial Office to negotiate for cession. For good measure he threw in the point that European possession in North America had been secured by conquest as often as by negotiation.

Within two weeks of the Bill's passing, the Bay of Islands press carried full reports, drawing attention to Maori independence recognised in Normanby's instructions, noting the fate of natives elsewhere, and wondering if Maori were similarly doomed.[15] According to Busby, these reports caused the 'greatest excitement and indignation' in the north. Information was also circulated by a Kaikohe Maori who had sat through some of the Sydney debates.

A deputation of Maori consulted the missionary, Davis, who assured them that their lands were secured to them by treaty.[16] Yet their fears remained. As one Maori perceptively observed, if Gipps were determined to take land from Pakeha purchasers by this means, then it was unlikely that he would spare Maori. 'Does he love us more than his own countrymen?' he shrewdly asked.

By December 1840, Clarke found that Gipps's Bill was causing concern among Maori in the Hauraki Gulf and the Waikato. Whakatiwae Maori wanted to know what right Gipps had to determine New Zealand affairs. Otawhao Maori demanded that government acts and intentions be translated into Maori because Maori were now a 'reading people' with as much right as Pakeha to be informed about laws; 'then we will think for ourselves,' they told Clarke. Despite Clarke's repeated assurances that the treaty remained the Maori 'Magna Charta', Maori scoffed at any suggestion that without the treaty they would have succumbed to the might of another foreign power. In most areas a fiercely independent Maori spirit was evident.[17]

Maori fears were rekindled when two land claims commissioners, Edward Lee Godfrey and Mathew Richmond, began their sittings at Russell in October 1841.[18] Inevitably, the hearings caused general excitement. One of the commissioners had to visit the locality of each claim and take the evidence of the European claimant, his witnesses and the Maori involved (those opposing the claim as well as those upholding it). Maori co-operation, so essential to government, was usually given willingly, yet the whole exercise was unsettling. The extent of early land sales was made plain, not only to Maori who attended the sittings, but to a wider public through the press, which published a description of each claim and the chiefs involved.[19] The press also publicised the resentment of old settlers who were anxious to justify the validity of their claims. They argued that their purchases had been made on terms prevailing before 1840 when New Zealand was an independent country recognised by the British government. The good faith of the Crown in recognising pre-1840 Maori sovereignty was called into question; the treaty, the proclaimed guarantee of Maori rights, was attacked as a fraud.[20]

The land claims investigations were probably the aspect of government that was most unsettling to both Pakeha and Maori in the early 1840s. Although Maori were prepared to support claims where the original sale had been fair and where it had been followed by occupation within a reasonable period, the investigations tended to generate dissatisfaction with all old sales. There were some exceptions; where speculative purchases were not upheld, Maori had the advantage of retaining both the land and the purchase price (or goods).[21] But in other decisions there was ample cause for dissatisfaction. The government decision that 'surplus lands' would revert to the Crown seriously shook Maori confidence, for Hobson and Busby had assured chiefs at the Waitangi treaty signing that 'all lands unjustly held' would revert to Maori ownership.[22] When a new governor, Robert FitzRoy, arrived at the end of 1843 he conveyed a similar impression.[23] From the Maori point of view it was not only difficult to see the logic of the government's decision, it also seemed to contravene earlier assurances. Maori were given good cause to believe that their suspicions of government intentions to acquire land by one means or another were justified, that the treaty guarantee had little worth.

Investigations in Auckland and elsewhere, and the appointment of a commissioner from England, William Spain, added to the uncertainties.[24] Problems were compounded by land transactions in the later 1840s and it fell to a settler government in the 1850s to deal with the matter. Not until 1862 were accurate surveys made, grants confirmed and 'surplus land' defined. Every time the question arose in the colony's first twenty years, Pakeha arguments were reiterated and Maori anxieties regenerated. A lingering suspicion that they had been cheated of their rights finally prompted Maori to appeal over the surplus lands and this resulted in a government commission in 1946–47, more than a century later, by which time investigators believed that no evidence of the early promises could be found.[25]

Tensions raised by Gipps's Bill and the land claims investigations demonstrated to the government that Maori were in constant and rapid communication with each other. To counter rumour and unsettling reports, the government decided to publish its own monthly newspaper in the Maori language, *Te Karere Maori*, the *Maori Messenger* or *Gazette*. The paper also attempted to meet Maori requests for information by periodically printing ordinances and regulations relevant to the Maori people. The result was a paper containing an odd collection of information; in the early 1840s, material usually related to current events, whereas in the latter part of the decade it concentrated largely on the arts of civilisation. Initially, 1,000 copies a month were printed, but the copies were passed around a far wider Maori readership for whom there was virtually no printed matter in Maori other than biblical or religious texts. Since the treaty and issues deriving from the assertion of sovereignty were matters of almost continuous public debate, Clarke printed the Maori text of the treaty in one of the first issues. From early 1842, then, the text of the treaty circulated in Maori communities.[26]

The government no doubt hoped that reassurances about the Crown's good faith would still fears, but issues other than the surplus lands problem caused Maori to fear for their future. Questions about land, law and authority – issues so closely related in the articles of the treaty – had to be worked out in government policies, and the task was not easy. In interpreting and implementing the treaty, confusion and doubt arose from the ambiguities of the agreement itself, from problems of communication between officials in England and New Zealand and, not least, from the conflicting pressures of the interested parties. The extent of Maori land ownership, in particular, gave rise to a prolonged and often bitter debate which involved all those connected with New Zealand – the imperial government, the colonial government in New Zealand (and for a time New South Wales), the New Zealand Company, the London-based missionary bodies, and many in the colony, both Pakeha and Maori.[27]

Gipps's first comments on the treaty indicated a difference of opinion. He suggested that Maori land ownership should be defined in the narrowest sense as applying only to lands occupied and cultivated. But Maori had accepted the treaty only because they believed that it guaranteed their rights to the whole of New Zealand. This was understood by Hobson, by those directly concerned in treaty-making, and by a large body of settlers. But when Hobson forwarded a copy of the treaty through Gipps to the Colonial Office, the complete possession guaranteed in article two slipped past Gipps. He approved the treaty as a whole. In subsequent correspondence between Gipps and Hobson, the point does not appear to have been clarified.[28] Lord John Russell at the Colonial Office, ignorant of any conflict of understanding, approved both the treaty and Gipps's comments on it. Neither Gipps nor Russell, then, understood the treaty as Hobson did and, had they done so, 'there can be little doubt that it would have been at once disallowed by Her Majesty's Government'.[29]

Hobson died in September 1842, his responsibilities being assumed by Willoughby Shortland until the arrival of the new governor, Robert FitzRoy, in December 1843. In England, Russell was succeeded by a new Colonial Secretary, Lord Stanley. Changes in government in New Zealand and in England did not help to resolve the land issue.

The problem of the land guarantee came to Stanley's notice in October 1842 in relation to claims of the New Zealand Company to lands purchased before 1840. The Company had initially acknowledged Maori land rights to be absolute, but in subsequent negotiations with the Colonial Office they shifted ground. Hard-pressed by settler demands and by financial problems, they urged that only a restricted right of Maori ownership should be ac-knowledged; this, they claimed, was the accepted practice with other indigenous races.[30] Protracted negotiations between the Company and the Colonial Office, held in abeyance to some extent by Spain's land claims investigations, climaxed in 1844 when the Company secured the appointment of a parliamentary select committee to examine its case. G. W. Hope, Parliamentary Undersecretary at the Colonial Office, submitted a draft report, recognising the extensive land rights held by the Maori people. But the committee, by a narrow majority, adopted a report by the chairman, Lord Howick, which described the treaty as 'injudi-cious' and recommended that Maori ownership of land be restrict-ed. He suggested a tax on all uncultivated land, with confiscation for non-payment. Although this was intended to control specula-tion, it threatened to abrogate the land guarantee as understood by the signatories.

Stanley did not feel obliged to implement the report, partly because of the narrow majority and partly because he genuinely doubted its wisdom. He observed that measures taken in New Zealand supported the land guarantee in its widest sense. A res-tricted interpretation was 'irreconcilable with the large words of the Treaty of Waitangi' and 'inconsistent with the honour, good faith and policy of the Crown'; the Maori people could not be treated like the Australian Aborigines. But having made this ac-knowledgement, he subsequently played with the idea of a land tax.[31] This inconsistency of approach drew criticism from New Zealand Company supporters in England. It also attracted protest from those committed to upholding the treaty, especially the missionary bodies and their men in New Zealand. Hope took a firm stand, threatening to resign if Stanley succumbed to Com-pany pressure, a move which would have embarrassed the Prime Minister, Sir Robert Peel, and his party, who were thus forced to find a way of settling New Zealand Company problems without sacrificing the treaty.

Stanley's decision at least allowed for the possibility that article two might be interpreted as the signatories understood it. He confirmed this in June 1845 in a three-day debate in the House of Commons, when the land issue was discussed at length. This debate finally forced a reluctant Colonial Office to define publicly its attitude to the New Zealand land question. Although Stanley still refrained from giving a firm definition on the land guarantee of the treaty, he did at last admit that Maori law and custom concerning land would have to be taken into consideration.[32] Meanwhile, despite this debate, the land guarantee was being interpreted in New Zealand through the implementation of pre-emption.

From the foundation of the colony, it was officially acknowledged in New Zealand that ownership of all land was vested in the Maori people, and in return the Crown had the sole right of buying Maori land. Both points were covered in the treaty's second article in the English text. Hobson, knowing that complete control over all land transactions was part of the government's plan,[33] followed up the treaty by making the necessary land ordinances. Land for settlement was to be bought at a low price from Maori and sold at a high price to settlers, the profits to be expended on further development and emigration. The aim was to minimise imperial government costs and to make the colony as financially self-sufficient as possible.

The concept of the government as the sole purchaser of their land was completely new to the Maori people. Until 1840 they had been accustomed to dealing freely with their land, and that they were prepared to restrict this freedom by agreeing to the pre-emptive clause of the treaty is surprising. Did they fully grasp that the government was going to be the sole purchaser? Or did they think that they had promised merely to give the government the first offer? And did they realise that if the Crown did not wish, or was unable, to buy, then the land could not be offered to any other interested party whatsoever?

The Maori text of the treaty simply referred to giving the Crown the 'hokonga' (the buying and selling, or the trade) in land. Hobson and the Colonial Office unquestionably intended to obtain the sole right of purchasing Maori land and were confident that the treaty conferred this. The treaty negotiations suggest, however, that the exclusive nature of pre-emption was not always clearly understood. Nor did Maori grasp the financial constraints that pre-emption might bring; it was presented, it seems, either as a benefit to be gained or as a minor concession in return for the guarantee of complete Maori ownership.

Maori understanding, at least at Waitangi, was possibly restricted by inadequate explanations, by absence from the meeting of 5 February when pre-emption was explained, or even by a chief's momentary cat-nap at the critical time. Henry Williams, questioned later on his explanation, was non-committal: 'The chiefs wishing to sell any portion of their lands, shall give to the

Queen the right of pre-emption of their lands.'[34] Colenso, a critical observer at Waitangi, was more informative, noting that a number of chiefs did not fully understand pre-emption, an impression left, too, with another onlooker, William Brodie.[35] At the meeting, only Moka, who queried the restrictions placed on Pakeha, demonstrated any grasp of pre-emption. Immediately after the signing, Colenso cited the chief Hara, who had offered land to individual, would-be purchasers since the signing. Hara had indignantly defended his customary right to deal with his lands as he pleased. Yet a Paihia chief, Tamati Wiremu, seems to have appreciated that the right of purchase rested solely with the Crown for he appealed to the governor in March 1840 to put a halt to overtures still being made by individual Pakeha. Tirarau, who went to the Bay of Islands to sign the treaty in early May 1840, was to refer to Hobson two weeks later for clarification on the very matter of pre-emption, but down the west coast at Kawhia, Whiteley was adamant that Maori signatories there had fully understood that they were to sell to the Crown alone.[36]

A good deal depended on the negotiator involved. Bunbury reported clearly on the explanations he gave on his trip south in May–June 1840. At Coromandel and Tauranga, Maori were told that the government wanted to 'check their imprudently selling their lands, without sufficiently benefiting themselves or obtaining a fair equivalent'. Pre-emption was 'intended equally for their benefit, and to encourage industrious white men to settle amongst them', to share their skills with Maori. Rather than allowing large areas of land to be alienated to absentee speculators who would not benefit Maori, it was better for the Queen to buy their lands herself 'at a juster valuation'.[37]

Henry Williams also seems to have justified pre-emption as a protection against land speculation, for he reported that chiefs to the south of Cook Strait and up the coast to Wanganui were 'gratified that a check was put to the importunities of the Europeans to the purchase of their lands'.[38] Williams and his fellow missionaries had been apprehensive of the encroachments of land purchasers well before Hobson's arrival.[39] Since most of the treaty negotiators were missionaries or, as in the case of Henry's son, Edward, closely associated with them, it seems reasonable to conclude that the general sense conveyed in explaining pre-emption was a protective one. It is quite likely that negotiators did not realise the full significance of pre-emption; Hobson may not have widely publicised the financial provisions for the colony and the part that pre-emption would play.[40]

Maori attitudes to pre-emption depended a good deal on their particular circumstances. In the southern districts, Maori were eager to secure government assistance in dealing with the New Zealand Company settlers who were exerting every means in their power, not excluding force, to lay claim to lands which Maori considered they had never sold. It does not seem to have occurred to Maori to question whether the government had sole right of purchase or only first offer. What southern Maori needed was government protection; with considerable patience, those in the Port Nicholson area appealed to the governor by letter and by deputation to settle their difficulties.[41]

By contrast, although a great deal of land in the north had been alienated before 1840, some Maori were initially not averse to selling more and saw in this an immediate benefit from the treaty. Many of the major chiefs in the Bay of Islands and Hokianga districts quickly made land offers to Hobson in 1840; by early May, he noted 'much impatience and discontent' among potential land sellers. Symonds confirmed this; Maori had even eased off work in anticipation of sales.[42] Hobson, though, was in no position to take up more land in the north. Apart from inadequate funding for setting up a small colonial administration, his financial problems were compounded by the decision to shift the centre of government to the Waitemata early in 1841. This required extensive purchases at Auckland in 1840, and forced him to refuse northern land offers. Northern Maori were naturally disappointed, and a reaction against pre-emption came to government notice in December 1841 at the Bay of Islands and in 1843 at Kaitaia.[43] The drying-up of the accustomed revenue from land sales contributed substantially to the tensions that climaxed in the war of 1844.

Where land sales did take place, as at Auckland, Maori rapidly realised the extent to which the government was benefiting from the margin between purchase and re-sale prices.[44] By the time FitzRoy arrived in December 1843, Waikato and Ngati Whatua chiefs were convinced that the pre-emption clause was unfair and should be reconsidered. Ngati Whatua representatives appealed to FitzRoy: 'At the meeting at Waitangi you [the government] said that we should be equal to the Pakeha and that we should sell our lands to the Queen. But we are now saying that it is up to the Queen to have the first say (offer) and if she doesn't want it, we should be able to sell it to any other Pakeha.' Waikato supported this view, and shrewdly countered the usual explanation of pre-emption as protection against speculators by pointing out it was the government itself that wanted extensive land blocks. Settlers usually required only small tracts which Maori were generally willing to alienate to encourage Pakeha to live among them.[45]

FitzRoy was aware that settler influence was responsible, at least in part, for encouraging these complaints. Maori had been 'repeatedly told' that they had given the Queen the 'hokonga' only, and that in the Maori text of the treaty this did not constitute a cession of the 'sole and exclusive right of purchase'. They had also been told that pre-emption was incompatible with article three of the treaty by which Maori were supposed to enjoy all the rights and privileges of British subjects, but, as long as they were unable to dispose freely of their own lands, this article was not effective – they were 'no better than slaves (taurekareka) taken in war, who have not the disposal of their own lands, while occupied by their conquerors'.[46]

The press was partly responsible for stirring up Maori unease. A steady campaign against pre-emption had been waged for almost six months before FitzRoy's arrival. In June 1843, the *Southern Cross* had complained about the effect of pre-emption on the Maori: 'The Parliament of Great Britain could not create such an anomaly as this; a being with all the rights and privileges of a British subject without the right of selling his land to whom he chooses.'[47] In August, the paper shifted its attack to the treaty as a whole. It printed the 'official' English treaty text of 1840 alongside what it called a 'literal and true translation' – a close rendering in English of the Maori text that most chiefs had signed. The main purpose of this stratagem was to cast doubt on the validity of the entire agreement: the Maori people could not have given their 'intelligent' consent to the treaty, as required by Normanby, because they had not fully understood its terms.[48] Although the newspaper showed that Maori perhaps had a different understanding from the one intended in the English text of 1840, it did not suggest that Pakeha might take this into consideration and acknowledge that it was the Maori text that had been negotiated and signed in that year. The emphasis was placed instead on the uselessness of the treaty to meet settler needs. The 'valid' treaty was assumed to be the English version, regardless of what Maori had signed or understood.

The newspaper campaign, backed by representations from Maori and Pakeha, was sufficient to persuade FitzRoy that the government would have to make some adjustment to pre-emption.[49] As FitzRoy confessed to Stanley, the facts of the Maori case went far to support their assertions. When Maori agreed to the pre-emption clause, they naturally expected that government would buy Maori land when it was offered. Given the official arguments of protection against speculation, it was also reasonable for Maori to anticipate that the government would give a fair price for land. Neither of these expectations had been fulfilled. Knowing that the government was making a profit from land sales, Maori offered new land at an increased price which FitzRoy found to be 'wholly out of the question'. The government could not consider new offers in any case, for it still had unsold land deriving from adjustments made with early settlers and with the New Zealand Company. Maori, unable to sell at all, or asked to sell at a price that was palpably unfair, justifiably felt betrayed by the workings of pre-emption and, as a result, by the treaty.[50]

Since the Colonial Office had allowed FitzRoy to exercise some discretion with regard to pre-emption, he decided to waive the restriction. Under the first waiver of March 1844, individuals could buy direct from Maori on condition that a fee of 10/- an acre was paid to the government. Certain areas, such as pa and sacred places, were to be withheld from sale and the details of each sale had to be scrutinised by Protectors. By the following October, however, such a small amount of land had been sold that FitzRoy decided to reduce the government fee to ld an acre. Under the first waiver, about 600 acres changed hands; under the second, 100,000 acres.[51]

When announcing the waivers, FitzRoy had taken care to stress that the aim of pre-emption had been to protect Maori interests – to check the purchase of Maori lands while their value was insufficiently known to their owners. This appeared to the settlers at Port Nicholson to be a deliberate misrepresentation of the real purpose of the measure, to which they drew Stanley's attention. As Stanley well knew, they noted, the real object of pre-emption was to apply in New Zealand the principles of sound colonisation.[52] The Colonial Office scarcely needed the reminder. They had accepted FitzRoy's March waiver with caution, anticipating that it would make Maori landowners competitors with the Crown, but the second waiver was unacceptable because it completely destroyed the economic purpose of pre-emption. When FitzRoy's successor, George Grey, took office in November 1845, he was directed to restore the Crown's pre-emptive right, except in those districts where the New Zealand Company stood in lieu of the Crown.[53]

Contemporary attitudes to pre-emption reveal that many had mixed opinions. The Anglican Bishop Selwyn, for example, was critical of the way pre-emption worked against Maori interests by creating funds to import settler labour which would supplant

Maori labour. Despite this, he favoured pre-emption for protective reasons. Chief Justice Martin, along with most missionaries, feared that Maori would sell their lands indiscriminately if pre-emption were abandoned and cited the rapid increase in lands offered under FitzRoy's temporary waivers, with Maori 'hawking' their lands in Auckland streets. And George Clarke was apprehensive, anticipating outbreaks of violence when disputed lands were offered for sale. Maori themselves were cautious. Although they had been pleased at first by the idea of a relaxation on government land regulations (some extolling the decision as 'ka pai'), some later expressed a wish to retain protection.[54]

Official thinking, too, varied. Hobson undoubtedly understood both the financial and humanitarian reasons for pre-emption, and realised also that regulated land sale was an orderly way of controlling settlement. FitzRoy, however, either undervalued the function of pre-emption in creating a land and emigration fund or was prepared to sacrifice it on grounds of humanity and justice. Yet, in the colony's first years, pre-emption did not produce substantial financial returns. It probably required that the government should have access to the extensive areas of 'waste land' obtained by force in Australia and by force and negotiation in North America.[55] But force was not practicable in New Zealand where humanitarian principles had been proclaimed and where Maori were capable of resisting any moves to acquire their land other than by purchase. The failure to supply adequate financial resources and reluctance to think carefully about the effects of pre-emption suggests a failure of policy over land transactions. At the least it indicates an inability to reconcile the conflicting interests of economical government and commitment to native welfare – the two areas in which new thinking had evolved in the decade preceding Waitangi.

When Grey restored pre-emption with the Native Land Purchase Ordinance of 1846, the *New-Zealander* attacked it as the 'first step towards the negation of the Treaty of Waitangi'.[56] The Ordinance was not concerned simply to restore Crown right of purchase; it also aimed to tighten government control over Maori lands. It became an offence for individual settlers to occupy or interfere with Maori land in any way. Leases were prohibited and restrictions were placed on taking timber and flax. Maori were now effectively prevented from utilising their lands freely. While the move was designed to curtail settler and Maori excesses, there was some truth in the press claim that it was a 'stealthy violation' of Maori rights. Maori had agreed to the treaty mainly because it guaranteed their rangatiratanga over their lands, forests, fisheries and other prized possessions. The Ordinance subtly undermined that rangatiratanga, it indicated a new firmness in government dealings with Maori in all respects and it paralleled a shift to bring Maori firmly within the compass of British law.

The establishment of British law and authority over the Maori people proved as contentious as the implementation of the treaty's guarantees on land. Because of the treaty, New Zealand was regarded as an unusual case, something of an experiment in colonial government. In other parts of the Empire the position of indigenous races had not been so clearly spelt out. In Canada, for example, Indians living on land which had not been secured by the Crown were left under the immediate authority of their own chiefs – a recognition by the Crown that they retained a degree of internal sovereignty.[57] But in New Zealand, article three of the treaty had placed on the government an immediate responsibility for many thousands of Maori subjects. Hobson had appointed George Clarke as Protector of Aborigines, but the immensity of his task, even when sub-protectors were added to his staff, could scarcely have been appreciated by the Colonial Office.

Hobson was not provided with any plan for the incorporation of Maori within the government's jurisdiction. Normanby and Russell were mainly concerned with outlining principles and guidelines for native policy. Both recommended that Maori custom be allowed, with the exception of cannibalism, but Russell was somewhat more specific. He suggested that some adjustment of English law might be necessary, that missionary work in civilising the Maori should be supported, and that force should be used only if needed to suppress unacceptable custom.[58]

This very general discussion left administrators in New Zealand with the responsibility of providing some practical plan of action.[59] Major questions were left unanswered. To what extent should Maori be subject to British law? Could they be exempt in certain circumstances? How far could Maori custom be tolerated in practice? How could the government enforce its authority with only a meagre staff of officials and few troops? Decisions on these and other problems were forced upon the government by the pressure of events.

Many chiefs were ready to co-operate with British law and government. They had signed the treaty, seeking some change; in accordance with their understanding of kawanatanga (governorship) they were often willing to allow government arbitration in petty disputes between themselves and settlers.[60] Theft, fraudulent trade deals, cattle trespass onto cultivations and unlawful removal of timber from Maori land were not uncommon. In some instances, appeals for intervention were made directly to the governor, but most requests were forwarded to the Protectors of Aborigines. Maori also began to bring cases before the colony's courts, sometimes with success.[61]

Where Maori were involved on both sides of a dispute, however, they often resented government offers of arbitration, though here too there were signs of change. Ensign A.D.W. Best found himself advising on an adultery case in Wellington in mid-1840, and Edward Shortland was caught up in a similar case in the Bay of Plenty.[62] In the Waipa, Te Waru, in a notable gesture of commitment to British law, submitted his daughter to a government official on a charge of murdering a slave (though the case was later dropped). He also stated his willingness to apprehend criminals.[63] Wiremu Neira Te Awaitaia, a Christian chief from Raglan, committed Maori in that district to deal with murder, 'or other heinous crime', through government officials and delivered an offender over to British justice. At Otawhao a magistrate had been asked for, because chiefs were 'united in hailing the coming of the Governor and the adoption of a new law with gladness'.[64] Even in those areas where government agents were seldom seen, Christian Maori were seeking out local missionaries or native teachers to act as mediators in a variety of tribal difficulties. Sometimes decisions might even be made by mission tribunals which imposed their own fines or punishments, such as expulsion from the pa community.[65]

But Maori compliance with British law had definite limits. While Maori proved fairly amenable to court decisions if the punishment was, or could be commuted to, a fine, when offences were likely to be punished by imprisonment or hanging Maori tended to protect offenders, particularly chiefs. There was one notable exception, however. A Bay of Islands Maori, Maketu, viciously murdered a Pakeha woman, her two children and a half-caste child.[66] Although there had been a previous case of a Pakeha murdered by a Maori, Kihi, it had been resolved by the natural death of Kihi before his trial.[67] Maketu presented a more serious problem. His apprehension, trial and hanging in March 1842 were regarded by Maori and Pakeha as a test case of Maori submission to British law. Pakeha felt heartened by what they saw as Maori co-operation. A number of northern chiefs publicly dissociated themselves from Maketu's action and asserted their commitment to the Queen's laws.[68] But the truth of the matter, as more perceptive Pakeha realised, was that Maketu had created the conditions for a major inter-tribal fight by killing the half-caste child of the chief, Rewa. To avert war, Maori had sacrificed Maketu to British justice.

Generally, a reluctance to submit to the law was evident when Maori feared that the government could not protect them if they abandoned customary methods, a situation that prevailed for many years after 1840.[69] Government authority was not a simple alternative to chiefly authority, nor were chiefs prepared to concede more of their power than was necessary. Chiefly power was needed to keep the tribes under control and, when this began to fail, Maori were concerned that the government was not supporting the chiefs.[70]

In the area of administration, land matters most often required government intervention. The new option of referral to government offered Maori a means of handling their endemic inter-tribal disputes – an extension of a trend evident in Busby's time. That Maori were eager to make use of this in the early years of the colony is evident in the number of Maori letters requesting government mediation. Even where this assistance was not sought, tribes felt encouraged to reject force in settling land disputes, in favour of asserting rights based on customary ownership, genealogies being more often cited as a consequence.[71]

Maori themselves acknowledged the gradual shift to peaceful mediation and presented cases either to the governor or to government agents. Te Wherowhero told FitzRoy that Maori were willing to seek assistance in even the most serious of long-standing disputes, such as Motiti Island at Maketu. There were advantages to be gained.[72] As Taipari of Tauranga pointed out to Best, 'if we [Maori] continue fighting our race will become extinct whereas Peace will increase it. It is now some years since I took any part in the quarrels of these parts & I find that whilst others become weak I am getting strong. The children of my Pah [*sic*] are not murdered in their youth and the boys are growing into men. I can now raise more fighting men than any Chief of Tauranga & I will use my strength to preserve peace.'[73]

But the shift to negotiation through government could serve quite another purpose, that of making the government a 'cat's-paw' in tribal quarrels. Hugh Carleton, Henry Williams's son-in-law, explained how a Maori would sell disputed land for a song, if the effect of the sale would be to involve the rival claimant in a quarrel with the English: 'He would have the double satisfaction of revenge, and of relief from the obligation of being bound in honour to maintain a troublesome and uncertain right.'[74] Clarke was aware of this possibility as early as 1840, when he reported that disputed land, often a border area between two adjacent tribes, was most likely to be offered first. To counter some of these problems, which could only become increasingly complicated, he recommended the compilation of a kind of 'Doomsday Book' which would record the major boundaries of the tribal areas and the internal divisions of a district as they existed at the inception of British sovereignty. The Thames chief Kahukoti endorsed this idea.[75] Similar suggestions were made a few years later by William Brown and Bishop Selwyn. By then, Clarke favoured the establishment of a land tribunal; the need for some such body had become more apparent as a result of the added confusion caused by FitzRoy's waivers, when the offers of kainga tautohe (debatable lands) increased.[76]

Throughout the country in the 1840s the government was involved in problems of disputed land. A typical disputed land case was that of Nopera Panakareao at Kaitaia. Land around the Mangonui Habour had been held in former days by Nopera's tribe, but for some thirty years a group of Ngapuhi, related to Hongi Hika, had been allowed to occupy it. These occupants had sold some of the land to Pakeha, thereby disregarding the traditional rights of the owners, and Nopera was determined to reassert his rights. He appealed to the government to intervene, in the meantime establishing some sort of claim on one side of the harbour where he hoisted the Union Jack. The government became involved in a long, bitter wrangle which encompassed not only the two rival Maori groups but also their associated tribes, the local settlers and other interested Pakeha. The Auckland *Southern Cross* charged Nopera with breaking the treaty, although it was not clear how it had arrived at this conclusion.[77]

Nopera's dispute was only one of many such cases throughout the country in the 1840s. In many areas old inter-tribal feuds continued. The land title situation had been complicated for some tribes by wars in the decades before 1840. With the arrival of government, Maori were provided with a new weapon in fighting a traditional power game. Missionaries bemoaned the government's incapacity to deal effectively with disputes which often resulted in considerable loss of life,[78] but given their limited manpower it is difficult to see how Hobson and his immediate successors could have coped adequately with a situation where traditional forces were still so strong. Indeed, some chiefs were well aware of the government's weakness and showed little confidence in the alternative of peaceful negotiation offered by British authority. This was particularly true of the Thames–Bay of Plenty area. Taraia, a Ngati Tamatera chief from Thames, expressed his willingness in late 1840 to welcome the government and to desist from fighting, but only on condition that he receive soldiers to protect him from his traditional enemies.[79]

It was, in fact, an issue involving Taraia in June 1842 that raised the question of the effectiveness of government authority.[80] Taraia attacked the Ngai Te Rangi of Tauranga over a boundary dispute, killed several and committed acts of cannibalism. The government felt obliged to act since Ngai Te Rangi had requested government protection. Taraia, however, argued that 'the Governor was no Governor for him or his people and that he had never signed the Treaty nor would he acknowledge his authority'.[81] More explicitly he told Hobson: 'With the Governor is the adjustment of European affairs and with us the adjustment of the natives.'[82] The government was at first inclined to deal forcibly with this blunt rejection of British sovereignty, but with insufficient troops to ensure success, it was decided to resolve the matter through negotiation which, fortunately, was accepted.

Within six months, the extent of government power and authority once more became an issue when a more serious dispute flared up between Ngai Te Rangi and Ngati Whakaue of Maketu.[83] Tohi Te Ururangi of Maketu drew attention to the fact that he, too, had not signed the treaty, and repeated Taraia's argument that the government had no right to interfere.[84] Willoughby Shortland, Acting Governor since Hobson's death in September 1842, contemplated using troops against Tohi, but the legality of such action was queried by officials George Clarke, William Martin and William Swainson. Swainson argued that British sovereignty in New Zealand was incomplete, that a prerequisite of asserting sovereignty had been the 'free and intelligent consent' of the Maori people; hence those who had accepted neither the treaty nor the Queen's authority in any formal way could not be considered British subjects and were outside the legal limits of British sovereignty. Clarke admitted this possibility but suggested that it would be 'an act of humanity' to both Maori and Pakeha to treat all Maori as British subjects. Where tribes had not yet ceded sovereignty, 'every honourable and humane means' should be used to get them to do so (a suggestion vetoed by Shortland), but to use force would be considered by Maori as a 'breach of faith'. Although the consensus among other officials favoured recognition of all Maori as British subjects, they were undecided over the use of force and the affair drifted into a negotiated settlement by March 1843.

But the matter had raised administrative problems relating to the treaty and to sovereignty. Swainson suggested subsequently that some areas could be constituted Native Districts where Maori custom might prevail.[85] Since these districts would still be under British sovereignty, he apparently favoured something akin to the autonomy allowed the North American Indian in unceded territory.[86] Native Districts, however, were to be merely temporary expedients; the overall aim of amalgamation was retained. The Native Districts idea was not acceptable to Clarke who had been convinced, even before Waitangi, that with settlement the only effective protection for Maori was to incorporate them within the rule of law. Separate Maori districts were opposed by others for quite different reasons. Shortland feared that they would lead to widespread rejection of Crown authority, and settlers resented the restriction on access to land for settlement that such districts would constitute.

Whatever scruples Swainson may have had about British sovereignty, the Colonial Office refused to countenance them. Stephen and Stanley stated that sovereignty had been publicly asserted by the Crown and announced to all foreign states. Any 'controversy' about it was 'utterly inadmissible' and ought 'to be repressed with a strong hand'. Stanley reinforced this with a lengthy dispatch stating the position of the Crown: 'All the territories comprised within the commissions for the government of New Zealand, and all persons inhabiting those territories are and must be considered as being to all intents and purposes within the dominions of the British Crown.' Stanley then conceded that within New Zealand there was no reason why Maori should not live under their own laws and usages in their dealings with each other (with certain exceptions such as cannibalism), as was the case in other areas of the Empire. Stephen pointed out that subjection to British sovereignty and subjection to English law were not 'convertible terms', that a temporary tolerance of Maori custom had been allowed for in Hobson's instructions, but that the colonial administration had not passed the necessary enactment.[87]

The perspectives of officials in London and New Zealand were different. Whereas the Colonial Office reacted to the debate over the Tauranga affair by asserting that sovereignty had been unquestionably secured against any claims of other nations, Swainson was more concerned with assessing the contractual nature of the treaty and its effects within New Zealand. Like other New Zealand officials, he was endeavouring to define the limits within which sovereign power and authority could be justly and effectively exercised. His preference for Native Districts probably came close to the Maori understanding of the treaty: Maori could retain a degree of autonomy and still be British subjects. It would be a situation not unlike the thinking of the King movement in the 1850s and certainly in line with later Maori aspirations. Maori would later search back for early official references to their customary rights, such as Swainson and the Colonial Office acknowledged, in vain attempts to gain official recognition for independent rights.[88]

As early as 1843, however, a more extensive recognition of limited Maori sovereignty was unacceptable in New Zealand. The third article of the treaty, granting Maori the rights and privileges of British subjects, was designed to serve the practical goal of settlement as well as to satisfy humanitarians. With two races living in close proximity, a qualification of the third article by entrenching Maori custom and by institutionalising independence in separate districts was most unlikely.

The debate did at least force the Colonial Office to clarify certain matters. The Maori people as a whole were to be subject to British sovereignty. The government reserved the right to intervene in disputes between Maori, although this was to be done with discretion; it was conceded that Maori custom should be allowed to prevail in dealings that involved only Maori or, in some circumstances, Maori and the government. From the distant Colonial Office, Stanley and Stephen saw no real problem in making allowance for Maori usages, as had been done elsewhere in the Empire, and directed New Zealand officials accordingly.[89]

Yet when FitzRoy arrived at the end of 1843, he was no more able than his predecessors to extend law and authority over the Maori people. The Colonial Office was not prepared to increase the troops at his disposal and the colony's financial position was worsening. Just as the British government's inadequate funding was preventing a fair implementation of its land policy, so it was jeopardising the establishment of effective administration and law. Maori continued to be more or less provisional British subjects, theoretically under British law but with few of its practical benefits.[90] As the contradictions of this situation became more apparent, there were signs of discontent among both races. Pakeha began to demand that Maori ought to be forced to comply with English law if they really were British subjects. Any refusal would constitute a breach of the treaty.

While FitzRoy shared the belief that, in the long term, Maori should be treated as British subjects, he appreciated that some immediate adjustment of the law to Maori needs was called for. He took advantage of a visit from a deputation of chiefs attending a mighty inter-tribal gathering at Remuera in May 1844 to outline part of his proposal. To accommodate the Maori abhorrence of imprisonment, he proposed that compensation be paid instead, with chiefs acting as guarantors.[91] In July this proposal was incorporated in the Native Exemption Ordinance, together with other concessions to Maori custom. Several other ordinances of 1844 were modified in minor ways to meet Maori needs.[92] Fitz-Roy also requested Chief Justice Martin (the only senior official conversant with Maori), to draw up for publication a Maori language lesson-book containing instructions on English laws and customs.[93] This fulfilled, to some extent, the Maori request to be kept informed about the law and supplemented the publication in the *Maori Messenger* of the occasional ordinance. In addition, Clarke consciously used the *Maori Messenger* as a medium of instruction in the processes of the law, reporting important court cases and explaining the official action taken.

Exhortation, however, was no substitute for good government. As FitzRoy's term of office progressed, it became apparent to both Maori and Pakeha observers that the government was too weak to adhere to a strong line of policy. Maori were unable to practise fully native custom or ritenga, yet no system of law had been provided as an alternative. Beyond the immediate vicinity of towns, Maori custom continued to prevail. Settlers were dependent more on the protection of local chiefs than on the government and were still liable to the penalties attached to a breach of Maori custom.

Maori, for their part, were aware that their situation had improved little with the advent of British authority. The presence of an alternative source of power in the land increasingly compromised chiefly status and authority. The position of a chief and the customary tribal restrictions that had exercised some restraint over out-settlers and over restless Maori youth were now no longer so respected. 'This anomalous state of things renders the present position of the settlers and the natives much worse than it was before the regular colonization of the country,' Clarke lamented.[94] As a result, Maori gradually lost faith in the government and its ability to implement its promises, and fell back on traditional methods of handling affairs.

For Pakeha, however, the situation was intolerable; a consensus in the community – official, missionary and settler – began to favour the adoption of a stronger policy towards the Maori people. Even Colonial Office officials, who had regularly advised the government to adopt a mediatory role, shifted to a less indulgent position when news of FitzRoy's Native Exemption Ordinance reached London about the same time as the first reports of the stirrings in the north that would challenge British sovereignty.

Chapter Six

CHALLENGES TO SOVEREIGNTY AND
THE TREATY

The 'Governor's book [the treaty] was very good, likewise his talk; but they would watch his actions with some jealousy,' some northern Maori told Clarke in the early 1840s. The Protector of Aborigines was well aware that British sovereignty was on trial. All Maori, regardless of commitment to the treaty, were suspicious of government intentions. Although Hobson's record proved to them that, on the whole, he was well disposed, many feared that under subsequent governors Pakeha would be 'exalted' and Maori 'put down'. In view of the Australian experience, these were not unreasonable misgivings. Maori had allowed the British into the country, but they reserved their final judgement on the treaty for the future. In the meantime, many were caught up in the surge of activity accompanying the establishment of a British colony. In areas close to settlement, their produce found a ready market at good prices. Maori labour, too, was in demand to help settlers setting up home in a new environment. Maori were carried along in the sudden swell of activity, and, as Clarke later reflected, 'it might truly be said that their cup of temporal prosperity was "running over".'[1]

But the early prosperity did not last. As its attractions diminished and as the new authority increased, the possibility of a Maori challenge to British sovereignty became more likely. By 1842, 'old hands' like Busby and Henry Williams were uneasy about a possible Maori backlash. Williams admitted that he knew no chief who had not expressed his distrust of Pakeha: 'In this I consider their feelings as perfectly natural. What were the feelings and conduct of the ancient Britons towards the first invaders of the country?'[2]

Since the north felt the first impact of government, the first signs of serious unrest were likely to appear there also. Towards the end of 1841, a series of events unsettled northern Maori. In November, Hobson issued a proclamation forbidding the cutting of kauri. The move was intended to curb the wanton destruction of forests, but it contravened the treaty's guarantee of Maori possession of their forests and encroached upon an important source of revenue. The move provoked even Waka Nene to exclaim that if the governor were present in the Hokianga, he would cut down a kauri before him to see how he would react.[3]

In the same month, the first serious application of British law to a Maori offender occurred when Maketu was apprehended for multiple murder. Some Maori talked of the administration overreaching itself.[4]

At the same time, tensions were surfacing over land, in addition to the continuing disquiet caused by pre-emption and the old land claims investigations. Blocks of land allotted to Pakeha who had married into a tribe were now liable to title investigation. Difficulties also arose over the rights of Maori widows, and over inheritance involving half-caste children. Did the latter, for instance, enjoy the full rights of British subjects? If so, did the ruling on surplus lands apply? Or were they a special case with customary rights through their Maori mothers?[5] From a Maori point of view, government decisions on these and on other matters were not always satisfactory.

Maori were gradually being made aware that they were no longer free to dispose of their lands. They found it difficult to accept that, by a valid sale to a Pakeha, they had permanently disposed of their land and any rights over it. One buyer, for example, encountered Maori resistance to the removal of manganese from some Whangarei land in 1844. When he protested that the land was his by purchase, the local chief disagreed: the land had been purchased but not the stones. Although the Pakeha was willing to allow Maori access to the manganese, which was used for dye, he was finally forced to settle the matter by giving the young chief, 'by written agreement', a cask of tobacco. Since the chief spoke English and clearly understood the nature of a contract, it is difficult to know whether he was simply 'giving it a try' or whether he genuinely believed that he still retained residual rights in the land. Some years later, the missionary Thomas Chapman referred to a similar instance when the ownership of loose stones on CMS land in the Rotorua area was debated.[6]

Problems also existed where land was resold by settlers. The concept of land as a commodity which could be exploited through resale was new to Maori. With the exception of the speculative purchases just before 1840, Maori land had usually been alienated to secure the benefits of a Pakeha presence. The arrangement was a personal one and, not surprisingly, when land was resold after 1840, Maori sometimes demanded further payment from the new owner. Sometimes this demand might be sparked off by the original articles of purchase wearing out; sometimes it would be stimulated by a real or alleged settler trespass on a Maori sacred spot (wahi tapu), or an infringement of some other custom.[7] It was clear, however, that Maori accepted the concept of total alienation of land rights through sale only after considerable experience.[8]

In the early 1840s Maori in many areas were beginning to show a more cautious attitude towards land sales, some refusing to sell any land at all. Mohi Tawhai of Waima took this stand at once in 1840, and anti-land selling committees were formed in his area. By 1842, chiefs at Whaingaroa were refusing to sell.[9] The following year, Kaitaia chiefs adopted an even firmer line, protesting strongly against any more sales, declaring their intention to exercise their previous rights and privileges over their lands, and objecting to the government assuming any authority over their possessions, including 'surplus lands'.[10] Clarke had warned the government in 1840 that Maori were not prepared to sell land indiscriminately. They wanted to retain coastal areas and swamp lands for the resources associated with them. They were reluctant to alienate large tracts of land, for one of their major purposes in selling land was closer association with Pakeha, thereby stimulating the demand for Maori produce and services.[11] To achieve these aims Maori were prepared to tolerate settler provocation and to make concessions to government. The ideal situation in land dealings, as seen by Wiremu Neira, was one of reciprocity: 'We are now anxious that our lands should be secured by us, that a check should be put upon English urging us to sell those lands that we cannot part with; and when we do sell, we wish that the feeling of kindness should be mutual; when we dispose freely of our lands, let the English dispose freely of their property.'[12]

But there was a limit beyond which Maori refused to be pushed in land matters. In the New Zealand Company districts, Maori held out against pressure, refusing to concede the extent of land claimed by the Company. At New Plymouth, they insisted that their favourite lands should be withheld, a concession that Fitz-Roy made by reversing the decision of Commissioner Spain.[13] In the Wanganui area, Maori denied the sale of the eastern side of the river and warned the government: 'You may take our land, but you shall break our necks first.'[14] In Wellington, they fought to retain control of pa sites and cultivations in the face of settler might. Te Aro and Kumutoto chiefs appealed for government support and shrewdly courted official goodwill,[15] but the Kumutoto chief, Wi Tako, finally exasperated by one settler attack in the press, rose to the challenge: 'I ask you pakehas, what did the Queen tell you? Did she say to you, "Go to New Zealand and fraudulently take away the land of the natives?" You say No. Then why do you encroach upon lands that have not been fairly purchased?'[16]

Maori had good reason to feel that the Waitangi pledge to protect Maori rights was not being fulfilled. In the Wellington area, the government, forced by the New Zealand Company, was prepared to favour settler interests at the expense of the Maori people. The sudden influx of a comparatively large white population, assertive to the point of violence, was an unexpected development for Maori and made the Cook Strait region a potentially explosive area from the beginning of 1840.[17]

In June 1843, tensions between Maori and Pakeha led to confrontation at Wairau.[18] The Company decided to push ahead with the survey and settlement of land which they claimed in that area, but Maori demanded that it wait for a decision from Commissioner Spain. Twenty-two settlers were killed, including Captain Wakefield and the Police Magistrate from Nelson. The Maori group, led by Te Rauparaha and Te Rangihaeata, also suffered loss of life, including Te Rangihaeata's wife. The local settler community was outraged and the Wellington press cried out for the death of the two chiefs. But in February 1844, FitzRoy's final adjudication of the case, which the Colonial Office upheld, exonerated the Maori and laid the blame squarely on the settlers. Although the facts of the Wairau incident supported this judgement, the decision failed to meet the expectations of either race. Many Pakeha felt that it condoned and encouraged further Maori violence, while Maori people, expecting a demand for restitution, felt that it indicated government weakness.

The clash of interests at Wairau, made the more dramatic because the participants happened to be leading members of their communities, left a lasting impression on both races. A year afterwards, George Clarke (junior) noted that a 'deep-rooted prejudice and suspicion of each other's motives has been engendered in the minds of both races, and a settled determination on the part of the natives to resist what they may consider acts of aggression or injustice by the settlers, especially in reference to the question of land'.[19] That Pakeha should attempt to take Maori land by force was indeed a completely new experience. Maori responded with a new firmness that was apparent to Clarke in negotiations the following year. Tuhawaiki and Taiaroa refused to sell the Otago block as a whole; they insisted that village cultivations, burial grounds and reserves should be clearly defined and specified in the agreement as remaining in Maori hands.[20] This demand for a more rigorous attention to the detail of the contract was backed with a threat of force, an 'influential chief' assenting to the sale with the remark that 'if the pakehas did not make all straight, they had only to repeat the scene of the Wairau'.[21] Such remarks, coupled with a more resolute Maori stance in other areas such as the Hutt Valley, reinforced a growing conviction among the settler population that the government should take a firmer line with the Maori.

Some northern Maori also felt that the time had come to make a stand. In July 1844, at the instigation of the chief Heke, they cut down the flagstaff on Maiki Hill at Russell.[22] The staff was used primarily as a signal station for ships, but Heke took exception to it because he regarded it as a 'tohu' (sign) that New Zealand had passed into British hands. His attitude was confirmed by the government's insistence that the mast be re-erected, even when it was brought down three more times. The initial incident of July 1844 developed over the next eighteen months into a major confrontation between Maori tribes and British troops. Tribes in the north committed themselves to Heke or to the government (or remained neutral), while the government force of 90 regular troops was expanded to about 1,000 men. By the time an engagement with Heke's main ally Kawiti brought the northern affair to a close in January 1846, both sides had sustained losses; New Zealand's first permanent settlement at Russell had been destroyed and its inhabitants had fled.

Maori dissatisfaction with the government arose from many causes. The governor and the capital had shifted to Auckland; Ngapuhi had lost mana to Ngati Whatua and Waikato, their traditional enemies; land sales revenue had declined; overseas shipping had fallen off and port dues were now taken by the government; the demand for Maori labour and goods had declined; and the cost of imported goods had been increased by duties. Throughout the colony there was deepening financial depression.[23] Inevitably, many northern Maori contrasted this 1844 situation with their former wealth and independence, and held British intervention responsible.

For some years Heke had been a restless influence, but it became increasingly apparent that he resented the intrusion of British authority. He appears to have understood more clearly than others the abstract nature of sovereignty. While Maori generally sought reassurance by questioning whether the government's real intention was to seize Maori lands, Heke recognised that the British flag was a sign that the land, in a sense, belonged to the Crown.[24] In a series of letters, filled with obscure allusions, he repeatedly made one clear point to the government – that he wanted British authority to be removed. 'Do you return to your own country, to England, which was made by God for you. God made this land for us, and not for any stranger or foreign nation to touch.'[25] Attributing the loss of Maori independence to the treaty, Heke lost no opportunity of voicing his dissatisfaction with it, and blamed the missionaries for deliberate deception in inducing so many to sign. A small but important act emphasised Heke's stance. Before 1840, CMS prayers had been said for the Maori chiefs and their families; after 1840 prayers for the Queen and the Royal Family had been substituted. By 1845, Heke and his supporters refused to join in the responses when these prayers were said.[26]

Heke had a personal connection also with the Waitangi property, for he had been one of the owners of the Waitangi land sold to Busby. He had resented the slight to his mana when Busby's claim had to be approved by the land claims investigators.[27] He also asserted that he had a right in the pole used for the flagstaff on Maiki Hill, since it had originally been provided by him to fly the flag of the United Tribes of New Zealand, the Confederation of 1835. This claim has never been treated seriously by historians but it may be true.[28] The New Zealand flag certainly flew on the Waitangi side of the Bay and Te Kemara, the major Waitangi chief, recollected his sense of personal loss when it was moved to Maiki Hill. According to Nene and other Bay of Islands chiefs, the flag had been forcibly taken down upon Hobson's arrival and the staff later removed to Kororareka. Officials found it hard to persuade local Maori to re-erect the staff.[29]

In 1844–45, Heke attacked the flagstaff because he believed that the mana of the land should not be vested solely in the government, as the British flag implied, but in the Maori people as well. He favoured a display of the Union Jack only if the New Zealand flag was flown alongside it.[30] When the flagstaff was brought down again in March 1845, the missionary Alfred Brown observed that the Maori 'hoisted their own colour on a neighbouring height'. Even chiefs such as Nene who fought for the government had asked that the Maori be allowed to fly their own national flag.[31] Whether for or against the government, Maori appear to have believed that their rangatiratanga was recognised in that flag and in the 1835 Declaration. They do not seem to have perceived any contradiction in their request to allow both the New Zealand and British flags to co-exist after 1840.

In challenging British sovereignty, Heke may have had other motives. A mission-educated Maori, he was reputed to speak some English, to have visited Sydney, and to be well acquainted with the history of England and with the American War of Independence. Encouraged by Americans living at the Bay of Islands, he may have hoped that British authority could be overthrown and perhaps replaced by that of the United States, an ex-colonial power, expected to be more sympathetic to Maori interests. It was probably no accident that Heke's first attack on the flagstaff had been made soon after American Independence Day, which Americans always celebrated. The United States consuls at the Bay of Islands had been regarded as agitators by officials.[32] These men would have little sympathy with the British annexation, for it had placed restrictions on American commerce. Relations between the United States and Great Britain had been rather tense in the early 1840s and there had even been talk of war. The two nations had border disputes in North America and were longstanding rivals for the China–Pacific trade. American nationals may well have promised Heke more support in his stand than the United States government itself would have given.

Heke had only to look to the Pacific to find precedents for native difficulties with foreign powers. In Hawaii, where indigenous authority had been compromised for some time by British and American interests, there had been a serious incident in 1843 involving the destruction of the Hawaiian flag; at the time, the relative merits of British and American power and protection had been discussed. In Tahiti, in the early 1840s, the French forced on Queen Pomare a treaty of cession. The Tahitian national flag had been destroyed and the tricolour raised; much publicity had been given to the invasion of Tahiti's land rights. The Tahitians actively resisted from early 1844 to December 1846.[33] Missionary and shipping contacts between Tahiti and the Bay of Islands ensured that these events would be known, and the Tahitian situation received extensive coverage in the New Zealand press early in 1844, just before Heke's first attack on the flagstaff.[34]

In September 1844, at a major meeting at Waimate, FitzRoy expounded at length on the advantages gained by Maori in 1840. He emphasised a protective interpretation: it was at Maori request that the Crown had followed the missionaries to New Zealand, to protect the Maori people from France, Russia or the United States. New Zealand was particularly fortunate to have received this special attention; a Tahitian request for British protection had been turned down and the native flag had not prevented France from seizing Tahiti. Only the British flag could give Maori real security. It was the 'signal of freedom, liberty, and safety.... In sharing its advantages with you, we make you our brothers; we place you on equal terms with ourselves.' FitzRoy also touched very briefly on the protective aspect of pre-emption. The conclusion to be drawn was that the Maori people had incurred certain obligations when Britain had chosen to show them her special benevolence.[35]

Heke, who had not been present at Waimate, received similar assurances: 'The Treaty of Waitangi ... was agreed to by the chiefs, and then the British flag was hoisted to show that the British nation and the New Zealand people were one body, united as brothers and friends. That flag is now the flag of all those New Zealanders who wish to be brothers of Englishmen, to be part of the great British nation, which is like a faggot of sticks, strongly bound together.' The Queen had asked nothing in return except the right of pre-emption which was designed for Maori protection[36] – a considerable understatement given the cession of sovereignty sought in the treaty's first article.

Henry Williams also leapt to the defence of the treaty. He found himself in a peculiarly uncomfortable situation during the northern war, open at once to Maori criticism that he and other missionaries had deceived them in the Waitangi agreement, and Pakeha criticism that Heke's rising proved that he had failed to secure genuine Maori consent to sovereignty. Whatever Williams's motives may have been in 1840, in 1844 his overriding concern was to avert a major Maori uprising which he was sure would result in a Maori victory. He knew that all Maori, 'without exception', had considerable doubts about the designs of the government; the treaty was 'the grand question – whether or not the country was seized in consequence of the treaty'.[37] Williams, therefore, decided to 'fall back' upon the Maori treaty text, arranging for the printing of 400 copies. For many days he was engaged in showing the chiefs that 'this Treaty was indeed their "Magna Charta" whereby their lands, their Rights and Privileges were secure to them'.[38] Because it was a 'sacred compact' there was no possibility of the Queen or the Governor tolerating 'any tinihanga' (tricky nonsense) towards the Maori people.[39] In one explanation to a large group which included Heke, Williams emphasised the protective argument – the treaty had prevented another nation from taking over New Zealand; it had been made to stop internal anarchy and to halt speculative purchasing. Similar explanations were probably given elsewhere; for instance, at a large meeting which Williams attended at Paroa, Bay of Islands, in January 1845.[40]

The *Maori Messenger* supported Williams by reminding the Maori people of the words and actions of their ancestors which had committed them to the English nation, appealing to the traditional respect given tupuna. It also printed the vain appeal of Tahiti's Queen Pomare, asking Queen Victoria for British protection.[41] In addition, the government printed the treaty for circulation among northern chiefs who had asked for a copy.[42]

Much of this promotion involved a deliberate blurring of the meaning of sovereignty. That the cession would ultimately mean a significant loss of Maori power was played down in 1844, as in 1840, by emphasising rangatiratanga. Since the treaty guaranteed Maori ownership of land, nothing substantial had been lost to England. But Clarke, the Chief Protector of Aborigines, admitted that even the rights of rangatiratanga would ultimately have to give way to Crown authority, despite Maori confidence that the treaty had confirmed those rights.[43]

That there was a reluctance to convey to Maori an understanding of the transfer of national sovereignty is revealed by an exchange of letters between Waka Nene and Henry Williams in 1847, where Williams agreed with Nene that the northern war had been provoked by Pakeha claims that the 'sovereignty (mana)' of the country had passed from the Maori, and noted that these claims were untrue. After the war Williams admitted more openly the need to sustain this Maori understanding in order to keep the peace: 'By the Treaty alone ... the thoughts of the tribes who stood by the pakeha, and those who sat quietly, were kept straight.'[44] If the full import of the treaty had been appreciated by Maori, the future would have been placed at great risk. The missionaries would have been the first to suffer Maori vengeance, since they had played a crucial role in 1840 as guarantors of British good faith. Maori had repeatedly made this clear.[45]

Henry Williams was acutely aware of the missionaries' vulnerable position. When news of the 1844 Parliamentary Report had come to his notice, he feared that the missionary cause in New Zealand would be lost. Strong criticism of the treaty in the House of Commons debate of June 1845 followed by the dispatch recommending a tax on land, caused grave concern not only to Williams but to all the English missionaries. The colonial newspapers covered these events fully and reports circulated among Maori people even in the remotest areas, again raising fears about the government's honesty and the security of Maori land.[46] Such threats to abrogate the land guarantee of the treaty did not help to build Maori confidence in the government. Together with FitzRoy's unsuccessful peace proposal seeking a surrender of Maori land as punishment (or utu) for the war, these developments might well have been sufficient cause for a more widespread rising against British sovereignty.[47]

There were good reasons why this did not occur. Those who participated in the northern war clearly made a careful assessment of the advantages and disadvantages of British administration. Maori who aligned themselves with the government, including most of the Hokianga chiefs, feared that they would lose settlers and trade. They wanted to protect access to the benefits of the Pakeha world, even though their original expectations of the prosperity that would follow the treaty had not been fulfilled. A similar appreciation of the material benefits brought by Pakeha was expressed at the Waimate meeting. There, speakers also stressed the advantage of having a governor – one kind of chieftainship over all – to restrain inter-tribal quarrels. They feared that if they became involved in the war then their own chiefly power would be jeopardised.[48]

Maori in other areas were reluctant to be drawn into the affair. At the Wairau incident Te Rauparaha and Te Rangihaeata had received widespread Maori sympathy because of the unjustified settler aggression, but Heke's actions did not earn the same response. Most Maori believed that, since Heke had acted on his own initiative, it was his own fight, or at most a Ngapuhi concern.[49] Te Rauparaha wrote to Te Wherowhero recommending that, as senior chiefs, they should keep the peace in the land. Te Wherowhero refused to become involved, and rejected Heke's suggestion that the Mount Victoria flagstaff at Auckland should be cut down.[50] Some Tauranga and Rotorua chiefs tried to extricate tribal members. Closer to the north, Parore and Tirarau (related to Heke and Kawiti) opted to support the government; but, as Parore made clear, if land were taken by force, or if Maori were degraded, then he would fight. From the Kaipara came similar pledges, Paikea requesting a Union Jack 'as a badge or sign', one of many Maori requests for the flag; as a result of the northern war it became very popular.[51]

Support for the government stemmed from the conviction that it was Ngapuhi's fight, but it arose particularly in areas enjoying for the first time the benefits of Christianity and material wealth. While the north lost its prosperity in the early 1840s, tribes closer to Auckland inherited the benefits of expanding settlement.[52] Ngati Whatua, Uriohau, Waikato and, to a lesser extent, the Bay of Plenty tribes, were not likely to place this advantage at risk. For Waikato, disenchantment with British sovereignty would come later.

The British presence in New Zealand was not upheld by Maori everywhere, however. Taraia at Thames was ready to assist Heke with men and ammunition if called upon.[53] Chapman at Rotorua had been 'fully employed' at times in March–April 1845 'talking down as far as possible rising excitement' about the war. He found many Christian Maori 'very decided in their wish to acknowledge the Queen but the majority are equally decided against it'. The following September, when he accompanied a party of 400 Rotorua Maori on a peace-making meeting to Tauranga, he observed the 'shades of native jealousy' that were exhibited over the Queen's 'sovereignty'.

> A few of the Christian natives warmly urged her Sovereignty's being acknowledged, insisting upon the necessity of it, as until then, no laws could be enforced, no order continued, no peace certain. Others were in much doubt as to whether it would not prove, if acceded to, their ruin as an independent people. Others angrily opposed it. One said, 'You [the Christian party] are continually calling upon us to acknowledge one Head, Christ – let Him be Head of the Church, as you say – but we want no one [else] over us'. This speech was much approved, and here the matter dropped.[54]

At Taupo the anti-government attitude was more resolute. In 1845, Donald McLean, a Protector of Aborigines, found Mananui Te Heuheu defending Heke's cause since 'he considered him to be in the right; that he was asserting his freedom and that of his country ... that the British Government intended to deprive the New Zealanders of their lands, their liberty, and their rights as chieftains.... The English were an insatiable people, desirous of conquering all nations ... Napoleon Bonaparte would have been a match for them, had he not been taken by stratagem', he concluded. Iwikau, Mananui's brother, 'urged the same arguments' and recalled how he had observed Ngapuhi suspicions of British motives when Hobson arrived in 1840.[55] The following November, the missionary Alfred Brown was pestered by Mananui Te Heuheu, talking of nothing but Heke whom he 'vehemently' defended, stating that 'the Queen was not going to take this Island as she had done Port Jackson and other places'. But Ngati Tuwharetoa, an inland tribe blocked from the north by Waikato–Ngati Whatua strength, could do little for Heke. As a gesture of defiance, however, Te Heuheu and Iwikau strongly opposed any Pakeha settling among them, except traders who did not require land.[56]

Maori further away from the seat of government – in the Bay of Plenty, Rotorua and Taupo – showed a stronger sense of independence. Just as the swing to Christianity came later in these districts, so the commitment to British authority was a slower process. This uneven development of Maori relationship with the Pakeha world, often related to traditional jealousies and animosities, prevented an extensive combination of Maori strength in opposition to the government. There was also a fear in more remote districts that the government, after quelling the northern war, would exact satisfaction from other Maori areas, in accordance with Maori custom. McLean found this in Maori communities between Wanganui and New Plymouth, where the *Alligator* reprisal was remembered. Nene, too, was anxious that the government should dispel such false ideas among Waikato–Ngati Maniapoto.[57]

The active hostilities in the north came to a fairly rapid conclusion following the arrival of the new governor, George Grey, at the end of 1845. Provided with more money and troops, Grey immediately took a firm line, insisting that 'neutral' northern chiefs should declare themselves. The challenge to British sovereignty seemed to have been resolved when the chiefs in opposition, including Kawiti but not Heke, made a formal peace with Grey in 1846. At major meetings, Grey reiterated the promises of the treaty and his intention to see that they were upheld. The peace was uneasy, however, for Heke showed caution in submitting to British authority and Grey prolonged his indecision by insisting that Heke make his peace with other northern chiefs first.[58]

Heke did not waver in his conviction that the long-term intention of the British was to take the land. Until his death in 1850, he continued to create uncertainty in the north and was suspicious of government moves to open up land for settlement.[59] In 1848 the Auckland press carried several reports of a northern movement, akin to a Maori confederation, under Heke's auspices. A 'Bill of Rights' was circulated around North Auckland, which expressed friendly feelings towards old settlers, but noted with regret that the authority (manatanga) of the ancestors had been surrendered. It emphasised the need to consolidate Maori unity and to preserve remaining lands. Although this confederation has left little trace, its sentiments foreshadowed a similar, more widely representative northern movement in the 1870s.[60]

Heke made one final effort to assert the mana of his cause before his death. In July 1849, he wrote to Queen Victoria, recalling the original contact that his ancestor, Hongi, had made with the Crown and the wish expressed by the British monarch that New Zealand should be left in Maori ownership. He appealed to the Queen to make good the words of the King, 'for although he and Hongi are dead, still the conversation lives'. He told Victoria that 'it rests with you to restore the flag of my island of New Zealand, and the authority of the land of the people'. Grey transmitted the letter to England with the observation that it was yet another attempt by Heke to boost his mana.[61] Heke had already suggested that the flagstaff should be re-erected on Maiki Hill as a joint venture by the government and those Maori who had been in opposition, but the matter was allowed to lapse. Other moves over the flagstaff, such as one taken by Nene, were strongly resented by Heke; it fell to Kawiti's son, Maihi Paraone Kawiti, to take the initiative in the 1850s.[62]

The northern challenge to British sovereignty had barely been settled when a new crisis disturbed the colony. Earl Grey, now Secretary of State for Colonies, introduced a radical change in land policy, acting on principles that, as Lord Howick, he had set out in the 1844 Report. The 1846 instructions, accompanying a new Charter granting self-government to the settlers, asked that Maori lands be registered; valid Maori ownership was to be confirmed on the basis of occupation and labour expended on the land. Once such claims had been allowed, all other land was to become Crown land. These principles, Earl Grey noted, should have been followed from the proclamation of sovereignty; the governor was to look on them as the foundation of policy. Though this restrictive interpretation breached the treaty, Earl Grey added an impossibly contradictory admonition: 'No apparent advantage could be suffered to weigh against the evil of acting in a manner, either really, or even apparently, inconsistent with good faith.'[63]

The proposed measures were welcomed in the southern districts 'as disposing once and for all of "Treaty of Waitangi nonsense"'.[64] In the north, however, the reaction was different. Newspaper editors knew that Maori who could read would spread the news rapidly; it would spark a violent protest.[65] Initially they refrained from printing the objectionable land sections of the instructions. Later, the press began a sustained attack on the proposals, scoffing at any probability of their being enforced, partly to stiffen Pakeha resolve against their implementation, and partly to allay Maori fears.[66] The *New-Zealander* traced the history of the treaty and the repeated promises to the Maori people:

> For seven years and more has this agreement of Waitangi – the Runnimede [*sic*] of the Antipodes – passed for binding here: guaranteed by successive Ministers of opposite political opinions . . . conned over with the most painstaking scrutiny by the Natives themselves – complained of by themselves, as overreaching them with regard to the Queen's pre-emption right, imperfectly explained before ratification of the compact – still adhered to, in spite of the disappointing construction it was afterwards found to bear, by men who long had the power to have hunted us out of the country, had they thought fit to do so; and we now affect to call it 'a device to amuse savages'.

Readers were reminded that not only was the Queen pledged but the compact had been to British advantage in ensuring peaceful settlement, a crucial point for settlers who had recently fled the north. Auckland's other paper, the *Southern Cross*, stated that it was simply not worth having Maori stirred up to fight for their birthright.[67]

In December 1847 over 400 Auckland settlers signed a petition against the instructions and forwarded it to Earl Grey through the governor. In marked contrast to earlier attacks on the treaty, especially on pre-emption, settler interests now favoured upholding the agreement.[68] The Pakeha population of more than 3,000 in the Auckland district was vastly outnumbered, and Maori created much of Auckland's wealth through their trade. With the destruction of Russell as a concrete example of what could occur, settlers were taking no chances.

Governor Grey, too, feared that an attempt to carry out the instructions would result in war, but he was wary of giving a blunt rejection to Earl Grey. The governor temporised and allowed the protest to be taken up by public men in the colony – Selwyn, Martin and Swainson. Privately Grey may have been sympathetic, but publicly he dissociated himself from their protest and expressed disapproval of it. Apart from an initial caution, directed at the Secretary of State, that Maori tribes appeared to be unsettled by the news, Grey kept silent.[69]

The dispatch from England and Grey's silence were particularly embarrassing for the missionaries. Their credibility as men of trust and good faith, who had pledged the honour of England in the Waitangi agreement, was set at risk. The first mission protest was launched in July 1847 by Bishop Selwyn, 'as the head of the missionary body by whose influence and representations, the native chiefs were induced to sign'. Using the strongest possible terms (for which he was later criticised in England), he warned the governor that he intended to use 'all legal and constitutional measures' to inform Maori of their rights as British subjects and to assist them to uphold those rights.[70] Henry Williams, Maunsell, Hadfield and others joined the chorus of complaint. The Wesleyan missionaries added their criticism through their General-Superintendent in New Zealand, Walter Lawry, and through individuals such as John Hobbs and John Whiteley, who had played a major part in the treaty signing. Like the CMS missionaries, they were concerned to defend Maori rights, to promote the general welfare of the colony and, not least, to protect their own position and work.[71]

As the settler community had feared, information about Earl

Grey's instructions circulated rapidly among the Maori people. In the Waikato, Wiremu Tamihana Tarapipipi informed the CMS missionary, John Morgan, that Maori were saying that 'the Queen was going to take their island from them'. Morgan, who had not heard of the dispatch, strenuously denied that the Waitangi compact could ever be violated. In the Bay of Islands a similar report, 'very widely circulated', held that all uncultivated lands were to be taken by the Crown and that more troops had arrived to carry this out. It caused a 'great deal of excitement', especially with Kawiti, who went to Auckland to verify the news. He pointed out to Nene that it was in 'open violation' of Waitangi and in opposition to the statements of the governor. Nene suggested that an official circular in Maori be distributed to refute the report but this was not done.[72] Large meetings, involving Nene, Kawiti, Te Rauparaha and Te Wherowhero, were held at Te Wherowhero's cottage in the Auckland Domain. In November, Te Wherowhero and four other major Waikato chiefs presented Grey with a letter to the Queen which expressed their disquiet at the rumours and requested that the Queen herself confirm the repeated assurances given them by her governors.[73]

In retreat before this growing volume of protest from New Zealand, Earl Grey directed Governor Grey to assure the Maori people that there was no foundation to the rumours that the treaty would be violated by taking Maori lands. On the contrary, it had always been stated that the treaty should be 'most scrupulously and religiously observed', a reassurance that satisfied Te Wherowhero.[74] A similar reply was given to the Auckland petitioners in July 1848.[75] By that time the Secretary of State for Colonies had been subjected to parliamentary criticism by speakers 'primed' with correspondence from New Zealand.[76] He was also under pressure from the Wesleyan Missionary Society and the Aborigines Protection Society. The former received a lengthy Colonial Office reply which was forwarded to New Zealand.[77]

Evidence of an official change of heart allowed the governor to take the initiative. In May 1848, he casually dismissed the possibility that the government would have difficulty in acquiring Maori land by assuring Earl Grey that Maori would cheerfully recognise the Crown's right of pre-emption: 'they will in nearly all – if not all – instances dispose, for a merely nominal consideration, of those lands which they do not actually require for their own subsistence. Even further ... the native chiefs would cheerfully give such land up to the Government without any payment, if the compliment is only paid them of requesting their acquiescence in the occupation of these lands by European settlers'. This was a most misleading statement, yet Grey's optimism seemed to be justified by the end of his governorship when 30 million acres of land in the South Island and 3 million in the North had passed out of Maori hands. The methods and terms of purchase were none too scrupulous, however, and would lead to Maori resistance in the 1850s.[78]

Earl Grey's challenge to the interpretation of the treaty of Waitangi generated fresh debate and focused attention on the treaty when it might have quietly faded in importance. For more than two years the subject was aired in correspondence between the Colonial Office, Governor Grey and the protestors. Grey's silence in New Zealand, accepted at first by the protestors as necessary to protect his position, later stimulated their concern that he might be protecting Earl Grey at the expense of the treaty, and finally sparked their protest.[79]

Martin, the Chief Justice, was particularly disturbed. He believed that Earl Grey's instructions were so dangerous that they should be rescinded. He was also perturbed that the terms of the constitution excluded Maori and made them subject to a settler minority. Although Earl Grey suspended the constitution, Martin feared that as long as it remained on the statute book a settler representative assembly might implement the land measures. Colonial Office correspondence showed a distinctly ambivalent attitude.[80] Martin produced a seventy-page commentary on Earl Grey's dispatch. He argued that it constituted a breach of the national faith pledged at Waitangi and a violation of established law in dealing with native lands. The booklet was produced primarily for limited distribution in influential English circles, but five copies were passed around in the colony and its contents soon became public.[81] It was a most unusual step for a colonial Chief Justice to oppose actively the instructions of the metropolitan government, but Martin felt that the humanitarian values reflected in the 1840 treaty were endangered. The British press was in sympathy with Earl Grey and against the 'humbug Treaty'. *The Times*, which had shown little sympathy with the systematic colonisers in 1840, now supported the Earl and only belatedly criticised the move.[82]

News of Grey's dispatch coincided with reports of the final suppression of the uprising in Tahiti and the arrival of the first group of military settlers, the 'Fencibles', at Auckland.[83] The governor was putting pressure on missionaries to reduce their large land-holdings.[84] He had also sought a Supreme Court decision (The Queen v. Symonds), to invalidate purchases made under FitzRoy's pre-emption waivers.[85] In the course of the judgement, which re-asserted that the Crown alone was the sole source of title (a principle that had evolved in colonial law), the legal reasoning which had so irritated Maori during the land claims investigations was repeated – that the Maori people enjoyed only a 'modified dominion' over their lands, in the same way as the American Indians. While Martin had concurred in this judgement, given by Mr Justice Chapman, he had not been completely easy with it. In his booklet he defended Maori land rights, arguing that they were not only recognised in colonial law but had been specifically confirmed by treaty and given added insurance by Maori being made British subjects, a title which the Indians did not have.[86]

Martin's exposition of Maori rights differed little from conclusions reached by two London legal advisers commissioned by the Aborigines Protection Society. Shirley F. Woolmer's opinion was that Crown rights in the matter of land title had to be upheld, but that the treaty was 'the basis from which the rights and interests both of the Crown of England, and of the Natives of New Zealand must be ascertained'. Moreover, the Maori people 'being the ceding party ... their sense ought to govern the interpretation'. Joseph Phillimore was even more explicit. He stated 'that the Treaty of Waitangi is of binding obligation on the two contracting parties, and that it is to be considered as the corner stone, on which all our relations, with the Islands of New Zealand, must be founded'.[87] With the publication of these opinions, accompanied by a lengthy treatise by the Society's secretary, protest against Earl Grey's dispatch of December 1846 began to ebb. The Secretary of State himself reiterated that there was no intention of overturning the treaty. This was sufficient to still most outcry.

In the colony, however, the lapse of time before the arrival of news kept the matter in the press through 1849. Some were still concerned that verbal reassurances and the suspension of the 1846 Charter were not enough. Indeed, John Whiteley, in co-operation with the Chief Justice, continued to campaign after his Wesleyan superiors decided to let the matter rest. Whiteley feared that the move by Earl Grey would encourage others to attack the treaty. He was also uneasy about a comment in Grey's instructions that the treaty might not apply to all Maori since not all tribes had signed. He even suggested that the treaty, with its ambiguities, might be forgotten and a set of similar principles be substituted. These would then apply universally to Maori and carry a perpetual obligation.[88] This proposal, however, was never taken seriously, and the end of the decade brought a pause in the treaty debate.

Attitudes to the treaty remained unclear. An unusual and difficult situation had been created with the cession of an entire country and its people to the British Crown: this had not been encountered before, and led to a variety of interpretations of the treaty's legal status. The legal arguments of Martin in New Zealand and Phillimore and Woolmer in England recognised the treaty as the contractual basis of British sovereignty. (Woolmer also claimed, interestingly, that it should be interpreted as the ceding party, the Maori, understood it.) The official position was more complex.

Initially the Colonial Office acknowledged that the title of the Crown rested on the 'deliberate act and cession of the chiefs, on behalf of the people at large'. Hobson's proclamations of sovereignty received royal approval and were published in the *London Gazette*. In 1845 Lord Stanley referred to the treaty as having been 'ratified by Her Majesty's command'. Yet later Stanley and James Stephen also insisted that British sovereignty applied to all Maori whether they had signed or not, an approach which implied that the public assertion of sovereignty was more important than the treaty.[89] The 1844 report further confused the issue by claiming that, although it was a 'formal Treaty', it was 'little more than a legal fiction' since Maori were 'incapable of comprehending the real force and meaning of such a transaction'.[90]

In the colony's first years there was also much uncertainty over the treaty's terms, the result either of official misunderstanding or of reluctance to accept its terms. Even when Colonial Office officials finally conceded that Maori title to the land had to be interpreted in the widest sense, this decision was more an acknowledgement that any other interpretation would have prevented peaceful colonisation than a recognition of Maori rights and Crown obligations. Earl Grey's attempt to impose a restricted interpretation did serve one very important function, however: it created fresh publicity about the treaty, reinforcing the belief that New Zealand was a unique case in race relations. All publicity over interpretation emphasised the essential promises given Maori by treaty.

In New Zealand itself, the terms of the treaty were probably better known in the 1840s than at any time since. Repeated public statements by governors and officials asserted that the treaty would be upheld. In the colonial press the pros and cons of the agreement were vigorously discussed, the point of view shifting as settler interests changed. The text of the treaty was regularly in print. Apart from a government printing of both English and Maori texts in 1844,[91] sections of the document were reproduced in the colonial press from the earliest years. In 1843, it was printed in full in English by an Auckland paper, together with an alternative English translation of the Maori text.[92] There were other publications in the period, sometimes with translations in English; the missionary John Hobbs, for example, found the Waitangi text printed in an English periodical, the *Watchman*.[93] The Maori text appeared in the *Maori Messenger* in 1842, and Henry Williams produced additional copies in 1844.[94] The circumstances of the signings, even reports of the chiefs' speeches, were reproduced; the comment by Nopera Panakareao that the shadow of the land only had gone to the Queen enjoyed a wide circulation, at least among Pakeha.[95]

While the debate on the treaty and threats to overturn it had been unsettling to Maori, officials had regularly soothed their uneasiness by arguing that the treaty was a compact between the Queen and the Maori people; threats could be ignored for they did not emanate from the Queen.[96] This encouraged Maori to believe that they enjoyed a special relationship with Queen Victoria, and that her agents, the governors, fulfilled a special paternal function not unlike that of a supreme chief. This understanding was promoted by missionary counsels, by the *Maori Messenger* which directed Maori to appeal to the governor for redress of problems, and by the paternalistic language of governors.[97] Belief in a special relationship prompted several communications to Victoria in the 1840s – that of Te Wherowhero and the Waikato chiefs, a petition from southern Maori against a proposal to introduce convicts to New Zealand, and several letters and gifts. These were forerunners of more formal approaches that would be made in the 1880s.[98] This Maori view of government as benevolent was unrealistic, for it persisted into the period when responsibility for Maori welfare had passed to a settler assembly. It left Maori ill-equipped to cope with the impersonal and rigorous nature of the executive and legislative branches of government.

By 1850, the balance sheet of benefits and disadvantages of British administration might well have appeared favourable to many Maori. There appeared to be a place for Maori people in a variety of colonial activities. They profited from the increased pace of development as settlement expanded. Auckland and Wellington markets were well supplied with produce grown by Maori in neighbouring districts or, as in Auckland, supplied by tribes further afield in a coastal trade that built up gradually in the 1840s.[99] With the recession in the middle of the decade, Auckland Maori hawked their goods directly to households or sold them at stalls near the harbour's edge, their greater mobility giving them an advantage over Pakeha traders.

Through government employment on road and other public works, as well as through private contracts, Maori earned considerable amounts in cash. Earnings varied greatly; the Maori who assisted the Auckland harbour pilot, for example, made 7/- a day, while on the Epsom Road in Auckland, Maori were paid 1/6 per day (at a time when soldiers earned only 10d per day). In the south, contractors found it worth their while to pay Maori road-builders 2/6 a day.[100] In many localities, Maori workmen provided bush settlers with rush cottages thatched with grass, at charges ranging from 30/- to £12.[101] In negotiating contracts, Maori were quick to take care of their interests. About 350 Maori road-workers in Auckland went on strike in 1848, demanding 'full money payment' and not part in rations, as had been suggested. As one Auckland newspaper commented, the Maori workers had struck 'with as much unanimity as if they had been Newcastle colliers or Manchester spinners'.[102]

In some instances, Maori took the initiative – a hotel on the Waikato, townships at Herd's Point (now Rawene) and at the 'Portage' near Otahuhu, flour mills costing £80 to £500, in Coromandel, Kawhia, Waipa and Waikato. At Rangiaohia in the Waikato, Morgan described a flourishing rural community with 600 acres in wheat, a dozen cows, 50 horses, 10 ploughs, 7 carts and drays, and other equipment. To achieve economic goals, Waikato Maori, setting aside inter-tribal and inter-denominational differences, were increasingly prepared to co-operate.[103]

Money earned by Maori contributed in no small measure to the welfare of both Maori and settler. Maori purchased a variety of articles – blankets, clothing, hardware, tobacco, soap, paper, arms, ammunition, boats and canvas. They were careful buyers. Shops in centres like Auckland, which relied heavily on Maori trade, stocked their shelves to suit Maori tastes. Some Maori adopted a European lifestyle. By 1847, Hadfield's mission settlement at Otaki had 'good barns, huts with fireplaces, nicely fenced large gardens, extensive wheat fields beautifully tilled, numerous small paddocks of grass, and a variety of other comforts and conveniences'.[104] European table settings and food appeared in areas as far apart as Otaki and Kaitaia, and small settler cottages began to find favour with a few Maori owners.

Many Maori also participated in the social life of the colony. In the capital, they took part in regattas, attended levees and socials at Government House, celebrated the Queen's birthday and the colony's anniversary day with feasts provided at government expense.[105] On Hobson's death, so many Maori crowded into Auckland that a special copy of the *Maori Messenger* was printed to invite them to follow the funeral procession.[106]

The new authority in the land also gradually overcame some of the old tribal antagonisms and made it possible for tribes to mix and communicate more freely. In 1844 over 4,000 Maori met at Remuera, and numerous smaller feasts were significant enough to attract newspaper comment.[107] Te Wherowhero's cottage in the Auckland Domain became a place of call for visiting Maori, a forum where matters of concern could be aired and discussed. At Mechanics Bay, Auckland, and elsewhere, the government provided hostelries for the many Maori visiting the town for trade and other purposes.[108] Churches, too, were established for Maori worship in centres like Auckland, although missionaries noted the falling off in Maori attendance as trade increased.[109] Under Grey's administration, some of the long-promised welfare benefits were provided: hospitals were opened at Wellington and Auckland and an Education Ordinance provided for Maori education.

Maori participation in these benefits was uneven; tribes nearer settlement inevitably gained more than those in remote districts.[110] To some extent the benefits were offset by a keener awareness of the shortfall between Pakeha promise and performance, and a growing disillusionment. Complaints from two respected Maori, both in the Auckland district and both actively involved in the settlement's growth, illustrate this. Tamati Ngapora expressed his fears to Grey over the disintegration of the old social structure and the loss of chiefly control. To cope with the problems arising from new values and a new lifestyle he requested that some law be framed to strengthen the authority of chiefs, to the benefit of the colony as a whole.[111] Grey, however, did not favour the idea.

Epiha Putini (Jabez Bunting), who had at one time written to *The Times* in London to correct misrepresentations concerning Maori, criticised the government in 1850 for its incompetence in dealing with Maori problems. The chief had approached the Police Magistrate and the government-appointed Native Counsel in an unsuccessful attempt to get satisfactory payment for the sale of a piece of land. In a letter to the *Southern Cross*, he expressed his frustration: 'Now my thoughts during these many years have been that there was one law for both Natives and Europeans. Now, however, I fully understand that it is all deception, and that the Natives must still grovel in the mud. Now listen, friends, do not in future talk about the oneness (impartiality) of the law for the European and the Native.'[112]

Such doubts derived from practical experience of the Pakeha world and belied the claim that benefits were sure to accrue from amalgamation. What could Maori people do? Believe what their own experience was telling them? Or listen to the *Maori Messenger*? The paper encouraged Maori to continue believing that their situation would be different from that of other native races: 'When you gave the shadow (atarangi) of your land (oneone) to the Queen Victoria, you became brothers of Englishmen. Englishmen came among you, not to rob or to plunder you, but to buy and to sell with you and to instruct you in the arts of peaceful industry.' Australian Aborigines, the *Messenger* said, had lost their land because they were 'savages with no industry – no intellect', like 'brutes' and 'very inferior'. New Zealand, however, would be a greater country than Australia because of the Maori people. 'Believe it, dear friends, the English are here not for their own advantage only, but for yours.'[113]

Chapter Seven

A MATTER OF MANA

When Grey's first governorship ended in 1853, the treaty was still widely recognised in New Zealand and in England as having created a special link between Maori and the Crown. Through the pages of the *Maori Messenger* Grey sent a farewell message to the Maori people, urging them to co-operate with the government in the unique experiment of racial amalgamation; it would be a model for indigenous races elsewhere, if only Maori could prove it possible.[1] The language was patronising but the aim was genuine. Three years later, William Swainson, the colony's first Attorney-General, promoting New Zealand on a lecture tour of England, spoke confidently of the country as the exception among British colonies of settlement in its dealings with the indigenous race.[2] The optimism of Grey and Swainson was about to be challenged.

Throughout the 1850s, it became more difficult for Maori to reconcile government actions with official statements about the treaty's good intent, and there gradually emerged a strengthened resolve to resist the imposition of British supremacy. Maori, often referring to the sovereignty they wished to retain as the 'mana of the land', began to ask more searching questions about the extent of power and authority that could be exercised by chiefs and government. Such questions were central to the Waitara dispute and to the King movement. Each stimulated a lengthy debate on the matter of mana and the nature of sovereignty, a debate that was to move finally from a verbal to a military struggle. In that process, the tone of official statements shifted from acknowledgement of the treaty's humanitarian concern, to an insistence on the Maori people's moral obligation to uphold the treaty and to accept the rights it conferred on the government.

Changing attitudes to the treaty among settler politicians and administrators reflected changes in the colonial community at large in the 1850s. New settlements, organised on planned Wakefieldian principles, had been established at Otago in 1848 and at Canterbury in 1850. There and elsewhere, many colonists had come to a reluctant acceptance of the treaty as an unavoidable circumstance of the colony's first days. Alfred Domett, an early Nelson settler who had participated in the debate of the 1840s, thought the treaty's land guarantee 'unwise as well as impracticable to meddle with', at least in the meantime; more generally, he confessed an 'utter contempt' for the treaty.[3] Newer settlers sometimes revealed a greater degree of impatience. James Crowe Richmond, in Taranaki, anticipated the time when the treaty would be overruled and Maori claims to the extensive bush-lands would no longer be able to 'damp the ardour and cramp the energies of the industrious white man'.[4] Such opinions were often generated by irritation over land transactions, but as long as land purchase matched settler demand, the treaty was not generally seen as unduly obstructive to colonisation. If Maori owners refused to sell, of course, it would be a different matter.

A new dimension developed as the colony moved towards self-government. It had been apparent for some years that practical application of the treaty would have to be worked out in New Zealand. The 1852 constitution transferred the struggle for definition of the treaty from the desk of the Colonial Office to the floor of the colonial parliament.

The new constitution was not accompanied by any instructions on land such as had, in 1846, suggested a restrictive interpretation of the treaty's land guarantee. Indeed, the 1852 measure implicitly recognised the land guarantee by endorsing the Crown's right of pre-emption. The constitution also seemed to recognise some of the egalitarian principles behind the 1840 document, by allowing Maori a place in future government of the colony. The Secretary of State for Colonies gave an assurance that the 'whole spirit' of the measure was to put Maori on the same footing as settlers 'as completely as possible'.[5] Theoretically, no distinction was drawn between the two races with regard to the franchise. The qualification was to be male, over the age of twenty-one, having possession of either a freehold estate with an annual value of £50, or a leasehold estate of the annual value of £10, or the occupation of a dwelling of the annual value of £10 in a town or £5 in the country. It was intended to be virtually a male suffrage.[6]

Certain precautions were nevertheless built into the constitution. An annual sum of £7,000 was to be set aside for native purposes, in recognition of the inevitable exclusion from representation of some Maori at a time when Maori were substantial contributors to the colonial revenue; provision was made to define, if necessary, native districts where Maori laws, customs and usages would prevail, 'unless repugnant to the general principles of humanity'; and finally, any enactment of the central legislature which related specifically to Maori had to be reserved for Crown assent. These provisions were seen as a temporary acknowledgement of the special situation of the Maori people. The ultimate aim was still amalgamation, an objective which Grey's optimistic dispatches anticipated in the not-too-distant future. Indeed, participants in the British debates who perceived certain dangers were prepared to disregard them in view of the 'general fusion' of the races that seemed so imminent.[7]

Yet the provisions of the constitution did not pass without some criticism in England. The Aborigines Protection Society favoured an equality to be gained by establishing a policy of complete amalgamation. Noting the exclusion of Maori people from a real share in government during Grey's term in office and doubtful that a settler government would allow them a real share, the Society urged that Maori participate equally 'in all respects'.[8] 'Every step which the native advances in civilization, without sharing in self-government, renders more certain the permanence of his exclusion', it warned.[9] The constitution's provision for separate districts was seen as disadvantageous, for Maori would be placed outside the protection of British law.

In contrast, the Wesleyan Missionary Society sought to have treaty rights confirmed more explicitly by transferring the obligations of the imperial government to the colonial government. The Wesleyans hoped that this, a kind of colonial ratification of the treaty, might prevent any moves to evade the 'spirit and obvious meaning of the Treaty as understood by the natives at the time of its signing'. Pointing to Hobson's actions in proclaiming sovereignty on the basis of agreement by a limited number of chiefs representing the whole Maori people, they further urged that the protection and rights of the treaty be withheld from no Maori whatsoever.[10] Neither this protest nor that of the Aborigines Protection Society influenced proceedings. The Society indignantly complained that the Bill had been 'carried through its several stages with the rapidity of an ignominious flight, rather than the gravity of legislation.'[11]

The representations of the two societies showed a shrewd anticipation of settler unwillingness to concede rights to indigenous races. Both groups were aware too that the political climate of the early 1850s was less humanitarian.[12] The focus had shifted from native welfare towards settler development and self-government. Maori rights were not ignored altogether; they were simply being overtaken by new principles. The British politician William Gladstone exemplified the change of mood. His old friend Bishop Selwyn had prompted him to defend the Waitangi treaty in the 1840s; by the early 1850s he was more concerned to free the British government and taxpayer from burdensome responsibility

and cost; in the 1860s, this would lead him to respond indifferent-
ly, even unsympathetically, to humanitarian appeals on behalf
of the Maori.[13] The new trend towards a policy of colonial self-
sufficiency would markedly alter relations between England and
her colonies. The principle of trusteeship, although not unimpor-
tant as a continuing theme in British dealings with New Zealand
throughout this period, would never again enjoy the high point
reached in 1840. The protests over the 1852 constitution were not
sustained, partly because they met with little support in England
and partly because the constitution itself, on the surface, seemed
to recognise Maori rights to a reasonable extent.

When the constitution was introduced in New Zealand in 1853,
it became evident that many of the fears of the English humanitarians would be realised. Although the franchise qualifications
had not specifically discriminated against Maori, few held the individual title required to qualify; in addition, the electoral districts
excluded some areas of largely Maori population. Where Maori
were able to participate in elections, a number did so. But among
the colonists the cry was raised that the polls would be swamped
by Maori voters who, so it was argued, could not be expected to
be responsible voters since they lacked experience and were
vulnerable to manipulation. There was scarcely time to test such
assertions, however, for in 1858 a means was found by which
Maori voters could be disqualified on technical grounds.[14]

In various other ways Maori were disadvantaged by the constitutional process. The constitution allowed for self-government in
most colonial matters, providing for six provincial legislatures and
a General Assembly of Governor, an appointed Legislative Council and an elected House of Representatives. With ministerial
responsibility, Maori soon became subject to settler government,
despite the fact that responsibility for Maori affairs was retained
by the governor, a decision taken by Grey's successor, Thomas
Gore Browne.

On arriving in the colony in 1855, the new governor quickly
realised that amalgamation was not taking place, and that the
position had been misrepresented in England. New Zealand comprised two nations, Maori and Pakeha, many Maori living outside
the boundaries of effective government. Browne sought advice
from men qualified by experience in Maori matters, mainly settlers of long residence, and Anglican and Wesleyan missionaries.[15]
Their recommendation, that Browne keep control of Maori matters, was supported by several arguments: that the Crown had
accepted the responsibility of upholding Maori rights in 1840, that
Maori would be suspicious of control by the settler assembly, and

that politicians representing settler interests could not be relied upon to deal justly with Maori people.

This reasoning had been followed by the Colonial Office and governors since the founding of the colony. Based on the principle that the Crown's duty was to stand between settler and Maori, it assumed that settlers as a body were not to be trusted and that Maori were incapable of protecting their own interests. Now, in the 1850s, these assumptions endangered the ultimate ideal of one nation. There was no timetable for the political coming-of-age of the Maori people. Though it was generally recognised that the governor's control would be temporary, settler politicians had no assurance that they would be granted control over Maori matters if they demonstrated a maturity in Maori affairs. It was a situation that encouraged settler politicians to push for full control of Maori affairs.

The reservation of Maori affairs to the governor did not work well. The Assembly reluctantly accepted Browne's argument that the Crown was entitled to responsibility as long as the British government stood the cost of defence. But it curbed the governor's freedom in Maori matters by restricting the financial allocations necessary for an effective native policy and administration. Moreover, settler and Maori interests were so inextricably mixed that it proved impossible to determine the limits of Maori affairs. To politicians committed to the principle of full responsible government (especially South Island representatives), the arrangement was a constant irritant which led them to be excessively critical of Browne's advisers. In 1858 the Assembly attempted to seize the initiative by passing legislation to deal comprehensively with the Maori situation. When this received only partial assent from the governor, it became evident that the system of divided control was becoming unworkable.

By the end of the 1850s, the Colonial Office was arriving at similar conclusions. The difficulties experienced in British North America made British officials aware of the dangers, if not the impossibility, of attempting to restrict the powers of a colony once responsible government had been granted. In New Zealand, the attempt to reserve control over Maori affairs was to be complicated by the costs of defence, with the outbreak of war in 1860. The issue would not be resolved until all British regiments were withdrawn at the end of the 1860s.

Maori in the 1850s grew suspicious of the changes in government and in its operations. Authority and power were qualities they customarily ascribed to individuals; in the Crown Colony period rule by the governor had been an acceptable adjunct to traditional Maori authority structures. The personal relationship of governor and chiefs was fostered by Grey and (less adequately) by his successors. Approaches between chiefs and governor were direct and, in receiving a personal hearing, chiefs undoubtedly felt that they were being accorded the respect that was their due. Officials shrewdly used such occasions to reinforce the concept of a personal relationship between the Crown and the Maori people, promising to keep the Queen informed and noting the advance towards a united people. Maori, disposed by custom to favour reciprocity, often responded with expressions of loyalty, with the wish to be one with settlers, sometimes with a gift to be forwarded to the Queen.[16] By the 1850s there was also an occasional Maori appeal to the Queen for redress of grievances – the first trickle of what would later become a steady flow of Maori protest based on treaty rights.[17]

Settler government, however, confronted Maori with a new authority representing interests that they increasingly perceived to be opposed to their own. Excluded from the General Assembly, not comprehending the full import of parliamentary tactics and offended by the language of debate reported in the colonial press, sections of Maori opinion gradually became alienated from the government. In some districts, aggressive land purchase agents, perhaps the only representatives of central government known to those tribes, became the main cause of Maori irritation.

The growth of Maori unease in the 1850s was neither simultaneous nor universal, for the experience of contact varied considerably. Some tribes – south Taranaki, for instance – had never identified their interests with the government. In Rotorua, too, Maori would acknowledge neither Queen nor governor, some dissociating themselves from 'that pukapuka (treaty) which the Ngapuhi signed'. They asked the missionary Thomas Chapman if Ngapuhi considered Rotorua Maori to be merely slaves, that they had felt free to 'give away' the people and the land to Queen Victoria: 'don't call her *our* (to tatou) Queen – call her your (to matou) Queen', they told the missionary. Chapman recorded that when the customary prayers for the governor were said, Rotorua Maori made a point of refusing to respond with the 'Amen'.[18]

By contrast, Hokianga Maori, among the first to consent to the treaty, complained that the expected benefits of settlement, trade and employment for Maori, had not eventuated. They hoped that surveying the old land claims for settlement might rectify the situation.[19] Other tribes also hoped for government assistance. Waikato, whose agreement to the treaty had been partial (some signing but Te Wherowhero refraining), nevertheless looked to the governor for new institutions to meet changing circumstances; in particular they sought some code of law.[20] In part, it was government failure to fulfil this expectation that led to the election of the aged Waikato chief, Te Wherowhero, as the first Maori King, Potatau, in 1858.

The King movement, as it came to be called, had its beginnings in 1853 when two Otaki chiefs, Tamihana Te Rauparaha and Matene Te Whiwhi, introduced the idea to North Island tribes.[21] Its development was subsequently promoted by the Ngati Haua chief, Wiremu Tamihana Tarapipipi Te Waharoa, the 'King Maker', at several major meetings in the Waikato and near Auckland in 1857–58.[22] The move to select a king had previously come to government attention through other meetings, the most notable at Manawapou (Taranaki) in 1854, and in 1856 at Pukawa (Taupo) under the auspices of Iwikau Te Heuheu of Ngati Tuwharetoa. This latter meeting, which was vital to Te Wherowhero's final selection, involved central North Island tribes from the Waikato and Taupo districts, with a few Maori from the East Coast and Hawke's Bay.[23] Sympathy with the idea of setting up a king as a focus for Maori aspirations was more widespread. Other tribes gradually joined in – Taranaki, Ngati Ruanui and Wiremu Kingi's Te Atiawa people. Some remained aloof. The Arawa claimed that they could not take part because of their allegiance to the Crown, a commitment made in the mid-1850s and a reversal of their earlier anti-treaty stance.[24] But by 1860, a substantial section of North Island Maori looked to the King. The strength of this federation lay more in the identification of shared interests than in any organisational structure; tribal loyalties remained strong. Nevertheless, the movement was significant in being, in a broad sense, national, an effort to consolidate a sense of Maoriness in the face of encroaching settler government and colonisation and, most importantly, to restrict alienation of Maori land.[25]

Initially King leaders were concerned that their movement should be acceptable to the government. Strongly influenced by biblical concepts, the movement's most important leaders – the King himself, Wiremu Tamihana and Tamati Ngapora – conceived of a complementary relationship. The Queen's law, upheld by the governor's mana, would stand alongside the King's laws and mana, with both sides owing allegiance to God. This relationship was seen as mutually advantageous, with Queen and King each having a personal mana and acknowledging the mana of the other. Symbols signifying an equal Crown-Maori relationship characterise the King movement's early years: two sticks stuck in the ground, representing governor and King, with a third across them – 'the law of God and the Queen' – and a protective circle about the whole since the 'Queen is a fence for us all' (Maori and Pakeha).[26] Another used the image of a whare: New Zealand was the house, Pakeha the rafters on one side, Maori the rafters on the other side, with God as the ridgepole, an image first used by northern Maori in Busby's time.[27]

King movement leaders, not unreasonably, believed that the treaty's guarantee of rangatiratanga confirmed that a relationship of equality would continue, allowing Maori people a degree of autonomy. They desired to work with the settler government in a kind of 'conjoint administration'.[28] One symbol of continuing Maori identity was the 1834 flag of an independent New Zealand, flown at several of the King movement's major meetings.[29] There were, however, other more volatile elements, more or less hostile to the Queen's authority (mana), who threatened the movement from the beginning. Some wanted to rid New Zealand of the Queen's mana and of Pakeha in general. For these, the existence of the King provided a rallying point for Maori nationalism.

The reaction of the settler community to the King movement was twofold. Some saw it positively as the long-awaited Maori acceptance of self-imposed rules of law and order which would counteract the continuing internecine strife over land and related interests. Moreover, the fact that the movement had achieved an unprecedented degree of co-ordination in Maori society held out the promise that it might in time be fully incorporated into the government structure. It would then further the amalgamation process which remained the goal for the Maori people. Even if the movement could not be steered in this direction some thought it could do little harm and might lapse if ignored.

But a far larger section of the settler community, and finally the overwhelming body of public opinion, was hostile. The setting up of a Maori King was regarded with a suspicion that became more marked as the movement failed to diminish. These attitudes sprang from fear that the movement was a 'land league' which would impede the acquisition of further Maori land. Settler anger gave rise to allegations that the King movement rejected British sovereignty and the treaty, denied the Queen's mana, and would inhibit indefinitely the expansion of a thriving colony.

To extremists, the King movement was treasonable. To the more moderate, it introduced divisiveness that threatened the one nation ideal envisaged at the colony's foundation and which was said (with some truth) to have been pursued since then. Settlers apportioned blame for the emergence of the movement both to

Maori shortcomings and to the failings, or lack, of government policy. Two contemporary writers presented complementary views: Thomas Buddle, assessing the Maori point of view, described the movement as a struggle to preserve chiefly mana, while John Gorst, focusing on the Pakeha side, asserted that English caution and timidity had left the question of sovereignty unresolved, a matter now brought to a crisis.[30] Both were correct. The final struggle over the mana or sovereignty of the country was in the making.

The King movement could possibly have been accommodated under some form of association with the New Zealand government, had Browne and the Assembly encouraged this. A generously defined interpretation of rights deriving from the Maori text of the treaty could have given the movement status. The 1852 constitution had made provision for Maori districts, providing the option of embracing the King movement within the constitutional framework of the colony. Browne, however, after an initial wavering, refused to countenance a movement which he interpreted as a direct challenge to British sovereignty. Claims for Maori autonomy held no place in his interpretation of the 1840 agreement.[31]

Settler attitudes to Maori affairs hardened when fighting broke out in Taranaki in 1860. This was precipitated by the governor agreeing to purchase a piece of land at Waitara offered by Teira, although Wiremu Kingi Te Rangitake, senior chief of Te Atiawa, was actually living on the land. By virtue of his rank, Kingi was entitled to exercise his customary authority to veto Teira's sale, which he did. Browne chose to disregard the veto; when the government attempted to take up the offer, fighting broke out between Taranaki Maori and British troops. Since the point at issue was the definition of customary land title, in particular the degree to which a chief could determine disposition of land, attention once more focused on the treaty's guarantee of rangatiratanga or customary possession of land. When it became apparent that the government was becoming more deeply involved and Kingi was aligning himself with the King movement, the Waitara debate broadened to include the entire Crown–Maori relationship. Official justification of the government's action was based on Maori cession of sovereignty; Kingi's stand was interpreted as a violation of the treaty. Critics branded his attitude a defiant challenge to Crown authority, even an act of treason, while others justified the chief's position on the ground that it upheld rights confirmed in 1840. There was no avoiding a review of those rights.[32]

Inside and outside the General Assembly, in public and in private, in the press and in various publications, the debate was prolonged through 1860 and beyond. A parallel exploration of the issue in England reflected the shades of opinion in the colony and, because of the lapse of time in communications, often gave rise to renewed colonial debate. The entire question was broadened by the continuing activity of the King movement, which was suspected first of encouraging and then of actively supporting Kingi's stand. Europeans of various opinions came to the conclusion that a full assertion of British sovereignty was necessary to resolve the situation.

How the Waitara issue could be terminated and how the King movement should be dealt with posed problems for which Browne had no ready solution. Aware that the Waitara case would be scrutinised in the 1860 General Assembly session and sensitive to mounting criticism, Browne called a conference of major chiefs, ostensibly to consider certain government proposals on Maori affairs.[33] The governor's real concern, however, was to consolidate sovereignty by securing from the chiefs support for his actions at Waitara and condemnation of the King movement.[34] He would take considerable care to present these two matters to the conference within the context of the Crown–Maori relationship established by the treaty.

The conference at Kohimarama near Auckland in July and August 1860 was the most representative gathering ever held under government auspices; 200 chiefs from the North Island were involved, and Taiaroa had come from the South Island.[35] The conference revealed the nature of Maori comprehension of the agreement entered into twenty years earlier, particularly as many of the chiefs had signed the treaty. Great emphasis was placed on the treaty's humanitarian element; the governor opened by dwelling at length on the treaty's clauses, repeating the pledges made in 1840 by the Crown and by chiefs, and stressing that the treaty was the first fruit of a new British policy towards indigenous races, one which invited them to unite with the colonists and 'become one people under one law'. In this the Crown played a special role: 'It is your adoption by Her Majesty as her subjects which makes it impossible that the Maori people should be unjustly dispossessed of their lands or property. Every Maori is a member of the British Nation; he is protected by the same law as his English fellow subject; and it is because you are regarded by the Queen as a part of her own especial people that you have heard from the lips of each successive Governor the same words of peace and goodwill.' The treaty promises had been faithfully observed by the Crown, Browne asserted, but he concluded by issuing a stern warning that any acts contravening Maori allegiance would render the Maori people liable to forfeit the rights and privileges of British subjects.[36]

Some of the chiefs saw that Browne was threatening to make Crown obligations under the treaty conditional on Maori acceptance of government authority. Maori speakers, during the four weeks of the conference, began to express fears that the government might use the King movement to justify abrogating the treaty. Those long associated with Pakeha argued in favour of a renewed Maori commitment to Waitangi. Waka Nene compared New Zealand, where Maori enjoyed advantages derived from the treaty, with Tahiti where Pomare and the Tahitians were less favoured under French control (an argument used in 1840 that had become more telling with further French intrusions into the Pacific). The Ngati Toa chief, Tamihana Te Rauparaha, citing the attempts made in England to overthrow the treaty, urged the Maori people to make their commitment clear: 'Do not consent that the Treaty should be for the Europeans alone, but let us take it for ourselves and let it be a cover for our heads.' Mete Kingi from Wanganui agreed: 'Let this meeting be joined to the Treaty of Waitangi. Let us urge upon the Governor not to withhold this institution from us.'[37]

Support for the treaty was not general, however. One Te Atiawa chief from Wellington admitted that he had not appreciated the treaty's meaning and intent until government authority had extended into his district, involving local chiefs as assessors to magistrates. Other chiefs doubted the extent to which the treaty still applied – Paora Tuhaere, a Ngati Whatua, thought that it was merely 'Ngapuhi's affair', an opinion shared by others. Some reasoned that because Ngapuhi had broken the treaty it was no longer in force; others argued that the protection of the Queen was retained in spite of supposed treaty violations by Heke and others.[38] There was no unanimity in attitudes to the Waitangi treaty. But on one point there seems to have been consensus – regardless of what had happened since 1840 the treaty was by no means ignored by Pakeha. In the assembly's view, this alone made the treaty significant.

Northern Maori showed that they had a more developed understanding of the treaty.[39] Ngapuhi, aware that they had played the most significant part in the 1840 negotiations, also believed that the British government had become involved in New Zealand at their request, an interpretation that owed much to judicious reminders by Pakeha. Since 1840 there had been much discussion on the treaty in the north, and Heke's challenge had increased Ngapuhi consciousness of the Waitangi agreement. In 1858 when a flagstaff was erected again on Maiki Hill at Russell by those who had opposed the government in Heke's war, it was named 'Te Whaka-kotahitanga o nga iwi' (the union of the races), and recognised by Ngapuhi as a symbol of their renewed commitment to the treaty and the Queen, and as a rejection of King movement overtures. It was accepted as such by Browne when he visited the north in February 1858.[40] From Ngapuhi speeches at Kohimarama, it is clear that these events had contributed much to northern under-standing of the treaty.

Donald McLean, Native Secretary and Chief Land Purchase Commissioner, who presided over the meeting, decided at the end of the first week that some clarification of the treaty's terms was called for. His explanations, aimed at establishing the treaty as the foundation of sovereignty and government authority, were naturally designed to appeal – an exercise in diplomacy that distinctly resembled the 1840 negotiations. McLean stressed the protective nature of the treaty, urging the chiefs not to lose sight of that 'great boon'.[41] He read again the governor's opening address, which had deliberately emphasised the benefits of the treaty by beginning with the second and third clauses before citing the first whereby sovereignty had been ceded. This reordering and other small alterations (made in drafting the speech) played down the crucial transfer of power involved in the treaty-making. Nor was the transfer of power emphasised by McLean's translation of sovereignty as 'nga tikanga me nga mana kawanatanga katoa' (the authority and all the powers of governorship), which merely expanded on 'te kawanatanga katoa' in the Maori text of the treaty. McLean thus avoided an explicit definition of the more abstract national sovereignty understood by Britain to have been ceded in 1840. More importantly, he was skirting a highly explosive issue – the settler government's growing desire to assert undisputed authority throughout the country.

In steering the conference towards a favourable conclusion, the Native Secretary was determined to impress upon the chiefs a construction of the treaty that would be as advantageous as possible to the government. He would not accept that any tribes might not be bound by the treaty; nor would he countenance a suggestion that the treaty had been made 'in the time of ignorance' and was not understood;[42] this could have been construed as an official admission that Maori were not equal partners to the contract and that they were not bound by it.

He was able to turn one criticism to lasting effect. Tuhaere of Ngati Whatua, complaining that the Waitangi meeting had been unrepresentative, concluded that 'this [alluding to the conference] is more like it; this is the real treaty upon which the sovereignty of the Queen will hang because here are assembled Chiefs from every quarter and even from the other Island, to discuss questions and to seek out a path'. McLean was in complete accord with this idea, even referring to the conference as 'a fuller ratification', a notion first voiced by Tamihana Te Rauparaha.[43] Other chiefs agreed and the idea was reflected in a major resolution passed unanimously at the last session: 'That this Conference takes cognizance of the fact that the several Chiefs, members thereof, are pledged to each other to do nothing inconsistent with their declared recognition of the Queen's sovereignty, and of the union of the two races, also to discountenance all proceedings tending to a breach of the covenant here solemnly entered into by them.'[44]

The pledge was the endorsement the government had been seeking. For some tribes it confirmed their agreement to the treaty; in other cases it committed tribal groups, such as Te Arawa, who had not signed and whose allegiance to the Crown had been slow to emerge. To some extent this general commitment compensated for a lack of unanimous support for two other resolutions, one endorsing government policy on Waitara, the other condemning the King movement.[45] Many chiefs were quite critical of government failure to investigate Kingi's case with due care. There was a general feeling that Waitara could have been avoided if the government had sought the co-operation of the chiefs as mediators. And the question of the King movement obviously presented a problem to some chiefs. While willing to accept the Queen's authority, they were reluctant to admit that the movement was incompatible with the Queen's sovereignty.

The Kohimarama conference came to serve quite different functions for the officials and for the Maori people. From the government point of view, the conference was just one more attempt to deal with the Maori problem. While it sounded out Maori opinion more comprehensively than before, the gathering was not fully representative in that it excluded chiefs in open opposition to the government, particularly Taranaki and Waikato, the latter receiving invitations after proceedings had started.[46] It was also criticised as being merely a counter-demonstration to the large King movement meetings which were attracting many Maori supporters.[47]

As a response to the Waitangi treaty, however, the 1860 conference was undoubtedly one of the most influential Maori gatherings ever held. This became apparent when Maori treaty rights, understood to be confirmed by the Kohimarama conference, became a point of reference for the expression of organised Maori protest later in the century. Chiefs took away from the conference distinct understandings. The entire conference proceedings (in Maori and English) were also circulated to most chiefs of consequence.[48]

The most important idea retained by Maori from the 1860 conference was that Maori mana had been guaranteed. The recapitulation of the treaty had been influential, as had the official recognition given chieftainship by the government's convening such a meeting. The government's acceptance of a conference petition, that the meeting be made a permanent institution, may have further confirmed the impression of mana guaranteed.[49] Conference chiefs did not see this mana as in any way conflicting with that of the Queen, which they acknowledged. The Queen's mana was protective, the term maru (protect) being used as often as the term mana in reference to Crown influence; chiefly mana related to those situations over which chiefs had traditionally exerted authority. Indeed, speakers could see no conflict in the co-existence of several mana, or spheres of influence.[50] It was hardly surprising that the meeting was reluctant to condemn the King movement, for the concept of a shared authority, which the treaty seemed to allow for, was applicable to all chiefs and not merely to the King movement.

As a result of the conference also Maori were fully acquainted (possibly for the first time) with all the treaty guarantees. While the land guarantee had always been a critical point of discussion, forests and fisheries had not previously attracted the same attention. They were included in the English text but were not specifically referred to in the Maori text which most chiefs had signed. McLean's translation of Browne's opening speech expanded on the guarantee of the treaty's second article (the Maori text) to include lands (whenua, oneone), forests (ngaherehere), fishing places (wai mahinga ika) and all other possessions (taonga). Their inclusion may have always been assumed, but these explanations were explicit. The lack of comment when McLean later read the Maori text (which omitted these details)[51] showed that the chiefs now understood article two to cover all these areas. Clarification of these guarantees was important, for fisheries in particular were soon to become a cause of much tension as settlement expanded.

The final resolution of the conference, in effect a ratification of the treaty, came to be known as the Kohimarama covenant. The idea of a covenant, a solemn religious pledge, uniting Maori and

Pakeha as one people, had been proposed by a northern representative. More than other participants, Ngapuhi tended to refer
to the Waitangi agreement as the covenant (te kawenata) rather
than the treaty (te tiriti), indicating an understanding that had
been evident in their 1840 negotiations. It seems that they continued to regard the treaty as a sacred compact, in one sense
uniting all Maori tribes and, in another, acting as the bond of
union between the races. McLean shrewdly encouraged this,
speaking of the 'covenant' in preference to the 'treaty'.[52] The
governor's opening address also stressed that the Queen had entered into a 'covenant' with her chosen race, the Maori people.
The final pledge, therefore, represented far more than an extension of Maori commitment to the terms of Waitangi; it reaffirmed
the 1840 agreement as a most solemn compact, giving the covenant concept wider currency.

From the government's point of view, the conference had not
been entirely successful. Even while the meetings were still in
session, the General Assembly met in Auckland after a break of
two years, and it was clear from the tenor of debate that the
government would have to come up with some other plan. The
crux of the problem was that vast areas of the North Island
remained in Maori ownership and control, restricting settlement.
The difficulty, as seen by the Assembly, was to mollify Maori
opinion and at the same time to acquire land. One proposal put
forward in 1860 was the establishment of a Native Council. Like
the Kohimarama conference, this would later be interpreted differently by Pakeha and Maori.

It seems that the council suggestion originated with Henry
Sewell, a government member with wide legal experience. Like
many colonial politicians, he had long realised that, if a 'racial
explosion' over land was to be avoided, it was imperative to
terminate Maori title to large blocks of land in the North Island.
One effort to achieve this had resulted in abortive legislation in
the 1858 session.[53] Sewell now planned a council, nominated by
the governor, to inaugurate a new scheme for the bi-racial systematic colonisation of specified districts. The scheme would lead
to the closure of the Land Purchase Department, a body disliked
by the Assembly because it was responsible only to the governor
and unpopular generally because of its failure to overcome Maori
opposition to sales.[54]

Since Governor Gore Browne agreed that the scheme might
defuse a potentially explosive racial situation, a Bill incorporating
Sewell's ideas was referred to the British government for

enactment.[55] It looked at first as if the Bill might pass through the British Parliament, but a determined opposition was mounted, by colonist James Edward FitzGerald, formerly Superintendent of Canterbury. FitzGerald appealed to the Colonial Office to drop the Bill; it would effectively repeal the 1852 constitution for half the colony by creating an administrative system not responsible to the General Assembly – 'two Governments in one Colony'.[56] The Secretary of State for Colonies, the Duke of Newcastle, fearing that the Bill might result in the 'proverbial fate of a house divided against itself', decided to press it no further.[57]

The New Zealand General Assembly, alarmed by the prospect of the English Bill passing, attempted to provide a colonial substitute; Sewell proposed a General Maori Council with provincial and district councils. A modified form of Native Council Bill was passed and duly referred to the British government, but the move was half-hearted. The idea of creating a government separate from the General Assembly provoked the jealousy of colonial politicians. Moreover, prospective Pakeha council members were unhappy about its composition and anticipated interference from the Assembly.[58] The proposals went no further. Maori later interpreted these ideas as official recognition of a Maori right to separate government, a right derived from the 1835 Confederation of the north and from the treaty, and confirmed in the special constitutional provisions of 1852 allowing for native districts. This interpretation, however, reads into government moves an acknowledgement of Maori rights that the colonial government did not admit.

General Assembly discussion of a Native Council in 1860 was only a small part of an extensive debate on native affairs generally and on the Waitara issue in particular. The Assembly could achieve no consensus on Waitara; members often adopted arguments less from a conviction of their merit than for their value as political weapons. Since the Stafford Ministry was under pressure to defend the Waitara decision, government speakers cast about for justification of Browne's stand. The Native Minister, Christopher William Richmond, saw Wiremu Kingi's attitude as rebellion because the cession of sovereignty entitled the Crown to assert British law in land dealings; Kingi was retaining the land merely to keep out that law. For Kingi and his people the 'spirit' of the treaty was 'dead', J.C. Richmond asserted, because their actions dissociated them from the contract. It was a treaty, Francis Dillon Bell reminded the Assembly, that not only conferred rights but imposed duties – an imposition that Kingi was determined to resist.[59]

That Browne's decision over Waitara had violated the second article of the treaty was the major contention of those in opposition to the governor. Wellington politican William Fitzherbert alleged that it had caused 'an unholy and unjust war', a point of view shared by many members.[60] But criticism of the war did not necessarily indicate a concern for Maori rights. Many politicians were using the situation to attack the much disliked control of native affairs by the governor and by McLean, who was stringently criticised by William Fox as 'a medicine man, a Grand Lama, absolute in power and irresponsible to authority'.[61] McLean's purchase system, as Sewell correctly claimed, alienated Maori from government.[62]

While there was no unanimity on the Waitara issue, members at least agreed that the experience indicated a need to define Maori title, as it had been confirmed by treaty, through some kind of tribunal. Seen as either expedient or just, depending on the sympathies of individuals, the tribunal proposal would later be taken up by the government in the 1862 Native Lands Act. The Assembly resolved that the Native Land Purchase Department should be separated from the ordinary government administration of native affairs, with which it had been combined since 1856. But this, too, was left to the future. Discussion on both matters foreshadowed the policy that would be adopted the following year.

It was remarkable that no significant legislation was enacted in the 1860 session. The government was indecisive, but also believed that new legislation might rouse Maori suspicion of official intentions, and would make it difficult to secure further purchases. This was one reason for the failure of a Native Offenders' Bill directed at curbing settler trade with disaffected Maori, which met strong opposition both in and outside the Assembly on the basis that it would create further Maori hostility.

Only some politicians showed an awareness of Maori sensibilities in their public statements. During Assembly debates, for instance, both C.W. Richmond and Sewell agreed on the need to find methods of working round the treaty to acquire Maori land, but while Richmond baldly registered the need to extinguish native title, Sewell reaffirmed Maori land rights recognised by treaty.[63] Fox went further, urging that the interpretation to be put on the treaty 'ought to be in the sense in which it was understood by the Natives ... at the time the treaty was entered into'. Since he had not been a notable defender of the treaty, members found his about-face rather surprising; Weld cited Fox's earlier hostility to the treaty in his 1851 publication *The Six Colonies*. Fox, however, revealed that the text had actually been written by

Sewell, a charge that Sewell defended with the plea that 'he lived to learn'.[64]

The conclusion to be drawn from such public exchanges was not consoling to those anxious to uphold treaty rights. Politicians adopted positions on the treaty more from personal interest and expediency than on the ground of moral justice. The 1860 debates showed that reassurances about the treaty might be merely a means of appeasing the Maori people. This boded ill for the future of the treaty as Maori understood it.

Colonial politicians also 'aired' the treaty at this time as a means of retaining British support. In 1860 they needed funds to meet the expenses of the Taranaki war, the proposed militia and the probable confrontation with the King movement. Politicians argued that the British government was obliged to stand the cost of the war. By the treaty, that government had bound itself to secure to the Maori people the benefits of peace and good order, through a settled form of civil government. Because this had failed, the Maori had established a King. Such arguments, repeated throughout the 1860s as the costs of war escalated, were difficult to refute as long as responsibility for native affairs rested with the governor.

Politicians were anxious that the war should not be seen as a 'colonial' or 'settler' war, but as a matter of imperial defence. It was important that the colonial government's motives and actions should appear just and equitable to the British government. Press reports revealing the more extreme settler stances were both embarrassing and compromising; they were often reprinted or cited in the British press, and attention was even drawn to them in British parliamentary debates. War costs and the effect of adverse publicity were therefore of some significance in encouraging a public, official stance that upheld the treaty. There was always the slender possibility that the British government might respond to colonial importunities by rescinding responsible government – a proposition floated in English official circles in 1860–61.[65]

Outside the Assembly, this political chicanery raised misgivings among those who had earlier defended Maori rights. A campaign was now launched to safeguard the principles of the treaty. Long-serving Church of England missionaries took the lead, claiming a 'right of remonstrance' because of their role in the 1840 negotiations. The most public plea was made by Octavius Hadfield, the Otaki–Waikanae missionary who had enjoyed a close association with Wiremu Kingi. Hadfield spoke before the House of Representatives in 1860 and subsequently published several works on the issues.[66] With Selwyn and several other missionaries, he appealed against the Native Offenders' Bill of the 1860 session, which he believed would constitute a violation of the treaty's third article by placing Maori outside the protection of law. That settlers would have been similarly affected was an important consideration in the dismissal of the Bill.[67]

This defence of Waitangi principles was continued in the 1860s by Church of England leaders. Through private correspondence and the printed word, they sought support in the colony and in England.[68] The effect of their work was considerably weakened by the insinuation that it was unseemly for clergy to participate so openly in a political debate, that such a spirited defence of the Maori people cast doubts on the campaigners' loyalty and that it encouraged Maori opposition by providing them with a 'cause'. These criticisms were influential in England, with Newcastle and Gladstone for example, in detracting from the real weight of the campaigners' case.[69]

But one critic whose opinion could not be easily dismissed was Sir William Martin, once the colony's Chief Justice and now retired. Martin was so opposed to what he believed to be the injustice of the policy leading to the Waitara war that he spent several months writing *The Taranaki Question*, which he directed expressly to members of the British Parliament and the General Assembly.[70] Arguing that the issue at Waitara was basically a land quarrel, he outlined Maori tenure as he understood it to exist at the time of the 1840 treaty. Martin reasoned that the treaty had left that tenure as it was – a right of property held collectively by the chiefs and tribes, the chiefs retaining 'what they understood full well, the "tino rangatiratanga", "full Chiefship"' over all their tribal land. He pointed out that since 1840 the rights of tribes as collective groups, as well as of chiefs, had been repeatedly recognised, in word and in act, by successive governors. All past cessions of land to the Crown had this basis. He likened the chiefs' power and influence to a seigniorial right, whereas the rights conceded to the Crown, known in Maori as 'kawanatanga' or 'Governorship' and in English as 'sovereignty', were recognised by the Maori as only 'such rights as were necessary for the Government of the Country'.[71]

Martin saw the King movement as evidence of the progress of the Maori people towards the more ordered, lawful existence which they had been promised at the colony's foundation and he asked for tolerance towards it. The Waitangi covenant and the spirit in which it was entered into was the subject of an eloquent appeal:

Here in New Zealand our nation has engaged in an enterprise most
difficult, yet also most noble and worthy of England. We have undertaken to acquire these islands for the Crown and for our race, without
violence and without fraud, and so that the Native people, instead of
being destroyed, should be protected and civilised. We have coven-
anted with these people, and assured to them the full privileges of
subjects of the Crown. To this undertaking the faith of the nation is
pledged. By these means we secured a peaceable entrance for the
Queen's authority into the country, and have in consequence gradually
gained a firm hold upon it. The compact is binding irrevocably. We
cannot repudiate it so long as we retain the benefit which we obtained
by it.[72]

Martin was clearly not basing this appeal on legal grounds but
on the moral duty of every New Zealand settler to fulfil the
pledge of the nation, the solemn compact made in 1840. The plea
was a strong one, clearly and concisely presented in the humanitarian tradition, but in the early 1860s government and settler
attitudes were not sympathetic.

Because of Martin's standing in the colony, *The Taranaki Question* was subjected to a critical analysis by Browne and government ministers.[73] This reply argued that Martin took an unduly
narrow view of the subject by treating 'as a question of title'
what was in fact 'a question of sovereignty'. The criticism was
not entirely ill-founded. Martin carefully avoided discussing
sovereignty by simply translating the treaty's Maori terms into
their literal English equivalents. Readers were left to conclude that
there might well be a wide divergence between Maori and English
understanding of the document's terms, especially of 'sovereignty'. Martin was side-stepping the issue just as the government had
chosen to evade the point at Kohimarama.

Even as Martin worked on *The Taranaki Question*, another
commentary was being penned by one of the colony's judges, Mr
Justice Johnson. The judge adhered solely to the English text of
the treaty, making no concession to the divergence of the texts.
He admitted that the chiefs had enjoyed both mana over the land
and the right of usufruct before 1840, but concluded that the
treaty would have been an absurdity unless the chiefs, on behalf of
their tribes, had absolutely abandoned all possible claims to their
sovereign rights or to quasi-sovereign rights that might be called
their 'mana' over the land.[74] No doubt many in the government
and the settler community wished that this understanding of the
treaty had obtained in 1840, but those who fully appreciated the
treaty-making and the colony's early history knew differently. As

Sewell observed, Johnson was 'imperfectly acquainted' with the case; the government published his opinions nevertheless.[75]

Through the latter half of 1860 and well into 1861, new writings less clear than those of Martin and Johnson further confused the issues. C.O. Torlesse recommended isolating the Maori until they agreed to a new treaty; Fox blamed the governor for the mess over Waitara and advocated full settler responsibility for Maori affairs.[76] Busby, bursting into the limelight again in a press debate on the treaty, published his own reply to Martin.[77] The ex-Resident, for some twenty years a self-appointed but increasingly inconsistent authority on the treaty, presented an emotional argument, asserting that there was 'no evidence of New Zealanders ever having any rights with the exception of those which were created by the Treaty of Waitangi'.[78] Had Busby intended his statement to mean that the treaty conferred legal rights under the Crown on the Maori people, then his argument might have commanded some respect, but his reasoning was unclear. George Clarke, former Chief Protector of Aborigines, felt compelled to print a defence of Martin in which he pointed out Busby's errors and reiterated that Maori rights, as they existed in 1840, had been confirmed by treaty and not conferred as Busby implied.[79]

It is difficult to determine the extent to which this discussion, with all its confusion and contradiction, affected Maori. Settlers were uneasily aware that at least some of it reached Maori ears. To counteract its effect, the government's *Maori Messenger* had been mounting its own campaign for some time. The King movement had come under special attention; the newspaper admonished its readers to uphold the Queen's mana, which the treaty had given them, and which left no room for allegiance to the King. It was repeatedly stressed that only under the Queen's mana could Maori and Pakeha be one people. The paper published an open letter from Busby to the Maori people, which outlined the treaty's protective features and repeated the idea that the shadow of the land alone had gone to the Queen, the substance remaining to the chiefs. Busby reinforced the notion of the treaty as the spiritual 'covenant' between the Queen and the Maori people making them one. 'Take heed,' he warned Maori readers, 'that ye are not rebelling against God as well as against the Queen.'[80]

The important question of mana was taken up by the *Maori Messenger* against a background of growing public debate on the use of the term.[81] The paper reported on a King movement meeting near Auckland early in 1860 where speakers had discussed mana at length. It was not a new idea – the fear that Maori mana

over the land was passing to the settlers had been voiced intermittently by Maori throughout the 1850s[82] – but a section of the
movement now advocated asserting a Maori independence (te
tikanga whakamotuhake i nga iwi Maori). The *Maori Messenger*
voiced the opinion that the mana of New Zealand had gone to the
Queen already, but disingenuously asked: 'What is this mana? Is it
anything more than the right to protect?' Maori and Pakeha were
one people so one race could not say that the country was for
them alone; it was for both races. 'Ekore e penei, No matou a Niu
Tirani, engari, No tatou a Niu Tirani.'[83] Like Martin's work, this
journalism also evaded the issue of sovereignty.

In the first half of 1861, the colony appeared to be drifting towards a showdown on the question of sovereignty. Browne had
become more resolute in his condemnation of the King movement
when some Waikato became involved in the Taranaki fighting.
Following an uneasy truce in Taranaki in April 1861, the focus
shifted to Waikato where Tawhiao had become King following
Potatau Te Wherowhero's death in June 1860. In late May 1861,
the governor sent a proclamation to the Waikato people accusing
them of violating the treaty and requiring from all 'submission
without reserve, to the Queen's sovereignty and the authority of
the law'. Land 'combinations' were outlawed and plunder taken in
Taranaki had to be restored. As Browne's critics said, this was
tantamount to saying: 'Accept the Treaty of Waitangi or I will
make you.'[84]

From the Maori point of view, Browne's proclamation justified
long-held fears that Pakeha were not to be trusted: two months
before, in the *Maori Messenger*, Browne had actually denied two
rumours – that he was bent on depriving Maori of their land and
that he was determined to destroy chiefly influence. At the same
time, he had recited the second article of the treaty including the
guarantee of fisheries, adding with considerable solemnity: 'I repeat this assurance to you [Maori] again now, and I call upon all
true and faithful Maori to contradict any report, coming either
from European or Native, which throws doubt on this pledge.'[85]
Even the May proclamation had noted this second article, in
contradiction to the insistence on Kingite submission. In the face
of Browne's inconsistencies, Wiremu Tamihana Tarapipipi wrote
a thoughtful reply reiterating the understanding of the treaty that
the moderate wing of the King movement had held from the
beginning: that there was a place for an independent Maori body
in conjunction with the Queen's sovereignty or mana.[86]

Whether a degree of Maori independence should be tolerated

was now the crucial question upon which the governor, the press and the General Assembly concentrated in mid-1861, but without reaching a consensus. The governor and some ministers privately favoured carrying the war into the Waikato, and the possibility of a more representative Kohimarama conference was also talked about in government circles,[87] but a turn of events saved Browne and the ministry from either course.

In July 1861 the Stafford Ministry fell and Fox formed a new government. Within weeks, news arrived of George Grey's appointment as governor for a second term, a decision which the Colonial Office had felt obliged to make in the face of growing doubts about Browne's suitability. Browne postponed calling another Kohimarama conference, and when Grey arrived the proposal was dropped altogether. The new governor thought it would not be 'wise to call a number of' semi-barbarian Natives together to frame a Constitution for themselves'.[88] Grey probably reasoned that to give official recognition to a corporate Maori body while relations with the King movement had not been settled was tantamount to an official acceptance of Maori separateness. The government now turned to other alternatives to settle the matter of mana or sovereignty.

Chapter Eight

A WAR OF SOVEREIGNTY

'All questions between the British colonists of New Zealand and the Maoris are now merged in a war of sovereignty – probably of extermination.'[1]

This report in *The Times* of 16 December 1864 was a belated recognition of a state of affairs that had existed from at least 1861. That the question of sovereignty was the critical point of difference between the races had been widely acknowledged in New Zealand. As Frederick Weld, Native Minister in the Stafford Ministry, put it, the government was determined to assert British sovereignty, whereas it was clear that Wiremu Tamihana 'meant most distinctly a Maori nationality'. To Weld, this would spell ruin because the King movement 'combination' would block the expansion of law and order, a result that would ruin Maori progress too. Many members of the Assembly shared Weld's view. Like Weld, they were convinced that history showed the need to impose supremacy over native races by force. The 'inevitable hour of conflict must come,' warned C.W. Richmond; 'it was one of the necessities of colonization.'[2]

The government, nevertheless, needed to justify any attack upon the King movement, and Assembly members thought that they had found a cause in Tamihana's correspondence with the government. The chief's assertion of a Maori independence, deriving from the treaty's guarantee of chieftainship, enabled members to argue that Waikato would not submit to British sovereignty.[3] It was an easy step to suggest that the King movement's very existence constituted treason.

Among the public at large, the general impression by the early 1860s was that the country was heading for a 'war of races'. Differences of opinion lay only in how and when the war might begin. Sewell feared that the tone of public vindictiveness was sufficiently strong in 1861 for a war of extermination to break out that year.[4] Yet settlers were not unanimous in their support for war; some still hoped that it could be avoided. Lady Martin assured an English friend that 'independent quiet men who had been in the country for many years were to a man opposed' to the idea.[5]

In early 1861, however, 'moderates' like Sewell, 'sick and indignant' at the belligerent tone of the governor and the Assembly, were a minority voice.[6] In spite of the uneasy truce that brought

Taranaki hostilities to a temporary halt in April 1861, neither civil nor military leaders were disposed towards a peaceful solution. The issue of sovereignty now moved centre stage in political events. Sometimes sovereignty and the terms of the treaty were the focus of attention; at other times, treaty rights were implicit in government decision-making, inextricably entwined in the extension of authority and settlement. The 1860s were a crucial decade when official decisions determined both the understanding of the treaty that would prevail and the means by which the treaty could be given effect.

How to proceed against the King was the essential point for Browne and the ministry in the first half of 1861, but the 'babel of opinions' had led to no action when the Stafford Ministry fell in July.[7] William Fox, who led the new ministry, criticised the previous ministry for the recklessness with which they had taken steps leading to war and their 'sham negotiations' with the King movement. But he was no more averse to force than his predecessors, if official overtures to the King movement failed to bring Maori submission. His caution was less a concern to avoid war than a desire that any war should be seen as a war for British supremacy and hence an imperial responsibility.[8] Skilled at adapting his political stance to the needs of the moment, Fox had previously shown a disconcerting shiftiness on the treaty.[9]

With the arrival of Grey in September came the first signs of Crown withdrawal from the principle of trusteeship. Although the responsibility, expressed as part of the British commitment in 1840, had not always been shouldered, it had been recognised up to the 1860s by reservation of Maori affairs to the governor. But from October 1861, responsibility was shifted increasingly to the colonial government. The process would be an untidy, ill-defined retreat for Britain; not until the last British troops left the country in February 1870 could it be said that Britain had completely resigned its control.[10] In the intervening years, uncertainty in the British–colonial relationship gave rise to distrust and antagonism between the two governments. The losers in this struggle were the Maori, for no formal transfer of treaty obligations was made or even considered.

Britain's colonial policy in the 1860s was subject to Treasury pressures for reduction in expenditure. Colonial responsibility for self-defence was regarded as a logical corollary to self-government. Newcastle, Secretary of State for Colonies from 1859 to 1864, was fairly pragmatic, aiming at a balance between security for settlers, justice for the Maori people and the demands of economy. His successor, Edward Cardwell, was more ruthless, however, seeking to curtail costs and disengage Britain from New Zealand responsibilities.

In spite of new attitudes to colonial administration, neither Secretary of State was really indifferent to Maori rights. Cardwell had defended the treaty in the 1840s and had urged Browne to uphold it. Newcastle, too, was not entirely deaf to the pleas of the humanitarian lobby in New Zealand during the Waitara war.[11] The problem for both men was how to control policy effectively from a distance of 12,000 miles – a dilemma made more acute in the 1850s by self-government. Newcastle became convinced that the best hope for the Maori people lay in placing responsibility for Maori affairs squarely on the colonists, forcing them to carry the burden with greater prudence.

At first the Fox Ministry seemed willing enough to accept responsibility for day-to-day administration of Maori affairs. McLean's Native Department had long been disliked as a law unto itself, and McLean had already resigned in June 1861.[12] The ministry did not accept full responsibility in Maori affairs, however, partly in recognition of Grey's right to determine policy where imperial interests were involved, and partly from a wish to avoid financial responsibility. The arrangement was that where Grey and the ministers disagreed, the matter would be considered by the Assembly. Within weeks, ministers found Grey to be disconcertingly ambivalent in attitude and devious in dealings. It was evident, said Sewell, now Fox's Attorney-General, that the governor intended to have the determining say in Maori affairs, yet hold the ministry responsible – a 'sham' responsibility.[13] Grey also allowed Newcastle to assume that the ministry had accepted full responsibility, while Newcastle believed that Grey still had some controlling influence.

With the co-operation of the Fox Ministry, Grey embarked on a policy which aimed to bring Maori within the compass of British authority. The ultimate objective was undisputed control over the whole country. First, peace negotiations in Taranaki were resumed, along with overtures to the King movement, while military preparations were also continued; and second, an improved administrative structure was proposed, the 'new institutions' or the Runanga system.[14] By persuasion or by force Maori were to be brought to submission. It was to be a war of sovereignty on two fronts – political and military.

The Runanga system, said to be based upon the traditional Maori runanga, endeavoured to bring Maori usages under government control.[15] Village Runanga were to be under the direction of Resident Magistrates assisted by Maori assessors, and district Runanga under Civil Commissioners; all appointees were to be salaried. Legislative sanction was provided by the 1858 Native Districts Act and Native Circuit Courts Act. The system, implemented in only a few districts, had mixed success. In the Waikato, where the government hoped it would supplant the King's institutions, it was treated with understandable suspicion. The King movement was asserting independence, while Grey was offering indirect government thinly disguised as self-government. He had, in fact, rejected two possible alternatives – a Maori Council or another Kohimarama-style conference – as too close to an official admission of Maori independence. The 'new institutions' were favoured as the training ground for the eventual incorporation of the Maori people into a unified political community. In a subtle form, the government moves were yet another version of 'amalgamation'.

Settler society, shaping up for a fight, did not welcome the new institutions. From sheer racial prejudice, settlers more often than not refused to abide by Runanga resolutions, even in predominantly Maori districts. In squatter districts such as Hawke's Bay, the ability of the local Runanga to dictate terms for rents and seasonal labour was resented. Even more irritating to settlers was the failure of the Runanga system to free land for purchase. The Runanga had been intended to define tribal, hapu and individual interests in land; once title had been confirmed by the Crown, the Runanga would be free to authorise alienation to settlers. The proposal had the merit of retaining 'corporate tribal authority', thereby sustaining traditional rights guaranteed under the treaty. In practice, however, Maori were reluctant to alienate any land. When settlers realised that the title would be tribal, not individual, they bitterly denounced Maori 'communism in land'. Settler antagonism defeated a Native Lands Bill (drafted by Sewell and introduced by Fox), designed to confirm the power of the Runanga.[16] A storm of criticism over the handling of Maori affairs, much of it dwelling on the treaty, led to the fall of the Fox Ministry.

The settler cry for rapid individualisation of Maori title and direct dealing between individual Maori and settler was answered by the new ministry, led by Alfred Domett, with the Native Lands Act, 1862. The work of the Native Minister, Francis Dillon Bell, this Act was the most serious attack on Maori land ownership so far, although the preamble recited the Waitangi treaty and stated that land rights thus guaranteed should be 'ascertained, defined and declared'.[17] To carry this out, the Act allowed for a court (presided over by a European magistrate) which would determine ownership and issue a certificate of title in favour of the appropriate tribe, community or individuals. Purchase could then proceed direct from Maori to settler because the Act also waived the Crown's right of pre-emption. On paper, the court seemed to be 'practically the ratifying tribunal' that a later Native Minister claimed it to be.[18] Its real intent, however, was to speed up settler purchase of land and the amalgamation of the Maori. Maori were later to complain bitterly about the Act's terms which had altered treaty provisions and abrogated Maori rights.

Some Assembly members, too, complained that the treaty was being violated, but their concern was not with Maori rights. Their fear was that direct purchase of land would drastically cut provincial land revenue in Auckland, Wellington and Hawke's Bay. The promoters of direct purchase also resorted to the treaty, airing old arguments about pre-emption, claiming that it was never intended to mean an exclusive right of purchase vested in the Crown, and that it had prevented Maori getting value for their lands. Various other skeletons were dragged out of the closet, and the debate demonstrated forcibly how the treaty could serve opposite goals.[19]

On one point, however, all members were in agreement: that native title would have to be determined by some properly constituted tribunal. For some years, this had been acknowledged by the Colonial Office, the New Zealand government, settlers and, latterly, by Maori groups alarmed by the Waitara dispute. Although politicians often railed against the treaty's guarantee of Maori ownership of all land, most accepted that this right was so entrenched by 1860 that it would have to be circumvented by legislation.[20] Licence for the change had been given by Grey and Newcastle; the latter assured Grey that the Colonial Office would assent to 'any prudent plan for the individualization of Native title, and for direct purchase under proper safeguards'.[21] Although this last injunction was largely ignored, the Act received the Royal Assent, making the imperial government a partner in this major threat to treaty-guaranteed rights.

Sewell, ever watchful of colonial legislation, feared that the Assembly had been manipulated by an Auckland business combination. He estimated that Thomas Russell, one of the governing clique and Minister of Colonial Defence, would make 'a certain £10,000 a year before five years'. According to Sewell, he represented 'the true mind of the old land-sharking interest'.[22] But the Auckland 'birds of prey' and Australian speculators were not able to make an immediate 'rush' on Maori land as Sewell forecast.

The implementation of the 1862 Native Lands Act was postponed when the Domett government and Grey led the colony into the anticipated war of sovereignty in 1863.[23]

Through 1862 Grey's efforts at 'peace-making' did not encourage Maori confidence in the government. Grey and the Domett Ministry were looking for unqualified submission of the King's followers. With government and the King movement adhering to different views of sovereign rights, a meeting of minds was near impossible. The King movement, however, tried to get Grey's agreement on terms at Taupiri in January 1863. The King's control was to be upheld in the Waikato, Grey's road-making – 'cutting the land's backbone' – was to stop at the Mangatawhiri Stream and no armed steamers (then being built by the government) were to be allowed up the Waikato River. These terms were based on the treaty's guarantee of Maori mana over lands, forests and fisheries. Kingites warned that if settlers proved troublesome they would be sent out of the Waikato.[24] Grey was evasive in dealing with these points; the negotiations became as much a sham as those conducted under Browne. In March, John Gorst, Resident Magistrate in the Upper Waikato, was evicted by Ngati Maniapoto for his attempts to subvert the King movement. His publication *Te Pihoihoi Mokemoke*, a counter-move to a Kingite paper *Te Hokioi*, was viewed by Waikato Maori as deliberate provocation, a 'paper war'.[25]

In Taranaki, Grey had decided to return the Waitara block which he was convinced had been unjustly purchased. Unfortunately he moved first to seize the Tataraimaka block, Crown land occupied by Maori during the war; the action predictably led to renewed fighting. The decision to reverse Browne's stand on Waitara irritated politicians and public, and the lack of investigation and consultation over Waitara did not allay the Maori sense of injustice.

Between May and July, rumours circulated in Auckland that Waikato Maori intended to launch a surprise attack on the town; Ngati Maniapoto did propose the move but moderate Kingites restrained the extremists and endeavoured to keep communications with the government open and to avoid fighting. At Mangere, Tamati Ngapora pledged his life as a guarantee of Auckland's safety – 'Ko au ano te utu'[26] – but Kingite attitude to the south were stiffening. At Ngaruawahia CMS missionary, Benjamin Ashwell, had noticed a mounting aversion to prayers for the Queen, and in March 1863 *Te Hokioi* had printed an account of the progress of the native people of Haiti towards independence; parallels with Maori experience were drawn.[27] With both races there was unease.

Grey now determined to strike a pre-emptive blow and the Domett government enthusiastically agreed to his plans. He proposed to advance into the Waikato, set up military posts, clear the land of its Maori occupants from Auckland to the Waikato River, and confiscate territory which would be used for military settlements and to defray war costs. Belatedly, a proclamation warned Kingites that those who 'rebelled' would forfeit their land rights guaranteed by the treaty. Before this reached the Waikato, however, British troops had crossed the Mangatawhiri Stream on 12 July. Both sides recognised that war had begun.[28]

The New Zealand wars developed into a series of engagements which steadily expanded the area of fighting.[29] In 1863–64, British troops pushed further up the Waikato than was justified by the extent of Maori opposition. Early in 1864, a new operation was begun at Tauranga and from the end of 1864 a punitive campaign was launched in south Taranaki. Designed to make Taranaki habitable for settlers by 'pacifying' local tribes, the campaign was intended to punish the independent-minded Ngati Ruanui; it resulted in new extremes of fighting on both sides. Further complications arose from the emergence of the Pai Marire cult in south Taranaki and its spread to other North Island districts.[30] This movement, beginning in 1862 as an attempt at peaceful adjustment to change, took a more violent form from 1864, an indication of the pressure of war upon certain Maori groups.

The war changed in character from the mid-1860s. Set-piece warfare, most often the norm in the Waikato, gave way to protracted guerilla campaigns on the North Island's west and east coasts. New leaders – Te Kooti and Titokowaru – appeared later in the decade as the war dragged to an uncertain and untidy end. What had started as moves against Taranaki and Waikato had affected almost all North Island districts, directly or indirectly.

From the outset, the struggle was an unequal one. A build-up of British troops from 1860 had ensured superior numbers in the field. These men were amply supported by military supplies and by the material assistance of the settler population, for many of whom the war was a commercial boon. Early in the Waikato fighting, the war effort was augmented by the addition of colonial forces whose ranks were swelled by volunteers recruited in Australia. These colonial forces gradually supplanted the British troops, who began to withdraw in 1865. Maori who fought on the Queen's side played an increasingly important part, taking the opportunity to settle old scores against traditional enemies, a factor that marked the last stages of the fighting with bitterness and desperation.

Against this war effort, Maori who resisted were ill equipped to effect a lasting victory. They were outnumbered in every major confrontation, and they maintained their lines of supply only with difficulty. Yet Maori skill in adapting to changing circumstances of warfare confounded the opposition, especially in the early stages of the fighting. Demonstrations of Maori chivalry and Christian courtesy challenged any Victorian notions the troops might have had that they were fighting barbarism and savagery. As the war dragged on, a conviction grew among the imperial troops and their officers that they had been committed to fight a war for the land on behalf of settlers, against an enemy who had earned the troops' respect. The Colonial Office gradually arrived at a similar conclusion. Legislation passed by the General Assembly provided statutory powers to carry out the war of sovereignty – an attack on the political front to support the military effort.

The political attack was mounted by a new ministry. The Domett Ministry had postponed calling the parliamentary session as long as possible while war measures were pushed through in the latter half of 1863. But by October, when the Assembly met in Auckland (it had met in Wellington in 1862), there was an uncomfortable feeling that the colony might have bitten off more than it could chew. The Domett Ministry resigned, releasing its members from accountability for the events of 1863.[31] The Whitaker–Fox Ministry remained an Auckland-dominated combination. Russell, the real power in the previous ministry, continued as Colonial Defence Minister; his legal partner, Frederick Whitaker, now became government leader in the Council and Attorney-General. Described as a 'cold shrewd subtle reckless man, careless of means, and careless of consequences', Whitaker was able to bend Fox to a ruthless line of policy.[32] When the Assembly was not in session, Fox having returned to Wellington, the real power lay with Whitaker and Russell. Unscrupulous men were now in a position to legislate against Maori rights.

Whitaker was responsible for three related pieces of legislation – the New Zealand Settlements Act, the Suppression of Rebellion Act and a Loan Act.[33] The New Zealand Settlements Act allowed for confiscation of Maori land as a punishment for the war, while the Suppression of Rebellion Act sanctioned extreme colonywide measures to deal with a 'rebellion' that involved only certain areas. Both Acts raised serious questions about the status of the

Maori people and their land rights, about the standing of the treaty of Waitangi and about powers being assumed by the colonial government. The measures were rushed through parliament, giving members little time to consider the implications, on the assumption that the government needed unusual powers to deal with an unusual situation. The justification cited in the Acts was that Waikato Maori, indeed most Maori, had been engaged in a plot to exterminate the settlers. As Sewell observed, this was a 'gigantic lie'.[34]

The New Zealand Settlements Act did grievous damage to Maori–Pakeha relationships, for it left the Maori people with a deeply felt sense of injustice that still rankles. The Act, aptly described as the 'keystone' of government policy,[35] authorised the confiscation of lands from those in 'rebellion' in any district of the colony whatsoever. Settlers would be established on these lands in sufficient numbers to deter Maori from further resistance; whatever land remained would be sold to defray war costs. Fox calculated that about 4 million acres would have to be taken in the Waikato, the Thames–Piako valley and Taranaki. The Act, however, left the government dangerously free to deal with all Maori land almost at will, because confiscation could be extended beyond these named areas at any time. Confiscation, moreover, dispossessed friendly Maori along with the 'rebels', leaving them the doubtful benefit of compensation to be decided later by a court of arbitration.

The only opposition to the Act came from FitzGerald in the House of Representatives, and Sewell and Swainson in the Legislative Council.[36] FitzGerald asserted that confiscation was a violation of the treaty's land guarantee, and in opposition to the Constitution Act (section seventy-two) which denied the Assembly rights over Maori lands before title had been extinguished.[37] Swainson argued that the Crown was *in loco parentis* to the Maori people and would break faith with them under the treaty by allowing the Act to pass. He noted a recent comment from Newcastle that 'the course of the Government should be regulated with a view to the expectations which the Maori have been allowed to base on the Treaty of Waitangi'.[38] No one attempted to answer this objection; the legislation was clearly in defiance of Newcastle's demand.

Whitaker maintained that the right to confiscate 'for public works' was part of the rights of sovereignty ceded by the treaty; Maori, as British subjects 'in rebellion', had no right of compensation. He cited legal opinions in justification.[39] To silence critics who might claim that Maori were *not* British subjects – and thus not 'rebels' – he placed Maori in a dangerous position beyond the protection of British law. He cited Vattel who propounded the principle that if one party to a treaty violated it then the other party was discharged from all obligations.[40] Whitaker was out to make the law fit the need and, as he well knew, he had the backing of the Assembly. The New Zealand Settlements Act did not include a clause reserving it for the Royal Assent, as required for legislation of that nature; it could take effect immediately. As Sewell observed, the imperial government might object, but distance would prevent effective interference. If the deed of confiscation were carried out, it would be too late to withdraw, so Whitaker chanced it.[41]

Sewell, silent in the debate, within weeks launched an attack by publishing an open letter to his English patron, Lord Lyttelton.[42] He aimed to embarrass the New Zealand government and to prod the English political and moral conscience. In the crisis of the 1860s, Sewell perceived that New Zealand stood at the crossroads.

The essential question to be resolved was 'what are the respective rights and obligations of two races placed in political relation to each other'.[43] Beyond any doubt, he reasoned, the treaty had reserved to Maori their full territorial rights; but as to the cession of 'kawanatanga, the governorship – or sovereignty', Maori must have understood that they would retain 'the right of self-government over their internal affairs'. The acknowledgement of sovereignty by the Maori was 'the same ... as in the case of the American Indians.... It carried with it the exclusive right of pre-emption over their lands, and the exclusion of interference of foreign nations'. From this he argued that the Crown had limited rights of authority over the Maori. It did not have the right to inflict penalties unjustly and prematurely, as in the case of confiscation for so-called rebellion.[44] At most, the Crown had a right to extend roads through Maori territory, but compensation was obligatory and Maori consent desirable. The sovereign power, moreover, rested with the imperial executive and not with the New Zealand government.

Thus far Sewell's assessment of relative sovereign rights within the country came close to Maori understanding of rights confirmed in the treaty. Yet he went on to assume that in New Zealand the treaty had imposed a duty on the Crown gradually to extend British law over the Maori and that Maori self-government would be temporary, an understanding certainly not conveyed in the guarantee of rangatiratanga. Sewell's argument represented the humanitarian, gradualist approach to relations with the Maori to whom the Crown stood as guardian. At most, this allowed Maori the exercise of limited and temporary internal sovereign rights. It was at least preferable to Whitaker's precipitate application of an absolute Crown authority.[45]

The effect of the New Zealand Settlements Act on Maori land, Sewell felt, constituted a 'revolution'. He knew Whitaker's legal opinion in some detail from a disagreement with him earlier in 1863 on the land issue. Whitaker's view was that Maori lands were 'Demesne lands of the Crown', subject only to occupation and use by the Maori; that Maori land title was not 'cognizable' in a Court of Law, and could be overridden by an Act of the colonial legislature; that an imperial treaty was not, as American jurists held, a fundamental part of the law of the colony limiting the legislature's power; that in a case of conflict between the two, a positive enactment of the colonial legislature would prevail over the terms of the treaty. Sewell dissented from these 'doctrines' with the comment that if they could be maintained, 'the territorial rights of the Natives are held upon a slender tenure'. This, unfortunately, proved to be the case.

The Assembly was not as ready to accept the Suppression of Rebellion Act. This Act authorised the governor to arrest and detain indefinitely any persons suspected of complicity in the 'rebellion'. Trial by court martial and suspension of habeas corpus were allowed. Punishment of offenders might be death, penal servitude, or corporal punishment such as whipping. It was difficult to convince members that such extreme measures were needed, and that they should apply throughout the whole country and (in theory at least) to both races. Some members saw the Act as potentially an interference with their civil liberties.[46] Although the measure passed, the voting indicated a small but strong opposition. Similarly, there was opposition to the Loan Act; £3 million was sought to cover the costs of confiscation and the war. South Island members resented charging war costs to the colony at large, but since the Act complemented the other legislation it was let pass.

Whitaker had gambled on a favourable response from the Colonial Office and this paid off; the three Acts of 1863 were not disallowed.[47] Cardwell, who had just taken over from Newcastle, was concerned to reduce the British commitment, and Grey convinced him that confiscation might achieve this by giving Maori a 'short, sharp shock', rapidly bringing the war to an end. Cardwell also hoped that Grey would restrain the Whitaker–Fox Ministry. Several conditions were made: that the New Zealand Settlements Act be limited to two years, that confiscation be carried out only if an attempt to persuade Maori to cede land failed, and that adequate provisions would be made to treat the Maori fairly. To hasten British abdication of responsibility, Cardwell agreed to a modified loan arrangement, but made it clear that the colony must accept a reduction and eventual withdrawal of British troops. It would have to plan for its own defence and bear the cost.

Before this advice reached New Zealand, moves had begun to establish military settlements in the Waikato and at Tauranga on confiscated land. An official confiscation proclamation was issued in December 1864.[48] Cardwell's provisos were ignored. Nearly 3¼ million acres were confiscated in the Waikato, Bay of Plenty and Taranaki. Though about half of this area was subsequently paid for or returned to Maori ownership, the confiscation fell unfairly on many Maori.[49] Waikato lost almost all their lands, while Ngati Maniapoto territory went untouched; Ngati Haua, Tamihana's tribe, lost a section of their land as did Ngai Te Rangi at Tauranga. Both friendly Maori and 'rebels' were penalised. The King and his followers, virtually homeless, retreated into Ngati Maniapoto lands where they could never be more than guests. This breach of the treaty, as it came to be seen by most Maori, left a permanent legacy of bitterness.

Meanwhile, a controversy was raging over some 200 Maori prisoners taken in various engagements. Again, the question of Maori rights under the treaty was involved. Whitaker and Fox contemplated bringing charges of high treason against the prisoners, or at least against a selected few, but could not decide whether the cases should be heard before the Supreme Court or by court martial under the Suppression of Rebellion Act. Sewell tried to reason with them, suggesting that when Maori were capable of understanding moral distinctions, they should be made amenable to British law, but where they could not understand the moral guilt, as with treason, it would be 'cruelty' to punish them. Again, Sewell took his stand on American legal decisions involving the Indians, arguing that it was absurd to give sudden effect to rights of sovereignty over internal affairs when differing laws and customs were involved.[50]

While Grey and the ministry haggled, and Whitaker had second thoughts about using the Suppression of Rebellion Act, the prisoners remained in confinement for months, first on an old coal hulk in Auckland Harbour and then on Grey's island home at Kawau near Auckland. They escaped in September 1864, making their way back to the Waikato. Grey and his ministers indulged in mutual recriminations, leaving the status of the Maori people still an open question.

The drift of opinion toward imposing on Maori the responsibilities (and penalties) of British subjects went further under the next ministry, led by Frederick Weld from September 1864. Sewell was once more Attorney-General. It was a ministry devoid of Auckland men; Weld and Sewell were determined to shift the capital to Wellington, hoping that wiser counsels might prevail if the Assembly were distanced from the war.[51]

Sewell hoped for moderation in government dealings with the Maori but it was immediately evident that Weld intended to take a no-nonsense approach. As Stafford's Native Minister for eight months in 1860–61, he had become firmly convinced that the Waitara issue was a question of sovereignty and not a land quarrel as Martin and the humanitarian lobby argued. Resolutions to this effect were passed, with Weld's persuasion, during the 1863 session of the Domett Ministry. Weld's main contention was that sovereignty had been largely nominal and had not been put fully into effect by actions in New Zealand; the remedy was to enforce government authority firmly, yet with justice.[52] He accepted the position of premier in 1864 with this end in view. A person of considerable integrity, Weld perceived no contradiction in his attitudes towards the Maori. He had no grasp of the complex Maori values relating to land. To his way of thinking, Maori interests could best be served by individualisation of title, secure property ownership and growth towards political enfranchisement – attitudes liberal for their time, but nevertheless serviceable to settler interests.[53]

When Weld took office in 1864 his aim was full control of Maori affairs. British troops were to be withdrawn, because, as long as they remained, responsibility for Maori affairs had to be shared between Grey and the ministry – a system of 'double government' that led to conflict.[54] Two pressing issues faced the new premier: how to settle confiscation and how to end the war. Several measures were quickly passed. An amendment to the New Zealand Settlements Act extended the duration of the original Act to December 1865 and left it open for further extension.[55] Weld was flexing the muscle of colonial independence. This legislation failed to meet any of Cardwell's requirements. Weld and Grey reached a decision on the Waikato confiscations and a proclamation was issued. A Public Works Lands Act was hurried through to give the government authority to make Taranaki habitable for settlers, by making a road between Wanganui and

New Plymouth through territory dominated by hostile Ngati Ruanui. The Act authorised the taking of Maori land, with compensation only where title derived from the Crown – another form of confiscation. Weld's lack of sympathy for Maori sensitivities was clear in his rough treatment of one objection – that the Act was an infringement of the treaty. In yielding sovereign rights, he asserted, Maori had given the government power to take land for roads, 'even ... a road through a graveyard'.[56]

By early 1865, Weld's line of policy was clear. Those Maori who wanted peace would be treated with moderation; those who resisted would be 'pacified' so that settlement could proceed. By mid-1865 even the cautious Sewell, disheartened by events, was prepared to overlook the fact that there was a contradiction in a policy which aimed to make peace by waging war.[57] That year, Weld's uncompromising attitude led to an expansion of the war. On the west coast, near Wanganui, operations began to open up Taranaki, with colonial forces playing a more prominent part. On the east coast, where sporadic fighting in 1864 had disturbed areas largely uninhabited by settlers, a new front was opened up following the murder of the missionary Carl Volkner at Opotiki in March 1865. Under the direction of Donald McLean, now Superintendent of Hawke's Bay, a colonial force of settlers and 'friendly' Maori was organised to put down disturbances and seek out Volkner's murderers. Weld's instructions to McLean gave him wide discretionary powers and revealed a determination to treat 'rebels', many of them Pai Marire adherents, with greater ruthlessness.[58]

In Taranaki, a punitive campaign in which both innocent and insurgent Maori suffered the destruction of their dwellings and cultivations, created a bitterness towards the government as lasting as that already caused in the Waikato. The subsequent confiscation of the entire coastal strip of the province dispossessed large numbers of Maori. As in the Waikato, many Taranaki Maori considered the moves a breach of the treaty; in the latter part of the 1860s even Maori not directly involved in confiscation agreed. Such a serious attack on the treaty made many Maori feel that the race as a whole must be involved in the consequences.

In the meantime, Weld's aim of doing away with 'double government' and securing full control over Maori affairs was running into trouble. The shift of the capital to Wellington early in 1865 produced treble government. Although the government had begun work in Wellington in early 1865, Grey remained in Auckland for some time, while General Cameron, commanding the British troops, was at Wanganui. Communications between the three were difficult and the divided authority structure did not encourage firm decision-making and policy implementation. The Weld ministers became disappointed with Cameron and distrustful of Grey. Grey clashed with Cameron over their fields of responsibility and took the unusual step of joining battle with the Maori himself. Cameron was not at ease with either Grey or the ministry. All three parties had to take account also of the authority of the British government.

Sections of opinion in Canterbury and Otago, resentful of war expenditure, voiced a preference for a divided colony with responsible government only in the south and perhaps at Wellington. At the same time, a powerful Auckland lobby sought reversion of that province to Crown Colony control, with Grey acting as a kind of 'dictator' in association with the provincial authorities. Hard-nosed colonial politicians finally came to the conclusion that separation would not improve the colony's financial credit-rating and the matter was dropped.[59]

The Auckland lobby may have got wind of a suggestion by Sewell and Sir William Martin that would have created semi-autonomous Maori districts in the centre of the North Island, outside Auckland's jurisdiction.[60] Sewell believed that the King movement was still upholding independent rights, and concluded, correctly, that the problem of sovereignty had not been solved.[61] The King was issuing his own war 'honours', King supporters were refusing to accept confiscation boundaries recently defined, and there was strong objection to further road-making – 'this sap of the Governor'.

As an alternative, FitzGerald proposed a new Maori Provinces Bill, based on the premise that a degree of Maori independence should be tolerated until British law was fully accepted. As such, it was not a recognition of independent Maori rights. It encountered such strong opposition that it had to be dropped.[62] Settler self-interest was a significant factor operating against the toleration of a separate Maori authority.

With the issues of sovereignty and Maori resistance uppermost in 1865, the position of Native Minister was a critical one. Weld appointed first Walter Mantell and then James FitzGerald, both known for their Maori sympathies. During Mantell's term from December 1864 to July 1865, the treaty was scrutinised closely. Until then, the several original treaty sheets seem to have been ignored. After a narrow escape from fire in 1841, they had been kept in an iron safe in the Colonial Secretary's office, moving from Auckland to Wellington with the shift of government. In early July 1865, William Baker of the Native Department completed brief notes on the treaty signing, but his notes were mainly a short summary of the official reports.[63] He also attempted (unsuccessfully) to make an accurate listing of chiefs who had signed.

Mantell, administrative head of Native Affairs as well as Minister, was steadily losing confidence in the Weld Ministry's commitment to improve the Maori situation. He evidently wanted to clarify what Maori rights were under the treaty and the extent of Maori commitment. Mantell had been personally involved since the 1840s in government dealings with Ngai Tahu lands in the South Island, trying unsuccessfully to ensure justice for the Maori. He had long been convinced that unless the government really meant to honour its treaty pledges and confer the benefits of British subjects on Maori, it would be better to drop the pretence of talking about one people. He was disturbed that Sewell's advocacy of a degree of separation for the Maori modified their status as British subjects. This would nullify the treaty, whereas the crucial point had been the promise to confer the rights of British subjects on the Maori as well as pledging that native title would be respected.[64]

By the middle of 1865 Mantell was distressed that Weld was prepared to allow Dunedin's Princes Street Maori reserve to be taken over arbitrarily by the Otago Provincial Council. Mantell had made the reserve himself in 1853 as a landing place and central market for local Maori. If the Weld government sacrificed the land, now greatly increased in value, to settler interests, Mantell feared that his credibility among Maori as Native Minister would be undermined. Before the 1865 parliamentary session opened in late July he resigned. His main reason was the government's crooked dealing with the reserve, but he also had reservations about Weld's Maori policy generally and about proposed legislation for 1865 which tended towards separatism and the discriminatory treatment of Maori people. This trend, Mantell feared, would weaken Maori claims for equality before the law, as promised in the treaty.[65]

Mantell called for a copy of Baker's listing of signatories to the treaty and his annotations to be laid on the table of the House.[66] A week later, other members, seeing the relevance of the request, pushed the matter further. The Assembly requested that there be laid on the table of the House 'the original Treaty of Waitangi, with all the signatures attached thereto, and any contemporaneous papers explanatory of it', held by the government. Comments passed in debate indicate that members were considering carefully the discrepancies between the Maori and English treaty text and the implications of Maori commitment to honour the agreement. Hugh Carleton, Henry Williams's son-in-law, emphasised that the Maori text showed clearly that the full rights of chieftainship had been guaranteed, and that this had an important bearing on government relations with the Maori. They had signed a treaty in the Maori language; some members felt that they should be bound by what they had actually signed. Carleton, however, took care to note that though one text must have been written first, neither was supposed, at the time, to have precedence.[67] And there the matter rested.

In the latter half of 1865, efforts to subjugate the Maori had intensified. Moderation was now represented in the Assembly by FitzGerald, who succeeded Mantell. He was chosen as much for his prestige with the Maori people, which the government hoped to turn to good account, as for his abilities. Both as a Christchurch newspaper editor and as a parliamentarian, he publicly espoused an idealistic and egalitarian relationship between Maori and Pakeha. He had been so outspoken in support of Maori rights in the past that his appointment as Native Minister was greeted with consternation by many in the Assembly. But could the visionary come up with practical policy?[68] In the midst of the war tensions of 1862, FitzGerald had moved resolutions affirming 'entire amalgamation . . . into one united people' and claiming for the Maori people full and equal enjoyment of civil and political rights. The treaty of Waitangi had made New Zealand different from other countries, FitzGerald had argued at that time.[69] This in fact embodied an element of settler self-interest, for he reasoned that only in the 'fusion' of the two races under the one law could there be safety for both. FitzGerald's attitudes were essentially paternal. He could show liberality and yet, at times, an appalling insensitivity to Maori grievances (such as the South Island claims) and an impatience bordering on vindictiveness when Maori actions thwarted his idealistic notions.

FitzGerald's inconsistencies, coupled with Weld's no-nonsense approach, produced a mixed bag of legislation in 1865. Humanitarian vision was not absent, but Weld's desire to subjugate the Maori was the dominant theme. FitzGerald did not prove the 'wild' visionary in office that many had feared. Nevertheless, when he launched the 1865 legislation in August, he admitted that the war was one of sovereignty in which both sides had mixed motives; on the settler side, there was greed for land and the 'incidental advantages' of a war. Where coercion by force had failed, he believed that the coercion of law might succeed; it was to be a 'policy of suppression ... and a liberal and a generous policy' at the same time.[70] As FitzGerald explained it:

> Two rules are deeply fixed in my mind. 1. To expect men to respect law who don't enjoy it is absurd. 2. To try and govern a folk by our courts and at the same time to say that our courts shall take no cognisance of *their property* is amazing folly. Two-thirds of the Northern Island is held under a tenure which is ignored by our law. Is it *possible* to govern any people by a law which does not recognise their estate in land?

> I blame no man for the past, but for the future I take this as my guide that a people cannot be governed by a law which pretends to be powerless to deal with their property; and that one race cannot govern another as a pariah class – make laws for them, and so [*sic*] on ignoring their right to partake in the making of those laws.

> You may mock me as to Maoris sitting in parliament. My dear Friend, I am not a fool nor attribute to political forms mysterious virtues, but I know all that the sitting in parliament brings in its train and I say that ignore tenure to land and ignore the sitting in parliament and all that belongs thereto and the alternative is war, extermination to the weaker race and financial disaster to the stronger.

FitzGerald was touching on the financial mess that the war had caused in the colony, a problem that dogged the Weld Ministry and continued for some years. Shrewdly, he perceived that financial constraints could possibly be a powerful moderating factor, and so, he concluded, 'if men will not do right for right's sake they are made to do so by the punishments vice invokes'.[71]

FitzGerald's approach was influenced by Weld's ideas of firmness and justice in dealing with the Maori. Weld had moved to repeal the 1863 Suppression of Rebellion Act immediately on taking office in 1864, considering it offensive and a blight on the New Zealand Statute Book. (It was due to lapse anyway and was said to have been a 'dead letter'.) In its place, an Act of Indemnity absolved from responsibility those who, during the war, had committed acts under government direction for which the law might normally hold them accountable. Weld's Attorney–General, Sewell, thought that the distinction between the earlier legislation and the new Act was significant. The Suppression of Rebellion Act was 'a kind of plenary indulgence beforehand for violence or excesses of any kind or degree committed under colour of authority' whereas the new Act was 'a Constitutional form of absolution for things done under special emergencies'. The Act nevertheless gave absolution for acts of violence against Maori at a time when the distinction between crime and acts of war was not always clearly drawn; a second Act was passed the following year.[72]

To suppress crime committed by Maori, FitzGerald introduced the Outlying Districts Police Bill. In Maori districts, where crimes had been committed against civilians, the onus was placed on chiefs to surrender culprits such as murderers; failure to do so made the district liable to land forfeiture. Sewell thought that, 'judiciously used', the measure might bring law to areas such as Opotiki where the missionary Carl Volkner had been murdered a few months earlier. Not surprisingly, the Bill was opposed by Mantell and William Martin, and condemned by the Colonial Office as dangerously close to an outright confiscation Act and allowing too much licence to punish unjustly.[73]

The Weld Ministry took a hard line on confiscation. The time limit was extended to December 1867.[74] New and more extensive confiscations were proclaimed in Taranaki; settler interests had prevailed. Neither Sewell nor FitzGerald was perturbed about these moves, which earlier might have sparked their opposition. Even the moderate, humanitarian wing of the government had become inclined to let the end justify the means. As critics of the Weld government predicted, these measures would lead to further fighting before peace could be restored.

Meantime, the Assembly, having always been averse to separate Maori institutions or districts, took a positive step towards the alternative – effective Maori enfranchisement. The Native Commission Act enabled the governor to convene an assembly of chiefs to sound Maori opinion on the best means of introducing Maori parliamentary representation. FitzGerald carefully avoided requiring allegiance to the Crown from participants; the assembly was to be a consultative and not a law-making body. The measure was a halfway house; because it did not commit the government to anything definite, members were able to agree to it. Nevertheless, that agreement accepted the principle that Maori should be incorporated into the governing structure. This was a positive vote in favour of 'amalgamation' which some members saw as a Maori right but which most simply accepted as inevitable. The dissenting voice of Colenso, prominent at the 1840 Waitangi meeting and now member for Napier, was out of place when he suggested an alternative, that Maori meet annually with the governor, 'the Great Father, as the American Indians met with the President of America'.[75]

That Maori were British subjects, as the Waitangi treaty stated, was a principle recognised in the Native Commission Act, but FitzGerald wanted it asserted beyond all doubt. His Native Rights

Act of 1865 incorporated this assertion. The law was to be extended to Maori so that they could bring cases involving their persons or property, especially land, before the Supreme Court. The measure reflected the Native Minister's idealistic approach, but he was forced to admit that Maori land ownership would have to be determined by the Native Land Court before it could be considered by the ordinary law courts. Whether the Supreme Court could overrule the Land Court decisions, FitzGerald thought should be left to the law profession to 'settle or dispute'.[76]

To members, however, this was a piece of fine theory that could not be implemented. 'It was calculated,' said J.C. Richmond, 'to cause some disappointment' among the Maori. Although many government people thought it was a timely public declaration to the Maori race about their rights, Richmond's prediction was correct. The Supreme Court consistently refused to reconsider Land Court decisions and could be resorted to effectively only after a Land Court decision.[77] In practice, the Act was not the protective instrument that FitzGerald desired. The Assembly willingly accepted the principle that Maori were British subjects, and subsequently enforced obligations on them when it suited. FitzGerald's attempt to give legislative recognition to the treaty's third article turned out to be something of a two-edged sword.

An integral part of FitzGerald's policy in 1865 was a new Native Lands Act. It supplanted the 1862 Act (and an 1864 amendment), but was essentially the same in principle: Maori land ownership was to be determined so that customary title could be extinguished and the land brought within the law.[78] Some important changes in procedure were made, however. The 1862 Act had been brought into operation only north of Auckland. The Court was operating well there, with knowledgeable Maori leaders playing a key role. In a runanga situation, there was a fair chance that accurate evidence would be given to determine ownership. William Martin favoured the continuation of this system and tendered his advice to the Weld government at some length, although he feared it would be disregarded.

Decisions had already been made. Weld and Mantell had appointed Francis Dart Fenton as Chief Judge of the Land Court in early 1865 and had given him a free hand to organise a new system. The runanga committee of inquiry was abandoned and a court was established along more formal lines reminiscent of the Supreme Court. Maori assessors were still to assist the judge, but the new procedures of witnesses and formal evidence had their origins in European practice and were foreign to Maori usage. The Court was to award a certificate of title once ownership had been determined. The 1865 Act sanctioned these arrangements and gave the Court new powers of deciding succession where Maori owners died intestate.[79]

While the debates on the first Native Lands Act of 1862 revealed a brutal settler bias against Maori people and a determination to circumvent the treaty's land guarantee, the 1865 debates were quiet affairs. Settler pressures on the legislature were, however, considerable. Landed interests in the Assembly were complaining about a lack of action. Weld, convinced that the treaty should never have recognised Maori land ownership so extensively, wanted to see Maori land holding rapidly reduced.[80]

FitzGerald was forced to compromise: the Act was 'a medium course between those who dreaded the land-purchases being put into common operation, and those who were in favour of the sale of lands'.[81] The latter got the best of the bargain. Under the Act's provisions, any one Maori with a claim to a particular block could initiate investigation of title before the Court, thus forcing an entire tribe to defend their rights. A tribe as a whole was not to be granted certificate of title unless the block was larger than 5,000 acres, a provision that in practice was seldom used. In the initial operation of the Act, it was normal to specify ten chiefs in whom title could be vested. In theory, these ten were to act as trustees for the tribe but in practice they were legally able to alienate their interest. The legislators had ignored cautious counsels: Martin's recommendations that land, after determination of title, should be sold by public auction and that some of the proceeds be compulsorily invested, were not included in the Act; nor was Fenton's suggestion that land dealings before title definition should be made not only invalid but illegal. Leases were no longer a contravention of the law, as they were under Grey's 1846 Native Land Purchase Ordinance.

The 1865 Native Lands Act effectively severed the threads of Crown protection and nullified the treaty's second article. With the abandonment of Crown pre-emption, the way was opened for settlers to force Maori to relinquish their land. From the Maori point of view, pre-emption had not always worked to their advantage, but it had served as some kind of safeguard against the alienation of land. The new Act introduced revolutionary change. Coupled with the move to establish Maori political representation, it was 'essentially the abandonment of the system of protectorate or dry-nursing'.[82] 'Amalgamation' and equality of rights were now the justification for encouraging a rapid 'Europeanisation' of land. It was often claimed that the policy was in the best interests of the Maori race but, as with the former protective policy, it could be made to operate to settler advantage.

If there was any truth in FitzGerald's claims that the 1865 policy was 'liberal and generous' as well as being an assertion of sovereignty by force, Maori could scarcely be expected to see things in the same light. Wiremu Tamihana Tarapipipi was wary of government overtures in the Weld period. He laid down his arms in 1865, but he refused to have his loyalty to the government bought by bribes of land grants. He held consistently to the argument that the Queen and the King could both stand, with the law as the unifying factor. But his confidence in achieving justice through lawful means was greatly shaken by the Waikato confiscations. In 1865 and 1866 he petitioned the Queen and the New Zealand parliament. The 1865 petition noted that, under the Waitangi covenant, Maori understood that they retained their rangatiratanga and their mana but the confiscations appeared to violate this. Tamihana asked for a commission of inquiry to be appointed by the Queen. His cry was for reassertion of the Queen's mana – 'give us back our land, our chieftainship, and our mana of which the colonists and the Governor are seeking to deprive us'.[83] He asked the Assembly to return all confiscated Waikato lands. After a heated debate, the Assembly agreed grudgingly to receive his petition as a gesture of recognition that Maori had the rights of British subjects, but nothing came of it. Tamihana came to the conclusion that he was merely being passed from one to another – from governor, to Assembly, to Queen – in a hopeless merry-go-round of political buck-passing.[84] With the full realisation of the magnitude of confiscation weighing heavily upon him, he returned to Waikato.

The Weld Ministry fell in October 1865. In spite of professed intentions of ending the war and gaining the confidence of the Maori people, they had not succeeded. General Cameron had been replaced by the hard-line General Chute in the middle of the year and his ruthless Taranaki campaign was pushed to its conclusion. On the East Coast, fighting continued. When a general amnesty was announced in early September, it did little to restore Maori confidence and offended Europeans by freeing some Maori who had already been brought to trial and convicted. Facing strong opposition in the Assembly over finance and the separation issue, Weld resigned.[85] No one expected the incoming premier, Stafford, to survive for long, but he saw out a three-year term, more because the annual turnover of ministries in the previous five years was finally recognised as inimical to the country's interests than from any particular talent in governing.

The Stafford Ministry had nothing new to offer in the field of Maori affairs. As one historian puts it, the ministry comprised 'untried non-entities' with a 'policy of negatives'.[86] In effect, Maori would be left alone unless 'outrages' were committed. In 1868, the government had its hands full with Titokowaru on the west coast and Te Kooti inland from Poverty Bay. Severe as some of this fighting was, no one doubted that government authority would eventually be established. Yet New Zealand's resources were being stretched to the limit; by the end of the decade there was a widespread yearning for an abiding peace.

Sir George Bowen replaced Grey as governor in February 1868. The Colonial Office had resolved that its commitment in New Zealand would be more quickly ended by ridding itself of the devious Grey whose sympathies had increasingly been on the side of the settlers. Bowen brought a different approach. As he reflected later, it seemed 'more politic and humane' to outlive the Maori troubles than to fight them.[87] After 1867, the remaining British troops were gradually withdrawn and the Armed Constabulary, full-time colonial volunteers, took their place. The last British forces pulled out in February 1870.

When the Fox Ministry took over in mid-1869, the policy of 'amalgamation' was firmly established. A Maori Representation Act in 1867 had made allowance for four Maori members to sit in the House and, with the later addition of Maori to the Legislative Council, gave the race the political representation that FitzGerald had determined upon in 1865. Maori were entitled to sit on juries in certain circumstances; generally the Maori people were subject to the law administered by European magistrates and judges. But some allowance was made for differences in the Maori situation. Special provision was introduced for Maori education, schools that would lead ultimately to an English-speaking population. Maori children were soon to enter the colony's ordinary primary schools too. The Native Department, which had survived through the 1860s, was re-organised and allowed to continue, with Donald McLean as Native Minister. With flexible and conciliatory tactics, he gradually brought the troubled districts to a more settled state. It was a return to a gradualist approach, a recognition by McLean that sovereignty had either not been properly interpreted to Maori in 1840 or had not yet been fully accepted by them.[88]

As late as 1869, there had been a tussle between the New Zealand and British authorities over the status of Maori. Should disaffected Maori be treated as belligerents or rebels? Were they to be considered as aliens in foreign warfare or as British subjects in rebellion? The opinion of New Zealand's Attorney-General, that they were rebels (and therefore liable to have a price put on their heads), ran counter to the argument of the Secretary of State for Colonies that the normal courtesies of warfare should apply. For New Zealand, the British stand, with its explicit censure of colonial practice, was like a red rag to a bull.[89] Maori status had been firmly defined by the Weld Ministry: Maori were British subjects and were to be treated accordingly. The storm raised by this question late in the 1860s demonstrated that New Zealand had travelled far along the path of consolidating a national identity of interests that differed from those of the Motherland. In most respects, those interests were selfishly Eurocentric, but a place had at least been found for the Maori people within the mainstream of colonial development. That this had its price, however, was shortly to be spelt out.

Mantell, now in the Legislative Council, was prompted by events in 1869 to take up the treaty question again. His interest was aroused by a question before the House: who owned the foreshore adjacent to Maori land? The question, far more complicated than it seemed at first sight, concerned gold-mining rights to the Thames sea beach. To determine Maori rights in relation to those of the Crown, Mantell asked that a 'literal copy of the original Treaty of Waitangi in Maori', together with William Baker's notes made in 1865, be tabled as a preliminary step to seeking a legal opinion on Maori rights. A week later, Mantell proposed a new motion expanding on his first request, that there be tabled and printed 'a copy of the English version of the Treaty of Waitangi, as printed by authority of the Government in 1840, and a careful translation thereof into Maori; also, a literal translation into English of the original Treaty, already ordered to be laid on the table; also, if procurable, a copy of such original draft in English as may have been prepared for translation by Governor Hobson or by his authority'. Baker's notes and his listing of signatories were also requested.[90]

Although the Colonial Secretary, William Gisborne, doubted if some of these documents could be found, Mantell was particularly insistent that a translation of the English text into Maori should be made, since the original was 'in execrable Maori'. In the new translation the original 1840 rendering of 'the rights and powers of sovereignty' by 'kawanatanga' (governorship) became 'nga tikanga me nga mana katoa o te Rangatiratanga' – all the customary powers and mana of chieftainship. The second article, too, was different. The 'possession', originally rendered as 'rangatiratanga' (chieftainship), became 'tuturutanga' (absolute guarantee).

This was not merely a new translation; it was a different treaty. Whatever understanding the British negotiators might have intended to convey in 1840, the Maori treaty text had certainly not conveyed to Maori an all-embracing relinquishment of Maori rights. When the new Maori text, together with the other documents requested, was tabled, the Colonial Secretary, William Gisborne, noted that the 'original draft in English' could not be found either in the Native Office or the Colonial Secretary's office. The translation, then, must have been made from the printed English version.[91]

The new Maori text made by a Native Department translator, T.E. Young,[92] was in line with government thinking. In 1869, government and public attitudes were harsher towards Maori generally. Maori had to be struck with the 'full force' of their position as British subjects and not allowed to escape the consequences of their actions by pleading ignorance. This was evident in the latter half of 1869 as batches of Maori, followers of Te Kooti and Titokowaru, were tried for high treason (rather than murder) under the Summary Trials in Disturbed Districts Act. About 100 Maori were sentenced to death although, with two exceptions, the sentences were commuted to imprisonment.[93]

Against this background, with its strong element of vindictive anti-Maori feeling, it was hardly surprising that Mantell was anxious that Maori rights should be clarified. The new translation had spelt out the official resolve to impose government supremacy and Mantell no doubt hoped that Maori would grasp its implications. The printing of the new Maori translation, with the other material, at least made public the understanding of the treaty that the government wished to promote. With Maori members sitting in parliament, awareness of the change probably moved into the Maori community gradually.

As far as it is possible to identify a particular point in time when events and political decisions led New Zealand to adopt one line of policy in Maori affairs and to reject another, then Weld's term of office and the principles of amalgamation then confirmed has a strong claim. Under Weld and FitzGerald colonial cries for independence had taken on a new note. Neither Weld's self-reliant policy nor FitzGerald's assertions of liberality derived entirely from events in the colony, however. Both owed a good deal to the two men's sensitivity to British criticism of the prosecution of the war. In the British parliament and the British press during the

1860s, comments on the New Zealand government's treatment of the Maori had been often hostile and scathing.[94] London's major newspapers, especially *The Times*, shifted from a guarded tolerance of Britain's commitment in New Zealand to an increasingly critical questioning of the war, seen now as serving settler interests.

The humanitarian lobby, too, was vocal. When CMS efforts to defend the Maori lapsed in the early 1860s, the Aborigines Protection Society took up the cause with vigour, sponsoring several publications on the New Zealand situation – 'exceptional in the modern history of colonization' because of the treaty, an 1864 tract reminded readers.[95] The Society appealed to Grey to modify the confiscations, openly expressing its sympathy for the Maori people; its secretary, F.W. Chesson, entered into public debate with William Fox in the London press. There is no evidence of substantial change in colonial attitudes but it was galling and uncomfortable to colonial politicians to see the adverse press comment which the government's London agent sent regularly to the colony.[96]

Yet embarrassment over censure from abroad is not by itself a satisfactory reason to explain changes in colonial attitudes to Maori rights in the 1860s. That thread of idealism, present in the treaty-making, was still evident. Even in the midst of war and outrage, amalgamation was still seen as possible. Some thought it a paradox of New Zealand history that two races who held each other in high esteem should have been driven to fighting. To many thoughtful settlers it was obvious that a sector of Maori society had remained good friends of the Pakeha throughout the war; even Maori in resistance had often enough earned respect. The dilemma, however, was how to get Maori to accept what settlers saw as the inevitable solution – a full acceptance of the Crown's sovereign rights, with all the responsibilities this entailed. Various shades of political opinion on Maori rights had come together on this one point – that if force failed, then law must succeed in achieving the desired supremacy.

Maori were not quick to accept that a complete submission to sovereignty might mean a relinquishment of their mana of chieftainship. This was a new, retrospective interpretation of the treaty. It was also some time before Maori fully comprehended the implications of the transfer of responsibility in Maori affairs from the British to the New Zealand government. It was inconceivable to them that both the Queen and her parliament had washed their hands of the Waitangi covenant. But they had.

Chapter Nine

THE QUEST FOR LOST RIGHTS

As the structure of a new colonial society emerged in a burst of immigration and development after 1870, the treaty receded from settler consciousness. Busby's fight to have his early land claims recognised had helped to keep the treaty intermittently in public view, but in 1869 his claims were finally settled. A few years later, other old settlers from the pre-1840 period voiced a last protest. Resenting the restricted land holdings allocated to them in the early claims investigations, they petitioned the government for redress, but without success.[1] For the new society at large, with little knowledge of early New Zealand, the treaty was now largely irrelevant, a part of the country's history.

The government did not want the treaty resurrected; the growth in the non-Maori population, surpassing the Maori population before 1860, had made it feasible to argue that New Zealand was a British colony by virtue of its occupation. Pakeha numbered 256,393 in 1871 and would continue to increase, whereas Maori totalled only some 45,470 in 1874 and were declining steadily.[2] The prospect of a country with only a few Maori survivors no doubt encouraged the view that the treaty had served its purpose. Yet the treaty could not be completely ignored; difficulties over Maori land were enmeshed in the land guarantee. Moreover, when Maori protest increased in the late 1870s and 1880s the government was forced to discuss the 1840 agreement publicly. Government statements seldom praised the treaty; they disparaged it, or insisted that the contract bound Maori to obey the law. It was a far cry from the ideals expressed at Waitangi.

For the Maori people, however, the treaty became more relevant than ever after 1870. Government jurisdiction and Pakeha settlement began to touch the most remote Maori villages, providing Maori with a common cause and partly overriding tribal divisions. Whether or not tribes had signed the treaty, the agreement increasingly became the touchstone for protest. Despite the fine words of governments, both British and colonial, treaty promises had not been fulfilled. Disappointed and frustrated, many Maori forged a unity of purpose, looking to the treaty as their support in conflicts with the government, now that warfare had failed. Maori grievances, diverse and sometimes confused, found kotahitanga (unity) in the treaty.

After the wars, the most serious attack on the vitality of Maori life stemmed from the Native Land Court set up under the Act of 1865. By the early 1870s, it was evident that the methods of the court, as they had evolved under the direction of Chief Judge Fenton, were adverse to Maori welfare. Maori were disturbed by the ease with which the land could be prised from their grasp. Crippling court charges, survey costs and additional expenses often encouraged sale to discharge debts. Although the 1873 Native Lands Act introduced some reforms, the safeguards and controls suggested by Donald McLean, William Martin and Edward Shortland (formerly Civil Commissioner and Native Secretary) were dismissed or neutralised. This Act slowed down alienation but, in spite of further amendments and legislation, Maori land holding continued to diminish. Government purchases, financed largely under the provision made by the Immigration and Public Works Act 1870, amounted to over 5 million acres between 1870 and 1892; by 1892 Maori retained only a little over a third of the North Island, nearly 11 million acres, of which 2½ million were leased to Pakeha.[3] The accompanying loss of Maori morale was great, if more difficult to measure.

In order to settle their difficulties and grievances over land, Maori were encouraged, officially and privately, to have recourse to the law, a suggestion vigorously taken up in the 1870s. Some cases dragged on for years as they passed through either the Native Land Court or the colony's usual judicial channels. In the 1880s, more than a thousand Maori petitions were presented to the General Assembly. The treaty figured prominently in many of these actions, indicating that it was an important point of reference for Maori.

Experience in the courts, however, demonstrated that the treaty afforded Maori little protection. The central Dunedin reserve was lost to Maori use through judicial and administrative manipulation in the 1860s. Reserves did not give Maori the expected benefits, because of complications of title and a culpable failure on the part of government to take effective steps to secure the land in Maori ownership.[4] One important case, in 1877, involved Wi Parata (a Legislative Councillor) and the Bishop of Wellington. For some time, efforts had been made to have a land grant revert to its former Maori owners because the terms of the original grant (that it be used for educational purposes) were not being fulfilled. This case was likely to call into question all similar religious, charitable and educational trusts in the colony, a point that had been drawn to the government's attention the previous year. In giving his decision, Chief Justice James Prendergast declared that the treaty was a legal 'nullity' because it had not been incorporated in domestic law. Prendergast's comment, which ignored Maori rights in favour of Pakeha interests, set a precedent for subsequent cases which cited the treaty.[5]

The failure of the country's ordinary law courts to recognise the treaty's land guarantee found a notable parallel in the Native Land Court's decisions on the Rangitikei–Manawatu purchase. According to Court use, the treaty was understood to have guaranteed ownership to the occupants of any given land area, as at the date of the treaty signing. The Rangitikei–Manawatu lands had been gained not long before by Ngati Raukawa through conquest from Ngati Apa, Rangitane and Muaupoko. In 1840 the conquered groups had been squeezed into the interior, but in the 1860s they began to sell their 'lost' lands to the Wellington Provincial Council. The Court, in a 'highly contentious judgement' in 1869, awarded most of the block to Ngati Apa on the ground that they were still resisting in 1840. The decision left Ngati Raukawa with little land, although concessions were subsequently negotiated. In a later judgement the Court held that Ngati Raukawa, having left their Waikato lands, had lost their rights there too; 'they were denied a place both in their homeland and the district they had conquered'.[6] This violation of the treaty's second article stirred Henry Williams's son, T.C. Williams, to protest in a pamphlet, *The Manawatu Purchase completed, the Treaty of Waitangi broken.*[7]

From the 1860s fishing and food-gathering rights confirmed by the treaty were also threatened. For the first twenty years or more of the colony, such rights were given some recognition by the government. The Protector of Aborigines had noted the significance of eel preserves. Such possessions were much prized, with right of access or transfer of rights often negotiated for.[8] In early land sales Maori fishing rights were sometimes specifically acknowledged. George Clarke (junior) reserved fishing places in Wanganui during the settlement of the New Zealand Company purchase there, and similar recognition was made in the South Island. But verbal agreements were more usual, and without a written or legal guarantee such assurances were whittled away.[9] In time, it seems to have been accepted that when land was alienated, all rights, including fishing rights, were transferred.

Maori also had to fight to retain fishing rights that were more or less independent of land – offshore, in foreshores, lakes and rivers. From the 1850s, harbour development raised questions about coastal ownership and use of the coast.[10] Regulations to control the taking of shellfish were particularly objectionable. So too were the drainage works in areas such as the Wairarapa Lake where Maori understood that their rights had been settled with the government in various negotiations.[11] Fishing and food-gathering were affected by the importation of foreign fish and by the introduction of game birds – pheasants, quail, swan, geese and other species – mainly in the 1860s. Protective legislation was an additional irritant to Maori people.[12] With these developments, Maori naturally looked to the treaty and scrutinised its terms with a new interest. Questions of sovereignty and land rights had been the most critical issues but now fisheries and forests were to figure in Maori protest.

In 1872, the treaty's fishing guarantee was further eroded when Prendergast, the Attorney-General, ruled that title to the lands below high-water mark rested with the Crown.[13] The decision emerged from a conflict of interest between companies seeking gold-mining rights on the Thames foreshore and Maori owners of adjacent land. Certain Ngati Maru hapu had rights to fish the mud-flats which were famous flounder grounds. As a government agent observed, Maori fishing rights to mud-flats and offshore had not been seriously questioned before. At Katikati Harbour, for instance, one tribe fished within the line of tide-rip, another outside it.[14] In the Thames case, the Shortland Beach Act provided for purchase below high-water mark, but payment was presented as compensation; it was not to be construed as a precedent for any further Maori claims to tidal land.[15] The Act, however, related to a specific piece of land and did not assert Crown prerogative to foreshore rights throughout New Zealand. Prendergast's 1872 ruling spelt this out.

From then on, the best that Maori could obtain was a special, though seldom exclusive, usage right to fisheries in specific instances. This was allowed for in the 1877 Fisheries Act and its later amendments and re-enactments. The Act dealt with salt and fresh water fisheries. Section eight referred to the treaty: 'Nothing in this Act contained shall be deemed to repeal, alter, or affect any of the provisions of the Treaty of Waitangi, or to take away, annul, or abridge any of the rights of the aboriginal natives to any fishery secured to them thereunder.'[16] In practice, this meant very little; unless some special enactment or provision was made, no fishing right could rest secure on the 'provisions' of the treaty alone. From time to time some allowance was made for Maori fishing rights, but this was small compensation for the loss of extensive rights understood to derive from the second article of the treaty. It was a policy of compromise. Customary Maori fishing needs could be tolerated, because they were destined to fall into disuse; amalgamation and a declining Maori population would carry New Zealand closer towards the attainment of that other Waitangi promise of one people under one law.

Maori also perceived dangers to their rights from government and local body works, the steady encroachment of settlement and the law. Seemingly innocent adjuncts to settlement, such works were a real or at least an imagined threat to Maori. They considered themselves penalised by local body rates, and seldom participated in local body elections or administration. Rates on roads were seen as contraventions of treaty rights, although Governor Bowen, on a 'progress' of the North Island in 1872, assured chiefs that their mana was not affected either by new roads or by the taxes.[17] The Public Works Acts of 1864 and 1876, with their provisions for taking land compulsorily for public development, were seen as in direct contravention of Maori rights.[18] And the building of the main trunk rail link through the centre of the North Island encountered strong Maori opposition that was only gradually whittled away by the government.[19] The 1880 Dog Tax Registration Act, designed to reduce the packs of uncontrolled, Maori-owned dogs that threatened sheep flocks, was resented by Maori as infringing individual rights, especially when dog tax inspectors attempted to collect fees in Maori villages.[20]

By the 1870s it was becoming clear to Maori that the extent of the treaty's protection was limited by court decisions, by various shady dealings and by legislation. Maori such as Wi Tako, who were well versed in Pakeha methods, quickly drew the lesson that Pakeha kept 'the body of the law' and gave Maori only 'the ghost of it'.[21] This was a conclusion that many Maori formed as their experience of settlement broadened. Sometimes Maori rights were infringed by sheer official incompetence, while in other cases there was official manipulation of administrative and judicial systems to Pakeha advantage. Sometimes the executive and administrative arms of government were in conflict over Maori issues, to the detriment of Maori welfare. Even under McLean, possibly the most sympathetic of the Native Ministers after the wars, there was an ambivalence, a disconcerting compromise of Pakeha and Maori interests, that inevitably disadvantaged Maori.[22]

Above all, it gradually became apparent that the treaty was being interpreted in a way that increasingly restricted the autonomous rights of the Maori. By the 1880s Maori were saying that their mana was passing away or had already been lost. This conclusion was arrived at only after a great deal of soul-searching and self-assessment in a series of Maori runanga. These would finally lead in the 1890s to a union of Maori identity under the treaty of Waitangi in the Kotahitanga movement.

The runanga, traditional gatherings to resolve issues, increased in frequency after the wars, both at hapu and tribal level. Occasions such as marriages and funerals were used as opportunities for extended debates. As the size of these meetings grew, there was an increase in the building of new and sometimes elaborately decorated meeting houses.[23] The runanga served two major purposes: to reform, consolidate or re-affirm tribal associations after the disturbances of the 1860s and, more broadly, to determine hapu and tribal relationships with the government. The two factors were related. Maori awareness of the need to come to terms with the Pakeha world was stimulated by the basic problem that affected all tribal groups – the expansion of the workings of the Native Land Court, and the need to settle land claims and control alienation. A variety of other matters, usually of local interest, also took up runanga attention, so that committees of a semi-permanent nature were maintained, giving the runanga some continuity of identity and purpose.

The difficulty of dealing with central government and its agencies was a new stimulus to the runanga system from the 1870s on, leading to meetings which involved and committed first whole tribes and then many tribes. Runanga were reported from almost all areas. On the Wanganui River in the early 1870s there were at least three large meetings, attended by chiefs representing other tribal districts. Their object was to unify the Wanganui tribes and to establish a lasting friendship between the races. At the same time, Tuhoe hapu were attempting to form a 'Union of Mataatua' that would guard the land, an objective successfully achieved in the 1870s and 1880s. At Ohinemutu a 'Great Native Committee' held lengthy sittings in 1880 to resolve land problems. There was extensive runanga activity on the East Coast too, and Taupo Maori expressed a wish to organise local runanga of leading chiefs elected to determine Maori needs and to present them to the government. Wairarapa runanga were also meeting regularly.[24]

Some, if not all, of these areas were influenced by the Hawke's Bay Repudiation movement.[25] The primary objective of the movement, popular in the 1870s, was to obtain compensation for fraudulent land dealings, but it was not successful. By the end of the 1870s the movement had foundered.

The Repudiation movement placed a significant emphasis on the treaty. The ultimate objective of its leader, Henare Matua, was that 'all the tribes of this island should unite . . . in "the bond of love"'.[26] Specifically, unity or oneness of purpose (often referred to as kotahitanga) in dealings with the government was sought. Interest was directed towards the treaty (and sometimes the Kohimarama covenant),[27] both as a bond of union for all Maori and as the basis for a continuing Maori relationship with a personal Crown to whom appeals could be addressed. Their petitions to the General Assembly professed loyalty to the Crown, and suggested petitioning the Queen to appoint 'a trustful and upright man', a kind of ombudsman, through whom representations on Maori problems would be made to the monarch.[28]

Te Wananga, the Repudiation movement's newspaper, printed the Maori text of the treaty in 1876, accompanied by a translation into English, prepared 'with great accuracy, so as to express as clearly as possible the sense and spirit of the original'.[29] According to this new English version, the Queen had been given 'chief rulership' over all, while the Maori people were confirmed and guaranteed in the 'full chieftainships' of their respective territories and the 'full dominion' of their lands and all their property. This was probably very close to the Maori understanding of 1840, but by 1876 it was evident to many Maori that their right to autonomy based on the treaty was strictly limited in the government's interpretation. This new translation promoted the treaty 'as the "Magna Charta" of their [Maori] constitutional rights'. It was consistent with Matua's increasing preference for separate Maori institutions – the withdrawal of the Maori representatives from the Assembly, the closing of the Native Department and the Land Court, and the establishment of a separate Maori parliament.[30]

Other areas of the country were not so revolutionary in their demands, but the government was repeatedly requested to give some recognition to the Maori committees and runanga. Since the government did not respond positively, Maori groups, in particular Ngati Whatua and Ngapuhi, began to take further initiatives. These and other moves would later be linked with the Repudiation movement to form a national body, the Kotahitanga of the Treaty of Waitangi. This new focus of activity, as it expanded from the mid-1870s, brought the treaty into greater prominence. In most districts it does not seem to have been as central to tribal awareness as it was at Kohimarama, Auckland and in the north, where runanga (or parliaments as they came to be called) were to make the treaty their particular point of reference. Three major meetings were held at Kohimarama – in 1879, 1880 and 1881 – and Ngapuhi treaty parliaments, beginning in 1881, met through to the 1890s.

The idea of reconvening the Kohimarama conference was put to the government first by Tamihana Te Rauparaha of Otaki, and then by Paora Tuhaere of Auckland, both active participants in 1860.[31] The suggestion was first voiced during the 1869 debate over Maori status and encouraged by the visit of Queen Victoria's son, the Duke of Edinburgh. Maori were especially dissatisfied with their participation in national politics. Many felt that they were underrepresented by the four Maori members, who were considered incapable of identifying with the varied interests of several dozen major hapu in the four electorates. Numerous appeals were made in the 1870s for increased representation.[32] Maori also felt that their members did not keep them adequately informed about General Assembly business. The first incumbents, inhibited by a lack of fluency in English, were not talkative participants in debates (one observer remarking that they sat there merely 'as specimens of carved images').[33] To bridge the communication gap the government appointed interpreters.

The reconvening of the Kohimarama conference was also justified by the old argument that the troubles bedevilling the country could be avoided through government consultation with chiefs. In a traditional Maori manner, the conference would allow Maori to sort out their problems before presenting them to the government. Since the government was still endeavouring to quell disturbances and to re-establish relations with the King movement (even seeking the co-operation of Tuhaere and Ngapuhi to achieve this),[34] the conference request was not unreasonable. But because of official reluctance to allow Maori to consolidate privilege and power, no action was taken. Numerous Maori requests in the 1870s, that runanga and committees be given legislative recognition and extended powers, were also refused.[35]

In the absence of government response Tuhaere took the initiative and convened a large conference in March 1879, at Orakei near Auckland.[36] Some 300 attended; Ngapuhi and other tribes were represented. Links with the earlier 1860 conference were evident: the hall, built for the occasion, was called Kohimarama, and in his opening speech Tuhaere cited the 1860 meeting as setting a precedent for the new meeting to discuss the treaty.

For almost half the nine-day conference, Tuhaere kept discussion rigorously centred on the 1840 agreement and its interpretation. The treaty itself was read aloud, as was Browne's address to the 1860 gathering when the treaty had been fully explained and its protective aspects emphasised, including the guarantee relating to fisheries. Tuhaere stated that his reason for examining the treaty was to keep it in 'living remembrance' for the sake of those at the conference and their descendants; he wanted, too, 'to understand the real intent and meaning of the terms'.[37] He noted that although the treaty had been ratified on the Maori side (as had the Kohimarama covenant), Maori people were disillusioned with the trends of government policy.

Conference members were invited to comment on the treaty and its effects. Benefits were weighed against disadvantages. Most speakers favoured adherence to the treaty, partly because of tribal allegiance given to the agreement in 1840,[38] and partly because of the real advantages which they believed they had received as a people, especially the gifts of peace and protection: the treaty had shielded them not only from foreign invasion but also from inter-tribal warfare. Participants noted that the conference was the kind of co-operative unified action which would not have been possible for different tribal groups before 1840. For this reason, the treaty was seen as a covenant of peace and unity, satisfying man's temporal welfare just as the law of God provided for man's spiritual well-being. Furthermore, the treaty was considered by the conference to be the essential bond of unity between the races: under the Queen, Maori and Pakeha would stand united in almost every sense.

Speakers also cited the guarantee that the Queen would protect the Maori people and that they would maintain their mana over their lands, forests, fisheries and other possessions. These promises had been repeated at Kohimarama, but the mana had been lost and the Queen's protection had passed away. The loss of mana over the land was attributed mainly to individualisation of ownership through Crown title.[39] This in turn had led to loss through sale, and to liability for rates, survey costs and mortgages on the land. Some claimed to have been affected by unjust confiscations following the wars; others noted the infringement of Maori rights or mana caused by the protective game laws. There were also unresolved irritations of cattle trespass on cultivations, of the illegal felling of timber on Maori land and of Maori cattle killed by the railway.

In addition, many were concerned about the loss of fishing rights, an aspect of the treaty that was especially relevant to the coastal Maori from the Thames–Manukau to the tip of the North Auckland peninsula. Complaints were made about Pakeha trespass on foreshores, about restrictions on the taking of shellfish, about the ruling on ownership of land below high-water mark and about specific areas such as pipi beds on the Manukau Harbour. The subtlety with which the treaty's fishery guarantee had been undermined clearly confused Maori. Unlike lands or forests, where some agreement normally had to be arranged, fisheries had simply been 'taken away', in spite of the treaty's words.[40]

The conference did not find it easy to apportion blame. Most speakers seemed reluctant to attribute the diminution of mana to the treaty itself. Alternatives were sought and found – usually in the failings of the law to protect the Maori people, and in the operation of the Native Land Court, which some felt should be restricted in its powers or abolished altogether. Others blamed the missionaries for their failure to explain the law. They were hard critics of themselves: if mana had gone, then Maori people had to take a share of the blame for letting the land go. The finger was not pointed at the British government or the Queen. In fact, only one or two speakers criticised the Queen personally. In the final assessment, it was the New Zealand government that the conference held primarily responsible for Maori problems.

In spite of the firm chairmanship of Tuhaere, no conclusive resolution on the Waitangi agreement emerged. Compared with the 1860 Kohimarama conference, however, the assembled Maori clearly had a firmer grasp of the main principles of the treaty. Some were still confused over the finer details of interpretation but in 1879 there was no evidence of the vagueness that had surrounded the 1860 discussion. Speakers referred confidently to the treaty clauses they considered had been violated and related these to their current grievances. They could pin-point problems of interpretation – the ambiguity of the treaty, for instance – and use these to stress the government's failure to give effect to particular promises. Maori knowledge of the treaty had advanced remarkably since 1860. Undoubtedly this was partly the result of government efforts made at the time to circulate information, but the events of the intervening years and Tuhaere's deliberate emphasis on the treaty at the 1879 conference had played their part.

Although Tuhaere had hoped to influence government opinion, the conference's effect on government policy was minimal. Sir George Grey, twice governor and now premier, together with Native Minister John Sheehan, had given their official blessing to Tuhaere's assembly: they hoped that Tuhaere and other Ngati Whatua might act as conciliators with the King movement at a forthcoming meeting with the government. Grey found it useful to fall back on the treaty, promoting it as he and other governors had regularly done for nearly forty years in various circumstances, and for varying reasons. This encouraged the conference to work towards that treaty ideal of a unity of races which the King movement was said to be betraying. When the Grey Ministry fell later in 1879, however, a new ministry with John Bryce as Native Minister was to assume a harder line towards Maori grievances.[41]

While the conference's effect on the government may have been slight, it was to have a significant influence on the standing of the treaty itself. For although the assembly could not reach a unanimous decision on action to be taken with the government, they were at least concerted in their desire to see the treaty implemented. It now became the symbol for a new unity of purpose and gave some sense of cohesion to the diversity of tribal, hapu and individual aspirations.

Plans were made for two further annual conferences, which were held at Orakei, Auckland in March 1880 and March 1881.[42] Again, participants took the Waitangi treaty and the 1860 Kohimarama covenant as their point of reference. In 1880, however, the British acceptance of the 1835 Declaration of Independence was recalled. Conference members noted that in 1835 the kaumatua (elders) had resolved to hold an annual runanga where laws for New Zealand might be laid down by the chiefs. They reasoned that, since the treaty had recognised the 1835 Confederation and had guaranteed rangatiratanga, the British government seemed to have confirmed Maori chiefs' entitlement to a degree of autonomy. Thus the annual conferences and the whole concept of a Maori parliament were given the hallmark of constitutional validity.

This belief gained in popularity as the parliament movement expanded; it was particularly important for Ngapuhi who had been the major signatories to the 1835 document. Ngapuhi had welcomed the Pakeha first, but they shared responsibility with Ngati Whatua who had also allowed the Pakeha to 'light their fires'. From the north and from the Waitemata the 'smell of that fire' had spread throughout the country.[43] This placed a special responsibility on these two tribal groups for the consequences of Maori agreement to the treaty. They saw their responsibility as deriving also from the Christian religion: New Zealand was a Christian community and 'if one part of the body is in pain, the whole body is affected', a metaphor capturing the concept of one people under God's law.[44] Conference speakers, many of them Christian, applied this as much to Maori–Pakeha relationships as to the difficulties affecting one tribe and not another. While this Christian sense of corporate responsibility did not override tribal loyalties, it supplied another basis for Maori union.

One of the main anxieties at the Ngati Whatua conferences was the government's handling of Te Whiti's passive resistance in Taranaki. This chief had established a flourishing pacifist community on land officially confiscated after the wars but not occupied immediately by settlers. Reserves had been promised but had not been made. A commission of inquiry was appointed, but government attempts to settle the land and to oust Te Whiti from Parihaka led to the detention of Maori without trial (and eventually to the forceful destruction of Parihaka in November 1881).[45] Maori were naturally disturbed at the trend of events. They viewed the government's actions as a repetition of the mishandling that had led to the Waitara dispute and to the wars of the 1860s. That the King movement had not been reconciled with the government was another concern. Both issues, aftermaths of the war, were related: they arose from confiscations which contravened the land guarantee of the treaty. Maori leaders felt that force could have been avoided if chiefly advice had been sought.

The Ngati Whatua conferences clarified the reasons which were later the basis for a Maori decision to appeal personally to the Crown. The erosion of chiefly power had been evident for some time but government retrenchment under the Native Minister, John Bryce, struck a direct blow by dispensing with the paid services of chiefs as assistants in court and other official business. The elimination of various government grants of aid had the same effect.[46] These measures seemed a deliberate decision on the part of government to distance itself from the Maori people and to ignore the four Maori MPs. Government policies were leading to an estrangement of the races. The conferences resolved that the idea of one people, expressed so often officially from 1840, should be brought to government attention once more.

Ngapuhi had come to the same conclusion. In the 1870s they began to attract government attention to the treaty by building up Waitangi as a centre for inter-tribal discussions on treaty-related matters. This activity was not on the site of the official treaty meetings but on land on the Paihia side of the Waitangi River mouth, known today as Te Tii marae.[47] Since Maori groups attending the 1840 treaty meeting had camped there, debating the treaty through the night of 5 February, it was a fitting venue for discussion of the treaty. In 1875, when a large tribal gathering celebrated a significant marriage, a hall was built at Te Tii. The gathering of 500 Maori and 100 Pakeha, probably the largest held on the spot since the 1840 meeting, was organised by Ihaka Te Tai Hakuene who continued to promote the marae as a place for tribal meetings.[48] While the hall and the 1875 gathering did not appear to Edward Williams (now the local magistrate) to have any organised political motivation, the opportunity was nevertheless used to hold an evening meeting where discussion turned to the treaty. It was decided to call the new hall 'The Treaty of Waitangi'.[49]

There was more to the naming of the hall than the remembrance of the treaty. Ngapuhi had evidently been spurred to action when other tribes had invited them to attend runanga where problems affecting the Maori people were aired. One communication from Rotorua had been received as an affront, tantamount to a challenge, by some Ngapuhi because it referred to the treaty as 'he Tiriti Paraikete' (a treaty of blankets) and of no mana or effect. Since this reflected poorly on the wisdom of the kaumatua who had signed in 1840 (the parents of many present at the 1875 meeting, including Te Tai), Ngapuhi's role in the treaty-making and the value of the treaty were bound to be defended. The senior chief, Kerei Mangonui (Rewa's son), claimed with some exaggeration that the northern elders had placed New Zealand under the Queen's mana in full knowledge of what they were doing; in view of the 'unjust' gibes from southern tribes, the hall had been named for the treaty as a renewal of commitment to the Waitangi covenant.

Mangonui rejected the notion of Ngapuhi becoming involved in the affairs of the country as a whole, citing earlier efforts at peace-making that had failed. He recommended that problems be adjusted at tribal level before wider consultation. In this he undoubtedly spoke for other chiefs. For some two years, the matter had been discussed in correspondence between Maihi Paraone Kawiti and Aperahama Taonui, senior chief and tohunga of the Northern Kaipara–Hokianga district. Taonui, with the personal mana of having signed the treaty as well as his prestige as a tohunga, had advanced the same policy as Mangonui.[50] It was not a permanent rejection of inter-tribal politics; the timing was not right.

The treaty, however, gradually became the focus of considerable political activity among Ngapuhi. When the governor visited the north in 1876, Te Tii was used as the main place of assembly, and an appeal was made for government assistance to erect a new building.[51] This request was repeated in an 1878 petition to the General Assembly from a group of Ngapuhi 'thoughtful of the covenant made by the Treaty of Waitangi'.[52] They went further and proposed that the house should be used as a place where the governor might explain the instructions of the Queen for the Maori people, and where the chiefs could 'return thanks' for the benefits they had received. By May 1880, at the instigation of Hare Hongi Hika, a descendant of the famous Hongi, sufficient funds had been collected to enable work to commence on a new, larger building which would be known again as 'The Treaty of Waitangi'.[53] In August a monument, also commemorating the treaty, was ready for erection in a commanding position on the marae. It stood roughly sixteen feet high; on its base was inscribed the full text of the treaty in Maori with an accompanying note that it had been signed by 512 chiefs.[54] By March 1881 the site was ready for the first of several major inter-tribal gatherings to be held in the 1880s.

Meanwhile local political issues kept attention focused on the treaty. Continuing difficulties arising from the 1873 Native Lands Act and other land legislation were constant sources of acute irritation and distress, stimulating endless debate.[55] Maori responded heatedly to the dog tax because it was directed so clearly at Maori dog owners. Magnified out of all proportion, it was construed as just one more government measure to oppress the Maori people. Throughout the north, both government and private development were causing additional tensions. By 1881 Kawiti was entangled in long-standing disputes involving various issues – a land grant, a surplus lands question and public works projects at Opua – none of which was settled to his satisfaction.[56]

At the same time, the government's dealings with Te Whiti were drawing Ngapuhi's attention towards national politics. Northern chiefs had earlier expressed to the government their concern about the injustice of the confiscations.[57] In 1880 the withdrawal of the Hokianga chief Hone Mohi Tawhai from the commission of inquiry into Taranaki confiscated lands reflected a widespread lack of Maori confidence in the government's impartiality.[58] The arrests and detainment without trial of those Maori who had acted with Te Whiti to prevent settlement of the lands heightened Maori suspicion towards all government measures. From Hokianga the Resident Magistrate reported a noticeable 'feeling of sullenness and distrust' towards Pakeha generally.[59]

The north had been further drawn into Te Whiti's problems in August 1879 by the association of two northern chiefs – Hori Karaka Tawhiti and Maihi Paraone Kawiti – with a national committee of chiefs.[60] Te Whiti's stand had opened up the whole question of confiscation, an old sore to a great many Maori. The committee proposed to inquire into the validity of confiscations under the 1863 New Zealand Settlements Act. It intended to take legal proceedings to the Supreme Court and even to the Privy Council if necessary. The committee called on those Maori involved in the confiscations to let the dispute be settled by legal processes rather than by force.

The same sense of corporate responsibility was evident at the opening of the new 'Treaty of Waitangi' meeting house in March 1881. Chiefs in the Bay of Islands district were proposing to seek full implementation of the treaty. Part of the task would be to protect the 'remnants' of land remaining to the Maori people. They proposed to establish a runanga or parliament of kaumatua with a second subordinate runanga – an organisation not unlike the two-house structure of the General Assembly. The parliament, to be set up first in the north, would ultimately be a national body supplementary to the Assembly.[61]

When the meeting convened, four chiefs were named as the main trustees for the Bay of Islands – Hare Hongi, Maihi Kawiti, Kingi Hori Kira and Kerei Mangonui; Heta Te Hara was elected chairman. All were descendants of famous chiefs and representative of major divisions within the Ngapuhi federation. Intra-tribal divisions could still cause tensions, and to override this factor, Aperahama Taonui, a chief from outside the bay, had acted as mentor and facilitator of the treaty movement for some time. By his own account, his role was to inaugurate the movement and to open the new 'Treaty of Waitangi' house, but to leave the bay chiefs from then on to work out their own affairs.[62]

Taonui had strongly influenced the northern efforts to act on the treaty. Although he had signed the treaty in 1840, it is part of northern tradition that he had then been disappointed by a point of etiquette – the treaty document had lain on the Union Jack and not on a Maori cloak which would have been fitting in the circumstances.[63] Fearing that this might augur badly, Taonui had kept a watch on relationships with the government. For many years his faith in the Crown's good intentions was sustained, until land problems and legislation affecting Maori welfare, including his personal interests, had shaken his confidence. Aware that he was one of a dwindling number who had signed the treaty, the chief committed himself to see positive steps taken towards fulfilment of the treaty's promises. He had first directed Kawiti to select leaders who would look into Maori problems; later he assisted him in drawing up a set of draft resolutions,[64] which were ready for the March 1881 meeting and embodied proposals drawn mainly from Kawiti's group of hapu.[65] The resolutions set out the need for Maori management of Maori affairs through a separate parliament.

When the meeting opened on 23 March 1881, the demand for a Maori parliament was put to government. Wi Katene said that the assembly favoured an elected body that would deal with all questions affecting the Maori people. It should have the power of veto in all measures affecting them. Three other proposals followed: that the confiscated lands should be restored to the tribes 'on the ground that the Treaty made no provision for the forfeiture of the lands in case of rebellion'; that the question of rights to the foreshores be opened up, because sovereignty over those areas had not been forfeited and indeed had been guaranteed by the treaty; and finally, that the dog tax be waived. Kawiti took up the appeal, expounding on these points at some length, drawing on the resolutions framed earlier and reading the treaty aloud. He argued that a parliament was necessary to weld Maori into a united and strong body to fight for treaty rights, for the government of New Zealand had disregarded it. It had 'milked the cow that was sent by Queen Victoria as a covenant to the tribes of New Zealand'. Other chiefs expressed the general disillusionment with government and its record on the treaty, and supported the parliament proposal. Among these were Tuhaere (whose own runanga at Orakei had only just closed), and two senior Wanganui chiefs, Mete Kingi and Kawana Paipai.[66] The meeting made it clear that the parliament proposal was not a gesture of disloyalty to the Crown. On the contrary, the Union Jack flew over the marae.[67] Association with government on Maori terms was sought, not a separation of the Maori people from government.

The size of the Waitangi meeting and the presence of representatives from further afield ensured that the parliament proposal and its relationship to the treaty received wide publicity. The meeting was believed to be the largest gathering in the area since February 1840. An estimated 3,000 Maori were present, together with a large number of Pakeha including Mrs Busby and members of the old missionary families. The hospitality provided was lavish: a wall of 2,756 kits of potatoes, topped with 500 dried sharks, stretched for nearly a quarter of a mile, with several hundred pigs and other items. Ihaka Te Tai and a committee were the organisers; Kawiti took care of press publicity. Even the local Kawakawa newspaper, often scathing about Maori grievances and shortcomings, was impressed.[68]

The government's response was disappointing. Sir Arthur Gordon, the governor, had been invited and his attendance at such an important meeting was fully expected. Expectations ran high, until the appearance of the Native Minister, William Rolleston, confirmed that the governor would not be present. Gordon, sympathetic with Maori grievances to the point of alienating the ministry of the day and a good deal of public opinion as well, was not likely to absent himself deliberately. He had already committed himself to a tour of the South Island, but it is possible that the government exerted pressure on him to prevent his attendance.[69] His non-attendance was taken as a deliberate slight. Plans to unveil the monument on which the treaty was inscribed were apparently cancelled. Taonui had designed a ceremony to symbolise Maori and Pakeha uniting in the treaty. The monument was first to be covered by a Maori cloak, then with a Union Jack, laid by Hariata (Heke's widow) and by Kawiti; finally there was to be a scripture reading on the theme of Christians as servants of the New Covenant.[70] The commemoration of the 1840 covenant was to set the seal on the new campaign to have the treaty implemented, but without the governor much of its significance was lost.[71]

Although Rolleston had served for only a few weeks as Native Minister, he was fully aware of the sensitive nature of contemporary Maori issues, especially the Parihaka affair and its relationship to the meeting's demand for the return of confiscated lands. His response to the meeting's demands was irritatingly evasive. He brushed aside the Maori proposals and lauded the very ideal which the meeting claimed was not being achieved, that Maori and Pakeha through the treaty were 'as one people under the Queen'. He told the meeting plainly that there could be only one parliament, that its law on confiscation was a fait accompli and that the foreshores, 'by the law of nations', were for the use of everyone. The only concession was on the dog tax, which he thought might be modified. Maori at Waitangi responded civilly but coolly, reaffirming their eagerness to have a parliament and airing a variety of grievances by way of justification.

From the point of view of even well-disposed politicians such as Rolleston, the Maori population of less than 50,000 did not seem to justify the requests for separate political bodies. At most, such runanga were tolerated by the government as safety valves for Maori grievances. Occasionally they might serve useful political ends, such as dealings with the King movement or the investigation of land problems. The government would not encourage any Maori political organisation outside its control. When Ngati Whatua assistance in Waikato peace-making was sought, Tuhaere's 1879 conference had been recognised, but recognition was withheld in the following year.[72] And with only half-hearted commitment, the government allowed a Native Committees Act to pass in 1883, whereby the Maori committees operating all over New Zealand might be given some government support. The legislation proved an unsatisfactory solution to Maori demands and the government deliberately frustrated the Act's intent.[73] According to the 1891 government-appointed commission on native lands, the Act was nothing but a 'hollow shell' that 'mocked' the Maori people with a 'semblance of authority'.[74]

By the latter half of 1881, it was clear that Maori aspirations for a separate parliament had no hope of gaining a favourable hearing.[75] With Bryce once more Native Minister, the government moved rapidly to its final show-down with Te Whiti, first issuing an ultimatum and then brutally destroying his village of Parihaka with a 2,000-strong force. Against a background of deepening financial trouble and unemployment, the government's actions received wide public support and went almost uncriticised by the colonial press. The proceedings against Te Whiti had been authorised by the 'pliable' Attorney-General Prendergast while Gordon was briefly out of the country.[76] Gordon thought the affair had been 'disgracefully unjust', but believed that, as governor of a constitutional colony, the most he could do was to acquaint the Colonial Office with the affair. The Colonial Office, for its part, made its position public: colonial affairs, including dealings with the Maori, were the colonial government's affair.

The attitude of the British government to the Parihaka affair revealed beyond any shadow of doubt that Britain no longer accepted any official responsibility for fulfilment of the terms of the Waitangi treaty. Britain had no right to intrude in the affairs of a self-governing colony and was unable to do so effectively. According to Gordon, interest in the welfare of indigenous races was generally at a low ebb in Britain at this time.[77] It seemed that Britain had washed its hands of the 1840 treaty. At about the same time, too, members of the New Zealand government considered that the treaty had largely served its purpose. It could not be dismissed entirely, partly because of its relationship to Maori land problems and partly because the treaty remained the traditional basis for demanding Maori loyalty to the Crown.

The degree to which the treaty could be manipulated to justify government policy was made clear in the late 1870s, when William Fox, long-standing politician and twice premier, became involved in the government-appointed commission of inquiry into Taranaki confiscated lands. The commission report, which admitted some government responsibility for the Taranaki situation, kept strictly within the terms of reference established for it by the 1879 Confiscated Lands Act. It did not raise questions concerning the Queen's sovereignty, the treaty or the origins of the confiscations. But because the commission was in part a response to the 1879 national Maori committee which was threatening to take legal action to test the validity of the confiscations, Fox felt it incumbent upon him to justify the government's actions taken up to the time of the inquiry. He wrote a lengthy exposition which covered the treaty, the 1863 legislation leading to confiscation and its relationship to the Te Whiti issue.[78] Ngati Ruanui, at this time, were using the treaty in their fight to hold Taranaki lands. They claimed that since they had not signed the treaty (which was true) they were not bound by it, could not be classed as 'rebels' and were not liable for confiscation. To refute their argument, Fox was forced to review the treaty as the purported basis of Crown authority in New Zealand.

He first turned the Ngati Ruanui claim to immunity from the treaty against them, arguing that it would be 'so much the worse' for them if they were not parties to the treaty for, according to the law of nations, all the lands 'not actually used and cultivated' passed by right to the discovering nation. He reasoned that Britain's rights of sovereignty had been established by Cook's 'discovery', and that the 1834 flag and the 1835 Declaration of Independence, which had formed the 'groundwork' for the treaty, were a 'sham'. He found fault also with the treaty negotiations, criticising Maori understanding and stressing the lack of unanimous Maori assent. Such 'questionable means' had been forced on Britain, according to Fox, by a combination of humanitarian and missionary influence.

Having dismissed the treaty, Fox then performed something of an about-face by stating that 'no one' would 'deny the validity of the Treaty'. Presumably this line of argument was necessary to enforce loyalty to the Crown, for Fox argued that articles one and two of the treaty were reciprocal. If Maori rebelled, they forfeited their lands; loyalty pledged under the first article ensured protection under the second. If Ngati Ruanui came under the treaty, they were rebels and stood to lose their land; if they denied the treaty, they lost their land by virtue of discovery. Either way, the tribe could not win.

Towards the end of his exposition, Fox began to admit his real concern, that there might be some technical or legal point on which the confiscations could be overturned. For this reason, officials had not allowed the 1879 Maori committee to initiate legal proceedings against the government. A great deal of land was involved and the government feared that to open up the matter would cause a panic among Pakeha landowners. No 'practical injustice', however, had been done, Fox blandly claimed, and the extent of the war had more than justified the extent of the confiscations. Moreover, if Maori custom required that confiscated territory should be occupied to validate government claims, this would be overridden by legislation. As a final shot, he threw in the justification that 'turning the wilderness into a garden' gave Pakeha a special mandate.

Fox very clearly favoured the government and Pakeha interests against the rights of the Maori people. He was acting the advocate, of course, giving a retrospective interpretation of events, doubtful in its accuracy and coloured by the current needs of the government. The case for the Maori, by contrast, had no prospect of success because the government was its own advocate, judge and jury.

Maori were aware of the impossibility of their situation. The threat of the 1879 Maori committee to take its appeal beyond New Zealand was no idle boast. For years there had been talk of English trips and appeals to the English authorities, but no one had taken the idea seriously. Nor were Maori aware that full local responsibility for internal affairs since the 1860s indicated that Britain had completely abdicated responsibility for the treaty. It was to test the long-promised protection of the Crown, by personal appeal in England itself, that the Maori people turned their energies in the 1880s, seeking that autonomy through which they hoped to determine their future and secure their interests.

Chapter Ten

A STRUGGLE FOR AUTONOMY

As New Zealand moved into the 1880s, public opinion towards Maori grievances cooled further. This was evident in government policy, in hostile press statements and in day-to-day contacts between the races. Unable to get a hearing at home, Maori leaders considered the possibility of a personal appeal to the Queen. Victoria had been a young monarch when the Waitangi treaty had been negotiated, and much emphasis had been given to the personal nature of the compact between the 'Great Mother' and the Maori people. The idea of sending a Maori deputation to England had long been promoted by sympathetic Pakeha – sometimes government agents, occasionally men with some legal expertise and more commonly, simply people with Maori contacts and interests. Their role as sympathisers and stimulators of Maori activity was paralleled in England by the Aborigines Protection Society. It had kept contact with New Zealand affairs for many years, but in the 1880s contacts multiplied as Maori interest in protest heightened. The Society now served a function carried out by governors in the early years of the colony – that of reassuring the Maori that there were bona fide rights under the treaty that could be invoked. The Society, like the governors, knew that such assurances were worthless, but Maori had to find this out by hard experience.

Two Maori deputations made their way to England in the 1880s. The first came from Ngapuhi in 1882; the second, a year later, was from Waikato and included the Maori King. Both groups claimed to represent the interests of the Maori people as a whole and both based their petition on the treaty. Neither appeal was successful, although each attracted a good deal of public interest. More importantly, they promoted among a wide Maori public the idea of seeking redress on the basis of the 1840 agreement. The appeals were also part of a groundswell of activity in the 1880s that was to lead a major sector of Maori society towards organised, united political activity.

The notion of a Ngapuhi appeal to English authorities had been mooted at a March 1881 meeting at Waitangi, but northern support was not unanimous. Opinion was divided on the general direction that the Treaty of Waitangi movement should take. By the end of the year, however, the task of organising a visit to

England had been taken up by Hirini (Sydney) Taiwhanga of
Kaikohe.[1] This fifty-year old son of Rawiri, an early Christian
convert associated with the Paihia mission, was well educated,
fluent in English and experienced in government business. Government officials considered him a troublemaker, but among a
Maori public increasingly frustrated with government policy he
attracted a following. Although not of great personal mana, he
had made his mark at various gatherings with vigorous denuncia-
tions of government policy and articulate demands for redress of
grievances relating to the treaty. This persistent promotion, as one
observer shrewdly remarked, kept the treaty alive for a considerable number of Maori whose knowledge and understanding was
still somewhat 'vague and loose'. Taiwhanga picked up many
of his ideas on Maori protest at the Orakei parliaments and other
runanga, and was later able to synthesise them into a set plan.[2]

Early in 1882, an aged northern chief from Kaihu, Parore Te
Awha, provided Taiwhanga with the financial backing to take a
Ngapuhi petition to the Queen. Taiwhanga, the main spokesman,
would be accompanied by Parore's nephew, Wiremu Reweti Te
Puhi Hihi Te Awha, and Parore's grandson, Hakena Parore, both
of better standing than Taiwhanga though less skilled in politics.
Government agents in the north were sure that Parore had only
sponsored the proposal so that his descendants might see the
monarch. They also believed that Taiwhanga was out to further
his political career, although they grudgingly admitted that he was
genuinely committed to promoting Maori welfare. Whatever the
motives of the participants, the appeal was endorsed by several
major chiefs connected with the Treaty of Waitangi movement –
Aperahama Taonui, Maihi Paraone Kawiti, Hare Hongi, Kerei
Mangonui and Kingi Hori Kira.[3] In fact, the 1882 Waitangi parliament endorsed the idea of a deputation to the Queen, though not
necessarily under Taiwhanga's leadership.

The petition presented in England rested on the basis that the
'sole authority' concerned with the Waitangi treaty was vested in
the Queen. There were two main requests: that the Queen
appoint a 'Royal English Commission' to investigate and rectify
laws that contravened the treaty, and that permission be given to
establish a Maori parliament which would restrain the New Zealand government in its endeavours to set aside the treaty. A long
exposition covered the confiscations, the Native Land Court, local
body taxes and government ill-treatment of Te Whiti. It listed
legislative acts and ordinances that were said to be 'against the
principles contained in the Treaty'. It also outlined the history of
Pakeha–Maori strife over land; the establishment of the King

movement was described as a legitimate act to protect Maori lands in accordance with the treaty's provisions. The appeal based its stand squarely on the treaty.[4]

When the Taiwhanga mission arrived in London in mid-1882, it soon established contacts with the Aborigines Protection Society. The Society and a long-standing benefactor of northern Maori, a Miss Dorothea Weale, jointly sponsored the mission.[5] Through F.W. Chesson, the Society's secretary, the petition was forwarded to the Colonial Office with a request for an interview with the Queen. The Secretary of State for Colonies, the Earl of Kimberley, first hesitated, then refused. His decision was influenced by the hostile attitude of the New Zealand government. New Zealand's Agent-General in London, Francis Dillon Bell, took pains to belittle the appeal and discredit the petitioners, but Kimberley decided finally that it would be diplomatic to receive the group himself since the visit had attracted so much public interest. On 18 July 1882, therefore, the three Maori were accompanied to the Colonial Office by a large group of Society members, parliamentarians, and some churchmen with New Zealand experience. The Maori urged that the treaty be upheld and applied to Pakeha and Maori alike, that measures for unifying the two races be taken, and that Te Whiti be released from custody.[6]

Kimberley, at first evasive, explained that he could not give any answer to the deputation since the proper procedures – forwarding the appeal through the New Zealand authorities – had not been followed. He firmly denied any responsibility on the part of the British Crown or government and pointed out that the British government no longer had any right to interfere in New Zealand's internal affairs. The interview concluded with Kimberley dismissing the treaty as a 'very simple' agreement: it had 'provided that the possession of land was to be respected', a responsibility now held by the New Zealand government, and the confiscations were in no way related. Clearly Britain had abdicated responsibility for the treaty and for Maori affairs.

The Taiwhanga mission had failed completely but pride was salvaged in various ways. John Gorst, an old New Zealand hand, agreed to present the petition to parliament, although in the face of colonial government opposition, it was evident that nothing could come from such a move.[7] Other well-meaning politicians tendered their advice: a company that would handle Maori land transactions to the benefit of both shareholders and Maori was suggested, and of greater importance was a proposal that Taiwhanga bring another petition to England, having first taken it through all the required channels in New Zealand.[8] With this encouragement, the group returned to New Zealand. They were lavishly entertained before their departure, given financial assistance, and taken to see minor royalty, but one poignant request had to be refused. The group had asked to 'rest their eyes' on the treaty to see the signatures of their ancestors, but the Colonial Office held only a copy of the treaty; the original was in New Zealand.[9]

By the time the deputation left England in September, the New Zealand government had begun to make out a case against the appeal;[10] the Premier, Frederick Whitaker, forwarded a memorandum to the English authorities in December.[11] Government leader at the height of the 1860s wars and deeply involved in land speculation in 1882, Whitaker showed no sympathy for the petition. He denied any contravention of the treaty, claiming that there had never been 'anything on the statute-book of the Colony, or in the conduct of the Colonial Legislature' to which 'reasonable exception' could be taken.[12] The petitioners were dismissed as lacking any chiefly status, and the petition represented as having no foundation of truth, at least as far as the colonial government was concerned; for, as Whitaker slyly pointed out, some of the complaints related to dealings in the period when native affairs were an imperial responsibility.

Whitaker was concerned less about the appeal itself than its effect on English public sympathy at a time when the Te Whiti affair was still topical. Even as the deputation made its way to England, Governor Gordon was struggling to bring to public notice the injustice of the Te Whiti case; Kimberley, however, chose to withhold Gordon's dispatch criticising the affair.[13] Like the Taiwhanga appeal, the Te Whiti case raised queries about the treaty and confiscation which embarrassed the government. Bell, Agent-General in London, realised during Taiwhanga's visit that it might become necessary to counter adverse publicity, a task he carried out in the latter half of 1882 through informal contacts amongst London's official circles.

New Zealand politicians were given an opportunity to air their opinion on the colony's history, including the treaty, at London's Royal Colonial Institute where a paper by William Fox was presented for discussion at the end of 1882. The Institute's policy was to elicit the most reliable information on the colonies and to present authoritative papers; Fox's paper was ensured a hallmark of veracity. But Fox was by no means a disinterested party. His paper disparaged the treaty and defended the settler record. Truth or historical accuracy were not the prime concerns; rather the need was to create a favourable impression upon a distinguished assembly.

Sovereignty, Fox argued, had been secured by Cook's discovery. But in as much as the treaty was a valid agreement, Maori rebellion had justified confiscation. As for Maori groups who claimed not to be bound by treaty, the law of nations allowed land seizure from belligerents after a war of conquest. Any legal imperfections relating to confiscations could be 'logically reconciled'; imprisonments in the Te Whiti affair were 'preventative not punitive'.[14] Fox was supported by two other colonial politicians, Sir Charles Clifford and Charles Pharazyn; Clifford attested to Fox's character, recited early New Zealand Company allegations that the treaty was 'a sham, a delusion, and a snare', and claimed that the confiscations had 'ended in great benefit' to the Maori people because of the increased land values brought by settlement.

F.W. Chesson of the Aborigines Protection Society pointed out that Fox had done 'scant justice' to the treaty by disregarding the circumstances surrounding its making: the Maori had been made well aware in 1840 of what rights they could expect from it, but attitudes had changed in the forty years since. The Royal Colonial Institute nevertheless published Fox's paper, together with the discussions and a copy of the treaty (in English). In April 1883, the Taiwhanga petition was finally dismissed and northern Maori were duly informed. Officials no doubt hoped that protest had been silenced; it was clear that by the 1880s the government strongly resented efforts to measure government policy by the yardstick of treaty promises.

The official response to the first personal Maori appeal to the Queen was of great significance for Maori. That the imperial and colonial governments could jointly reject an appeal relating to the treaty and rights claimed under it was a tangible proof of the extent to which officialdom could set the treaty aside. There was little chance of official action being taken unless the colonial government's attitude could be changed, or unless the Maori people themselves could hit upon some effective strategy that would influence public opinion in favour of Maori rights. Maori protest nonetheless persisted. The turnover of government personnel in London and in New Zealand held out some promise of change in official attitudes. It was important, too, that the Queen had not rejected Maori claims deriving from the personal character of the Waitangi covenant. With the continuing patronage of the Aborigines Protection Society to encourage them, various

Maori groups were ready to believe that appeals were always worth attempting.

Taiwhanga had come to this conclusion even before the 1882 mission returned to New Zealand. On 8 December 1882, he put two suggestions to a meeting at the Waitangi marae, that they adopt the land scheme proposed by English politicians and that another appeal should be made. The land company was rejected – it was far too reminiscent of crooked dealings with Maori land, all too familiar by the 1880s[15] – but the idea of a second petition was adopted. Within a month, subscriptions for the new appeal totalled £600 of some £3,000 needed. By April a petition had been printed, ready for circulation throughout the entire country.[16] It resembled Taiwhanga's petition in most respects, although there were two new proposals: the petition asked that committees of chiefs, under the authority of the treaty, investigate land ownership, and replace the Native Land Court; it also requested that the mana of foreshores and fisheries be returned to the Maori people (a point raised at the 1881 Waitangi parliament).[17] Throughout 1883 Taiwhanga travelled with the petition to marae around the North Island. The response was not great, partly because of Taiwhanga's lack of mana and partly because of adverse publicity about his private life.[18] Moreover, the Aborigines Protection Society had determined to dissuade Ngapuhi from appealing again (a 'waste of time', Chesson wrote).[19] They agreed reluctantly by 1885 and the petition was dropped. By then, other appeals had caught the public's attention.

The idea of appeal was taken up by the four Maori members of the House of Representatives in 1883. In July they wrote to the Aborigines Protection Society seeking help and expressing frustration at their total lack of influence in the New Zealand parliament.[20] Their message was that the 'Bond of Waitangi', in particular the land guarantee, was continually being broken by the colonial government which 'being a party to a suit in the question of lands acts also as the judge'. They proposed that Maori lands be vested in an elective body, with legislative and administrative functions, subject only to the governor. One of its responsibilities would be to oversee the leasing of Maori lands as an alternative to continuing loss through sale. Each of the four Maori representatives had experienced government action in his own tribal area which justified this request for Maori control, although the immediate provocation was the government's determination to open the King Country to settlement. But when referred to the New Zealand government for comment, the letter was dismissed by Native Minister John Bryce as irresponsible and not indicative of the real sentiments of the four 'loyal' Maori members, an allegation without supporting evidence. The new governor, William Francis Drummond Jervois, unlike his predecessor Gordon, backed the colonial government. Against such odds Maori efforts had no chance of a hearing. Yet the same year a more prestigious appeal to England was being planned by the second Maori King, Tawhiao, who had succeeded Potatau in 1860.

By the early 1880s Tawhiao, who had long resisted the intrusion of government and settlement in the heart of the North Island, saw that his position was being undermined as the government sought to induce Ngati Maniapoto to open their land for survey.[21] The King played for time but it was clear that with official persistence and Ngati Maniapoto's weakened resolve the independence of the King could not be sustained much longer. Confronted by mounting pressures to change his attitude towards the government, Tawhiao responded by breaking out of his isolation in 1881 and embarking on a round tour of the North Island in 1883. New negotiations with the government also began in mid-1882 although nothing definite was concluded. In May 1883, Tawhiao decided to try an appeal to England.

Taiwhanga's appeal was, of course, being publicised at the same time. He hoped that the King would associate himself with it, giving it his mana as well as additional funding, but Tawhiao rebuffed him. At a meeting early in 1884, the King revealed that he would go to the Queen in his own right. By February, plans were finalised; a tour by Tawhiao in March netted more than £3,000. Efforts were made to secure as representative a deputation as possible. Paora Tuhaere of Orakei was too unwell to travel, but the King's group was joined by two non-Waikato Maori, Topia Turoa and Hori Ropihana, the former from the upper Wanganui–Taupo district, the latter (also known as Ropiha) from Hawke's Bay. Their participation attracted interest in the voyage from tribes beyond the area of the King's closest support in the Waikato–Maniapoto–Hauraki triangle, a factor that was later to prove useful in securing wide commitment to kotahitanga (unity) on the basis of the treaty. The group also included Patara Te Tuhi, responsible for issuing the King's proclamations, and Wiremu Te Wheoro, member for Western Maori since 1879. The King sailed on 1 April in a blaze of publicity. Because of his mana, he was confident of success. New Zealand public opinion, as it was revealed by the press, was equally certain that the trip would fail.[22]

In many respects, the visit was a repetition of Taiwhanga's

experiences. The Aborigines Protection Society gave hospitality and assistance to the visitors. The appeal itself, based on a letter from Tawhiao to the Society written before he left New Zealand, asked, on behalf of the Maori race, the Queen to 'confirm her words given in that treaty'. Lamenting the political impotence of the Maori people, the petition made concrete proposals: a Maori parliament, to control land matters, would operate separately from the Wellington parliament; a commissioner, a Queen's appointee, would act as an 'intermediary', a kind of all-purpose ombudsman, able to represent Maori interests. The petition also requested an independent commission of inquiry into the confiscations, to determine either compensation or restitution.[23] Like Taiwhanga's appeal, the King's petition pointed out that clause seventy-one of the 1852 constitution could be interpreted as allowing provision for Maori custom and government. But compared with the earlier northern appeal, the King's petition was more coherent and specific in its demands. It was a fully fledged scheme for separate Maori self-government.[24]

The King's mission was more irritating to the colonial government than the Taiwhanga visit, for the opening up of the King Country was a sensitive issue in New Zealand.[25] The King retained influence in Ngati Maniapoto and Waikato territory where the government was attempting to break down Maori resistance to land sales; he could not be dismissed as lightly as the northern Maori. The government, determined to thwart the mission, reminded the British authorities that the King was merely a private subject of the Queen, that he represented at most only 1,000 Maori, and that responsibility for dealing with him rested with the New Zealand government.[26] The new Secretary of State, Lord Derby (son of Stanley who had refused to let the treaty be set aside in the 1840s), was less willing to co-operate with the New Zealand government than his predecessor Kimberley. He refused an audience with the Queen, but personally received the delegation which included over forty British politicians and sympathisers.[27]

Derby's reception of the King's party was an admirable gesture but it could be no more than that. Like Kimberley he had to admit that control over internal affairs had been handed over to New Zealand many years before and could not be taken back, 'even if it could be shown ... that those rights had not been used in the best manner'; the petition would have to be referred to the New Zealand government.[28] Derby, however, admitted the importance of the treaty, acknowledged the 'conflict of interests, and ... a conflict of ideas' between Maori and Pakeha, and finally assured the group that, when the New Zealand government had answered the complaints, the British government would 'endeavour to do justice', as far as their power went. Since the British right of interference in Maori affairs no longer existed, these assurances simply created false hopes.

Bell had feared this. He was highly critical of Maori sympathisers, such as the Aborigines Protection Society, who encouraged Tawhiao and Maori generally to believe that there was a 'party' in England that might promote Maori aims successfully.[29] He was also no doubt aware of the possible impact on Maori thinking of the recently completed British settlement with Cetawayo, the Zulu King whom the British had reinstated (although only to a small part of his former kingdom) after he had visited England.[30] Bell knew that a similar situation would not be tolerated by the New Zealand government. The Waikato war had been fought to destroy the King's power, and the objective of governments since had been ultimate amalgamation of the Maori and the opening-up of the whole country to settlement.

Tawhiao made one more attempt to secure an audience with the Queen, explaining that since the treaty the Maori race had looked up to the Queen as the 'great Mother'; now 'it is as if we were cast away as a race who had nothing to do with the Queen'. Even at this late hour, he might have been successful but for the firm attitude of Bell, and the prejudice of R.M. Herbert, Permanent Undersecretary for Colonies, who noted that the Queen seldom saw colonial governors, let alone Maori chiefs.[31] Tawhiao was left to enjoy a farewell by London's Lord Mayor – little consolation for the great effort of the English journey. Yet the Aborigines Protection Society continued to boost Maori expectations by assuring the visitors that they were 'leaving behind friends who would conscientiously represent their interests, and who ... would do their utmost to promote a lasting and satisfactory settlement of any difficulties that might still exist between the Maoris and the colonists of New Zealand'.[32] Well-meaning as this all was, it was really a 'delusion', as Bell noted.

When the King's party left England in late August, Te Wheoro remained behind, hoping for a reply when the British government had communicated with New Zealand. But in August there was a change of government in New Zealand. The new Native Minister, John Ballance, was slow in acting upon Derby's request for information, and Bell pleaded for time to make a report to the Colonial Office concerning the Maori grievances.[33] Te Wheoro, ill, returned empty-handed to New Zealand at the end of 1884. Tawhiao had already held a major meeting of Waikato tribes in

November where reports were given by members of the deputation; a major resolution was the decision to hold to the cause of the treaty. By March 1885, some 4,000 signatures had been forwarded to the Aborigines Protection Society in support of the petition presented in 1884. It was left to the Society to press the British government for an answer. Te Wheoro kept up a flow of correspondence to the Society.[34]

John Ballance, the new Native Minister, embarked on a tour of the central North Island in January and February 1885 to sound out Maori opinion before communicating with England. A series of meetings was held, Ballance moving from Wanganui up to the Waikato, to Thames, Rotorua, Tauranga and Gisborne. The meetings provided Maori with ample opportunity to air their grievances which varied little from one area to another. There was a hard core of Maori discontent which took its stand on treaty rights. There was great sympathy for the King's appeal, even if some had reservations because of tribal rivalries, fears of the King's ambitions, or caution about the New Zealand government's reaction.

In going out to the Maori people, Ballance had two main objectives – to discourage protest based on the treaty and to promote a policy for Maori affairs that might win Maori support for the ministry. He suggested that the management of Maori lands be controlled by committees of owners, that the number of Maori representatives in the Assembly be increased proportionate to the Maori population, and that any proposed legislation affecting Maori be subjected to Maori scrutiny before it went before parliament. He also hinted at the possibility of a conference of chiefs in Wellington later in the year, suggested that Maori might pick up contracts for the proposed extension of the railway through the King Country and noted that legislation restricting rights of assembly and movement, passed in relation to Te Whiti, had lapsed.[35] This was all calculated to appease Maori feelings, just as assurances to Tawhiao about government handling of land questions at Kawhia were designed to secure his agreement to construction of the main trunk railway.

But on the essential matter of the treaty, Ballance was unbending. He put forward the erroneous view that the New Zealand government had 'nothing to do' with the confiscations of the 1860s, because the colony's native affairs at that time (1865) were still under the control of the governor. As for a separate parliament – a request discussed at length when Ballance met the King in February 1885 – the minister argued that the treaty did not allow it.[36] The 'meaning' of the treaty was that it committed

Maori to the Queen's laws in return for a guarantee of protection and possession of property; at most, 'large powers' of self-government might be allowed but these would have to come under government authority. Perhaps the Maori committees, set up under legislation in 1883, could have their powers extended.

Tawhiao and his supporters refused to accept this interpretation of the treaty, and advanced the alternative Maori view. Te Wheoro told Ballance plainly that it was 'not correct' that 'all power' had been given by treaty to the Pakeha. 'It was given to both of us.... It was understood that the Maoris would be allowed to govern themselves in the same way that the Europeans are allowed to.' Te Wheoro agreed that it was certainly true that Maori had dealt initially with the British government and had actually never given the colonial government a right to govern – all the more reason, argued the chief, for allowing the Maori demand for separate government. Since the treaty had given Pakeha and Maori equal rights, it followed that there could be two parliaments, each with the Queen as its head. After further consultation, Te Wheoro agreed that the Maori parliament should submit laws for ratification to the New Zealand parliament, a belated concession which Ballance hailed with satisfaction, although he still rejected the whole notion of a separate Maori body.

It was left to the premier, Robert Stout, to pen the official rebuttal of Tawhiao's complaints in the petition to England. The reply, cool to the point of rudeness, echoed the response to the Taiwhanga appeal. Stout suggested that it would 'least embarrass' the British government if comments were made only on the period after 1865, when the New Zealand government had been left to manage affairs 'without interference', for since then it was 'quite certain' that there had been 'no infraction of the Treaty of Waitangi'. As for the years before 1865, the Queen's advisers could 'arrive at their own conclusions'. Stout dismissed the proposal to set up a Maori parliament, noting that Maori already had parliamentary representation. Section seventy-one of the constitution (by which it was suggested that the Maori parliament could be set up) was only a temporary measure; the Native Land Court now supplied the need for recognising the 'laws, customs, and usages of the Natives'.[37]

Before Stout's reply reached England, Gorst and other British politicians began to put pressure on the British government by asking questions in parliament about the status of the treaty and the fate of the King's appeal. Predictably, the Colonial Office relied upon the argument of non-interference, although Derby stated that the British government could still 'use its good offices with the Colonial Government with the view of obtaining for the Natives all the consideration which can be given to them'.[38] Even if this softened the blow of failure for the Maori petitioners, it unwisely raised false hopes again. Kingites and other Maori groups seized upon Derby's reply and turned what was really a refusal of aid into a promise that grievances might receive further consideration. It would have been 'most merciful', said Bell, to have given the Maori a 'clear statement' in reply to their allegation that the treaty had been infringed by the New Zealand government – that neither the Queen nor the British government would interfere at all in Maori affairs.[39]

This pattern, of English sympathisers raising Maori hopes while the New Zealand government remained deaf to Maori requests for a share in the administration of their own affairs, was to continue. The statements on Maori affairs made in the British parliament in June 1885 were sent by the Aborigines Protection Society to Te Wheoro for circulation among the Maori population. Maori naturally were 'appreciative', because their cause had been defended in the imperial parliament in language that was exciting, if misleading. Gorst had claimed that the British government was bound to support Maori in their problems; Randolph Churchill had contended that Britain retained a right of interference where native rights appeared to be infringed; Gladstone, the Prime Minister, had also entered into the discussion, musing on the possibility of implementing section seventy-one of the constitution. A turnover of ministries, bringing the Conservatives to power in June 1885, raised new hopes.[40]

Certainly there was some reflection at the Colonial Office on the fact that the colonial government 'did not come out well' in the matter of Tawhiao's appeal, but this did not alter the harsh truth that Maori needs were to be left to the colonial government. It was a lesson that the King and other Maori were not ready to learn. They hoped that something might still be achieved. Further deputations would go to England over the years with false expectations. The most influential result of all this activity was the carefully preserved detailed record, often in translation and widely circulated, an encouragement to prise open what Maori would refer to as the 'never-open door'.[41]

In North Auckland, talk about English appeals quietly died in 1885. In a printed letter of early 1885, part of the government's efforts to curtail Maori protest, Ballance urged that such efforts were pointless.[42] Taiwhanga's enthusiasm was tempered, mainly by the cool reception the Aborigines Protection Society gave any new proposals after the King's visit. His energies were now directed to winning the Northern Maori seat, which he did in 1887.[43]

Ngapuhi turned in new directions. They established, at the 1884 meeting at Te Tii (Waitangi), independent committees under the authority of the treaty. These were given extensive judicial powers, proceeded to adjudicate on a variety of subjects and continued to function through the 1880s and 1890s.[44] Their exact relationship to government agencies, such as the Native Land Court and committees established under the 1883 legislation, remains undetermined. It appears, however, that the two sets of committees and the Land Court functioned simultaneously in the north. The 1883 committees were not well received by Ngapuhi, but the treaty committees were supported and their decisions upheld. Their main purpose was to determine ownership of blocks of Maori land before investigation by the Court. The committees represented a compromise response to one request of the 1883 Ngapuhi petition for the abolition of the Court and the adjudication of land issues under the authority of the treaty,[45] a petition that was dropped along with the plan for a second English journey.

Early in 1885 Ngapuhi invited the King to join in a bond of union based on the treaty. Promoted by Taiwhanga, the aim was to draw up a 'document of union' at a meeting on 23 April, when it would be signed by Tawhiao and ultimately by all the 'oldest chiefs of each New Zealand tribe'.[46] The suggestion that unity was essential to the Maori cause had been made by Aborigines Protection Society members who, like most Europeans, found Maori tribal differences distressingly divisive. But inter-tribal tensions proved difficult to surmount. Tawhiao, accompanied by over a hundred followers, consulted with Ngapuhi for a week. The Waikato chiefs, for their part, were seeking Ngapuhi signatures to add to the King's petition, still a major concern to them, but succeeded only with the Ngati Hao and Popoto hapu from Hokianga, headed by Ani Kaaro, grand-daughter of Patuone.[47] The Ngapuhi document of union, drawn up over three days, seemed to have more chance of gaining unanimous support, but mutual jealousies separated Waikato and Ngapuhi. While the document, 'an everlasting covenant', was signed by the King, Te Wheoro, Kawiti, Taiwhanga and a number of other Ngapuhi, most northern Maori were critical of Tawhiao signing as 'King', the term implying an unacceptable subordination of Ngapuhi to Waikato.[48] The efforts of Kawiti and others to prevent the disintegration of the fragile union failed in the face of tribal differences. Even while sharing a unity of purpose based on the treaty, each tribal grouping took a separate path to establish a separate Maori parliament.

In the Waikato the King movement continued to preserve its independent identity. An independent King committee was set up in November 1885, in opposition to a committee at Kawhia, which was co-operating with the government. In April and May 1886, Tawhiao appealed to Ballance to grant requests similar to those embodied in the 1884 petition.[49] The King invoked clause seventy-one of the 1852 constitution as the basis for an annual Maori Council. Existing Maori committees would be brought under its jurisdiction, it would have wide-ranging administrative powers and be financed by existing Maori taxation. In this way the government could secure to the Maori those rights guaranteed by the treaty, and continually reaffirmed down to the 1860 Kohimarama conference. That was the time, Tawhiao pointedly reminded Ballance, when Governor Gore Browne had assured chiefs that the Queen had instructed governors before him, and all who would follow him, to 'maintain the stipulations of this Treaty inviolate'. In a polite reply, Ballance refused the requests, claiming that the government knew what was best for the Maori, that the majority of chiefs wanted the Land Court retained.

For several years after the 1884 appeal, the King party kept pressuring English sympathisers to follow it up. Some action was begun, but the New Zealand government's attitude did not change.[50] In fact, Ballance's moderate and subtle stance was more effective than the brutal rebuttals of his predecessor Bryce, for it appeared in England that Ballance was doing all he reasonably could to meet Maori demands. But while he was giving assurances that the King's power was really in decline, evidenced by the so-called 'desperate' appeals to England, government policy was rapidly divesting Tawhiao of his remaining control over Waikato land.[51]

For a time, it seemed as if the King party would be part of a widespread movement to form a national Maori parliament. Taiwhanga attempted to sustain the bond between the north and Waikato. Tuhaere, linked by marriage with both areas, often acted as Tawhiao's representative at northern runanga; sometimes the King party sent its own representatives to serve on committees and speak at meetings. But the King gradually became more isolated. Although he was kept informed of other tribes' continuing efforts to set up a Maori parliament, his own inclination, encouraged by his followers, was to retain authority in his own right so that something could be built on this foundation, even if the land base had gone. This stand, however, detached him from the union to which he was attracted in 1885, for other tribes would not consent to the King's claims of precedence. His Maori Council proposition to Ballance, for example, set up the King as overseer of the national council, a position that few other chiefs would have tolerated.[52]

Having failed to secure independent Maori government through appeals to both governments, the King set up his own council, or Kauhanganui, in the early 1890s. A constitution, published in 1894, outlined a governmental structure with wide-ranging administrative functions.[53] Under the premiership of Tana Taingakawa, a relation of Wiremu Tamihana Te Waharoa, the two-house Kauhanganui operated from Maungakawa near Cambridge. It published its own newspaper, *Te Paki o Matariki*, which discussed the 'covenant of union' formed by the King movement, emphasising that it was not in conflict with the covenant of the Queen in the treaty.[54] Part of the paper's emblem, however, was the King's motto, 'Ko te mana motuhake' – a separate, independent power. This aspiration represented the Maori point of view that relationships between Maori and Pakeha should be ordered under the treaty, on a basis of equality. Although a logical result of efforts to establish autonomous Maori government, the Kauhanganui was specifically the King's solution; others were seeking a different way.

By the mid-1880s, most tribes wanted to forge a unity of purpose in the treaty. The two appeals to England had stimulated considerable tribal interest; tribes all over the North Island had been visited, and their financial support sought. There had been extensive debates on the treaty and on the propositions incorporated in the two petitions, and keen interest in the outcome of the appeals – an interest prolonged when Maori optimistically interpreted Derby's reply in a way it was never intended. Expectations that English sympathisers could still do something for the Maori race, although treated with a degree of scepticism by some, were widely disseminated.[55] So, too, was the subsequent lack of response from either British or New Zealand governments. The sum effect was a heightening of Maori aspirations for greater participation in government and a better appreciation of how this might be fulfilled.

The government's unfavourable attitude, although a stumbling block, tended to unite Maori groups. It encouraged greater communication between tribes, especially during the tenure of the much-hated Native Minister Bryce. Maori found Bryce un-approachable, ruthless and insensitive to their values and customs. By contrast, his successor Ballance appeared to be well-meaning, was more tactful and was prepared to hold meetings in most tribal areas. This consultation was appreciated, although Ballance was just as determined to advance unacceptable government policies. His methods also fostered Maori unity, partly because of the opportunities he provided for sharing information, and partly because of legislation he introduced, especially the Native Lands Administration Act of 1886.

The Act was a great disappointment. Many Maori had hoped that it would restore the mana of the land by giving them full control, unencumbered by official restriction – in effect, fulfilment of the second treaty article. Hopes had been raised by the extent of consultation: in draft form, the Bill had been considered by a major meeting, called by Ngati Kahungunu, which had brought representatives from all parts of New Zealand to Hastings in January 1886.[56] The new measure stopped individual dealings with Maori lands. It preserved the principle of Maori communal ownership by allowing for an incorporation of owners of a block into one legal entity; an elected block committee, holding executive powers, would determine terms of sale or lease. The land, however, had to be entrusted to a government commissioner. The Act was made optional and Maori, objecting to loss of control over their lands, refused to bring land under the legislation. Committee powers, although extended as Maori had long requested, were a far cry from the independent control that they demanded in a Maori parliament.[57] Consultation had had little effect, and the Bill in its final form was received by Maori as yet one more government attempt to take the land.

By the end of Ballance's term, Maori had strengthened their resolve to act independently. Ballance had not fundamentally revised Bryce's policy of reducing expenditure and curtailing the special machinery for Maori administration. Although patient in public, privately he expressed a cynicism about Maori grievances; he also overrode divisions in Maori society, ignoring dissenting voices in the matter of the 1886 Act, claiming that the government was 'carrying out the principles of the Treaty of Waitangi' in seeking to consult at all.[58] The logic of such justification is difficult to see.

While the Ballance period was a disappointment to those hoping for Maori self-government, worse was to follow. When Edwin Mitchelson became Native Minister after a change of ministry in 1887, the temporary respite in land sales came to an end; the Native Land Act of 1888 restored direct purchase and in the next three years Maori land holdings diminished further. Maori expenses relating to the Land Court increased. At the same time Maori received less from the Native Department as expenditure decreased in pursuance of the policy of finally abolishing this branch of government (carried out in 1893). This direction in policy, coupled with a spate of legislation that ignored Maori rights to a hearing from government, was to lead to the final formation of the Kotahitanga, or union under the treaty movement.

Tuhaere of Orakei, Auckland, played an important part in the last stages of this process. For some years he had acted as a bridgehead between Ngapuhi and Waikato without achieving the unity of action he desired. He had also sought consensus, unsuccessfully, at several Ngati Whatua parliaments held at Kaipara in the mid-1880s.[59] Then in 1887 senior chiefs and tribes from the lower part of the North Island asked Tuhaere to take responsibility in the north for initiating discussions on the government's legislation and to encourage moves to union. Four meetings were held in 1888 – at Waitangi, Waiomatatini, Omaahu and Putiki – representing Maori interests in the north, east, south and west.[60] Tuhaere's mandate was to be exercised at the Waitangi meeting in March 1888, when he acted as chairman.

His involvement injected new vigour into the northern movement. Although Ngapuhi had long recognised that other areas were looking to them to take up the cause of the treaty with the government, participants at the annual meetings at the Waitangi marae from 1881 onwards had not been prepared to act in a concerted way beyond the Ngapuhi area itself. Nor was opinion united on what action should be taken in the north. In fact, some influential chiefs held aloof from the whole idea of a treaty of Waitangi movement.[61] By 1888, however, Maori MPs and government office-holders, both current and past, were prepared to participate in Maori moves to unite. The support of such men was needed, not only for the expertise they brought to tribal gatherings, but also because many of the initiators of action on the treaty were ageing.

The main work of the Waitangi meeting was to revise the 1886 Act so that it would provide for Maori control of their affairs.[62] But Tuhaere proposed to build the assembly up into a body capable of reviewing all proposed legislation and able to submit its own proposals to government. Once worked out in the north, the scheme could be applied to the rest of the country. Tuhaere reasoned that the progressive extension of Maori government from Waitangi was fitting, since the treaty had been forged at that spot and had gone forth from there. The sanction for the scheme was Maori mana, first recognised by Britain in granting the national flag and in the 1835 Declaration of Maori Independence, then in the treaty, and subsequently in clause seventy-one of the 1852 constitution. Tuhaere believed that, unless this Maori mana was officially recognised, Maori law-making would lack authority.

Tuhaere's exposition of the need for unity was well supported by the Waitangi meeting. So, too, were the precedents for the exercise of Maori mana. Kawiti read aloud the 1835 Declaration of Independence, a text which had previously been invoked by the Waitangi parliaments. The Declaration, stressing the separate and independent nature of New Zealand which the Crown had recognised in 1840, was of prime importance to the meeting in validating Maori claims to autonomous rights. The Maori text, however, was not the one prepared by Busby in 1835, but one which rendered Maori independence as mana motuhake – a term used from then on by many Maori.[63]

The resolutions of this Waitangi meeting, and of similar meetings held at Waiomatatini and Omaahu, were taken to a large inter-tribal meeting held at Putiki, Wanganui, in the last week of April and early May 1888.[64] Here it was finally agreed that inter-tribal differences should be overridden by all the tribes of the North Island forming kotahitanga. A national Maori parliament was to be established so that the Waitangi treaty could be properly implemented; in particular land would be controlled almost entirely by Maori. A new covenant had now been entered into, whereby chiefs and people would work towards restoring Maori welfare. Some chiefs hailed the agreement as more significant than the treaties of Waitangi or Kohimarama. The compact, likened to the solemn covenant in a Christian marriage, was recognised by the symbolic action of a general partaking in a 'giant' cake, pieces being sent to all parts of the North Island to symbolise the decision.[65]

This commitment to kotahitanga bore fruit almost immediately. A representative committee of chiefs was elected to represent Maori interests to the Wellington parliament. Well-known men figured on different occasions – Te Rangihiwinui Kepa (Major Kemp) from Wanganui, Maihi Paraone Kawiti from the north, Paora Tuhaere and more than a dozen others. It operated like an unofficial Maori council, trying to scrutinise proposed legislation and influence the government, and keeping information flowing back to tribal areas. In 1888 it attempted to curtail the government's law-making on Maori matters.[66] Proposed legislation had caused grave concern at the Wanganui meeting in April, particularly as the Native Minister seemed reluctant to allow Bills to be considered by tribal meetings. Tuhaere and other committee chiefs appealed to the Assembly to let the Bills be held over for consideration at the usual Waitangi parliament scheduled for March 1889. Tuhaere also spoke to the Wanganui resolutions that the Land Court's powers be drastically reduced and that the 1883 committees be allowed to operate independently of the government.[67] It was a repetition of the long-standing request for greater control, for the return of mana under the treaty. As before, the government ignored the request. Tuhaere and the committee then appealed to the governor to ask the Queen to disallow the 1888 Native Lands Act but it was implemented nevertheless.[68]

At the Waitangi meeting in March 1889, while the usual discussion of grievances took place, an important new development was the drawing up of a pledge of union under the treaty.[69] Those who signed the pledge committed themselves to kotahitanga and recognised the mana of the treaty under which a Maori government would be set up. From Waitangi, the document was sent to all tribes for signing, following the precedent set by the signing of the treaty in 1840. A week later the document had been signed by a large number of chiefs and over 400 others. By 1898 kotahitanga followers claimed that the pledge had the adherence of thousands of Maori.[70]

Tuhaere held a second conference in March 1889 at Orakei – a venue more convenient for both Maori and Pakeha – to consolidate and extend the work done at Waitangi.[71] About 500 Maori attended, including Te Rawhiti and Patara Te Tuhi, representing the King, Major Kemp from Wanganui, Wi Parata from Wellington and other major chiefs. Among the Pakeha were the Premier, Harry Atkinson, the Attorney-General, Whitaker, and the Native Minister, Mitchelson – an impressive representation. Since Pakeha had profited by Maori divisiveness, the prospect of an extensive combination of Maori interests, a development that Pakeha had consistently believed to be an absolute impossibility, was seen as a threat.[72] Maori land was still a hot political issue, despite the alienation of some millions of acres in the North Island since 1870.

Tuhaere and Kemp, impressive orators, told government representatives that one major aim of the movement was to unify the two races as the treaty had intended, that the two might be one people; their other aim was to achieve unity of purpose among

Maori, a need made more urgent by continuing Maori exclusion from government. Most important, the meeting made clear that it wanted the New Zealand government to ratify the Waitangi agreement on the basis Maori understood to have been agreed by both parties in 1840 – that there should be equality and a sharing of mana in New Zealand. This was not a concession that the colonial government was prepared to grant. Predictably, Pakeha MPs defended the Pakeha record from their understanding of the treaty: that it had given the British a mandate to rule and that they had 'done well' by the Maori people, especially in regard to land.

Because the government continued to stone-wall Maori appeals, efforts to achieve kotahitanga continued. The north and the west had confirmed their initial commitment, but there was still uncertainty about the south and east.[73] Even in the north there were problems. At the March parliament, Kawiti had directed Ngapuhi to consult so that Maori, like the Jews of the Old Testament, might be delivered from their 'afflictions'.[74] The injunction took on new significance with Kawiti's death soon after, but another year passed before the structure of the northern kotahitanga was finally worked out at a meeting at Omanaia in May 1890.[75]

The meeting, representative of all the north, was chaired by Hone Mohi Tawhai. Though aloof from the treaty movement in the early 1880s, Tawhai had shared with Aperahama Taonui a sense of spiritual revelation: both men had the prophetic vision of a solution of Maori difficulties through he tikanga nui (a great law) to be worked out in 1890, a time laid down in 1880, forty years after Waitangi. Maori were like the Jews who had wandered in the desert for forty years, but deliverance would come.[76] The choice of Tawhai as chairman and the meeting place as Omanaia (a spot sacred to Taonui's followers) were not accidental.[77] Before the meeting concluded, the organisational structure, the funding of permanent appointees, and an organising committee to be chaired by Te Hara of Ohaeawai (chairman and anointed head of the north's treaty movement) had been worked out. The most important decision, however, was the appointment of Raneira Wharerau to travel through New Zealand to establish kotahitanga. It was the final acceptance by Ngapuhi of their role as initiators, especially in relationships with the Pakeha; specifically, the tribe accepted a special responsibility to see the treaty implemented.

On 22 April 1891, Heta Te Hara presided over the first meeting of the northern kotahitanga at Kaikohe. Unlike the original Waitangi parliaments, which had been supported mainly by Ngapuhi from the Bay of Islands and its hinterland, the Kaikohe meeting embraced Te Rarawa, Te Aupouri and Ngati Whatua, as well as a wider representation of Ngapuhi. It resolved to name the body that they formed 'Whakakotahitanga' – the act of being one in purpose – but when the first national parliament opened at Waitangi in April 1892, the new organisation came to be known as Te Kotahitanga o te Tiriti o Waitangi – the Unity of the Treaty of Waitangi.[78]

Other tribes had organised along similar lines and had their representatives ready for the 1892 meeting.[79] Although this Waitangi gathering was known as the first of the Maori parliaments, the first Kotahitanga parliament proper was convened at Waipatu in Hawke's Bay, in June 1892.[80] It operated under an organisational structure laid down at Waitangi before the April parliament. While retaining the traditional runanga principle of consultation and deliberation, the parliament adopted more European procedures. There were electoral districts based on tribal boundaries and the parliament itself had two houses, an upper house of fifty chiefs and a lower house of ninety-six younger men. Debate was to follow the pattern of the General Assembly. The Maori parliament was designed not to supplant the Wellington parliament but to supplement it.[81]

The formation of the Kotahitanga parliaments represented the culmination of years of struggle to secure that degree of autonomy to which Maori felt entitled under the treaty. The parliaments operated for some eleven years before gradually losing support. They never secured the complete Maori union they sought. Tawhiao had gone his own way in setting up his Kauhanganui parliament about the same time as the first Kotahitanga parliament met, and Te Whiti had resolutely kept away from the organisation, despite attempts by Taiwhanga to draw him in. Yet the pledge of union was numerously signed, an indication that many Maori identified with the aim of the Kotahitanga movement in the latter part of the 1890s, even if they did not always actively participate. Such support was an indictment of official dealings with the Maori people in the half-century since the signing of the treaty.

Chapter Eleven

A RESIDUE OF GUILT: 1890–1987

From 1890 to the present, the treaty has continued to play an important part in Maori and Pakeha thinking about New Zealand's past. It has been a touchstone for both races, Maori at first but from the 1930s increasing numbers of Pakeha. Both have used the treaty in identifying their present concerns and expressing their hopes for the future. Most typically, those concerns and hopes have diverged, but there are also convergences. In the last ninety odd years, there has been continuity with the trends and interpretations evident in the pre-1890 period, but at the same time new aspirations have given the treaty fresh meanings.

Maori struggles to secure rights and a measure of control over their affairs have continued since 1890, but the government has been reluctant to make concessions or to relinquish control of Maori affairs. To accede to Maori demands for autonomy would indeed be proof that the goal of 'one people' has not been . achieved. And for many New Zealanders that remains the most significant aspect of the treaty, the ideological base for the claim that New Zealand has treated its indigenous race well. Maori protest, therefore, has been regarded as a challenge to the nation's special identity. Yet continuing Pakeha sensitivity over Maori claims suggests that a residue of guilt remains. This gives New Zealand a 'moral imperative' to make the practice in race relationships fit the 'one people' ideal[1] – paradoxically the very position which many Maori have continued to challenge since the nineteenth century.

The Kotahitanga movement of the 1890s was the most comprehensive nineteenth-century effort to secure the autonomy guaranteed by the treaty. To most Kotahitanga followers, the treaty had cemented a reciprocal agreement: the Crown would hold the mana of government while chiefs were confirmed in their authority. This understanding allowed for a sharing of authority, a partnership within the new nation. The movement's leaders hoped to secure legislative recognition of the Kotahitanga parliaments and allow full Maori participation in the functions of the state, as equals of the Pakeha. Another train of thought within Kotahitanga argued for an independent Maori authority, recognised by Britain before 1840 and confirmed by the treaty, which could exercise autonomous rights quite independently of government. In both attitudes, the treaty was crucial.[2]

In the 1890s, several attempts by the Kotahitanga to secure government sanction failed and the movement began to falter. Its last formal gathering was at Waiomatatini in 1902. Some Liberal measures had initially given grounds for hope. The Native Land Laws Commission of 1891 had condemned the legislation of the previous thirty years and the record of past land transactions. The Commission's Report seemed to promise a radical change, comparable with other Liberal measures, but in practice little was done. The Maori Lands Administration Act and the Maori Councils Act, both passed in 1900, allowed a small degree of local control rather than the wide powers requested. Restrictions on land alienation proved temporary and any resolve to assist Maori welfare gave way to pressure of Pakeha needs. By the end of the Liberal period, just before World War One, another 3 million acres of Maori land had passed out of Maori ownership.[3]

While the Kotahitanga declined from around 1900, the Kauhanganui (the King's parliament) continued with regular meetings at which Maori autonomy (mana motuhake), treaty rights and government failure to fulfil them were aired. In 1907, disillusionment with the Liberals' record prompted members of the King movement to draft an appeal to the British monarch. The petition was part of a renewed effort at a comprehensive kotahitanga that would embrace all Maoridom. A meeting of 3,000 people at Waahi (Huntly) made a pledge 'to maintain and uphold all the rights and privileges enjoyed by our race in the year 1834, signalized by the flag of 1836 [sic] and maintained until the enactment of the New Zealand Constitution Act of 1852.'[4]

This attempt at union under the treaty foundered on divisions within Kingitanga (a term increasingly used for the movement), and on differences with tribes outside it, but in 1909 the idea was picked up again by Tana Taingakawa, one of Wiremu Tamihana Te Waharoa's sons. Taingakawa drafted a new petition, for the governor to forward to England. It complained that the mana granted the Maori people by the second and third articles of the treaty had been nullified by the New Zealand government's enactment of a 'systematic series of laws', which were listed. In the Kotahitanga tradition, it sought absolute autonomy and control of all lands that had not been alienated. Taingakawa was bidding for the 'mana of absolute chieftainship'. Twenty years before, such an appeal might have gained the backing of the majority of Kotahitanga leaders who found their strength of purpose in chiefly mana, but by 1909, the first generation of Kotahitanga chiefs had died and younger men were not prepared to back the appeal. Significantly, the petition did find support in the Urewera where isolation had delayed the pattern of government intrusion and Maori adjustment.[5]

In 1913, another appeal to have the treaty implemented was prompted by Tupu Taingakawa, Tana's younger brother. He persuaded the King movement to fund a mission to England, to appeal to the Crown to rectify breaches of the treaty; in particular, to settle the matter of the post-war confiscations that had deprived Waikato of their lands. The visit achieved no more than Tawhiao's trip in 1884. Te Rata, the fourth Maori King, accompanied by Tupu Taingakawa and two others, received no satisfaction from the British authorities; their appeal was referred back to the New Zealand government. A small satisfaction was that, unlike earlier missions to England, they were accorded an audience with King George V and Queen Mary, but this had been made conditional: no grievances were to be voiced.[6]

Meanwhile, other Maori leaders were emerging for whom these separatist aspirations had little attraction. Known collectively as the Young Maori Party, the most well known were Apirana Ngata, Maui Pomare and Te Rangihiroa (Peter Buck). All were university graduates and all Members of Parliament. Buck captured the Northern Maori seat in 1909 and held it until 1914, Pomare held the Western Maori seat from 1911 to 1930 and Ngata represented Eastern Maori from 1905 to 1943. The three men were convinced that survival for the Maori race lay in shedding those aspects of the traditional way of life that retarded Maori acceptance of the modern world. All were committed to working within the administrative and legislative framework of government. There was no questioning the sovereign rights assumed by government; the challenge was to make that power work for the advancement of the Maori people.[7]

In 1922 Ngata, concerned about the extent to which Maori protest still relied upon the treaty, wrote an 'explanation' of it for the Maori people.[8] Because of Ngata's mana, this explanation was most influential in shaping Maori attitudes. He reasoned that until the meaning of the treaty's terms – 'government' and 'chiefly authority' – was made clear, no one could 'consciously understand' the full meaning of the compact. Ngata, however, took the English text and ignored the Maori version. He defined 'government' as 'te tino mana' or 'absolute authority' over the people, which he said had been conceded to the Queen and her parliament by the first article. The tribal ancestors had transferred their 'chiefly authority' to the Queen for ever, and the embodiment of that authority was now the New Zealand Parliament. For that reason, all the demands for 'Absolute Maori Authorities' (such as the Kotahitanga and Kauhanganui) were just 'wishful thinking'. The second article confirmed only rights of possession; the Native Land Court carried out this provision by adjudicating on Maori ownership. The distinction between the first and second articles he summed up by citing Nopera Panakareao's well-known 'wise words' that it was 'the shadow of the land which had been given to the Queen while the soil remains' – a reference that was not particularly apt either in the light of his foregoing explanation, or in view of the Kaitaia chief's subsequent reversal of this opinion.[9]

Ngata's objective was to steer Maori towards accepting the English treaty text. The government had translated it into Maori in 1869 to make its meaning clear, but subsequent Maori protest had adhered to the Maori text. Ngata believed that Maori energies would be wasted on a hopeless cause instead of being directed towards securing those benefits from the treaty that might reasonably be expected from the government. Fishing rights, for instance, had been an uncertain issue for many years, with Maori rights gradually whittled away. In 1922, the courts were considering the Arawa claims to fresh water lakes. In Ngata's view, the treaty's guarantee of fishing rights constituted a responsibility for the Crown that was morally, if not legally, binding. He admitted that there was conflict between the second article guaranteeing fishing rights and the third article which imposed laws that denied them, but there he left the issue, clearly hoping that favourable decisions might be made.[10]

Ngata's explanation merely added to the confusion surrounding the treaty's meaning and effect and this was compounded by a reprint of his pamphlet, in English, in 1963.[11] His 'explanation' is still cited as if it were a reliable, authoritative statement of the Maori understanding in 1840. It is not. The pamphlet perpetuates other erroneous notions – that there had been no law and order in New Zealand before 1840 and that Crown protection had prevented a French invasion and a later Russian attempt to take the country (possibly the 'scare' of the 1880s). Ngata also adopted the long-held and generally accepted Pakeha stand that the government had been justified in the post-war confiscations, which he likened to utu, although he conceded that there had been error in their implementation.

Three other pamphlets on the treaty were published in 1922, all produced by Alexander Francis McDonnell, an Auckland printer, specifically for a Maori-reading public. One, called simply *Ko te tiriti i tuhia ki Waitangi, 1840*, gave a brief exposition of the benefits and disadvantages of the treaty to the Maori race since 1840.[12] Like almost every Maori writing that dealt with contraventions of the treaty, it traced the legislative steps by which problems had been created. The second pamphlet reprinted the correspondence (in Maori and English) between Te Wherowhero, the Queen and the governor in 1847–48, concerning Earl Grey's instructions which had seemed to overturn the land guarantee.[13] It had no commentary. Possibly the extracts were intended to speak for themselves, for Governor Grey had used the occasion to prove to the Maori people that the Queen paid heed to Maori complaints. The reply from the Queen, moreover, was the oft-cited justification for Maori claims that the government had no right to confiscate land: 'it was never intended that the Treaty of Waitangi should be violated by dispossessing the tribes which are parties to it, of any portion of the land secured to them by the Treaty without their consent.'[14] The third publication was a comprehensive collection of documents and extracts relating to the treaty, among them the 1835 Declaration of Independence, petitions based on the treaty, Hansard speeches and writings referring to the treaty.[15]

This burst of publication coincided with a quickening of Maori interest in the Waitangi compact. By Ngata's account, it was 'widely discussed on all maraes'; it was 'on the lips of the humble and the great, of the ignorant and of the thoughtful'.[16] The revival of activity related to the treaty at this time arose from several developments – the Arawa tribe's success in having their lake rights recognised by the government, the opening of a new building at Te Tii marae, Waitangi, and two political parties – Ratana and Labour – adopting the treaty as part of their platforms. In the Arawa case, the government finally conceded Maori fishing and burial rights in the tribe's fresh water lakes, making an offer of compensation and setting up special arrangements to put the agreement into effect. It enabled Arawa to form the Arawa Trust Board to administer the newly recognised interests and the compensation payments.[17]

These events naturally stimulated much discussion of Maori rights and the treaty among Maori everywhere. Whether as individuals or as tribal groups, they had previously received no real satisfaction from various attempts to secure fishing rights. Government agents, too, had drawn attention to the problem, one report in 1885 noting that the 'constant gathering and wholesale destruction by the Europeans of the oysters on the foreshore of the Bay of Islands is causing a considerable amount of uneasiness; the Natives asserting a claim to the shell-fish under the Treaty of Waitangi'. At best, a claim to rights in a specified tidal fishing ground might be recognised by special provision. In general, however, such rights were not admitted in law as deriving from the treaty, a point spelt out by Chief Justice Robert Stout in a 1914 case: 'until there is some legislative proviso as to the carrying out of the Treaty, the Court is helpless to give effect to its provisions.... Even if the Treaty of Waitangi is to be assumed to have the effect of a statute it would be very difficult to spell out of its second clause the creation or recognition of territorial or extra-territorial fishing rights in tidal waters.' Securing rights in lakes and rivers had posed similar difficulties. The Arawa case, there-fore, was encouraging. By the end of the 1920s the government had made a similar agreement with Ngati Tuwharetoa over their rights to Lake Taupo and adjoining streams.[18] These advances were conceded only after considerable Maori effort; they were not granted readily, as of right. This pattern would continue, with Maori grievances usually based upon treaty rights that were being ignored or inadequately acknowledged by the government.

Within a day of the government's offer to Arawa in late March 1922, the Prime Minister, William Massey, accompanied by Nga-ta, Sir James Carroll and other MPs, opened a new meeting hall at Te Tii marae, Waitangi. The last big meeting at Te Tii had been the Kotahitanga parliament of 1899 when the governor, the pre-mier and other officials had been present. As Kotahitanga support had subsequently fallen away, activity at the marae had declined and the hall, erected for the first Waitangi parliament of 1881, had gradually fallen into disrepair. Plans to restore it gave way to a full-scale rebuilding scheme when, in 1917, the shaky structure collapsed in a gale. The stone monument, with the treaty's words inscribed on it, survived intact for the 1922 opening. (It still stands.) Massey expressed the hope that the new building 'would ... be held sacred by both races'. He also promised to grant any measure that would put the Maori people 'on a footing of equal-ity' with Pakeha, a promise made too late in the day for many Maori: the government had not included Maori returned service-men in rehabilitation schemes after World War One.[19]

Perhaps for that reason, three of the Maori MPs had forwarded a copy of the treaty to the British government in 1919. It had been received with some puzzlement because a copy was 'already on careful record', but was added to the 'archives' and acknow-ledged. Massey had assured Maori that the treaty remained sacred, and his attendance at the Waitangi marae appears to have been a gesture to support his words by action, but Maori seem to have indicated their dissatisfaction with Reform's record by their absence from the 1922 ceremony; preparations costing some £5,000 had been made to receive an expected 3,000 Maori, but only 1,000 attended. The new development at the marae was important, nevertheless, because the hall, constructed in more permanent materials, now stood squarely beside the monument to become a focal point for later protest related to the treaty.[20]

The Ratana movement, which was to challenge Maui Pomare for the Western Maori seat in the 1922 election, also drew attention to the treaty.[21] Tahupotiki Wiremu Ratana had emerged in 1918 as a faith-healer with remarkable powers, attracting a wide range of Maori followers. He believed that he had a two-fold mission: to transcend the barriers of tribe and religion in order to unite the Maori people in one God; and to advance the temporal welfare of the race. With neither strong tribal nor religious affiliation, nor any advanced education, Ratana became for his followers the Mangai, the mouthpiece of God, the bearer of revelations in the tradition of earlier Maori prophets. By the end of 1920, over 3,000 Maori had been drawn to his farm near Wanganui, and a makeshift village had taken shape. By 1925, the settlement had become the centre of a thriving church community.

Ratana formed a political party in the early 1920s, concentrating on current social problems and past grievances. The party's objective was to have the treaty incorporated in legislation, an aim often referred to as 'ratification'. This was promoted as the answer to all grievances sustained by the Maori race. That this rallying call had considerable appeal was shown by the support given to Ratana's son Tokouru in the 1922 election. Although the sitting member, Maui Pomare, retained the seat with 3,835 votes, Tokouru Ratana secured 3,037 and might have won but for the support given a third candidate, Rangi Mawhete. Standing as an independent, though sympathetic to Labour, Mawhete was also committed to securing treaty rights and polled 827 votes.

Having failed in the 1922 election, Ratana took a petition to England in 1924. The petition, basing Maori right of appeal on the treaty, sought the appointment of a Royal Commission from England which would make an independent investigation of Maori grievances. These included the return of confiscated lands and resembled those of earlier petitions. Ratana had intended to present the petition to the British monarch, but the well-established pattern for dealing with such appeals was followed. It was referred back to the New Zealand authorities.[22]

Ratana turned to winning the four Maori seats with candidates pledged to uphold the treaty. The first Ratana member, Eruera Tirikatene, entered parliament in 1932, stating immediately that his policy was 'to stand for the rights and privileges of the whole Maori race, as embodied in the Treaty of Waitangi'. In November 1932, he presented to parliament a petition containing over 30,000 signatures asking that the treaty be made statutory, but no government action was taken. The strength of Ratana's commitment to the treaty was sustained nonetheless. The four seats were held by Ratana men from 1943 onwards, each candidate pledged to promote the treaty. That pledge alone, together with the Ratana party's continuing success at elections, ensured that agitation over the treaty would continue.[23]

Another important factor was the activity of the Labour party from about 1922. In its search for votes, Labour made a policy statement in 1925 designed to appeal to Maori. If Labour became the government, it promised to set up a Royal Commission to investigate land claims 'arising out of and subsequent to the Treaty of Waitangi'. It promised a Maori Council which would secure, perhaps, the degree of autonomy so long sought.[24] This policy emerged from numerous meetings at which Rangi Mawhete, a descendant of Peeti Te Aweawe, chief of Manawatu, aligned himself closely with Labour and acted as a liaison between the party and interested Maori groups. At the 1925 election, Mawhete stood as a Labour candidate in Western Maori, with Labour candidates standing also in Northern and Eastern Maori. In spite of the party's promises, and a publication by Mawhete reviewing Maori rights under the treaty, electoral support was not strong.[25] Grass-roots organisation was thin and traditional tribal patterns of Maori support for their MPs prevailed.

By 1931, both Labour and Ratana recognised that co-operation would be desirable. Labour needed Maori backing; Ratana had that backing but had not won a seat in the 1928 and 1931 elections. Their policies were similar, both espousing the cause of the ordinary man, Pakeha and Maori, and both committed to implementing the treaty. When Tirikatene won the Southern Maori seat in a by-election in 1932, Labour and Ratana began a parliamentary alliance which lasted for nearly half a century and which ensured that the treaty would become a more important part of the European political scene than it had been for many years. After Labour became the government in 1935, the Ratana members worked inside the party to implement earlier Labour promises on the treaty and the Maori Council. For a long time, their work had little practical result, but it kept alive the objective of incorporating the treaty into law. Before that was achieved, however, Pakeha interest in the treaty had been stimulated by an unexpected development.

In May 1932 Busby's house at Waitangi, together with an adjacent 1,000 acres, was gifted to the nation by the incumbent Governor-General, Lord Bledisloe, and his wife. For the previous fifty years, Pakeha interest in the treaty and the Waitangi site had been minimal. By the 1930s, both 'had almost gone out of the public mind', according to Vernon Reed, who had tried unsuccessfully since 1908 to stimulate government and public interest. Reed encouraged the Bledisloes to purchase the Waitangi property, which was to be made 'a national memorial'. They added another 1,300 acres to the original gift and launched an appeal for funds for restoration by donating £500.[26] More than any other single factor, these actions contributed to a renewal of Pakeha interest in Waitangi and the events of 1840.

The development of the Waitangi site was important, too, in encouraging Maori awareness of the treaty and the Waitangi property. Maori representatives were appointed to the Trust Board and Maori now took the initiative in bringing forward ideas to commemorate the Bledisloe gift.[27] Ngapuhi resolved to build a whare runanga in the grounds of the treaty house (as it came to be known). The Maori building, standing beside the European house, was intended to symbolise the relationship established at Waitangi in 1840 and confirmed by Hobson's words – we are now one people. The idea was adopted by other tribes and became a national project. It was decided to lay the foundation stone for the whare runanga during a great hui which would celebrate the ninety-fourth anniversary of the treaty's signing.[28]

The gathering, hosted by Ngapuhi in early February 1934, was centred on Te Tii marae. It drew a massive tribal representation of some 10,000 people from throughout New Zealand. Among the guests was the Maori King Koroki, whose attendance was seen by some as a significant gesture of friendship for the government. The presence of members of the government, with the Bledisloes playing a prominent part, added mana to the occasion. The Department of Internal Affairs and the Native Department under Ngata jointly assumed a large measure of responsibility for organisation of this first official gathering at Waitangi. The occasion fell into two parts – the Maori welcome and festivities on Te Tii marae, and a subsequent ceremony in the treaty house grounds where the Trust Board had erected a flagpole, situated approximately where the treaty was signed. (The exact spot was in doubt: a cairn had marked it during the Busby family's occupation; later it was sometimes thought that a large Norfolk pine pin-pointed it.)[29]

The pattern set at this official ceremony was to endure over the years – a government steamer anchored in the bay (later there would be naval vessels), the Union Jack unfurled from the flagpole and the recitation of a prayer composed by Bledisloe, that God 'grant that the sacred compact then made in these waters may be faithfully and honourably kept for all time to come'. A second prayer added the plea that the union of the two races as one nation might be achieved through Christianity.[30] Bledisloe's first prayer became the accepted expression of national commitment to the Waitangi ideal for some fifty years, it sustaining the notion that a 'sacred compact' had been forged in 1840, and nurturing the concept of one people formed of two races. But the second prayer (and its significance) has been overlooked.

The 1934 celebrations, from the Maori point of view, were not merely an anniversary of the signing of the treaty. They also marked the centenary of Britain's acknowledgement of Maori sovereignty in 1834 with the gift of a national flag which became known as the flag of the United Tribes of New Zealand. In 1934, a replica of that flag was apparently unfurled at Waitangi in addition to the Union Jack, although this was not noted in the published record of the celebrations.[31] The Maori understanding of the treaty as an agreement recognising Maori independence was, therefore, sustained in 1934, alongside Bledisloe's encouragement to regard the treaty as the foundation of New Zealand's nationhood. That there might be conflict between the two views of the past had been shown in the history of Maori protest and the persistence of the two notions indicated that there could be further conflict.

For the public at large, the 1934 celebrations were not particularly significant. Response to a public appeal to finance the Waitangi property's maintenance and development was disappointing. Bledisloe, a regular visitor to Waitangi and an active participant in Trust Board plans during his governorship, was keen to publicise the Waitangi property and its history. He was especially anxious that a nationwide consciousness might develop out of what was primarily, for Pakeha at least, an Auckland and Northland interest.[32]

All over New Zealand at this time there was a growing interest in the approaching 1940 centennial. A special committee was formed to organise the celebrations and to oversee a series of historical publications. Research unearthed much early, half-forgotten history, and this generated newspaper articles on historical subjects, all of which increased public awareness of the country's origins. Indications of the emerging national outlook were to be seen in the newly minted currency of the mid-1930s, the crown coin depicting the signing of the treaty, and in a campaign to have Thomas Bracken's poem, *God of Nations*, adopted as the national anthem. In 1940, then, it seemed fitting to hold a major centennial celebration at Waitangi. Bledisloe's gift made this possible. The treaty itself was thus accorded a central position in the national consciousness, in marked contrast to the 1890 anniversary when little thought had been given to the possibility of choosing 6 February for the official festivities to mark the colony's foundation. Auckland and Wellington had contended for the commemoration to be held on their provincial day, Auckland taking the prize.

As part of the 1940 celebrations, the treaty documents and other relevant papers were temporarily held at Waitangi. This was the first time they had been treated as significant. A remarkable paradox of New Zealand history was the official neglect of these documents even while they were said to have been so central to the nation's origins. In 1841 they had been almost destroyed by fire, George Elliott, the government records clerk, rescuing them from an iron box before the weatherboard cottage in Official Bay, Auckland, that served as government offices, went up in flames. Thereafter the treaty documents disappeared from sight until 1865 when William Baker of the Native Department, at the request of parliament, worked on them and produced a rather erroneous list of signatories.[33] They were called on again in 1869 at Mantell's request and then, in 1877, facsimiles of the several treaty sheets were made before they were put in storage. But when Dr Thomas Hocken, searching for historical documents, found the treaty papers in 1911 in the Wellington Government Buildings, several of the sheets had been damaged around the edges by water and two had also been nibbled by rats. Restored and mounted, the sheets were kept in special boxes from then on.[34] When they were sent to Waitangi in 1940, it was the first time that they had been on public show.

Because the Labour government was determined that the 1940 celebrations would be a great demonstration of national pride and unity, considerable time and money were devoted to planning the festivities. The outbreak of the Second World War in 1939 merely served to heighten Labour's commitment. Outwardly, the Waitangi celebrations appeared to be successful. Over 10,000 people attended, including many tribal representatives and a group from the newly formed Maori Battalion. An impressive re-enactment of the treaty signing was staged and speakers rose to the occasion with appropriate expressions of unity.

The Governor-General, Viscount Galway, referred to the First World War, claiming that a 'new compact . . . of heart and affection between the Maoris and their pakeha brothers' had been made then. Ngata spoke moderately of the treaty as 'a gentlemen's agreement which on the whole had been not badly observed'.[35] And the nation's newspapers had a field day with full-page spreads under headings that described Waitangi as the 'cradle of the nation', and the treaty as the 'Dominion's Magna Carta', the 'bulwark and foundation of nationhood'.[36] Some of these expressions were not new – the treaty had been likened to the Magna Carta quite soon after 1840 – but after 1940 expressions such as these were popularised through repetition at most Waitangi ceremonies.

Behind the facade, however, all was not so happy. Although the Labour government had poured more money into Maori affairs after 1935, especially into land development begun by Ngata, many Maori discerned a lack of sensitivity in government ranks and were disappointed by Labour's failure to implement promises. Compensation for the nineteenth-century confiscations in the Waikato, for example, had still not been finalised by 1940, although a commission of inquiry had determined the justice of the case in the 1920s.[37] Many Maori shrewdly seized upon the celebrations as a good opportunity to embarrass the government into action. They drew attention to claims and grievances, identifying the government's inadequacies and calling into question the nation's good reputation in race relations at a time when public opinion was most vulnerable.

Maori did not support the 1940 celebrations as they had the 1934 hui. Waikato, with their compensation claims not settled, refused to attend, although they had a hand in building the 100-foot long canoe that was launched at Waitangi; and Taranaki Maori, old sores still smarting, did not unanimously support the occasion. South Island Maori, on the other hand, set grievances aside and some 500 Ngai Tahu participated in southern festivities in April. In official speeches, however, they pressed home the point that they had waited over a hundred years for settlement of some claims which had been officially recognised since the 1850s, and that a final settlement would have been fitting in the centennial year. They were disappointed. So, too, was Hoani Te Heuheu of Ngati Tuwharetoa, who had hoped for a decision from the Privy Council in 1940 on an appeal case which involved rights under the treaty.[38]

Ngata used the occasion of the 1940 centenary to comment publicly on race relations. In a reversal of one of his previous comments on the treaty, he told parliament that the substance of the land had gone to the Queen by the 1840 treaty and that Maori retained only the shadow – a repetition of Nopera Panakareao's second thoughts on the treaty. Frank Langstone, Native Minister, refuted the allegation and chastised Maori for their lack of gratitude, telling them that in its dealings with an indigenous race, 'No other country in the world has such a [good] record' as New Zealand,[39] a claim that Pakeha would assert as often as Maori might query the record. At the Waitangi function itself, Ngata noted old grievances, asking the government to settle such issues so that Maori could 'close their eyes to the past'.[40] The Labour government, under Peter Fraser from 1940, was not indifferent to grievances, but war postponed any resolution.

War conditions did, however, allow for the satisfaction of one long-standing Maori request – the desire for a degree of Maori control over Maori affairs as a right under the treaty. As the nation's war effort swung into motion in 1940–41, it became accepted government policy not to enforce conscription with Maori. In the First World War, tribes who had suffered confiscation in the nineteenth century refused to volunteer at first and then resisted conscription. Arrests had been made in the Waikato, the only area where conscription was enforced. During the Second World War the government was aware that there was still bad feeling. Waikato were prepared to defend New Zealand, but they still saw no reason to fight for England: the treaty was 'a delusion to make the Maori people believe that the British people will keep their word of honour,' said the old chief Te Kanawa.[41]

In the hope that a new approach would break down this resistance, Labour established the Maori War Effort Organisation in 1941. Its main purpose was to encourage voluntary enlistment, but it also stimulated civilian support for the war effort and gave assistance with manpower. Under the leadership of Paraire Paikea, MP for Northern Maori, a national network of Maori committees was established. Although close liaison was kept with government and army, the War Effort Organisation gave Maori a degree of autonomy long sought after and provided scope for greater involvement within the mainstream of New Zealand life.[42]

After the war, legislation brought the committee structure under the control of the Native Department (from 1947 the Department of Maori Affairs). Fraser hoped that the change would not stifle Maori initiative and enthusiasm, but bringing the War Effort Organisation under firm government control did change its character. From being an autonomous body run by Maori, it became the welfare section of a department dominated by Pakeha, an orientation modified very little by the appointment of Tipi Ropiha as the department's head in 1947. The wartime committees were reorganised, leading to the establishment of a national Maori Council in 1962, but there was still a strong sense among Maori that the autonomy and power they sought had not been achieved.

This sense of deprivation was aggravated by events after the war. Successive governments failed to meet Maori requests and needs. The first Labour government, for example, assisted Maori with its general policies and special Maori affairs programmes, but in the final reckoning it did not measure up to its 1935 promise of 'equality with racial individuality'. The problems involved were considerable and became fully apparent only when Labour held office. In its fourteen-year administration, Labour did initiate changes in housing, education and social welfare that might lead Maori towards the promised equality but, like all New Zealand governments before and since, it would not advance Maori interests at the expense of electoral support. One casualty was Tirikatene's petition on the treaty. The original intent, to enforce treaty promises by having it incorporated in legislation, was supplanted in 1945 by a government decision to print the treaty and hang copies of it in every school and Maori meeting place in the country, 'as a sacred re-affirmation' of the 1840 agreement. The recommendation had come from the Maori Affairs Committee of the House, which had finally considered Tirikatene's petition (and two similar petitions) after a thirteen-year delay.[43]

This action, though not particularly satisfying to the Ratana– Labour Maori MPs, opened the way to a new initiative on the treaty just before Labour's second administration, from 1957 to 1960.[44] Labour's Maori Policy Committee, chaired for twenty-two years by Tirikatene, requested that 6 February should be declared a public holiday 'in view of its [the treaty's] historical significance and more particularly its influence on Maori land laws and Pakeha–Maori relations'. This became part of Labour's 1957 election policy. The committee also wanted a more vigorous policy on land development and a Minister representing the Maori race on the Executive Council, an appointment that had been allowed to lapse.

By 1960, these requests had not been acted upon. Walter Nash jealously guarded his role in Maori policy and gave the Maori

MPs a poor hearing. With an election coming up in late 1960, however, Labour found it expedient to act on the demand to commemorate the treaty by giving Waitangi Day official recognition. A threat by Tirikatene to introduce a private member's bill, if the government failed to act, no doubt carried weight. There was also talk of the Maori members showing their displeasure by withholding their support. The Waitangi Day Act 1960, however, was little more than a gesture. It declared that 6 February would be known as 'Waitangi Day', a 'national day of thanksgiving in commemoration of the signing'. Any area could now substitute Waitangi Day for a holiday already observed in the region, but the legislation did not allow for a national holiday as the Maori MPs wished. Without this provision the Act caused barely a ripple on the nation's waters.

In spite of this apathetic response, general public awareness of Waitangi was far greater than Bledisloe could have envisaged in 1932. His Waitangi gift had given a focus to what had been for years, to most Pakeha, and some Maori, merely a vague notion about the early history of their country. The gradual Pakeha rediscovery of the Waitangi treaty was closely related to the development of the Waitangi estate and to the anniversary celebrations. This growth of interest was mainly a post-war development. For four or five years after 1940, the Waitangi property was used by the army, who restricted public access, but in the meantime, Vernon Reed and the Trust Board, together with a small band of local people, continued to promote it. From 1948 an annual government grant augmented admission fees and other fund-raising efforts.

One change that was to have important influence was the erection of a new flagpole in 1946–47. When the old flagstaff was found to be rotten, the navy offered to erect and maintain a new one. From 1947, when the Union Jack was unfurled at an impressive ceremony, the tradition was established of holding an annual naval ceremony at Waitangi with naval vessels anchored in the bay.[45] This visible reminder of imperial might cast the annual commemoration of Waitangi in a distinctly new light. Maori protest in the 1970s made it clear that Maori resented the naval display as symbolic of over a hundred years of Pakeha domination.

From 1950, the Waitangi National Reserve, under its controlling authority the Waitangi Trust Board, was serviced by the Department of Lands and Survey. The property was now visited more often. In late December 1953 the Queen and the Duke of Edinburgh stopped at the grounds for an hour.[46] The visit, not included in the original tour proposal, had been indignantly requested by northern Maori, although the change of plans probably resulted not from Maori representations but from a direct approach by Bledisloe who, in retirement, maintained an interest in the Waitangi property.

It was the first time a reigning monarch had visited Waitangi, but what promised to be a momentous occasion was marred by friction. Northern Maori sought government financial assistance to present a suitable Maori reception, but this was refused. There were differences of opinion about the selection of Maori representatives to meet the Queen. E.B. Corbett, Minister of Maori Affairs, turned down a suggestion that Maori should discuss the treaty with the Queen, a proposal which originated with Whina Cooper, Maori Women's Welfare League President. It was 'quite improper', according to Corbett, although he appears to have seen nothing improper in his own trespassing on Maori protocol by insisting that he would present, on behalf of the Maori people, the formal address to the Queen at Rotorua.[47] Tensions remained below the surface for the Royal Visit, but the shape of later protest at Waitangi, and the role of Maori women in that protest, were foreshadowed in these exchanges.

The 1953 Royal Visit was significant for Waikato, too, because it was the first time that a reigning monarch had visited the 'King's headquarters' at Turangawaewae. The Holland government disapproved but the visit went ahead. The fact that a special address for the Queen, drawn up by the Tainui Maori Council, had to be 'presented' after the visit did not detract from the significance of the message. The address noted that although the first Maori King, Potatau Te Wherowhero, had not signed the treaty, the time had come to 'fulfil that which was left incomplete by Queen Victoria and Potatau in the Treaty of Waitangi'. The uncompleted business was Waikato's 'oath of true allegiance', a pledge that they were prepared to give now that the monarch was willing to come to Waikato.[48] The move did not therefore detract from the spirit of independence that continued to flourish within the King movement.

Though Maori felt some reservations, the public imagination seems to have been unreservedly captured by the Royal Visit. As the *Dominion* reflected: 'Thus at last Waitangi comes into its own to a degree worthy of its significance and New Zealanders must see that its status is maintained and heightened.'[49] From that year on, annual ceremonies on 6 February at Waitangi were attended by the Governor-General, members of the government and the armed forces. Subsequent Royal visitors regularly had Waitangi on their itineraries. From brief ceremonies of perhaps half an hour, the scope of the annual event began to expand. The Governor-General's speech became a feature, always reported by the press. Year after year it emphasised the legendary good relationship between Maori and Pakeha which the treaty was said to have initiated. The common theme was the forming of one nation from the partnership of two races, by the sacred compact: 'It brought together two fine races who settled down together to achieve full nationhood for a young and undeveloped country under the Queen's peace and law.' This was Cobham's expression in 1959; and in 1960, when the first evening ceremony was held before some 7,000 onlookers, he reiterated the theme – '120 years ago, the pattern was set and a new tapestry planned in which light and dark threads were interwoven to form the completed study of a new nation'.[50]

These ceremonies at Waitangi drew attention to the ideal of 'one people', providing good opportunity for Maori criticism of the shortfall between promise and practice. Inevitably, the government was attacked by Maori. Leaders joined in the opposition to an All Black tour of South Africa in 1960 that excluded Maori players – a problem not handled well by either Labour or the incoming National government. It was one of the first signs that Maori might be prepared to resort to new methods of organised protest to highlight their criticisms of government inadequacies in the area that was becoming known as 'race relations'.

Many Maori considered that there was good cause for protest in the 1950s and 1960s when National administrations held power for all but three years. The most offensive legislation was the 1953 Maori Affairs Act and an amendment in 1967. The provisions of both Acts, which related to Maori land, disregarded traditional Maori values and aimed at economic rationalisation and use. Although the land problem was serious enough for urgent attention, the imposition of such legislation without sufficient consultation was bound to give rise to protest. Other legislation in the National period – the 1953 Maori Trustee Act, the 1953 Town and Country Planning Act and the Counties Amendment Act 1961 – was also considered to have contravened the treaty. These Acts exacerbated tensions already caused by earlier legislation.[51]

Many Maori sensed a strong assimilative urge behind this legislation, a new variation on the old theme of creating 'one people'. The Hunn Report of 1960 crystallised Maori fears by assuming the ultimate demise of any separate Maori identity in New Zealand. Regardless of policy, Hunn observed, it was more than likely that intermarriage would create one people – and that people would be all Pakeha, some more brown than others. This was offensive, although Hunn had not intended it to be; his definition of integration did allow for a Maori contribution to the national identity, but this tended to be overlooked by critics.[52]

Through the 1960s and 1970s, increasing Pakeha and Maori interest in Waitangi and the treaty were not always in harmony. The focus of interest for each race was different. Pakeha interest continued to be based on the historical nature of the treaty. The Waitangi Day celebrations were televised, and broadcast annually to the nation. The 1968 broadcast was the longest single national link-up that television had carried out in New Zealand,[53] and in most subsequent years Waitangi received generous treatment from the media. A Maori academic, Koro Dewes, accurately observed the drift of national sentiment in 1968: 'There is no doubt that many New Zealanders are beginning to search for something to believe in which will credibly express their nationalism, and so the Treaty of Waitangi is becoming recognised as a symbol of our nationhood.' But Dewes, reflecting the opinion of an articulate section of Maori society, urged the 'Pakeha majority who have a veto on whether things are done or not' to follow up words with actions, to make the treaty a 'true symbol, with real meaning, and not just spurious sentimentalism'.[54]

Dewes recommended that Waitangi Day be made a full national holiday; the Labour–Ratana MPs, too, had been lobbying for this change. The idea had its organised supporters, both Pakeha and Maori, although Pakeha interest seems to have lacked any contemporary political significance of a radical kind. The New Zealand Founders' Society (founded in the 1940s to promote pride in the early European settlement of the country) advocated official recognition of an all-New Zealand national day on 6 February. By the end of the 1950s the Society was holding social functions to mark that date.

Maori requests for legislative recognition of Waitangi Day, however, were part of a long-standing struggle to have the treaty made enforcible in law. Official recognition of the date was seen as a first step towards more comprehensive legislation, although this was not always evident. A gathering of some 15,000 at Carlaw Park, Auckland, organised by the Auckland Waitangi Day Trust (an amalgam of several Maori groups), seemed to the press merely to be 'celebrating' the 1968 Waitangi Day, and seeking to have a public holiday to ensure subsequent like events.[55] The latent political purpose went unrecognised.

By the 1970s the thrust of organised Maori activity was towards both a national holiday and 'ratification' of the treaty. The challenge to Pakeha was made explicit by Maori leaders. Dewes asserted that 'for the Pakeha the Treaty meant very little, except that it helped to legalise his proclamation of sovereignty over these islands, that it created another outpost of the British Empire ... in the south-west Pacific and added another country in the red on world maps'. Pat Hohepa, of the University of Auckland, asked pointedly if the treaty was 'a promise or a betrayal'. Like many other Maori, he predicted, at the beginning of the 1970s, that race relations would deteriorate, given 'the continuing lip service to the farce that all is well, given a continuation of insipid platitudes and no practical remedial measures'.[56] This prediction seemed to be fulfilled as the volume of Maori protest swelled in the 1970s, with a small but articulate group of Pakeha sympathisers joining the cause. In 1971 the Waitangi ceremonies were disrupted by incidents, said to have been organised by the Tamatoa Council in Auckland.[57] (It was no coincidence that 1971 was United Nations year for the elimination of racial discrimination.) From then on protests continued as Maori sought to gain maximum publicity for their grievances.

Apart from the proliferation of government measures that continued to intrude upon Maori interests, both Maori and Pakeha sectors of the community were influenced by events and trends outside the country – the post-war decolonisation of Africa, Asia and the Pacific, the growth of the Black Power movement in the United States and the activities of the United Nations and its agencies, especially those dealing with the question of human rights. Maori watched with interest the assertiveness of non-European groups emerging in the newly independent countries. The rapid success of some of these groups in establishing the right to self-determination was in marked contrast to the Maori experience, a factor that added a degree of frustrated energy to Maori protest.

Maori also learned from the struggles of other minority groups with government structures. Indians in Canada and the United States were influential in sharpening Maori awareness of rights that might be conceded, and in demonstrating methods of protest that might strike at the weak points of the dominant culture. The success of some Indian claims in the 1970s added fuel to the Maori cause and underlined the marked differences between the Indian and Maori situations. In the United States, Indian treaties were protected by the constitution and thus came within the jurisdiction of the law, while in Canada, responsibility for Indian affairs was split between central and provincial governments. In both instances, Indians gained certain concessions.[58] By contrast, New

Zealand's constitution had never effectively protected the treaty. Unless incorporated in legislation, the treaty was not cognisable in law. From the Maori point of view, the Waitangi treaty seemed a poor tool to procure rights that Indians were obtaining with seemingly less remarkable treaties. This conclusion was reinforced by several modern law cases in which the Waitangi treaty was rejected as a basis for arguing rights.[59]

Maori protest in the 1970s owed much to the activities of groups and organisations born of increased Maori urbanisation and education. Young Maori were better able to articulate their grievances in terms calculated to force some response from the Pakeha majority and many were prepared to adopt the strategies of the modern activist movements. A succession of groups began to challenge the Pakeha record in fulfilling the treaty promises – Nga Tamatoa, Kotahitanga (revived in the 1960s), the Maori Organisation of Human Rights and, by the end of the 1970s, the beginnings of a movement that would lead to the formation of the Waitangi Action Committee and associated groups.

The cry of the modern protest groups was initially for a greater Pakeha awareness and acceptance of Maoritanga – the whole complex of Maori culture and identity – which they claimed the treaty had guaranteed. By 1980, the call of the more radical activists included a claim that Maori be clearly acknowledged as tangata whenua, the people of the land; they specifically claimed a Maori sovereignty that they wanted Pakeha to acknowledge.[60] There was little talk of the treaty as a sacred compact, a concept encouraged by Pakeha and, as a result, suspect.

Alongside this activity, well-established national organisations such as the New Zealand Maori Council and the Maori Women's Welfare League made submissions to the government, sometimes on request, about the Maori situation in relation to the treaty. Such documents were in themselves a challenge to government. Henare Ngata, for instance, concluded one report on the treaty by telling the National government in 1971 that 'those who approach it in a positive frame of mind and are prepared to regard it as an obligation of honour will find that the Treaty is well capable of implementation'.[61]

This clamour of the late 1960s and early 1970s challenged academics to take a more active role in researching the history and effect of the treaty. Their findings were more critical than earlier works. They discovered that most previous writers had over-emphasised the humanitarian concern in the original treaty negotiation, at the expense of a fair evaluation of the treaty's role in serving British and settler interests. Research also gave new insights into the Maori point of view; the historian Ruth Ross stressed the variance in Maori and English treaty texts and interpretations. Lawyers, too, began to re-evaluate the treaty and its standing in international law. The results of this research began to be published in the 1970s. Gradually, information about the treaty and its meaning to Maori has been disseminated more widely – a factor that has encouraged a growing circle of Pakeha to sympathise with, and sometimes support, Maori protest.[62]

In 1973 a Labour government responded to Maori requests by making Waitangi Day a public holiday on the day of the week on which it fell. It was a popular decision, given prominence by Prime Minister Norman Kirk's announcement at that year's Waitangi hui at Te Tii marae. The name Waitangi Day was altered to New Zealand Day.[63] Although the change caused little debate at the time, representatives of both Maori and Pakeha society subsequently objected strongly; it was felt that something of traditional significance had been quietly lost while little of national worth had been gained.[64] The 1976 Waitangi Day Act reinstated the name and, at the suggestion of Matiu Rata, the Labour–Ratana MP, a Maori text of the treaty was added to the English text already included in the schedule of the 1973 Act. Hastily put together on the night of the debate, the text was full of error, a point that escaped notice at the time.[65]

While the statutory recognition of Waitangi's anniversary day encouraged public awareness, the need for legislation to give effect to the treaty's promises remained a Maori concern. The Treaty of Waitangi Act 1975 seemed at first sight to provide the necessary framework, by setting up a tribunal to 'make recommendations on claims relating to the practical application of the principles of the Treaty and, for that purpose, to determine its meaning and effect and whether certain matters are inconsistent with those principles'. Both Maori and English texts of the treaty were appended as schedules. The obvious weaknesses were the limitations placed on the Tribunal: it had no powers of enforcing its decisions or recommendations, and had no authority to consider matters arising before the 1975 legislation. The Tribunal was immediately suspect as a piece of government 'window-dressing', a suspicion that gained substance when the incoming National government in 1975 delayed setting it up. After an initial spurt of activity, with sittings opening incongruously in the plush ballroom of the Intercontinental Hotel in Auckland, the Tribunal went into recess. Official and Maori interest turned to the incorporation of Maori rights within human rights legislation.

In the meantime, immigration from the Pacific Islands was

adding a fresh complication. In the 1970s official emphasis shifted towards using the treaty as the unifying symbol of an emerging multi-cultural society. Sir Keith Holyoake, Governor-General at the end of the decade, was especially fond of this notion, looking forward to the complete fulfilment of 'He iwi tahi tatou' by eliminating 'any form of distinction' between the races.[66] Many Maori interpreted this to mean the complete loss of a Maori identity and rejected such a proposition. They pointed out that until Pakeha had accepted the full implications of bi-culturalism, national aspirations of multi-culturalism were premature. Yet such ideas reached a wide audience. In the 1960s and 1970s the Education Department directed all schools to commemorate Waitangi Day; an official message was usually read which very often incorporated the notion of the treaty as the foundation of the nation's multi-culturalism.

In the face of strident protest at Waitangi ceremonies from 1979 to 1983, government reaction was first a greater caution in pressing the 'one people' theme, and then a resolve to move away from the concept of the day being a Maori–Pakeha 'celebration'; it would be the 'celebration of an historical event'.[67] This was administrative side-stepping, unlikely to ease tensions and typical of official evasion of treaty issues.

A number of Pakeha, however, including church leaders, began to show a willingness to reappraise the treaty and a reluctance to 'celebrate' the day as the government wished. A sympathetic understanding of issues which concerned many Maori gradually spread among a wider circle of Pakeha. The major religious denominations continue to promote group and individual study of the treaty.[68] While the public at large remained bemused or irritated by continuing protest, a random sampling of New Zealand opinion in March 1983 showed that most New Zealanders wanted to retain a day of observance to commemorate the signing of the treaty.[69] This was a far cry from the lack of Pakeha interest a century ago when one General Assembly member would happily have assigned the treaty to the wastepaper basket – 'about the only place it ought to be seen in'.[70]

By the early 1980s, Maori opinion on the treaty and on Waitangi Day had become more diverse than among Pakeha. The most extreme voice, a cry from an organised group of young activists, sought 'ratification' of the treaty. Maori were urged to 'boycott' the Waitangi ceremonies – a call first issued by Nga Tamatoa in 1972 – because successive governments had not honoured the 1840 agreement. Various protest groups, drawing on feminist, socialist and peace movements, made their presence felt at Waitangi from

1979 to 1985. By word and action, they challenged older Maori to rethink their long-held assumptions.

For the elders, especially those of Te Tii marae at Waitangi, which was thrust into the public eye by the protests, the challenge was not easy to accept. Eruera Stirling, although not a Ngapuhi, spoke for many kaumatua when he objected to the way young Maori were 'trampling on the mana of their elders and degrading the customs of their own people'. Condemning the call for a boycott, Stirling reproached the young for presuming to 'step over the covenant' which only men of chiefly line had a right to talk about. He asserted that 'when they trample on the work of their ancestors, they are also trampling upon themselves and upon us all', an opinion also held by some kaumatua.[71] Year after year, tensions at Te Tii showed the wide gap between this opinion and that of the protestors.[72]

In spite of their respect for the treaty, elders usually admitted that it was not altogether perfect – it restricted customary freedoms and led to land alienation – but they seldom condemned it outright. In their view, it was not the treaty that was at fault but the way it had been treated. Sir Graham Latimer, Chairman of the New Zealand Maori Council, after the violent protest of 1982, held to the view that Waitangi Day celebrations were worthwhile because they represented years of Maori struggle 'to get legislation changed and altered so that people could find some value in the document'.[73]

Many Maori, not necessarily active protestors, would have disagreed with Latimer's statement. The extent of Maori concern over the continuing alienation of Maori land and other problems was demonstrated by the impressive Land March in 1975. A new tone of resolve was apparent in stands taken at Bastion Point and Raglan over land disputes. And in 1979, the Ratana–Labour alliance came to an end with the resignation of Matiu Rata from the Labour Party. The Northern Maori MP, disillusioned with years of frustrated efforts to obtain redress for Maori grievances within the Labour structure, severed his connection and established the Mana Motuhake party.

As the name suggests, the party's aims were to secure self-determination for the Maori people, although within the mainstream of government structures. Rata took a stand in the Ratana tradition, seeking to have the treaty ratified, but in 1980 the party also favoured the tactics of protest, with a call to Maori to boycott the 6 February celebrations.[74] The attractiveness of the party, which had its roots in nineteenth-century Maori struggles with the government (Kotahitanga and the King movement) and recalled the 1835 Declaration of Independence, was shown by the 1981 election results: the party came second to Labour in all four Maori electorates. Though Mana Motuhake was not a serious threat, the Labour party could not entirely ignore such competition. In policy statements before Labour's win in the 1984 'snap' election, Labour appeared ready to give Maori opinion a fair hearing and, not surprisingly, the Mana Motuhake party did not poll well.

In February 1984, Kotahitanga was revived by a hikoi (march) to Waitangi in protest against 'celebrating' the day. Marchers included a large Waikato group as well as representatives of many tribes, churchmen and some Pakeha. Initially, some northern Maori leaders were not happy about the protest, in which they saw disrespect for a 'sacred document' signed by their ancestors.[75] In the final event, the march had organisational problems which confused both the media and the public. The Governor–General's two-hour wait to meet Kotahitanga leaders, and the failure of these leaders to come forward were interpreted as a failure of the hikoi as a whole. The important sense of oneness expressed in the march was generally not grasped.

That sense of unity, however, was demonstrated the following September when a major hui met at Turangawaewae, Ngaruawahia. At the initiative of the Maori Council of Churches, a committee representing a wide range of organisations had been set up to organise the gathering. The aim was to produce a Maori consensus on the treaty; workshop sessions were held, along with the traditional oratory of the marae. Pakeha were not encouraged to attend and press releases were carefully controlled to ensure accuracy. Resolutions covered the well-worn territory of earlier Maori requests, but official response was now more positive. With government assistance, a second hui was held at Waitangi on 5–6 February 1985. Resolutions confirmed the status of the treaty as 'unique and imbued with the mana of the tupuna'. While individual take (causes) covered a wide range of matters, there was a 'clear call' for no further Waitangi 'celebrations' until the treaty had been honoured. Only Tai Tokerau, for whom the treaty remained a special cause, dissented. Generally the hui acknowledged that the major challenge for the government in 'honouring' the treaty was to find a way of satisfying all interested parties.[76]

Meanwhile, the Treaty of Waitangi Tribunal had been active. Under the 1975 Act the Tribunal comprised a chairman (Chief Judge of the Maori Land Court) and two appointees, one a Maori, the other a Pakeha lawyer. Under the chairmanship of Chief

Judge Edward Durie, a rejuvenated Tribunal had brought out a remarkable series of reports. In 1983 it gave a sympathetic assessment of fishing rights in Taranaki. The Te Atiawa claim attracted a great deal of public interest when the National Prime Minister, Robert Muldoon, rejected the Tribunal's recommendations but subsequently reversed the decision. Legislation was passed to change the outfall of the Taranaki Syngas plant from Motunui to Waitara. It was a compromise solution but an indication that the Tribunal, though lacking powers of enforcement, could influence public attitudes and affect government decisions. The 1984 Kaituna report, again relating to discharging waste (this time into a river), was rather less successful. In 1985 the Tribunal produced yet another perceptive report on a Manukau Harbour claim which involved not only fishing rights but comprehensive usage rights.[77] The report drew a mixed response from government and public. An uneasiness, even a hostility shown by many Pakeha, suggests that satisfaction of Maori claims depends, as it always has, upon whether or not Maori and Pakeha interests coincide.

A further claim has also had a mixed reception. The Maori Language Board of Wellington wanted the Tribunal to recommend that Maori be recognised as an official language throughout the country. As hearings stretched over four weeks in late 1985, the longest Tribunal sitting to that date, the ramifications of what might have appeared a simple claim began to cast more than a ripple through the community at large. Whereas earlier claims had affected specific tribes and areas, the language claim had implications for everyone in the country, not only all Maori but all Pakeha too. The final report, released at the end of April 1986, was cautious in its recommendations, acknowledging the difficulties involved, but it did not shrink from suggesting that steps should be taken towards the end desired by the claimants. The 'taonga' guaranteed by article two of the treaty, the report noted, had incorporated the Maori language, because taonga (best translated as 'valued customs and possessions') included intangible as well as tangible things.[78] The Tribunal thus carried further its terms of reference which included the task of determining the treaty's meaning and intent, a task it had begun to address in previous reports.

With the passage of the Treaty of Waitangi Amendment Act in December 1985, the Tribunal constituted under the 1975 legislation came to an end; the warrants of the two appointees, Graham Latimer and Paul Temm, were allowed to expire. The new Act expanded the size of the Tribunal to six appointees, four being

Maori, while the Chief Judge remained chairman. The Tribunal's jurisdiction was broadened to allow the investigation of claims referring back to 1840. The new body, based on Canadian precedents, reflects a shift from a judicial-type court hearing towards a more informal commission of inquiry. Responsibility now rests with the Tribunal, with the assistance of a research team and consultants, to investigate the circumstances of claims brought before it. Admirable as these moves are, Maori expectations could be disappointed by delays.

The Labour government kept a fairly high profile on Maori affairs through 1985, but there was a marked reserve in official ranks by the end of the year, the government probably fearing that public opinion was not keeping pace with change. In late 1985 the appointment of New Zealand's first Maori Governor-General, Sir Paul Reeves, was generally accepted as recognition of the bi-cultural character of the nation. But Tribunal hearings on the Maori language claim, about the same time, created widespread unease. In addition, the government's proposal to incorporate the treaty in a Bill of Rights was not greeted with much enthusiasm by either race.

In December 1985, the Labour government decided to ease tensions over the treaty 'celebrations' by shifting the focus of events away from Waitangi. Waitangi Day 1986, therefore, was marked officially by a two-hour reception at Wellington's Beehive (Parliament Buildings). Entertainment reflected the multi-cultural nature of New Zealand society; the function had the flavour of a national day rather than a commemoration of the country's bi-cultural foundation and history. Protestors clashed with the police both at the reception and in the grounds where they greeted guests with cries that the treaty was a 'fraud'. Others, too, objected to the move, the Tai Tokerau people opting for a quiet ecumenical church service in the Waitangi grounds. The tone of the low-key commemoration was set by northern kaumatua, Sir James Henare, who prayed for reconciliation and harmony.

One of those present was the then Leader of the Opposition, Jim McLay, whose deputy, Jim Bolger, attended the Wellington function. If National hoped to satisfy Maori sensitivities by covering both events they probably failed, for Bolger's words were not well chosen. While noting that there was a responsibility to resolve outstanding Maori issues, he observed that solutions would not be found in 'picking over the bones of the past 146 years of New Zealand's history'. By contrast, Labour Prime Minister, David Lange, showed greater perception of the tensions surrounding the day and the treaty itself. He considered it ironic that the growing sense of identity that had led to 6 February becoming a public holiday from 1974 had encouraged a reassessment of the past which 'questioned the appropriateness of the treaty as cause for celebration'. And he added: 'We are not the poorer for the questioning. We are stronger in our understanding of ourselves and the way we live here.'[79] Since the Wellington-based Waitangi Day function had not been entirely satisfactory, the government, having consulted with Maori members of the Waitangi Trust Board, decided that a dual commemoration on Waitangi Day would be more appropriate. On 6 February 1987, therefore, there was an official commemoration once again at Waitangi, as well as the ceremony in Wellington. The latter, as in 1986, involved the diplomatic corps and was directed at recognition of the country's multi-national character, but this time Maori were fittingly acknowledged as the tangata whenua.[80] The two ceremonies, essentially a compromise, seemed generally acceptable to both Maori and Pakeha, although whether they continue to meet the varying aspirations of the two peoples remains to be seen.

Meanwhile, events in 1986 were leading to greater recognition of the status of the treaty. One implication of this was the assertion of Maori right to a stronger voice in government circles. This was apparent in June 1986 when *Puao-Te-Ata-Tu* (*Day break*), drafted in the main by Maori, was released. Known also as the *Report of the Ministerial Committee on a Maori Perspective for the Department of Social Welfare*, it not only suggested changes to that department; it also recommended that a comprehensive approach be adopted in all government dealings with Maori business and that the initiatives of the Maori people and the community at large be harnessed to help address problems.[81]

That Maori were not prepared to accept long-standing government paternalism was also demonstrated by widespread Maori irritation over a loan 'scandal' which first became public in December 1986. Maori were generally reluctant to accept allegations of incompetence in top Maori administrators. They repeated their long-standing call for a 'new-look' Department of Maori Affairs, one geared to better co-ordination of government agencies and a greater participation of the Maori community at all levels of government administration. Not surprisingly, some Maori saw the loan affair as part of the wider struggle to secure mana Maori motuhake (now referred to more often as self-determination than as autonomy).[82]

In the latter half of 1986, other issues drew public attention to the treaty, in particular to fishing rights. In a reserve decision from the Christchurch High Court in August, Mr Justice Williamson upheld traditional Maori fishing rights based on custom in quashing a conviction against a Maori fisherman, Tom Te Weehi, caught with under-sized paua in January 1984. Williamson noted that the point at issue was section 88(2) of the Fisheries Act 1983 which stated that 'Nothing in this Act shall affect any Maori fishing rights.' In reaching his decision he reviewed both fisheries legislation and other Acts that had referred to Maori fishing rights as well as the history of legal cases involving such rights. Drawing comparisons with the latter, he observed that the case before him was not based on ownership of land, or on an exclusive right to a foreshore or river bank; the claim was a 'non-territorial' one, and the right limited to the Ngai Tahu tribe and its authorised relatives for personal food.[83] The decision, nevertheless, was seen by disconcerted fishing industry officials as a 'landmark ... judgment [which] may put Maori fishermen outside fishing controls and make industry management pointless'.[84]

The issue of fishery management and treaty rights re-emerged in a claim before the Waitangi Tribunal early in 1987. The claim, brought on behalf of the five tribes of the Far North of the North Island, covers customary fishing rights in the area from Whangape Harbour on the West Coast up the Aupouri Peninsula (including Ninety Mile Beach) and down the east coast as far as the Mangonui River. The claimants maintain that they are entitled to recognition, enforcement and relief of their customary rights under the treaty. Since the claim also includes traditional fishing grounds within twenty-five miles of the mainland coast, regulation of commercial fishing is a major point at issue, involving several government departments. Like a claim brought by the northern Ngati Kahu and heard by the Tribunal a few months earlier, the Muriwhenua claim (as it is called) has brought the Tribunal into the public spotlight. More significantly, it has called government departments and local bodies to account for their actions.[85]

With the passage of the State Owned Enterprises Act in December 1986, the possibility of conflict between government departments and Maori interests was heightened. The Act's object was to create in the place of a number of government departments a group of state-owned commercial enterprises on 1 April 1987. This required the transfer of certain Crown assets to the enterprises, including extensive land holdings. The Act took Maori interests into account to the extent of making provision for lands that were the subject of a claim before the Waitangi Tribunal.

But, more important, it clearly incorporated recognition of the treaty by stating that 'Nothing in this Act shall permit the Crown to act in a manner that is inconsistent with the principles of the Treaty of Waitangi.'

With the principles of the treaty thus plainly incorporated in statute it must be recognised by the country's law courts, a point that enabled the New Zealand Maori Council to bring a case to the Court of Appeal in May 1987. The Council sought to restrict the exercise of statutory power to transfer any Crown asset, a move which, even with the precautions built into the Act, the Council found would put Maori interests at risk. As Queen's Counsel David Baragwanath told the Court: 'New Zealand history after 1860 is such an accumulation of statutes and executive acts in breach of the principles of the treaty that the Crown cannot properly assume that in transferring any particular asset it will not act inconsistently with those principles.' Baragwanath argued that the Crown was obliged to act positively to protect the interests of the Maori partners to the treaty. This would require consultation concerning any action which might effect taonga (treasured things).[86]

The case, of high interest from the historical and practical point of view, was conducted under the scrutiny of a court filled to capacity with Maori elders, scholars and interested parties. It stimulated a flurry of research activity as data was assembled. This, as much as the case itself, leaves a legacy of promise. New Zealand's history has suddenly assumed a high profile in the public domain. Just as the Law Commission has been required to undertake intense research into the history of Maori fishing rights, so have other groups and individuals been spurred to activity not merely in historical research but in reassessing the historical record.[87] That record provides both a guide for understanding the present and a justification for changing it.

APPENDICES

Appendix 1: *He Wakaputanga o te Rangatiratanga o Nu Tireni (A Declaration of the Independence of New Zealand)*

1. Ko matou, ko nga Tino Rangatira o nga iwi o Nu Tireni i raro mai o Hauraki kua oti nei te huihui i Waitangi i Tokerau i te ra 28 o Oketopa 1835, ka wakaputa i te Rangatiratanga o to matou wenua a ka meatia ka wakaputaia e matou he Wenua Rangatira, kia huaina, Ko te Waka-minenga o nga Hapu o Nu Tireni.

2. Ko te Kingitanga ko te mana i te wenua o te wakaminenga o Nu Tireni ka meatia nei kei nga Tino Rangatira anake i to matou huihuinga, a ka mea hoki e kore e tukua e matou te wakarite ture ki te tahi hunga ke atu, me te tahi Kawanatanga hoki kia meatia i te wenua o te waka-minenga o Nu Tireni, ko nga tangata anake e meatia nei e matou e wakarite ana ki te ritenga o o matou ture e meatia nei matou i to matou huihuinga.

3. Ko matou ko nga tino Rangatira ka mea nei kia huihui ki te runanga ki Waitangi a te Ngahuru i tenei tau i tenei tau ki te wakarite ture kia tika ai te wakawakanga, kia mau pu te rongo kia mutu te he kia tika te hokohoko, a ka mea hoki ki nga tauiwi o runga, kia wakarerea te wawai, kia mahara ai ki te wakaoranga o to matou wenua, a kia uru ratou ki te wakaminenga o Nu Tireni.

4. Ka mea matou kia tuhituhia he pukapuka ki te ritenga o tenei o to matou wakaputanga nei ki te Kingi o Ingarani hei kawe atu i to matou aroha nana hoki i wakaae ki te Kara mo matou. A no te mea ka atawai matou, ka tiaki i nga pakeha e noho nei i uta, e rere mai ana ki te hokohoko, koia ka mea ai matou ki te Kingi kia waiho hei matua ki a matou i to matou Tamarikitanga kei wakakahoretia to matou Rangatiratanga.

Kua wakaaetia katoatia e matou i tenei ra i te 28 Oketopa, 1835, ki te aroaro o te Reireneti o te Kingi o Ingarani.

[There follow the marks or signatures of chiefs.]

Note: The original is held by National Archives, Wellington. This text and the English text below have been copied from Facsimiles of the Declaration of Independence and the Treaty of Waitangi, *Wellington, 1976. The Declaration was first signed on 28 October 1835 by thirty-four chiefs. The last name was added on 22 July 1839, making a total of fifty-two chiefs.*

A Declaration of the Independence of New Zealand (English text)

1. We, the hereditary chiefs and heads of the tribes of the Northern parts of New Zealand, being assembled at Waitangi, in the Bay of Islands, on

this 28th day of October, 1835, declare the Independence of our country, which is hereby constituted and declared to be an Independent State, under the designation of The United Tribes of New Zealand.

2. All sovereign power and authority within the territories of the United Tribes of New Zealand is hereby declared to reside entirely and exclusively in the hereditary chiefs and heads of tribes in their collective capacity, who also declare that they will not permit any legislative authority separate from themselves in their collective capacity to exist, nor any function of government to be exercised within the said territories, unless by persons appointed by them, and acting under the authority of laws regularly enacted by them in Congress assembled.

3. The hereditary chiefs and heads of tribes agree to meet in Congress at Waitangi in the autumn of each year, for the purpose of framing laws for the dispensation of justice, the preservation of peace and good order, and the regulation of trade; and they cordially invite the Southern tribes to lay aside their private animosities and to consult the safety and welfare of our common country, by joining the Confederation of the United Tribes.

4. They also agree to send a copy of this Declaration to His Majesty the King of England, to thank him for his acknowledgement of their flag; and in return for the friendship and protection they have shown, and are prepared to show, to such of his subjects as have settled in their country, or resorted to its shores for the purposes of trade, they entreat that he will continue to be the parent of their infant State, and that he will become its Protector from all attempts upon its independence.

Agreed to unanimously on this 28th day of October, 1835, in the presence of His Britannic Majesty's Resident.

> [Here follows the signatures or marks of thirty-five Hereditary chiefs or Heads of tribes, which form a fair representation of the tribes of New Zealand from the North Cape to the latitude of the River Thames.]

English witnesses –
(Signed) Henry Williams, Missionary, C.M.S.
       George Clarke, C.M.S.
       James C. Clendon, Merchant.
       Gilbert Mair, Merchant.

I certify that the above is a correct copy of the Declaration of the Chiefs, according to the translation of Missionaries who have resided ten years and upwards in the country; and it is transmitted to His Most Gracious Majesty the King of England, at the unanimous request of the chiefs.

          (Signed)   **JAMES BUSBY,**
                   British Resident at New Zealand.

Appendix 2: *Te Tiriti o Waitangi (The Treaty of Waitangi)*

Ko Wikitoria te Kuini o Ingarani i tana mahara atawai ki nga Rangatira
me nga Hapu o Nu Tirani i tana hiahia hoki kia tohungia ki a ratou o
ratou rangatiratanga me to ratou wenua, a kia mau tonu hoki te Rongo ki
a ratou me te Atanoho hoki kua wakaaro ia he mea tika kia tukua mai
tetahi Rangatira – hei kai wakarite ki nga Tangata maori o Nu Tirani –
kia wakaaetia e nga Rangatira maori te Kawanatanga o te Kuini ki nga
wahikatoa o te wenua nei me nga motu – na te mea hoki he tokomaha ke
nga tangata o tona Iwi Kua noho ki tenei wenua, a e haere mai nei.

Na ko te Kuini e hiahia ana kia wakaritea te Kawanatanga kia kaua ai
nga kino e puta mai ki te tangata maori ki te Pakeha e noho ture kore ana.

Na kua pai te Kuini kia tukua a hau a Wiremu Hopihona he Kapitana i
te Roiara Nawi hei Kawana mo nga wahi katoa o Nu Tirani e tukua
aianei amua atu ki te Kuini, e mea atu ana ia ki nga Rangatira o te
wakaminenga o nga hapu o Nu Tirani me era Rangatira atu enei ture ka
korerotia nei.

Ko te tuatahi

Ko nga Rangatira o te wakaminenga me nga Rangatira katoa hoki ki
hai i uru ki taua wakaminenga ka tuku rawa atu ki te Kuini o Ingarani ake
tonu atu – te Kawanatanga katoa o o ratou wenua.

Ko te tuarua

Ko te Kuini o Ingarani ka wakarite ka wakaae ki nga Rangatira ki nga
hapu – ki nga tangata katoa o Nu Tirani te tino rangatiratanga o o ratou
wenua o ratou kainga me o ratou taonga katoa. Otiia ko nga Rangatira o
te wakaminenga me nga Rangatira katoa atu ka tuku ki te Kuini te
hokonga o era wahi wenua e pai ai te tangata nona te wenua – ki te
ritenga o te utu e wakaritea ai e ratou ko te kai hoko e meatia nei e te
Kuini hei kai hoko mona.

Ko te tuatoru

Hei wakaritenga mai hoki tenei mo te wakaaetanga ki te Kawanatanga
o te Kuini – Ka tiakina e te Kuini o Ingarani nga tangata maori katoa o
Nu Tirani ka tukua ki a ratou nga tikanga katoa rite tahi ki ana mea ki
nga tangata o Ingarani.

[signed] W. Hobson Consul & Lieutenant Governor

Na ko matou ko nga Rangatira o te Wakaminenga o nga hapu o Nu
Tirani ka huihui nei ki Waitangi ko matou hoki ko nga Rangatira o Nu
Tirani ka kite nei i te ritenga o enei kupu. Ka tangohia ka wakaaetia
katoatia e matou, koia ka tohungia ai o matou ingoa o matou tohu.

Ka meatia tenei ki Waitangi i te ono o nga ra o Pepueri i te tau kotahi
mano, e waru rau e wa te kau o to tatou Ariki.

*Note: This treaty text was signed at Waitangi, 6 February 1840, and thereafter
in the north and at Auckland. It is reproduced as it was written, except for the
heading above the chiefs' names: ko nga Rangatira o te Wakaminenga.*

The Treaty of Waitangi (English text)

Her Majesty Victoria Queen of the United Kingdom of Great Britain and Ireland regarding with Her Royal Favor the Native Chiefs and Tribes of New Zealand and anxious to protect their just Rights and Property and to secure to them the enjoyment of Peace and Good Order has deemed it necessary in consequence of the great number of Her Majesty's Subjects who have already settled in New Zealand and the rapid extension of Emigration both from Europe and Australia which is still in progress to constitute and appoint a functionary properly authorized to treat with the Aborigines of New Zealand for the recognition of Her Majesty's sovereign authority over the whole or any part of those islands – Her Majesty therefore being desirous to establish a settled form of Civil Government with a view to avert the evil consequences which must result from the absence of the necessary Laws and Institutions alike to the native population and to Her subjects has been graciously pleased to empower and to authorize me William Hobson a Captain in Her Majesty's Royal Navy Consul and Lieutenant Governor of such parts of New Zealand as may be or hereafter shall be ceded to Her Majesty to invite the confederated and independent Chiefs of New Zealand to concur in the following Articles and Conditions.

Article the first

The Chiefs of the Confederation of the United Tribes of New Zealand and the separate and independent Chiefs who have not become members of the Confederation cede to Her Majesty the Queen of England absolutely and without reservation all the rights and powers of Sovereignty which the said Confederation or Individual Chiefs respectively exercise or possess, or may be supposed to exercise or to possess over their respective Territories as the sole sovereigns thereof.

Article the second

Her Majesty the Queen of England confirms and guarantees to the Chiefs and Tribes of New Zealand and to the respective families and individuals thereof the full exclusive and undisturbed possession of their Lands and Estates Forests Fisheries and other properties which they may collectively or individually possess so long as it is their wish and desire to retain the same in their possession; but the Chiefs of the United Tribes and the individual Chiefs yield to Her Majesty the exclusive right of Preemption over such lands as the proprietors thereof may be disposed to alienate at such prices as may be agreed upon between the respective Proprietors and persons appointed by Her Majesty to treat with them in that behalf.

Article the third

In consideration thereof Her Majesty the Queen of England extends to the Natives of New Zealand Her royal protection and imparts to them all the Rights and Privileges of British Subjects.

[signed] W. Hobson Lieutenant Governor

Now therefore We the Chiefs of the Confederation of the United Tribes of New Zealand being assembled in Congress at Victoria in Waitangi and We the Separate and Independent Chiefs of New Zealand claiming authority over the Tribes and Territories which are specified after our respective names, having been made fully to understand the Provisions of the foregoing Treaty, accept and enter into the same in the full spirit and meaning thereof in witness of which we have attached our signatures or marks at the places and the dates respectively specified.

Done at Waitangi this Sixth day of February in the year of Our Lord one thousand eight hundred and forty.

Note: This English text was signed at Waikato Heads in March or April 1840 and at Manukau on 26 April by thirty-nine chiefs only. The text became the 'official' version.

Commentary on the Text

The treaty signed at Waitangi and several copies are held by National Archives Wellington. All contain the signatures, moko or marks of chiefs who wished to signify their agreement to the treaty. The original and the copies differ from each other in various ways: some have a slightly different text, one was signed by Willoughby Shortland and not by Hobson, some have the government seal and others have no seal. All are in the Maori language expect for the copy that went to Manukau and Waikato Heads.

Some treaty negotiators took care to collect signatures and moko in an orderly fashion. Henry Williams was particular in this respect, his treaty copy having chiefs' names and their marks running neatly downwards in several columns. His brother William was also tidy, but he took signatures running across the sheet in threes, from top to bottom. Because both copies of the treaty are fairly easy to decipher, an assessment of the numbers on each sheet can be made with little trouble.

Other copies of the treaty are not so easy to read, however. In some cases the names of chiefs appear on a copy but do not have a mark of any kind beside them. In many places, names of chiefs are interspersed with names of hapu, but the distinction is not clear and further research is needed to present an accurate record. The Waitangi sheet is the most confusing of all. It bears over 200 names of chiefs from the north and the Auckland isthmus, but there are many uncertainties regarding names, dates of signings and numbers signing at different locations. There are, for example, conflicting reports of the number who signed at Waitangi on 6 February and immediately after; there may have been forty-three, forty-five or fifty-two. Hokianga presents similar problems. This makes it virtually impossible to state figures accurately. Information sometimes comes to hand from diaries, which shed light on dates of signing or on the parties who signed. This was helpful with the treaty copy that went to the East Coast and it indicated the approximate date of Tirarau's signing at the Bay of Islands, which can be fixed as between 8 and 15 May.

Hobson sent four copies of the treaty to his superiors:

1. An English-language copy in Hobson to Gipps, 5–6 February 1840, CO 209/6, 46–54.
2. An English-language copy in Hobson to Gipps, 16 February 1840, CO 209/7, 13–15.
3. English and Maori treaties enclosed in Hobson to Russell, 15 October 1840, CO 209/7, 178. The treaty spans two pages with the Maori on the left and the English on the right. A title at the top simply reads 'Treaty' and seems to apply to both. At the foot on the left it says 'signatures taken off' and on the right notes that there were 512 signatures. The dispatch says that it was a 'certified' copy. When it was printed in GBPP, 1841, (311), pp.98–99, 'Treaty' was placed over the Maori text and '(Translation)' over the English.
4. Hobson to the Secretary of State for Colonies, 26 May 1841, enclosed the treaty in Maori and signatures of the Manukau-Kawhia treaty copy. This was printed in GBPP, 1841, (569), pp.110–11.

It is not clear how the figure of 512 treaty adherents was arrived at, but it is certain that the total signing was more than this, possibly between 530 and 540.

Appendix 3: *George Gipps's 'unsigned' treaty, presented to several chiefs including Tuhawaiki, in Sydney, 14 February 1840*

MEMORANDUM of an agreement entered into between His Excellency Sir George Gipps, Knight, Captain, General, and Governor-in-Chief of New South Wales and its Dependencies, on behalf of Her Majesty, Queen Victoria, and the undermentioned Chiefs of New Zealand. WHEREAS John Towack, Towack, John White, Kicora, Ticowa, Tranymoricon, Terour, Towack, John White, Kicora, Ticowa, Trany-moricon, Terour, Shoubeton, Akee, and Adekee, Native Chiefs of the several Islands of New Zealand, have expressed their willingness and desire that Her Majesty, Queen Victoria, of the United Kingdom of Great Britain and Ireland, should take them, their tribes, and their country under Her Majesty's Royal Protection and Government. And WHEREAS Her said Majesty, viewing the evil consequences which are likely to arise to the welfare of the Native Chiefs and Tribes from the settlement among them of Her Majesty's subjects, unless some settled form of civil Government be established to protect the Native Chiefs and Tribes in their just rights, and to repress and punish crimes and offences which may be committed by any of her Majesty's subjects, has been pleased to appoint WILLIAM HOBSON, Esq., Captain in Her Majesty's Navy, to be Her Majesty's LIEUTENANT – GOVERNOR in and over such parts of New Zealand as have been or may be acquired in Sovereignty by Her said Majesty, Her heirs and successors, and has empowered the said William Hobson, Esq., to treat with the Native Chiefs accordingly, and it is expedient in compliance with their desire that a preliminary engagement, to be ratified and confirmed by the said Native Chiefs in manner hereinafter mentioned, should be immediately entered into between the said Sir George Gipps, Knight, on behalf of Her said Majesty, Queen Victoria, and the said Native Chiefs and Tribes.

It is therefore hereby agreed between the said parties that Her said Majesty, Queen Victoria, shall exercise absolute Sovereignty in and over the said Native Chiefs, their Tribes and country, in as full and ample a manner as her said Majesty may exercise Her Sovereign authority over any of Her Majesty's Dominions and subjects, with all the rights, powers, and privileges which appertain to the exercise of Sovereign authority. And Her said Majesty does hereby engage to accept the said Native Chiefs and Tribes as Her Majesty's subjects, and to grant Her Royal protection to the said Native Chiefs, their tribes and country, in as full and ample a manner as Her Majesty is bound to afford protection to other of Her Majesty's subjects and Dominions. And the said Native Chiefs do hereby on behalf of themselves and tribes engage, not to sell or otherwise alienate any land occupied by or belonging to them, to any person whatsoever except to Her said Majesty upon such consideration as may be hereafter fixed, and upon the express understanding that the said Chiefs and Tribes shall retain for their own exclusive use and benefit such part of their said lands as may be requisite and necessary for their comfortable maintenance and residence. And that out of the proceeds of the land which may be purchased from them adequate provision shall be made for their future education and instruction in the truths of Christianity. And the said Chiefs do hereby engage to ratify and confirm this agreement in the presence of their respective Tribes, and of Her Majesty's said Lieutenant-Governor William Hobson, Esquire, or the Lieutenant-Governor of Her Majesty's possessions in New Zealand for the time being. In testimony whereof the said Sir George Gipps, and the said Native Chiefs, have hereunto affixed their names and seals at Government House, Sydney, New South Wales, this fourteenth day of February, one thousand eight hundred and forty.

Note: Text from E.Sweetman, The Unsigned Treaty, *Melbourne, 1939, pp.64–65. (Original in the Mitchell Library, Sydney.)*

Appendix 4: *A Literal Translation into English, made in New Zealand, of the Maori Version of the Treaty*

Victoria, the Queen of England, in her gracious remembrance of the Chiefs and Tribes of New Zealand, and through her desire to preserve to them their chieftainship and their land, and to preserve peace and quietness to them, has thought it right to send them a gentleman to be her representative to the natives of New Zealand. Let the native Chiefs in all parts of the land and in the islands consent to the Queen's Government. Now, because there are numbers of the people living in this land, and more will be coming, the Queen wishes to appoint a Government, that there may be no cause for strife between the Natives and the Pakeha, who are now without law: It has therefore pleased the

Queen to appoint me, WILLIAM HOBSON, a Captain in the Royal Navy, Governor of all parts of New Zealand which shall be ceded now and at a future period to the Queen. She offers to the Chiefs of the Assembly of the Tribes of New Zealand and to the other Chiefs, the following laws:–

I. The Chiefs of (i.e. constituting) the Assembly, and all the Chiefs who are absent from the Assembly, shall cede to the Queen of England for ever the government of all their lands.

II. The Queen of England acknowledges and guarantees to the Chiefs, the Tribes, and all the people of New Zealand, the entire supremacy of their lands, of their settlements, and of all their personal property. But the Chiefs of the Assembly, and all other Chiefs, make over to the Queen the purchasing of such lands, which the man who possesses the land is willing to sell, according to prices agreed upon by him, and the purchaser appointed by the Queen to purchase for her.

III. In return for their acknowledging the Government of the Queen, the Queen of England will protect all the natives of New Zealand, and will allow them the same rights as the people of England

(Signed)   WILLIAM HOBSON
Consul, and Lieutenant-Governor

We, the Chiefs of this Assembly of the tribes of New Zealand, now assembled at Waitangi, perceiving the meaning of these words, take and consent to them all. Therefore we sign our names and our marks.

This is done at Waitangi, on the sixth day of February, in the one thousand eight hundred and fortieth year of our Lord.

Note: *Text from J. Noble Coleman,* A Memoir of the Rev. Richard Davis, *London, 1865, pp.455–56.*

Appendix 5: *The Treaty of Waitangi and the new translations printed in 1869 by order of the Legislative Council (from AJLC, 1869, pp.69–71)*

HER MAJESTY VICTORIA, Queen of the United Kingdom of Great Britain and Ireland, regarding with Her royal favour the Native Chiefs and Tribes in New Zealand, and anxious to protect their just rights and property, and to secure to them the enjoyment of peace and good order, has deemed it necessary, in consequence of the great number of Her Majesty's subjects who have already settled in New Zealand, and the rapid extension of emigration both from Europe and Australia which is still in progress, to constitute and appoint a functionary properly authorized to treat with the Aborigines of New Zealand for the recognition of Her Majesty's sovereign authority over the whole or any part of those Islands. Her Majesty, therefore, being desirous to establish a settled form of Civil Government with a view to avert the evil consequences which must result from the absence of the necessary laws and institutions, alike to the Native population and to Her subjects, has been graciously pleased to empower and authorize me, William Hobson, a Captain in Her Majesty's Royal Navy, Consul and Lieutenant-

Governor of such parts of New Zealand as may be or hereafter shall be ceded to Her Majesty, to invite the confederate and independent Chiefs of New Zealand to concur in the following articles and conditions:—

Article the First.

The Chiefs of the Confederation of the United Tribes of New Zealand, and the separate and independent Chiefs who have not become members of the Confederation, cede to Her Majesty the Queen of England, absolutely, and without reservation, all the rights and powers of sovereignty which the said Confederation or individual Chiefs respectively exercise or possess, or may be supposed to exercise or to possess, over their respective territories as the sole Sovereigns thereof.

Article the Second.

Her Majesty the Queen of England confirms and guarantees to the Chiefs and Tribes of New Zealand, and to the respective families and individuals thereof, the full, exclusive, and undisturbed possession of their lands and estates, forests, fisheries, and other properties which they may collectively or individually possess, so long as it is their wish and desire to retain the same in their possession; but the Chiefs of the United Tribes and the individual Chiefs yield to Her Majesty the exclusive right of pre-emption over such lands as the proprietors thereof may be disposed to alienate, at such prices as may be agreed upon between the respective proprietors and persons appointed by Her Majesty to treat with them in that behalf.

Article the Third.

In consideration thereof, Her Majesty the Queen of England extends to the Natives of New Zealand Her royal protection, and imparts to them all the rights and privileges of British subjects

W. HOBSON,
Lieutenant-Governor

Now, therefore, we, the Chiefs of the Confederation of the United Tribes of New Zealand, being assembled in congress at Victoria, in Waitangi, and we, the separate and independent Chiefs of New Zealand, claiming authority over the tribes and territories which are specified after our respective names, having been made fully to understand the provisions of the foregoing Treaty, accept and enter into the same in the full spirit and meaning thereof; in witness of which we have attached our signatures or marks at the places and the dates respectively specified.

Done at Waitangi, this sixth day of February, in the year of our Lord one thousand eight hundred and forty.

Translated from the original English by Mr T. E. YOUNG, Native Department.
Ko WIKITORIA te Kuini o Te Kingitanga★ kotahi o Kereiti Piritone† raua ko Airana‡ e titiro atawhai ana ki nga Rangatira Maori ki nga iwi o Niu Tireni, e hiahia ana hoki ia kia tiakina o ratou tikanga tika me o ratou taonga a kia whakatuturutia ki a ratou te tino ataahuatanga o te rangimario o te ata noho, kua whakaaro ia notemea he tino tini rawa nga

tangata o tona iwi kua noho tuturu ki Niu'l'ireni me te hono tonu o te u mai o nga tangata i Oropi[s] i Atareria[ll] e haere tonu mai nei, kia whakatuturutia kia whakaturia tetahi tangata whai mana hei whakariterite ki nga tangata Maori o Niu Tireni kia whakaaetia e ratou te mana Rangatira o te Kuini kia tau ki runga ki te katoa ki tetahi wahi ranei o aua Motu. Mo reira hoki te Kuini i runga i tona hiahia kia whakatuturutia tetahi ritenga Kawanatanga hei arai i nga tikanga kino e tupu ake i runga i te kore Ture, i te kore ritenga ki nga tangata Maori ngatahi me nga tangata o Tona* iwi ake, kua pai i runga i tona arohanoa kia whakamana kia tohutohungia Ahau a Wiremu Hopihona he Kapene o a te Kuini Manuwao hei *Consul* hei Kawana hoki mo era wahi o Niu Tireni kua oti te tuku ka tukua ranei a muri nei ki a Te Kuini, kia ui atu ahau ki nga Rangatira kua noho i runga i te whakaaro kotahi ki era atu Rangatira o Niu Tireni mehemea ka whakaae ngatahi ratou ki enei mea ki enei ritenga hoki.

Ko te tuatahi.

Ko nga Rangatira o nga iwi o Niu Tireni kua noho i runga i te whakaaro kotahi me era Rangatira e tau ke ana e noho ana i runga i o ratou ritenga ano kahore ano kia uru ki taua whakakotahitanga e tino tuku rawa ana ki Te Kuini o Ingarangi nga tikanga me nga mana katoa o te Rangatiratanga e whakahaerea ana e mau ana i taua whakakotahitanga e ia Rangatira hoki e whakahaerea ana i runga i o ratou whenua i runga i o ratou Rangatiratanga ake ki reira.

Ko te tuarua.

Ko Te Kuini o Ingarangi e whakapumau ana e whakatuturu ana ki nga Rangatira ki nga Iwi o Niu Tireni ki ia hapu ki ia tangata o aua iwi te tino tuturutanga o o ratou whenua o o ratou motu ngaherehere o o ratou wahi hiinga ika, o era atu rawa e mau ana i a ratou katoa i ia tangata ranei o ratou mo te wa e hiahiatia ai e ratou ki a puritia e ratou; Otira e tuku ana nga Rangatira o nga iwi kua whakakotahi era atu Rangatira hoki ki a Te Kuini te tino tikanga mana anake e hoko i te tuatahi nga whenua e hiahia ai nga tangata no ratou aua whenua kia hokona, mo nga utu e whakaritea e nga tangata no ratou nga whenua ki nga tangata e whakaturia ana e Te Kuini hei kai-whakariterite ki a ratou mo te pera.

Ko te tuatoru.

Mo runga i tera e tukua ana e Te Kuini o Ingarangi ki nga tangata Maori o Niu Tireni tona tiaki Rangatira, e hoatu ana hoki ki a ratou nga tikanga me nga painga katoa e tau ana ki runga ki nga tangata o tona iwi ake.

W. HOBSON, Kawana.

NA, ko matou ko nga Rangatira o nga iwi o Niu Tireni kua noho i runga i te whakaaro kotahi kua whakakotahi hoki kua huihui nei i roto i te Runanga i Wikitoria wahi o Waitangi ko matou hoki ko nga Rangatira e tau ke ana e noho ana i runga i to matou ritenga ake, e whai mana ana ki runga ki nga iwi ki nga whenua kua tuhituhia ki muri i o matou ingoa, i runga i te mea kua ata whakamohiotia rawatia matou ki nga ritenga o te Tiriti i runga ake nei, e whakaae ana e uru katoa ana matou ki taua Tiriti ki ana ritenga katoa, hei tohu mo to matou whakaaetanga kua tuhituhia o matou ingoa me o matou tohu i ia wahi i ia kua oti te whakahua ki raro nei.

I mahia i Waitangi i tenei te ono o nga ra o Pepuere i te tau o to tatou Ariki kotahi mano e waru rau e wha tekau.

*Kingdom.   †Great Britain.   ‡Ireland.   sEurope.   ‖Australia.

Translated from the original Maori by Mr T.E. YOUNG, Native Department.
VICTORIA, Queen of England, in her kind thoughtfulness to the chiefs and hapus of New Zealand, and her desire to preserve to them their chieftainship and their land, and that peace may always be kept with them and quietness, she has thought it is a right thing that a chief should be sent here as a negotiator† with the Maoris of New Zealand – that the Maoris of New Zealand may consent to the government‡ of the Queen over all parts of this land and the Islands, because there are many people of her tribe who have settled on this land and are coming hither.

Now the Queen is desirous to establish the Government, that evil may not come to the Maoris and the Europeans who are living without law.

Now the Queen has been pleased to send me William Hobson, a Captain in the Royal Navy, to be Governor for all the places of New Zealand which may be given up now or hereafter to the Queen; and he gives forth to the Chiefs of the Assembly^s of the hapus of New Zealand, and other Chiefs, the laws spoken here.

The First.

The Chiefs of the Assembly, and all the Chiefs also who have not joined in that Assembly, give up entirely to the Queen of England for ever all the government‡ of their lands.

The Second.

The Queen of England arranges and agrees to give to the Chiefs, the Hapus, and all the People of New Zealand, the full chieftainship‖ of their lands, their settlements, and all their property. But the Chiefs of the Assembly, and all the other Chiefs, give to the Queen the purchase of those pieces of land which the proprietors of the land may wish, for such payment as may be agreed upon by them and the purchaser who is now appointed by the Queen to be her purchaser.

The Third.

This is an arrangement for the consent to the government of the Queen. The Queen of England will protect all the Maoris of New Zealand. All the rights will be given to them the same as her doings to the people of England.

WILLIAM HOBSON,
Consul and Lieutenant-Governor.

Now, we, the Chiefs of the Assembly of the Hapus of New Zealand, now assemble at Waitangi. We, also, the Chiefs of New Zealand, see the meaning of these words: they are taken and consented to altogether by us. Therefore are affixed our names and our marks.

This is done at Waitangi, on the sixth day of February, in the year one thousand eight hundred and forty, of our Lord.

†He kaiwhakarite.   ‡Kawanatanga.   §Whakaminenga.
‖Tino Rangatiratanga.

MAP 2: MAORI TRIBAL LOCATIONS, c.1870

Major tribes are indicated and
some locations reflect movements
which took place between 1800
and 1850. Source: *Oxford History
of New Zealand*, ed. W.H. Oliver
with B.R. Williams (OUP, 1981).
The map is derived largely from
AJHR, 1870, D-23.

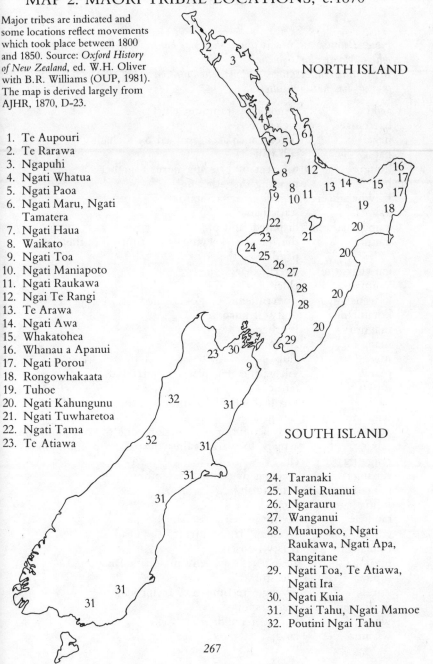

NORTH ISLAND

SOUTH ISLAND

1. Te Aupouri
2. Te Rarawa
3. Ngapuhi
4. Ngati Whatua
5. Ngati Paoa
6. Ngati Maru, Ngati
   Tamatera
7. Ngati Haua
8. Waikato
9. Ngati Toa
10. Ngati Maniapoto
11. Ngati Raukawa
12. Ngai Te Rangi
13. Te Arawa
14. Ngati Awa
15. Whakatohea
16. Whanau a Apanui
17. Ngati Porou
18. Rongowhakaata
19. Tuhoe
20. Ngati Kahungunu
21. Ngati Tuwharetoa
22. Ngati Tama
23. Te Atiawa

24. Taranaki
25. Ngati Ruanui
26. Ngarauru
27. Wanganui
28. Muaupoko, Ngati
    Raukawa, Ngati Apa,
    Rangitane
29. Ngati Toa, Te Atiawa,
    Ngati Ira
30. Ngati Kuia
31. Ngai Tahu, Ngati Mamoe
32. Poutini Ngai Tahu

GLOSSARY

Note: Because the Maori plural does not have 's', it has not been used where Maori plurals occur.
In the nineteenth century 'wh' was often written as 'w'. Where this occurs, the 'w' has not been altered.

ariki	senior or paramount chief
haeremai	welcome
haka	fierce dance accompanied by a chant
hapu	sub-tribe
hongi	to greet by pressing noses together
hui	meeting or gathering
kaiwhakahaere	organiser or facilitator
kainga	settlement
kainga tautohe	disputed land plots
kaituki	the person keeping the time for the canoe paddlers – the stroke
kaiwhakarite	intermediary
kaumatua	elder
kawanatanga	government, or governance
kotahitanga	unity of purpose
makutu	witchcraft
mana	authority or prestige
mere	club
marae	village meeting-place or surrounds
moko	tattoo
pa	fortified village, or more recently any village
Pakeha	European
powhiri	to welcome or beckon someone to come in
rahui	a mark to warn against trespass, a prohibition
rangatira	chief
runanga	meeting or council, assembly
rangatiratanga	chieftainship
taiaha	long club
taonga	highly prized possessions
tangi	weeping, lamenting for the dead
tinihanga	tricky nonsense
tohunga	an expert, especially in spiritual matters
tupuna	ancestor
utu	revenge, recompense, reciprocity
wahi tapu	sacred spot
whare	house or building
whenua	land

REFERENCES

INTRODUCTION

1. Robert FitzRoy, *Remarks on New Zealand,* London, 1846 (Hocken Facsimile ed. 1969), p.10.

CHAPTER 1: THE BRITISH CROWN AND THE MAORI PEOPLE

1. Peter Adams, *Fatal Necessity: British Intervention in New Zealand, 1830–47,* Auckland, 1977, pp.25–36.
2. Cook's Journals, published in the 1770s, were a mine of information. There were at least six other major publications up to the mid-1830s.
3. D. Ian Pool, *The Maori Population of New Zealand,* Auckland, 1971, pp.234–36.
4. J.M.R. Owens, 'Christianity and the Maoris to 1840', *NZJH,* II, 1 (1968), pp.18–40; J. Binney, 'Christianity and the Maoris to 1840, a comment', *NZJH,* III, 2 (1969), pp.143–65; J.M.R. Owens, 'New Zealand before annexation', *The Oxford History of New Zealand,* ed. W.H. Oliver with B.R. Williams, Oxford and Wellington, 1981, p.28.
5. E.g. H.A. Morton, 'Whaling in New Zealand Waters in the first half of the 19th century', PhD thesis, Otago (1977), pp.278ff; Augustus Earle, *A Narrative of Nine Months' Residence in New Zealand,* London, 1832, pp.18, 29, 172; Richard A. Cruise, *Journal of a Ten Months' Residence in New Zealand,* 2nd ed., London, 1824, p.93; J.S. Polack, *New Zealand: Being a narrative of travels and adventures ... between the years 1831 and 1837,* vol.2, pp.171–2, 215, 279–81; Robert McNab, *From Tasman to Marsden,* Dunedin, 1914, p.120; Dumont d'Urville, *The Voyage of the Astrolabe,* trans. Olive Wright, Wellington, 1955, pp.145–46.
6. Adams, *Fatal Necessity,* p.52; Mary Boyd, 'Cardinal Principles of British Policy in New Zealand', *The Treaty of Waitangi: its origins and significance,* Wellington, 1972, p.4.
7. John Ward, *British Policy in the South Pacific (1786–1893),* Sydney, 1948, especially Ch.4; J. Binney, *The Legacy of Guilt: A life of Thomas Kendall,* Auckland, 1968, p.25; McNab, *Tasman to Marsden,* pp.162–63.
8. Adams, *Fatal Necessity,* pp.52–53; Ward, *British Policy,* pp.39–40, Chs.6, 7.
9. Adams, *Fatal Necessity,* pp.25–26, 250; Robert McNab, *The Old Whaling Days: A History of Southern New Zealand from 1830–1840,* Christchurch, 1913, pp.298–9; R.P. Wigglesworth, 'The New Zealand timber and flax trade 1769–1840', Massey (1981).
10. Brown Journal, 6 March 1837, AUL; E.J. Tapp, *Early New Zealand: A dependency of New South Wales, 1788–1841* Melbourne, 1958, p.177.
11. C. Wilkes, *Narrative of the United States Exploring Expedition during the years 1838–1842,* London, 1845, vol.2, p.413; *The Whaling Journal of Captain W.B. Rhodes,* ed. C.R. Straubel, Christchurch, 1954, pp.xxiii–xxiv.

12. Adams, *Fatal Necessity,* pp.76–78; cf. Robert FitzRoy, et al., *Narrative of the Surveying Voyages of His Majesty's Ships Adventure and Beagle,* London, 1839, vol.2, pp.593–6; and J.S. Marais, *The Colonization of New Zealand,* Oxford, 1927, pp.92–97; Hobson to Liz, 25 August 1837, Hobson Papers, MS Papers 46, f.1, ATL.
13. McNab, *Tasman to Marsden,* pp.99, 102–3.
14. John Liddiard Nicholas, *Narrative of a Voyage to New Zealand,* vol.1, pp.30–33, 82–83; *The Letters and Journals of Samuel Marsden, 1765–1838,* ed. J.R. Elder, Dunedin, 1932, pp.80–81, 207; Tapp, *Early New Zealand,* p.32; McNab, *Tasman to Marsden,* pp.168–9.
15. Herbert W. Williams, *A Bibliography of Printed Maori to 1900, and Supplement,* Wellington, 1975 (reprint Government Printer), does not list this, but it is held at APL, listed as No. 4b.
16. Marsden, *Letters and Journals,* p.332.
17. *The Early Journals of Henry Williams 1826–40,* ed. L.M. Rogers, Christchurch, 1961, p.51; Earle, *Narrative of a Residence,* pp.194–200.
18. Binney, *Legacy of Guilt,* pp.54–57.
19. *Cruise Journal,* pp.27, 61–62, 107; Dacre to Busby, 3 October 1834, British Resident Papers, 1/1, NA; Sadler to Wood, 14 July 1836, CO 209/2, 378.
20. E. Fairburn, 'Maharatanga', NZ MS 91, APL; Hobson to Liz, 25 August 1837, Hobson Papers, MS Papers 46, ATL. On Titore's death, the suit passed to Hakiro, the letter to Whai: Bunbury to Hobson, 28 June 1840, GBPP, 1841 (311), p.100.
21. Polack, *New Zealand,* vol.1, p.184; Brown Journal, 1 May 1836, AUL; Marsden, *Letters and Journals,* p.1113.
22. Polack, *New Zealand,* vol.2, pp.127–8; *Cruise, Journal,* p.182; Kemp Journal, 5 July 1839, AUL; Dumont d'Urville, *Voyage of the Astrolabe,* p.125.
23. E.g. Nicholas, *Narrative of a Voyage,* vol.1, p.301; Shortland to Stanley, 18 January 1845, p.7, GBPP, 1845 (108).
24. E.g. Nicholas, *Narrative of a Voyage,* vol.1, p.165.
25. Adams, *Fatal Necessity,* pp.75ff; Williams, *Early Journals,* pp.191–2; Marsden, *Letters and Journals,* p.503.
26. Williams, *Early Journals,* p.192; Mrs Williams to her father-in-law, 3 October 1831, cit. Hugh Carleton, *The Life of Henry Williams,* Auckland, 1874, vol.1, p.92.
27. Petition encl. in Yate to Colonial Secretary, New South Wales, 16 November 1831, GBPP, 1840 [238], p.7. For similar petitions from Tahiti, see Ward, *British Policy,* pp.33, 69–70, 73, 92–93, 131.
28. Marsden to Darling, 18 April 1831, Marsden Family Papers, MS Papers 453, f.3, ATL; Marsden, *Letters and Journals,* pp. 498ff.
29. Goderich to chiefs, 14 June 1832, GBPP, 1840 [238], pp.7–8; Goderich to Bourke, 14

June 1832, *Historical Records of Australia*, Sydney,1923, vol.16, p.662; see also Bourke to Goderich, 23 December 1832, where he notes Darling's dispatches from August 1830 to September 1831 on NZ trade disruptions: *Historical Records of Australia*, vol.16, pp.482–3; James Busby, 'Memoir', CO 209/1, 197–9, and James Busby, *Authentic Information relative to New South Wales and New Zealand*, London, 1832, pp.57ff.

30. Eric Ramsden, *Busby of Waitangi*, Wellington, 1942, pp.56ff; Busby to NSW, 17, 30 May 1833, Busby Dispatches, q MS 1833–39, ATL.

31. Busby to NSW, 17, 25 May 1833, Busby Dispatches, q MS 1833–39, ATL, for the 'King's letter', Busby's address and translations of both.

32. Marsden, *Letters and Journals*, p.509.

33. The printing is Williams, *Bibliography of Printed Maori*, no.11 (a copy held at APL); see also White to Busby, 3 October 1833, BR 1/1, 97, ATL.

34. Ramsden, *Busby of Waitangi*, pp.39–46, 60–61, 85.

35. Bourke to Busby, 13 April 1833, GBPP, 1840 [238], pp.4–6.

36. For an eye–witness account, see William Barrett Marshall, *A Personal Narrative of Two Visits to New Zealand in His Majesty's Ship Alligator, A.D. 1834*, London, 1836, pp.149–301; Adams, *Fatal Necessity*, pp.69, 91.

37. Adams, *Fatal Necessity*, pp.69–70.

38. This is best indicated by letters in BR 1/2, 102 et al., NA.

39. Cit. Ramsden, *Busby of Waitangi*, p.221; FitzRoy, *Narrative*, vol.1, p.319.

40. Chapman to CMS, 6 August 1838, Chapman Letters and Journal, AUL.

41. BR 1/1, 92, 93 (September 1833), NA; J.M.R. Owens, 'New Zealand before annexation', *Oxford History*, p.48.

42. BR 1/1, 165, and 1/2, 5, 7a, 110, 127, 143, 144, 189, 202, NA.

43. Pomare to Busby, n.d. [1834?], BR 1/1, 158, NA; cf. Keith Sinclair, *A History of New Zealand*, Harmondsworth, 1959, p.69.

44. Busby to Papahia, n.d. [late 1838?], BR 1/2, 192, NA.

45. William Marshall Hau to Busby, December 1839, Hemi Kepa Tupe to Busby, n.d. [1839?], Herua to Busby, n.d. [1839?], and Fairburn to Busby, 20 December 1839, BR 1/2.

46. Wakena Rukaruka to Busby, n.d. [1839?], BR 1/2, 182, NA.

47. Ramsden, *Busby of Waitangi*, p.221; Alexander Busby evidence, GBPP, 1840 (582), pp.129ff.

48. Adams, *Fatal Necessity*, pp.249–50.

CHAPTER 2: MAORI SOVEREIGNTY AND ITS DEMISE

1. Bourke to Busby, 13 April 1833, GBPP, 1840 [238], pp.4–6. The instructions were included in Robert FitzRoy et al., *Narrative of the Surveying Voyages of His Majesty's Ships Adventure and Beagle, between ... 1826 and 1836*, London, 1839, vol.2, pp.198–202.

2. Busby to NSW, 13 May 1833, Busby Dispatches, q MS 1833–39, ATL.

3. William Yate, *An Account of New Zealand*, London, 1835, p.29; Busby to NSW, 13,20 May 1833, Busby Dispatches, q MS 1833–39, ATL.

4. Busby to NSW, 13 May, and 17 June 1833 enclosing specimen passport, Busby Dispatches, q MS 1833–39, ATL; Eric Ramsden, *Busby of Waitangi*, Wellington, 1942, p.64.

5. William Barrett Marshall, *A Personal Narrative of Two Visits to New Zealand on His Majesty's Ship Alligator, A.D. 1834*, London, 1836, p.108; Busby to NSW, 22 March 1834, Busby Dispatches, q MS 1833–39, ATL; Ramsden, *Busby of Waitangi*, pp.64–69; *Historical Records of Australia*, Sydney, 1923, vol.17, pp.412, 608–9.

6. British Resident Papers, 1/2, 96, 97, 114, NA, indicate registration of *New Zealander*, *Industry*, *Fanny*, *Trent*, *Mercury* and *Tokirau*; see also J. Walton, *Twelve Months' Residence in New Zealand*, Glasgow, 1839, pp.21–24; and Busby to Bourke, 23 July 1836, CO 209/2, 254.

7. Col. Sec. Van Dieman's Land to Busby, 23 October 1834, BR 1/1, NA; Robert McNab, *The Old Whaling Days*, Christchurch, 1913, p.101; E.J. Tapp, *Early New Zealand*, Melbourne, 1958, pp.58–60.

8. Busby to NSW, 22 March 1834, Busby Dispatches, q MS 1833–39, ATL; cf. Marshall, *Personal Narrative*, pp.107–12; also Busby to Hay, 3 April 1834, CO 209/1, 121–4, 213–36.

9. For Busby's address (English and Maori), see BR 1/1, NA.

10. Marshall, *Personal Narrative*, pp.108–9; Busby to NSW, 22 March 1834, Busby Dispatches, q MS 1833–39, ATL.

11. Marshall, *Personal Narrative*, pp.23, 108–12.

12. John Bright, *Handbook for emigrants and others*, London, 1841, pp.15–16; Edward Markham, *New Zealand or recollections of it*, ed. E.H. McCormick, Wellington, 1963, pp.73, 100, and see reproduction of flag facing p.57.

13. Ramsden, *Busby of Waitangi*, pp.91–94; S.M. Lange, 'Baron Charles de Thierry: Utopian coloniser', MA thesis, Auckland (1976), pp.3–9,51.

14. *Facsimiles of the Declaration of Independence and the Treaty of Waitangi*, Wellington, 1877 (reprint Government Printer, 1976). The original is held by National Archives, Wellington.

15. Glenelg to Bourke, 25 May 1836, CO 209/1, 268–70. A memo on the correspondence simply asks for it to be acknowledged: CO 209/1, 264–6.

16. Busby to NSW, 31 October 1835, Busby Dispatches, q MS 1833–39, ATL.

17. Ramsden, *Busby of Waitangi*, pp.95–96; for another view, see J.O. Ross, 'Busby and the Declaration of Independence', *NZJH*, XIV, 1 (1980), pp.83–89.

18. Ramsden, *Busby of Waitangi*, pp.114, 166; James Busby, 'Occupation of New Zealand 1833–43', p.8, Busby Letters and Papers, MS

46, AML; Busby to NSW, 22 March 1837, Busby Dispatches, q MS 1833–39, ATL.

19. Ramsden, *Busby of Waitangi*, p.97.

20. Busby to NSW, 3 July 1837, Busby Dispatches, q MS 1833-39, ATL.

21. BR 1/2: papers on file indicate Te Hapuku's presence in the north.

22. Herbert W. Williams, *A Bibliography of Printed Maori to 1900, and Supplement*, Wellington, 1975 (reprint Government Printer), nos.21 and 21a. W. Colenso, 'Day and Waste Book', MS 76, AML, records that 100 copies of no.21 were printed on 26 April 1837. Both printings are held by APL. See also A.S. Thomson, *The Story of New Zealand : Past and Present, Savage and Civilized*, London, 1859, vol.1, p.277.

23. John Ward, *British Policy in the South Pacific (1786–1893)*, Sydney, 1948, Ch.8 notes Tahiti and Hawaii.

24. Ramsden, *Busby of Waitangi*, pp.90–91.

25. Ramsden, *Busby of Waitangi*, p.91; McDonnell to Busby, 24 October 1835, BR 1/1, 37, NA.

26. Two did not sign unless by a different name and one, Te Morenga, had died.

27. See Appendix 1; Busby to NSW, 31 October 1835; Busby Dispatches, q MS 1833–39, ATL.

28. W.R. Wade, *A Journey in the Northern Island of New Zealand*, Hobart, 1842, pp.83–86; FitzRoy, *Narrative*, vol.2, p.590, vol.3, pp.501–2.

29. E.g. Richard A. Cruise, *Journal of a Ten Months' Residence in New Zealand*, 2nd ed., London, 1824; Marsden to Pratt, 24 February 1819, *The Letters and Journals of Samuel Marsden, 1765–1838*, ed. J.R. Elder, Dunedin, 1932, p.231; John Liddiard Nicholas, *Narrative of a Voyage to New Zealand*, vol.2, pp.222–4.

30. Harrison M. Wright, *New Zealand, 1769–1840: Early years of Western contact*, Cambridge, (Mass.), 1959, p.116 and fn.1.

31. Emerich de Vattel, *The Law of Nations*, London, 1758, 3 vols., trans. Charles G. Fenwick, Washington, 1916; *Imperialism*, ed. Philip D. Curtin, New York, 1971.

32. Brown Journal, 24,29 March 1837 and entries in April and May 1837, AUL; Ramsden, *Busby of Waitangi*, pp.167ff; Hugh Carleton, *The Life of Henry Williams*, Auckland, 1874, vol.1, pp.200ff.

33. Bourke to Glenelg, 20 April 1837, enclosing petition, CO 209/2, 318–24; Busby to Bourke, 16 June 1837, GBPP, 1840 [238], wanted Maori to appeal too, but the missionaries vetoed the idea.

34. Marsden to Baker, 6 August 1837, Marsden Family Papers, MS Papers 453, f.3, ATL.

35. E.g. J. Noble Coleman, *A Memoir of the Rev. Richard Davis*, London, 1865, pp.202ff; Busby to NSW, 28 March 1837, Busby Dispatches, q MS 1833–39, ATL; J. Binney, 'Papahurihia: Some thoughts on interpretation', *Journal of the Polynesian Society*, LXXV, 3 (1966), pp.321–31.

36. Busby to Bourke, 16 June 1837, GBPP, 1840 [238]; Coleman, *Richard Davis*, p.202.

37. Busby to NSW, 26 January, 20 February,

18 May 1836, Busby Dispatches, q MS 1833–39, ATL.

38. Busby to NSW, 25,30 January, 28 March 1837, Busby Dispatches, q MS 1833–39, ATL; Hobson to Bourke, 8 August 1837, GBPP, 1840 [238].

39. Ramsden, *Busby of Waitangi*, pp.169–70; Hobson to Bourke, 8 August 1837, CO 209/2, 30–37; Bourke to Glenelg, 9 September 1837, CO 209/2, 24–28.

40. Busby to Bourke, 16 June 1837, GBPP, 1840 [238]; James Busby, 'Memoir', CO 209/1, 197–9.

41. Peter Adams, *Fatal Necessity*, Auckland, 1977, pp.94ff; also J. Miller, *Early Victorian New Zealand*, London, 1958, Ch.1; Michael Turnbull, *The New Zealand Bubble*, Wellington, 1959.

42. Coates's evidence, GBPP, 1837–38 (680), pp.268–72; J. Beecham, *Remarks upon the latest official documents relating to New Zealand*, London, 1838; J. Beecham, *Colonization; being ... an Examination of the Proposals of the Association ... formed for colonizing New Zealand*, London, 1838. The latter is filed at CO 209/4, 209.

43. Adams, *Fatal Necessity*, pp.94–102 and Ch.4, where this period is discussed in detail.

44. Enderby to Glenelg, 18 December 1837, enclosing the petition of merchants to Melbourne, 16 December 1837, CO 209/2, 444.

45. Report from the Select Committee of the House of Lords, GBPP, 1837–38 (680).

46. Commons Committee on Aborigines (British Settlements), GBPP, 1836 (538) and 1837 (425); K. Sinclair, 'The Aborigines Protection Society and New Zealand – a Study in nineteenth-century opinion', MA thesis, University of NZ, Auckland (1946).

47. *The Colonial Intelligencer or Aborigines' Friend* carried reports.

48. For individual missionary opinion, see Adams, *Fatal Necessity*, pp.84–86.

49. For threats to block Wakefield's plan see W. White, *Colonization of New Zealand*, London,1838.

50. E.g. Torrens to Glenelg, 6 November 1839, CO 209/4, 297: a plan for government which pledged a willingness to negotiate with the Confederation and to recognise that the sovereignty of New Zealand rested with that body. Another plan incorporating Maori was proposed by de Thierry: S.M. Lange, 'Baron Charles de Thierry: Utopian coloniser', MA thesis, Auckland (1976), pp.40–41.

51. Miller, *Early Victorian New Zealand*, pp.8–9; [E.G. Wakefield and J. Ward], *The British Colonization of New Zealand*, London, 1837 [appendix by M. Hawtrey]; letter of the Rev. M. Hawtrey to Lord John Russell, December 1840, in *Extracts from the papers and proceedings of the Aborigines Protection Society*, February 1841, II, no.2, pp.49–57.

52. E.g. S. Motte, *Outline of a System of Legislation for Securing Protection to the Aboriginal Inhabitants of all Countries Colonized by Great Britain*, London, 1840. The scheme was originally drawn up by Saxe Bannister (at one time Attorney-General, New South Wales), two or three years earlier. It appears in CO 209/8, 426–37.

53. E.g. *Extracts ... Aborigines Protection Society*, London, May 1839, no.1, Article 6: Hodgkin to Hawes, 27 November 1837.

54. Draft instructions, 24 January 1839, CO 209/4, 203ff; Hobson to Glenelg, 21 January 1839, CO 209/4, 87–93.

55. Hobson to Liz, 25 August 1837, Hobson Papers, MS Papers 46, ATL.

56. Adams, *Fatal Necessity*, pp.124–5, 136ff., discusses the various groups and their negotiations with government.

57. Stephen to Labouchere, 15 March 1839, CO 209/4, 326–31; Adams, *Fatal Necessity*, pp.147ff.

58. Stephen minute to Labouchere, 18 May 1839, CO 209/4, 243–4; Draft instructions, n.d. [May?] 1839, CO 209/4, pp.221ff. Adams, *Fatal Necessity*, pp.148–9, believes that these were drawn up in May but there is no positive evidence to confirm this. Since they do not favour colonisation, they could have been a version drawn up when Glenelg was still in office. Either Adams's date is incorrect or Normanby was still wavering on the matter.

59. Draft instructions, n.d. [May?] 1839, CO 209/4, pp.221ff.

60. Adams, *Fatal Necessity*, p.155.

61. Normanby to Hobson, 14,15 August 1839, CO 209/4, 251–82, 157–63.

62. E.g. Bourke to Glenelg, 9 September 1837, GBPP, 1840 [238].

CHAPTER 3: THE TREATY AT WAITANGI

1. M.F. Lindley, *The Acquisition and Government of Backward Territory in International Law*, London, 1926, especially Chs.18,19; see also John Ward, *British Policy in the South Pacific (1786–1893)*, Sydney, 1948, p.31, fn.11.

2. E.g. Coates's evidence before the 1838 House of Lords Committee, GBPP, 1837–38 (680), p.243.

3. The term Pakeha is commonly used for a non-Maori New Zealander of whatever origin including those of mixed Maori-European ancestry who do not consider themselves Maori.

4. Guy Scholefield, *Captain William Hobson*, London, 1934, pp.80–81; Gipps to Russell, 9 February 1840, GBPP, 1840 (560), p.4.

5. Edward Sweetman, *The Unsigned New Zealand Treaty*, Melbourne, 1939, Ch.2; W. Williams to Colonial Secretary, 8 May 1840, GBPP, 1841 (311), p.101; Alexander Busby evidence, GBPP, 1840 (582), pp.129ff.; *Extracts ... Aborigines Protection Society*, II, January 1841, pp.17–18, letter from New Zealand (anon.) 19 December 1839; see also J.R. Lee, 'Historical Maps of the Bay of Islands', t.s., 1972, AUL.

6. John Miller, *Early Victorian New Zealand*, London, 1958, Ch.2.

7. Sweetman, *Unsigned New Zealand Treaty*, pp.55–59.

8. Gipps to Hobson, 15 January 1840, encl. in Gipps to Russell, 9 February 1840, CO 209/6, 24–27; Hobson to Gipps, 4 February 1840,

with Hobson's proclamations, encl. in Gipps to Russell, 19 February 1840, GBPP, 1840 (560), pp.6–9.

9. GBPP, 1840 [238], nos.16,17,18, cover Normanby's instructions, Hobson's queries and his supplementary instructions in reply.

10. Sweetman, *Unsigned New Zealand Treaty*, pp.59–60; and see below, p.95.

11. GBPP, 1840 (582), paras.256–75.

12. Scholefield, *Hobson*, pp.82–83; cf. T. Lindsay Buick, *The Treaty of Waitangi*, 3rd ed., New Plymouth, 1936, pp.703–5.

13. James Busby, 'Occupation of New Zealand, 1833–43', p.84, Busby Letters and Papers, MS 46, AML; Buller Journal, 3 February 1840, q MS [1838–44], ATL; Hobbs Diary, 25 January 1840, MS 144, AML.

14. Hugh Carleton, *The Life of Henry Williams*, Auckland, 1874, vol.2, p.11; Taylor Journal, 30 January 1840, MS 302, AML.

15. Taylor Journal, 30 January 1840, MS 302, AML; Mathew Journal, 30 January, 1,3 February 1840, NZ MS, APL; Scholefield, *Hobson*, pp.81–82, 101, 104–7.

16. Colenso Journal, 29 January 1840, Hawke's Bay Museum. Busby boarded the *Herald* as it anchored off Kororareka about 11 a.m. 29 January.

17. Hobson to [Baker?], 29 January 1840, Hobson Letters, MS 802, AML; Buick, *Treaty*, p.100.

18. Colenso, *The Authentic and Genuine History of the Signing of the Treaty of Waitangi*, Wellington, 1890 (Capper reprint, 1971), p.11; W. Colenso, 'Day and Waste Book', MS 76, AML; Busby to Colenso, 29 January 1840, encl. draft invitation, Colenso Papers, MS Col. 1833–63, IV, pp.57,58, ATL, and cf., Waka Nene's invitation in facsimile, Buick, *Treaty*, facing p.112.

19. For Hobson's queries to the Undersecretary, Colonial Office, and Normanby's reply, see GBPP, 1840 [238], nos.17,18.

20. Second set of draft treaty notes [by Freeman?] in *Facsimiles of the Declaration of Independence and the Treaty of Waitangi*, Wellington, 1877 (reprint Government Printer, 1976); R.M. Ross, 'Te Tiriti o Waitangi, texts and translations', *NZJH*, VI, 2 (1972), pp.132–3 and fn.24; Hobson to Gipps, 5 February 1840, GBPP, 1841 (311), p.8; Busby to Colenso, 'Friday morning' [31 January?], Colenso Papers, MS Col. 1833–63, IV, p.59, ATL; J.B.F. Pompallier, *Early History of the Catholic Church in Oceania*, Auckland, 1888, p.62.

21. James Busby, *Remarks upon a Pamphlet entitled 'The Taranaki Question, by Sir William Martin'*, Auckland, 1860, pp.3–4; Busby, 'Occupation of New Zealand 1833–43', p.87, Busby Letters and Papers, MS 46, AML.

22. See Ross, 'Te Tiriti o Waitangi', pp.132–3 and fn.24, where she identifies the writers. In all discussions of the treaty and its various copies, reference has been made to the Facsimile edition. The original treaty sheets are held by National Archives.

23. Another copy of the draft, evidently a first effort but identical in wording, has survived in

Busby Letters and Papers, MS 46, f.6, AML.
It has an annotation on it, 'Draft of the
Articles of a Treaty with the Native chiefs
submitted to Capt. Hobson, 3 Feby. 1840'.
24. Busby, *Remarks upon a Pamphlet*, pp.3–4;
Busby, 'Occupation of New Zealand, 1833–
43', p.87, Busby Letters and Papers, MS 46,
AML.
25. Cf., Ross, 'Te Tiriti o Waitangi', p.132.
26. Draft instructions, [May?] 1839, CO 209/
4, 238; cf. Draft instructions, August 1839 at
pp.260–1, where these comments are deleted
with a marginal note by W.L. [Labouchere?].
27. Busby to NSW, 31 October 1835; Busby
Dispatches, q MS 1833–39, ATL; see also
Robert FitzRoy et al., *Narrative of the
Surveying Voyages of His Majesty's Ships
Adventure and Beagle*, London, 1839, vol.2,
p.585.
28. See Appendix 3.
29. Normanby to Hobson, 14 August 1839,
GBPP, 1840 [238].
30. J.M.R. Owens, 'Missionaries and the
Treaty of Waitangi', *Wesley Historical Society
Journal*, (NZ), 1986, pp.17–40; Carleton,
Henry Williams, vol.2, pp.7–8.
31. Buick, *Treaty*, pp.98–100; Colenso
Journal, 29 January 1840, Hawke's Bay
Museum; Mathew Journal, 30 January 1840,
NZ MS, APL; Taylor Journal, 29,30 January,
3 February 1840, GNZ MS, APL; Buller
Journal, 3 February 1840, q MS [1838–44],
ATL; J. Buller, *Forty Years in New Zealand*,
London, 1878, p.78; Hobson to Baker, 29
January 1840, in Buick, *Treaty*, p.100. Fedarb
Diary, 2 February 1840, NZ MS 375, APL,
notes that Henry Williams preached at Paihia
the Sunday preceding the treaty signing – a
text suitable to the times: John I.5: 'And the
light shineth in darkness; and the darkness
comprehended it not.'
32. See Ross, 'Te Tiriti o Waitangi', p.133
and fn.27.
33. Carleton, *Henry Williams*, vol.2, p.12 and
note.
34. Ibid., pp.viii–xiv. Colenso Journal has no
entry for 4 February 1840, and he does not
mention giving assistance in his history of the
signing.
35. Cit. Carleton, *Henry Williams*, vol.2, p.12.
36. For the sake of clarity, the text is given as
it was at the time. It was usual to render the
'wh', as in whenua, as 'w'.
37. Ross, 'Te Tiriti o Waitangi', pp.133, 142
and fn.27.
38. Ross, 'Te Tiriti o Waitangi', p.137 and
fn.48; Charles Terry, *New Zealand: Its
Advantages and Prospects as a British Colony*,
London, 1842, p.181; William Yate, *An
Account of New Zealand*, 2nd ed., London,
1835, pp.228–31.
39. Early publications were checked. With
few exceptions the translations available before
1840 were made by the CMS and WMS
missionaries.
40. E.g. Ross, 'Te Tiriti o Waitangi', p.141.
41. John Hobbs to the editor, *Southern Cross*,
5 June 1860. It was Hobbs's emphasis.
Carleton, *Henry Williams*, vol.1, p.244, noted

that the meaning of mana had altered over the
years. The change in meaning or use,
especially with regard to the land, has been
noted also by A.R. Parsonson, 'He Whenua
Te Utu (The Payment will be land)', PhD
thesis, Canterbury (1978), p.70 and fn.23.
42. Normanby to Hobson, 14 August 1839,
and supplementary instructions, 15 August
1839, CO 209/4, 251–81; *Southern Cross*, 25
June 1858; and see Ross, 'Te Tiriti o Waitangi', p.144, for a discussion of pre–emption;
also Busby, 'Occupation of New Zealand,
1833–43', p.97, Busby Letters and Papers, MS
46, AML.
43. Apart from particular references that
are noted, the account of the Waitangi
proceedings that follows has drawn upon the
records of several participants or onlookers:
Colenso, *History*; Mathew Journal, 5,6
February 1840, NZ MS, APL; Taylor Journal,
5,6 February 1840, GNZ MS, APL; John
Bright, *Handbook for Emigrants and others*,
London, 1841, pp.136–42; Hobson to Gipps,
5, 6, February 1840, GBPP 1841 (311), pp.8–
9; Carleton, *Henry Williams*, vol.2, pp.11–15.
Colenso's account was checked by Busby
seven weeks after the events of early February
and several small notes added. The original
manuscript has been checked against Colenso's
History: W. Colenso, 'Memoranda of the
arrival of Lieut. Govr. Hobson in New
Zealand 1840', MS Papers 1611, ATL.
44. Fedarb Diary, entries for February 1840,
NZ MS 375, APL.
45. Colenso, *History*, pp.12–13.
46. Carleton, *Henry Williams*, vol.2, p.12.
47. Busby to Hobson, 19 February 1840,
transmitting the original Declaration, IA, 40/
42, NA.
48. Mathew Journal, 29 January 1840, NZ
MS, APL.
49. Colenso, *History*, pp.15–16.
50. Mathew Journal, 5 February 1840, NZ
MS, APL.
51. The account in Colenso's *History*, pp.16–
17, is taken almost verbatim from pencil notes
made during the meeting: 'Notebook', in
Colenso Papers, X, Hawke's Bay Museum.
52. Carleton, *Henry Williams*, vol.2, p.12;
Hobson to Gipps, 5 February 1840, GBPP,
1841 (311), p.8.
53. Colenso, *History*, pp.17, 19; see below,
p.97.
54. Colenso, *History*, p.19. There is no
evidence to support Moka's allegation.
55. *The Founding of New Zealand: The Journals
of Felton Mathew and his wife, 1840–1847*, ed.
J. Rutherford, Auckland, 1940, entry of 30
January 1840; for the Memorial, see encl.2 in
Hobson to Gipps, 3 February 1840, GBPP,
1840 (560), pp.6–9.
56. Colenso, *History*, p.24, notes that Hakiro
was Tareha's son, but that he spoke for Titore
who had died in 1837. Hobson to Gipps, 5
February 1840, GBPP, 1841 (311), p.8, refers
to 'Revewah' [Rewa?], 'Jakahra' [Hakiro?] and
'Kitigi' [Kaitieke?] a name by which Te
Kemara was also known.
57. Busby held the greater part of the Waita-

ngi peninsula from Te Kemara and other chiefs; Williams lived on the Church Mission land at Paihia originally known as Waitangi; the claim extended along towards the southern point of the Waitangi River mouth; Davis and Clarke had bought at Waimate where Rewa had held land; and Baker had land holdings on the Waikare River.

58. Colenso, *History*, p.20, note and p.23; see also Orton Journal, February 1840, Micro MS 90, ATL.

59. Colenso, *History*, p.18, note. The following section is drawn from Colenso.

60. Ibid., pp.18–19.

61. Ibid., pp.23–25.

62. Colenso, *History*, p.26; cf. Buick, *Treaty*, p.140, note, for a discussion on Heke and the conflicting accounts of his role at the treaty meetings. Colenso's account has been accepted for this information.

63. Bright, *Handbook for Emigrants*, p.141; Hobson to Gipps, 5 February 1840, GBPP, 1841 (311), p.8.

64. Mathew Journal, 5 February 1840, NZ MS, APL, notes that, on 4 February, Hobson had agreed to rent Busby's home for £200 per annum. Hobson did not follow the agreement up, but purchased Clendon's property at Okiato on the Kororareka side of the bay.

65. Carleton, *Henry Williams*, vol.2, p.14.

66. Colenso, *History*, p.30.

67. See above, pp.43–44; cf. Ross, 'Te Tiriti o Waitangi', p.133. In discussing this point, she suggests that the treaty considered at the meeting of 5 February differed from the treaty signed on 6 February. As evidence, she cites Carleton, Williams's son-in-law, who gave this explanation in NZPD 1864–66, p.292: 'An alteration was made while the draft was under consideration, and Mr. Taylor volunteered to write out the whole afresh.' Colenso confirmed this. But apart from the correction made at Busby's house on the morning of 5 February, there is no evidence to support Ross's line of argument that there may have been another alteration.

68. Taylor Journal, 5 February 1840, GNZ MS, APL; Ross, 'Te Tiriti o Waitangi', p.133, fn.28.

69. Colenso Journal, 6 February 1840, Hawke's Bay Museum.

70. Loc.cit.; Colenso, *History*, p.30; Ramsden, *Busby of Waitangi*, Wellington, 1942, pp.143ff., 166. In his Journal, Colenso noted that 'the great body of the Natives had dispersed', but his *History* makes reference to 'several' only, possibly the chiefs Waikato and Wharepoaka who had been involved in a land dispute at Whananaki some months before; and Kawiti who took exception to the distribution of tobacco in which he had missed out. None of these appears to have signed on 6 February. If they absented themselves, their followers also would have been absent – a possible explanation for the apparent discrepancy in Colenso's accounts. For Kawiti's attitude to the treaty, see *The Journal of Ensign Best 1837–1842*, ed. Nancy Taylor, Wellington, 1966, p.221.

71. Colenso's Journal and *History*, together with Taylor's account, all concur in this.

72. Buick, *Treaty*, p.116, mentions 1,500 Maoris but gives no reference.

73. Mathew is the only observer who recorded this.

74. Cf. Colenso, *History*, pp.31–32, and the Williams account in Carleton, *Henry Williams*, vol.2, pp.14–15; also J.B.F. Pompallier, *Early History of the Catholic Church in Oceania*, Auckland, 1888, pp.62–63.

75. Colenso translated 'te ritenga Maori' as 'the Maori custom, or usage', Williams's account spoke of 'Maori practices', but the contemporary attitude was probably best captured by Busby's 'heathen practices'.

76. Colenso, *History* pp.32–34; Mathew Journal, 6 February 1840, NZ MS, APL.

77. For this and subsequent sections see Colenso Journal, 6 February 1840, Hawke's Bay Museum; and Colenso, *History*, pp.32–33.

78. Colenso Journal, 6 February 1840, Hawke's Bay Museum. The correct rendering would have been: Sic transit gloria Novae Zealandiae.

79. Colenso, *History*, p.35.

80. A comparison of the 1835 Confederation document and the Waitangi treaty sheet indicates that a substantial number of signatories were from the Confederation as Hobson claimed. In this first treaty signing and in all subsequent ones, Maori agreement was given either by a signature, a moko or a mark, but various expressions have been used here to indicate Maori assent.

81. Hobson to Bunbury, 25 April 1840, GBPP, 1841 (311), p.17.

82. Hobson to Gipps, 6 February 1840, GBPP, 1841 (311), p.9.

83. Mathew Journal, 6 February 1840, NZ MS, APL.

84. *Missionary Register*, London, November 1840, p.509, cites a letter from Williams dated 13 February 1840.

85. Mathew Journal, 3, 4, 8 February 1840, NZ MS, APL.

86. Colenso, *History*, pp.34–35.

87. While Colenso records these words as 'He iwi tahi tatou', they are often said to be 'He iwi kotahi tatou'.

88. Colenso, *History*, p.34; Mathew Journal, 6 February 1840, NZ MS, APL.

89. Hobson to Gipps, 17 February 1840, GBPP, 1841 (311), p.10.

90. W. Colenso, 'Memoranda of the arrival of Lieut. Govr. Hobson in New Zealand 1840', MS Papers 1611, f.1, ATL; Colenso, *History*, p.34.

91. Busby, 'Occupation of New Zealand, 1833–44', p.91, Busby Letters and Papers, MS 46, AML.

92. Pompallier, *Early History of the Catholic Church*, p.62; Pompallier to Colin, 14 May 1840, Micro MS 669, r.3, ATL; Philip Turner, 'The Politics of Neutrality: The Catholic Mission and the Maori, 1838–1870', MA thesis, Auckland (1986), Ch.4.

93. E.g. R.G. Jameson, *New Zealand, South*

Australia and New South Wales: A Record of Recent Travels in these Colonies, London, 1841, pp.196-7.

94. Before 1840, Maori were becoming increasingly aware of the importance of documentation. They were cautious of signing land sales deeds, for example, because they were aware of the importance attached to them by Europeans. Certificates were sometimes sought by Maori as guarantees for their trustworthiness or to validate purchases of various items.

95. Carleton, *Henry Williams*, vol.2, pp.xliii-xliv; Peter Adams, *Fatal Necessity*, Auckland, 1977, pp.33-35; Hobbs Diary, 7,16 January 1840, MS 144, AML.

96. E.g. Carleton, *Henry Williams*, vol.1, pp.232-5 for various Anglican opinion, and Ironside Diary, 10 February 1840, Micro, MS 474, ATL; also Davis to Coleman, 13 February 1840, in J. Noble Coleman, *A Memoir of the Rev. Richard Davis*, London, 1865, pp.250-51; Hobbs Diary, 28 March 1840, MS 144, AML. For a good evaluation of the land sale situation in early 1840: Hobson to Normanby, 20 February 1840, CO 209/7, 27-33.

CHAPTER 4: EXTENDING THE TREATY
1. Normanby to Hobson, 14 August 1839, GBPP, 1840 [238].
2. Hobson to Bunbury, 25 April 1840, GBPP, 1841 (311), pp.17-18.
3. Discussions on the draft instructions, 24 January 1840, CO 209/4, 208ff.
4. Mathew Journal, (various entries), NZ MS, APL, and Taylor Journal, 9-10 February 1840, MS 302, AML.
5. Davis to Coleman, 8 February 1840, in J. Noble Coleman, *A Memoir of the Rev. Richard Davis*, London, 1865, pp.247ff; see map, p.62, and cf. T. Lindsay Buick, *The Treaty of Waitangi*, 3rd ed., New Plymouth, 1936, p.259.
6. Hobbs Diaries, 28 March 1840, MS 144, AML; Hobson to Gipps, 17 February 1840, GBPP, 1841 (311), p.11; Ironside Diary, 27 October 1839, Micro MS 474, ATL; Orton Journal, February 1840 entry, Micro MS 90, ATL.
7. Hobbs to Martin, 22 October 1847, in William Martin, *England and the New Zealanders*, Auckland, 1847, pp.73-74.
8. Speeches at the Hokianga meeting, encl. 2 in Shortland to Stanley, 18 January 1845, GBPP, 1845 (108), pp.10-11; Taylor Journal, vol.2, pp.361-66, MS 302, AML. Apart from the treaty sheet and the odd mention of chiefs' names in Hobson's report, these two sets of notes are the only sources which indicate the speakers at the meeting. Since the speeches lasted many hours, Shortland and Taylor evidently recorded only the most significant speeches.
9. Taonui cited the amount allowed for this; see encl. 2 in Shortland to Stanley, 18 January 1845, GBPP, 1845 (108), pp.10-11.
10. Hobbs to Martin, 22 October 1847, in Martin, *England and the New Zealanders*, pp.73-74.

11. Taylor Journal, 12 February 1840, MS 302, AML.
12. Hobson to Gipps, 17 February 1840, GBPP, 1841 (311), pp.10-12; Hobbs to Martin, 22 October 1847, in Martin, *England and the New Zealanders*, pp.73-74; Letter to J. Bumby, 29 May 1840, Hobson letters, MS Papers 813, ATL.
13. Hobson to Gipps, 17 February 1840, GBPP, 1841 (311), pp.10-12, talks of fifty-six Hokianga signatures but on the treaty sheet the number witnessed is forty-three.
14. The Journals of Taylor and Mathew, and Hobson's official report describe the events.
15. *The Founding of New Zealand: The Journals of Felton Mathew and his wife, 1840-47*, ed. J. Rutherford, Auckland, 1940, p.53; Taylor Journal, 14 February 1840, MS 302, AML. The chiefs and tribes involved were not identified.
16. Hobson to Gipps, 17 February 1840, GBPP, 1841 (311), pp.10-12.
17. *Journals of Felton Mathew*, p.55; Taylor Journal, entries 14-17 February 1840, MS 302, AML.
18. Herbert W. Williams, *A Bibliography of Printed Maori to 1900 and Supplement*, Wellington, 1975 (reprint), listed as no.52, whereas it is probably 52a; see R.M. Ross, 'Te Tiriti o Waitangi, texts and translations', *NZJH*, VI, 2 (1972), pp.129-57; W. Colenso, 'Day and Waste Book', 17 February 1840, MS 76, AML; Colenso Journal, 17 February 1840, Hawke's Bay Museum. W. Colenso, *The Authentic and Genuine History of the Signing of the Treaty of Waitangi*, Wellington, 1890, p.35, records that on 8 February he was 'busy in the printing office with ... two treaties', but there is no record of their printing.
19. Pomare's name appears above that of Hone Heke but J.R. Clendon, the witness, dated it 17 February 1840.
20. Charles Wilkes, *Narrative of the United States Exploring Expedition During the Years 1838-1842*, vol.2, pp.375-6.
21. Mathew Journal entries from 21 February to 4 March 1840, NZ MS, APL.
22. No indication was given of the exact site of this, but a memorial has been erected at Karaka Bay where a second Waitemata signing was held in July. The chiefs supposed to have signed there on 4 March are listed on the memorial. See map, p.62.
23. H.J. Ryburn, *Te Hemara, James Hamlin, 1803-1865: Friend of Maoris*, Dunedin, 1979, p.61.
24. S.P. Smith, *Maori Wars of the Nineteenth Century ... prior to the colonization of New Zealand in 1840*, 2nd ed., Christchurch, 1910, p.478.
25. Lane to Gipps, 28 March 1840, and Hobson to Secretary of State for Colonies, 25 May 1840, GBPP, 1841 (311), pp.14-15.
26. Symonds to Colonial Secretary, 12 May 1840, GBPP, 1841 (311), pp.101-2.
27. Mathew Journal, 4 March 1840, NZ MS, APL.
28. Symonds does not say where the meetings were held [Awhitu?].

29. Brown Journal, 1 April 1840, AUL; Hobson to H. Williams, 23 March 1840 and note, 23 May 1840, and W. Williams to Shortland, 8 May 1840; GBPP, 1841 (311), pp.17, 101.
30. Symonds to Colonial Secretary, 12 May 1840, GBPP, 1841 (311), p.101; Ryburn, *Te Hemara: James Hamlin*, pp.45ff.
31. H. Wily and H. Maunsell, *Robert Maunsell, L.L.D. A New Zealand Pioneer: His Life and Times*, Dunedin, 1938, p.69, where reference is made to Maunsell's visit to Awhitu in 1840, accompanied by Tipene Tahatika, to obtain Te Wherowhero's signature.
32. FitzRoy to Stanley, 25 May 1844, GBPP, 1845 (247), pp.13–14.
33. Symonds to Colonial Secretary, 12 May 1840, GBPP, 1841 (311), pp.101–2.
34. Symonds to Whiteley, 8 April 1840, GBPP, 1841 (311), p.102.
35. Brown Journal, 10 April 1840, AUL.
36. Hobson to H. Williams, 23 March 1840, GBPP, 1841 (311), p.17.
37. *The Turanga Journals 1840–1850 : Letters and Journals of William and Jane Williams*, ed. Frances Porter, Wellington, 1974, 5 May 1840, and entries from 17 February to March 1840; W. Williams to Shortland, 8 May 1840, GBPP, 1841 (311), p.101.
38. *Turanga Journals*, pp.85–86, 24 February 1840.
39. Ibid., 12, 20 February 1840. Details of the purchases are given at pp.149–50. W. Williams to Shortland, 8 May 1840, GBPP, 1841 (311), p.10l.
40. G. Clarke, [Jnr.], *Notes on early life in New Zealand*, Hobart 1903, pp.28–33; *Turanga Journals*, 16 May 1840.
41. Jane Williams, 13,15 April 1840, *Turanga Journals*; H. Williams to Hobson, 11 June 1840, GBPP, 1841 (311), p.105.
42. Hobson to Bunbury, 25 April 1840, GBPP, 1841 (311), p.18; H. Williams to Hobson, 15 May 1840, Official Correspondence relating to the . . . Treaty, q MS 1840, ATL.
43. Hadfield to 'My dear George' [?], 6 July 1840, Hadfield Papers, q MS 1833–1902, ATL.
44. Hugh Carleton, *The Life of Henry Williams*, Auckland, 1874, vol.1, pp.233, 239–40; *The Early Journals of Henry Williams, 1826–40*, ed. L.M. Rogers, Christchurch, 1961, pp.465–6, 16 December 1839; H. Williams to Hobson, 11 June 1840, GBPP, 1841 (311), p.105.
45. Gipps to Russell, 5 April 1840, GBPP, 1841 (311), p.4.
46. Hobson to Bunbury, 25 April 1840, GBPP, 1841 (311), pp.17–18, outlined Hobson's instructions.
47. For this and the following meetings, see Bunbury to Hobson, 6, 15 May, 28 June 1840, GBPP, 1841 (311), pp.100, 103–12; T. Bunbury, *Reminiscences of a Veteran*, London, 1861, vol.3; E.M. Williams, Journal of a Voyage in *H.M.S. Herald*, entries for April to

July 1840, MS 1840, ATL. The *Herald* anchored at Coromandel, 29–30 April.
48. Stewart to Bunbury, 3 May 1840, Official Correspondence . . . Treaty, q MS 1840, ATL; Williams Journal of a Voyage, 7,9 May 1840, MS 1840, ATL.
49. Hobson to Bunbury, 25 April 1840, and Bunbury to Hobson, 15 May 1840, GBPP, 1841 (311), pp.17–18, 103–4. Bunbury went inshore on the *Trent* and had to return to Mercury Bay to the *Herald*, before continuing southwards.
50. J.B.F. Pompallier, *Early History of the Catholic Church in Oceania*, Auckland, 1888, p.62.
51. Bunbury to Hobson, 15 May 1840, GBPP, 1841 (311), p.104.
52. Williams Journal of a Voyage, 19–20 May 1840, MS 1840, ATL; Morgan Journal, AUL, entries for February-April 1840; J.C. Bidwill, *Rambles in New Zealand*, London, 1841, [Capper reprint 1974], p.40.
53. Stack to Shortland, 23 May 1840, GBPP, 1841 (311), p.104; Brown Journal, 9 May 1840, AUL; Colenso to Hobson, 27 June 1840, Official Correspondence . . . Treaty, q MS 1840, ATL: Fedarb Diary, NZ MS 375, APL.
54. 'How Te Heuheu rejected the treaty', Best Papers, MS papers 72, f.73, ATL, (dictated on 26 May 1913 for Buick's publication, *The Treaty of Waitangi*). The information that follows relies on this account. An alternative account appears in J. Grace, *Tuwharetoa: The History of the Maori People of the Taupo district*, Wellington, 1959, pp.238, 437, but the facts given are contradictory. The Chapman and Morgan Journals and Diaries do not mention any meeting, but the entries in this period are not comprehensive in either instance.
55. *The New Zealand Journal, 1842–1844, of J.B. Williams*, ed. R.W. Kenny, Salem, [Mass.], 1956, pp.42–44. See also Pompallier, *Early History of the Catholic Church*, pp.66–67.
56. Colenso to Hobson, 27 June 1840, Official correspondence . . . Treaty', q MS 1840, ATL.
57. Freeman to Colenso, 1 July 1840, Colenso Papers, MS Col. 1833–63, IV, p.83, ATL.
58. Shortland to Brown, 7 May 1840, enclosing 'copies' of the treaty, IA, 4/1, no.35, NA.
59. Tupaea had been offered the treaty on 10 April, 12 May, and Buick, *Treaty of Waitangi*, p.229, makes reference to a further occasion at Manukau.
60. Bunbury to Hobson, 5 May 1840, GBPP, 1841 (311), p.100; Normanby to Hobson, 15 August 1839, GBPP, 1840 [238], pp.44–45; Hobson to Bunbury, 25 April 1840, GBPP, 1841 (311), pp.17–18.
61. Clarke, *Notes on early life*, pp.63–64.
62. Bunbury to Nias, 12 May 1840, Official correspondence . . . Treaty, q MS 1840, ATL. The Edward Williams diary entries date the *Herald's* movements.
63. Bunbury to Hobson, 28 June 1840, GBPP, 1841 (311), p.106. See also E. Shortland, *The Southern Districts of New Zealand*, London, 1851, pp.252–3, 256, 303.

64. Bunbury to Hobson, 28 June 1840, GBPP, 1841 (311), p.100; Williams Diary of a Voyage, MS 1840, ATL, entries from 30 May to 9 June 1840; cf. B. Howard, *Rakiura: A History of Stewart Island*, Wellington, 1940, p.106, and Edward's entry for 3 June 1840.
65. The site of the proclamation is unsure. See Howard, *Rakiura* pp.106-12; Buick, *Treaty of Waitangi*, p.233.
66. Bunbury to Hobson, 28 June 1840, GBPP, 1841 (311), p.107; Williams Diary of a Voyage, 9-11 June 1840, MS 1840, ATL.
67. Bunbury to Hobson, 28 June 1840, GBPP, 1841 (311), p.108.
68. This section and the following is drawn from E. M. Williams Diary and Bunbury to Hobson, 28 June 1840, GBPP, 1841 (311), pp.108-9.
69. Proclamations enclosed in Bunbury to Hobson, 28 June 1840, Bunbury to Parker, 4 July 1840, GBPP, 1841 (311), pp.112-3.
70. E.g. Harris to Busby, 21 January 1838, and Busby to Hapuku, 30 Jaunary 1838, British Resident Papers, 1/2 nos.101, 103, NA, and also Clayton to Busby, 8 October 1838.
71. Williams Diary of a Voyage, MS 1840, ATL; cf. Buick, *Treaty of Waitangi* p.262, who gives 23 June.
72. The circumstances of this signing have been collated from the several sources following: Taylor Journal, MS 302, AML; Johnson Journal, 23-28 April 1840, NZ MS 27, APL; Puckey Letters and Journals, AUL, various entries; Hobson to Gipps, 5 May 1840, and Shortland to Hobson, 4 May 1840, encl. Nopera's speech, GBPP, 1841 (311), pp.57-59; Shortland to Stanley, 18 January 1845, encl. the speeches of Kaitaia chiefs, GBPP, 1845 (108), pp.5-10.
73. Puckey Journal, 7 April 1837, 21 September 1839 and 12 June 1840, has comments on Nopera. The chief had a 'neat little weatherboard cottage' furnished in English style. The official party supped there at Nopera's invitation on the night of the Kaitaia signing: Johnson Journal, 28 April 1840, NZ MS 27, APL.
74. George Clarke [Sen.], *Remarks upon a pamphlet ... by James Busby*, Auckland, 1861 (reprint 1923), p.9; Johnson Journal, 27,28 April 1840, NZ MS 27, APL. Nopera's words, well known in New Zealand from the 1840s and often cited, were given by Johnson verbatim from the translation rendered by Puckey. No source has been found for Nopera's words in Maori, as spoken by Nopera. For the word 'shadow', writers have suggested wairua, atarangi and atakau.
75. Johnson Journal, 28 April 1840, NZ MS 27, APL; Taylor Journal, 28 May 1840, MS 302, AML.
76. *The Journal of Ensign Best, 1837-1842*, ed. Nancy Taylor, Wellington, 1966, pp.219-222, records this and the subsequent meeting. Since Bunbury was at the first meeting it must have been held between the time of his arrival in New Zealand on 16 April and his departure of 28-29 April on his treaty trip to the south.
77. Shortland to Tirarau, n.d. 1840, (Maori), MS Papers 2493, ATL; Buller Journal, 9 April 1840, q MS [1838-44], ATL, records the receipt of letters from Shortland to Tirarau, Parore and Mate, whom Buller was to persuade to go to the Bay. Colenso Papers, MS Col. 1833-63, IV, p.106, ATL, gives a copy of Tirarau's letter undated.
78. D. Rough, 'Early Days of Auckland', articles from the *NZ Herald*, 11-25 January 1896, AML.
79. The flag is held by the National Museum, Wellington. One of Hobson's proclamations of sovereignty dated the Waitangi signing as 5 February; in the other, which proclaimed sovereignty over all New Zealand, the latitudinal limits were erroneously defined as from 34°30' north to 47°10' south. Hobson to Secretary of State for Colonies, 25 May 1840, GBPP, 1841 (311), p.15.
80. Ibid., p.18.
81. Hobson to Gipps, 5-6 February 1840, CO 209/6, 46-54, which includes the English copy; and Hobson to Gipps, 16 February 1840, CO 209/7, 13-14, which includes the copy certified by H.W. Williams; cf., Hobson to Russell, 15 October 1840, CO 209/7, 178, where the two copies were enclosed; and the printed copies in GBPP, 1841 (311), pp.98-99. See also Ross, 'Te Tiriti o Waitangi', p.134, which notes the copies sent to Hobson's superiors as well as the various duplicates held in New Zealand. In one instance, a copy is said to have been included in Hobson to Russell, 25 May 1840, but this seems to be an error made by Ross when interpreting the text of an enclosure in the dispatch. Ross also notes the minor differences in the English texts which are of no great importance except for one text that omits forests and fisheries.
82. Russell to Hobson, 10 November 1840, CO 209/7, 53-54. The reports of individual treaty negotiators were enclosed in Hobson to Russell, 15 October 1840, and printed in GBPP, 1841 (311); cf. CO 209/7, 102ff, for marginal comments about how much should be published. This dispatch enclosed the Maori and English text of the treaty with copies of chiefs' moko and signatures. The names were removed.
83. Shortland to Hobson, 6 May 1840, encl. in Hobson to Secretary of State for Colonies, 10 November 1840, CO 209/7, marginal comment [Russell?], p.259.
84. Buick, *Treaty of Waitangi*, p.256.
85. The incident involved HMS *Pelorus*. Correspondence is in British Resident 1/2, nos.119-121, 123, NA.
86. Wilkes, *Narrative of the United States Exploring Expedition*, vol.2, pp.375, 380.
87. Maunsell to Hobson, 14 April 1840, encl. in Hobson to Russell, 15 October 1840, GBPP, 1841 (311), p.99.
88. Hadfield to Mrs H. [Hadfield?], 17 January 1842, Hadfield Papers, q MS, ATL.

89. Wilson to Brown, 24 April 1840, *Turanga Journals*, p.157, fn.40.

90. See GBPP, 1841 (311), pp.100, 101, 111; and Colenso to Hobson, 27 June 1840, Official Correspondence ... Treaty, q MS 1840, ATL.

91. E.g. Johnson, Journal, 28 April 1840, NZ MS 27, APL.

92. Carleton, *Life of Henry Williams*, vol.2, p.17; Colenso Journal, 13 June 1840, Hawke's Bay Museum.

93. The name appears on the Waitangi sheet close to Rawiri [Taiwhanga?]. Like Rawiri she had lived at the Paihia station since 1831.

94. H. Williams to Hobson, 15 May 1840, Official Correspondence ... Treaty, q MS, 1840, ATL.

95. The name appears on the Williams sheet simply as Rere. Rere's son was Rangihiwinui, better known as Major Kemp. A section of the Wanganui River near the present town is named after her.

96. See Bunbury to Hobson, 28 June 1840, GBPP, 1841 (311), p.108, where Bunbury included it in his report.

97. Taylor Journal, 28 April 1840, MS 302, AML. The speaker was given as 'Wartona Wera'.

98. *Bay of Islands Observer*, 7 July 1842.

CHAPTER 5: EARLY YEARS OF DOUBT AND DEBATE

1. A.H. McLintock, *Crown Colony Government in New Zealand*, Wellington, 1958, pp.49–50.

2. Hobson to Stanley, 22 July 1840, Hobson Papers, MS Papers 46, ATL; Stanley to Hobson, 17 September 1840, GBPP, 1841 (311), pp.81–82; Philip Turner, 'The Politics of Neutrality: The Catholic Mission and the Maori 1838–1870', MA, Auckland, (1986), pp.92–93.

3. Proclamation, 30 January 1840, in Hobson to Gipps, 4 February 1840, CO 209/6, 24–27.

4. McLintock, *Crown Colony Government*, pp.120–21, 130–32.

5. Hugh Carleton, *The Life of Henry Williams*, Auckland, 1874, vol.2, pp.20–29, for some of the early missionary feeling. Clarke's letter of acceptance, April 1840, IA 1/106, NA.

6. For Clarke's assessment of the Protectorate and his work, with Grey's comments appended, see Clarke in Grey to Stanley, 12 June 1846, and Grey to Earl Grey, 4 February 1846, GBPP, 1847 [837], pp.13ff.,35; C.H. Wake, 'George Clarke and the Government of the Maoris, 1840–45', *Historical Studies Australia and New Zealand*, X, 39 (1962), pp.339–56.

7. Clarke Report in Gipps to Russell, 7 March 1841, GBPP, 1842 (569), pp.97–100; Carleton, *Henry Williams*, vol.2, pp.28–29.

8. Johnson Journal, 7,8 April 1840, NZ MS 27, APL; Clarke Report in Gipps to Russell, 7 March 1841, GBPP, 1842 (569), p.96.

9. Proclamation, 27 April 1840, (Maori copy),held at APL.

10. Clarke Report in Gipps to Russell, 7 March 1841, GBPP, 1842 (569), pp.94–98.

11. See Gipps's Speech in Council, 9 July 1840, in Gipps to Russell, 16 August 1840, GBPP, 1841 (311), pp.63ff.; E. Sweetman, *The Unsigned New Zealand Treaty*, Melbourne, 1939, Chs. 4–6.

12. Claims had to be lodged within six months; a schedule was provided whereby values could be computed: before 1824, land was to be valued at 6d an acre; between 1825 and 1829, from 6d to 8d; in 1835, from 1/- to 2/-; and in 1839, from 4/- to 8/- an acre. Goods given for land were to be valued at three times their Sydney prices. Absentee purchasers were more heavily charged than residents.

13. Gipps referred to Chancellor Kent, Justices Storey and Marshall, and the judgement in Johnson v. McIntosh.

14. Sweetman, *Unsigned New Zealand Treaty*, Chs.4, 6, cover Wentworth's case in detail.

15. *NZ Advertiser and Bay of Islands Gazette*, 13 August 1840. Debates on the Bill covered the period 28 May to 9 July, the Bill passing on 3 August 1840.

16. Busby to Hope, 17 January 1845, GBPP, 1845 (108), p.15.

17. Clarke Report in Gipps to Russell, 7 March 1841, GBPP, 1842 (569), pp.94–98.

18. For a history of the land claims problems see Surplus Lands Commission, AJHR, 1948, G-8, esp. pp.25, 48ff., which trace the legislation affecting the issue; also Rosemarie V. Tonk, 'The First New Zealand Land Commissions, 1840–1845', MA, Canterbury (1986). Gipps's Land Bill of August 1840 became inoperative when New Zealand became a separate colony, but Hobson re-enacted the measure with few changes on 9 June 1841. There was further legislation in 1842, 1844, 1846, 1849 and 1856. See also Sweetman, *Unsigned New Zealand Treaty*, Ch.2; and Report of the Land Claims Commissioner, AJHR, 1862, F-1.

19. E.g. *NZ Herald and Auckland Gazette*, 24 July (suppl.), 4 September, 23 October 1841, and 19 January, 22 January 1842.

20. *Bay of Islands Observer*, 13 January, 24 February, 3 March, 14 April, 5, 12 May 1842. Hobson had anticipated that settlers would take this line of reasoning: Hobson to Under-Secretary, Colonial Office, August 1839, GBPP, 1840 [238], p.42.

21. AJHR, 1948, G-8, p.42; see also *Southern Cross*, 16 September 1848, where a Maori is reported as having returned the purchase money.

22. See above, p.47. Nopera may have been given the same idea: *Southern Cross*, 28 April 1849; H.T. Kemp to Clarke, 10 February 1843, GBPP, 1844 (556), Appendix 4, p.125 and Godfrey to Col. Sec., 10 February 1843, in FitzRoy to Stanley, 18 December 1844, GBPP, 1845 (369), p.73.

23. *Auckland Chronicle and NZ Colonist*, 27 December 1843; *Southern Cross*, 30 December 1843; Waimate meeting, MS 430, AML.

24. *NZ Herald and Auckland Gazette*, 29 December 1841, 29 January, 2,5,12 February 1842.

25. Surplus Lands Commission, AJHR, 1948, G-8, pp.60–62; Peter Adams, *Fatal Necessity*, Auckland, 1977, p.192.

26. *Te Karere*, February 1842. Referred to hereafter as the *Maori Messenger*, the paper was published under government auspices from 1842 to 1863 with a few interruptions. It had a print run of only 1,000 copies in 1842–43 but a very wide circulation. Kemp Report, 2 March 1843, MA-2, 43/24, NA; G. Clarke Jnr to Col. Sec., 28 December 1842, MA 4/58, NA.

27. For a detailed analysis, see Adams, *Fatal Necessity*, pp.176–87.

28. See Gipps to Russell, 5 March 1841 and correspondence enclosed, GBPP, 1842 (569).

29. G.W. Hope, Permanent Under–Secretary Colonial Office, cit. Adams, *Fatal Necessity*, p.180.

30. Ibid., pp.189–92, and Appendix 4; for comment, see F.M. Brookfield, 'The Constitution in 1985: The Search for Legitimacy', unpublished paper, Auckland, 1985, p.16 and fn.48.

31. Stanley to FitzRoy, 13 August 1844, GBPP, 1845 (1); Stanley to Grey, 27 June 1845; GBPP, 1846 (337), p.72.

32. GBPD, 81, 17 June 1845; Stanley to Grey, 27 June 1845, GBPP, 1846 (337), p.75.

33. Normanby to Hobson, 14 August 1839, GBPP, 1840 [238], pp.41, 44; Hobson to Under–Secretary of State for Colonies, August 1839, where he states that the explanation was 'very clear and satisfactory'.

34. Selwyn to Williams, 30 June 1847. Ross, 'Te Tiriti o Waitangi, texts and translations', NZJH, XIV, 1 (1980), p.149; Williams to Selwyn, 12 July 1847, Carleton, *Henry Williams*, vol.2, p.157; see Adams, *Fatal Necessity*, p.198 where he refers to an anonymous letter which might have been penned by Henry Williams in 1861, where the writer explained that pre-emption was described at Waitangi as follows: 'The Queen is to have the first offer of the land you may wish to sell, and in the event of its being refused by the Crown, the land is yours to sell it to whom you please.' Adams doubts the reliability of this evidence. Colenso queried Maori understanding, not the accuracy of the explanation given.

35. Colenso to CMS, begun 24 January 1840, CN M11, 715–16, AUL; Report of Select Committee on New Zealand, GBPP, 1844 (556), Minutes, p.39.

36. Colenso to CMS, begun 24 January 1840, CN, M11, 715–16, AUL; Ross, 'Te Tiriti o Waitangi', pp.145–6; Buller Journal, 30 May 1840, q MS [1838–44], ATL; J. Whiteley, 18 April 1856, in GBPP, 1860 [2719], p.274.

37. Bunbury to Hobson, 6,15 May 1840, encls. 3 and 6 in Hobson to Russell, 15 October 1840, GBPP, 1841 (311), pp.100, 103.

38. H. Williams to Hobson, 11 June 1840, encl. 8, in Hobson to Russell, 15 October 1840, GBPP, 1841 (311), p.105.

39. E.g. W. Williams's petition in Coates to Russell, 9 March 1841, GBPP, 1841 (311),

p.139; Morgan to CMS, 26 October 1840, Morgan Letters and Journals, AUL.

40. Busby to Hope, 17 January 1845, GBPP, 1845 (108), p.15, where Busby states that neither he nor H. Williams really grasped the full significance of pre-emption. A notice from the London Land and Emigration Commissioners, announcing the passage to New Zealand of several shiploads of emigrants, had taken them by surprise.

41. E.g. Entry Island letter, April 1840, MA-2, NA; Clarke Report in Hobson to Stanley, 13 November 1841, GBPP, 1842 (569), p.171; encls. A and B in FitzRoy to Stanley, 15 April 1844, GBPP, 1845 (131); Clarke to Col. Sec., 21 December 1843, encl. 2 in FitzRoy to Stanley, 20 August 1845, GBPP, 1846 (337), p.115.

42. Adams, *Fatal Necessity*, p.201; and see Register of inwards letters for 1840, MA-2, NA.

43. Petition of Kororareka residents, 15 December 1841, CO 209/14, 312–21.

44. Adams, *Fatal Necessity* p.205: 'By 1841, the Colonial Government had paid £1,445 for land which it sold at £25,431; by 1844, £4,054 had been paid for land sold for £40,263. William Martin, *England and the New Zealanders*, Auckland, 1847, p.64, calculated that the average price per acre paid for land purchased by the Crown to the end of 1844 was 4½d. For prices in the 1841 Auckland sales, see encls. 1 and 2 in Hobson to Russell, 5 August 1841, GBPP, 1842 (569), p.511.

45. *Southern Cross*, 30 December 1843: Ngati Whatua letter, translation into English by G. Clarke, and Waikato letter, translation into English by Thos. Forsaith, each certified 'true copy'. These translations suggest that Maori understood at Waitangi that by pre-emption they gave the Crown the first offer only, but the original Maori letters are not so explicit: see *Maori Messenger*, January 1844, where Waikato seem to reject the sole right interpretation as unfair, rather than as an inaccurate rendering of the original agreement.

46. FitzRoy to Stanley, 15 April 1844, GBPP, 1845 (131), p.24; FitzRoy to Stanley, 14 October 1844, GBPP, 1845 (369), p.20.

47. *Southern Cross*, 3 June 1843, p.3.

48. Ibid., 26 August 1843. S.M.D. Martin, the editor, appended these two translations to the following publication: S.M.D. Martin, *New Zealand in a series of letters*, London, 1845.

49. See encl. 1 in FitzRoy to Stanley, 14 July 1844, GBPP, 1845 (247), pp.21–23; FitzRoy to Stanley, 14 October 1844, GBPP, 1845 (369), pp.20ff; and encl. 1 in Grey to Gladstone, 29 September 1846, GBPP, 1847 [837]; cf. Stanley to Grey, 13 June 1845, GBPP, 1846 (337), p.72.

50. FitzRoy to Stanley, 15 April 1844, GBPP, 1845 (131), p.22; and for an earlier comment see Johnson Journal, April 1840, NZ MS 27, APL.

51. FitzRoy to Stanley, 15 April 1844 and encl. 0, GBPP, 1845 (131), pp.18, 44–45;

FitzRoy to Stanley, 14 October 1844, GBPP, 1845 (369), pp.20–21, 25ff.

52. Encl. 0 in FitzRoy to Stanley, 15 April 1844, GBPP, 1845 (131), pp.43–44; Memorial to Stanley, 10 October 1844, GBPP, 1845 (378), pp.13–19.

53. Stanley to FitzRoy, 30 November 1844, GBPP, 1845 (131); Stanley to Grey, 14 August 1845, GBPP, 1846 (337); Grey to Stanley, 14 April 1846, GBPP, 1847 [837], p.1; Hope to Ingestre, 7 August 1845, GBPP, 1845 (661), p.3.

54. Selwyn to FitzRoy, November 1845, G19/1, NA; Martin, *England and the New Zealanders*, p.53; Ashworth Journal, n.d. [December?] 1843, MS 1841–45P, ATL; Encl. 0 in FitzRoy to Stanley, 15 April 1844, GBPP 1845 (131). pp.43–44.

55. Official thinking on the utilisation of 'waste land' as a colony's resource had been evolving for some years, but when the Australian Colonies Waste Lands Act was passed in 1842 it was criticised in New Zealand as being unsuitable for local conditions where lands were not 'waste' as in Australia: Minutes and Proceedings of Legislative Council, 17 July 1844, encl. in FitzRoy to Stanley, 20 August 1844, GBPP, 1845 (247).

56. *New–Zealander*, 21 November 1846, and 28 November 1846 which reported a public meeting concerning a petition to the Throne against the Ordinance.

57. J.S. Molloy, 'The era of civilization: British policy for the Indians of Canada, 1830–1860', D Phil. thesis, Oxford, (1978), p.11.

58. Russell to Hobson, 9 December 1840, GBPP, 1841 (311), p.27. For a criticism of the 'airy speculation' of the imperial government, see McLintock, *Crown Colony Government*, pp.110, 125–9; for a contemporary criticism, Morgan to CMS, 26 October 1840, Morgan Letters and Journals, AUL.

59. Hobson was sent Grey's writings on the Australian Aborigines but there is no record of the effect, if any, that these made on Hobson: GBPP, 1841 (311), p.43.

60. Alan Ward, *A Show of Justice: Racial 'amalgamation' in nineteenth century New Zealand*, Auckland, 1973, p.48. Ward gives a detailed treatment of the law and its application to the Maori throughout the nineteenth century. For 1840–1847, see Adams, *Fatal Necessity*, Ch.7.

61. E.g. Ward. *Show of Justice*, pp.45–50; Brown Journal, 16 February 1847, AUL.

62. A.D.W. Best, *The Journal of Ensign Best, 1837–1842*, ed. N. Taylor, Wellington, 1966, pp.227–8; E. Shortland, *Traditions and Superstitions of the New Zealanders*, London, 1856, pp.237–40.

63. *Journal of Ensign Best*, pp.294–6.

64. Ibid., pp.287, 350.

65. Ward, *Show of Justice*, p.54; Brown Journal, 24–29 July 1843, AUL.

66. Hobson to Russell, 16 December 1841, GBPP, 1842 (569), p.191.

67. Johnson Journal, 20–23 April 1840, NZ

MS 27, APL; Ward, *Show of Justice*, p.47; Carleton, *Henry Williams*, vol.2, pp.21–22.

68. Carleton, *Henry Williams*, vol.2, p.35; *NZ Herald and Auckland Gazette*, 19 January 1842, printed letters from chiefs; see also *Maori Messenger*, 1 January 1842.

69. E.g. Brown Journal, 24–29 July 1843, AUL; *Maori Messenger*, 31 October 1859.

70. Clarke to Col. Sec., 1 July 1845, in Fitz-Roy to Stanley, 17 September 1845, GBPP, 1846 (337), p.134.

71. Register for 1840s, MA-2, NA; Chapman Journal, 2 February 1846, and 30 November 1845, AUL, where he observed the use of a genealogical rod.

72. FitzRoy to Stanley, 25 May 1844, GBPP, 1845 (247), p.8.

73. *Journal of Ensign Best*, p.394.

74. Carleton, *Henry Williams*, vol.2, p.61; A.R. Parsonson, 'The Expansion of a Competitive Society', *NZJH*, XIV, 1 (1980), pp.45–60.

75. Clarke Report in Gipps to Russell, 7 March 1841, GBPP, 1842 (569), p.96; Clarke to Col. Sec., 1 June 1843, encl. in FitzRoy to Stanley, 20 August 1845, GBPP, 1846 (337), p.113; and see Ward, *Show of Justice*, pp.49–50.

76. Stanley to Grey, 28 November 1845, transmitting a letter from W. Brown, GBPP, 1846 (337), p.101; Selwyn to FitzRoy, November 1845, G 19/1, NA; Martin, *England and the New Zealanders*, p.49.

77. Nopera began to stir in May 1840: *NZ Advertiser and Bay of Islands Gazette*, 22 July 1840; May letter and others in 1840 from Nopera, Register, MA-2, NA; Godfrey to Col. Sec., 10 February 1843, in FitzRoy to Stanley, 18 December 1844, GBPP, 1845 (369), p.73; *Southern Cross*, 10 June 1843.

78. A.R. Parsonson, 'The Expansion of a Competitive Society', *NZJH*, XIV, 1(1980), pp.57–58; Chapman to CMS, 26 January 1848, Chapman Letters and Journals, AUL.

79. Clarke Report in Gipps to Russell, 7 March 1841, GBPP, 1842 (569), pp.95–96.

80. For various discussions of this affair see Adams, *Fatal Necessity*, p.219; Ward, *Show of Justice*, p.58; Ian Wards, *The Shadow of the Land*, Wellington, 1968, pp.60–62; Report, GBPP, 1844 (556), Appendix, pp.192ff.

81. *Journal of Ensign Best*, p.364.

82. Cit. Wards, *Shadow of the Land*, p.61, fn.4; Taraia and Takanini to government, June 1842, Register, MA-2, 42/81–82, NA. Another letter, 22 June 1842, 'numerously signed', protested against the Queen's sovereignty, MA-2, 42/67, NA.

83. *Journal of Ensign Best*, pp.380–400, various entries December 1842-February 1843, and a reconstruction of the affair, pp.63–67 and Appendix 20; Adams, *Fatal Necessity*, pp.220–22; Ward, *Show of Justice*, pp.58–59; Wards, *Shadow of the Land*, pp.64–68; and Report, GBPP, 1844 (556), Appendix, pp.456ff.

84. Report, GBPP, 1844 (556), p.458, and p.469 for translation.

85. Ward, *Show of Justice*. pp.61ff. discusses the fact that Native Districts were later allowed for in both the 1846 Charter for self-government and the 1852 Constitution.
86. E.g. Martin, *England and the New Zealanders*, pp.22–28, where he refers to the American experience in his analysis of the New Zealand case. The *Bay of Islands Observer*, 7 April 1842, suggested that the government distinguish between territories ceded and those not ceded, so presumably the idea had some currency.
87. *Journal of Ensign Best*, Appendix 20; Adams, *Fatal Necessity*, pp.220–22.
88. E.g. 'Notes of the Treaty of Waitangi Movement', Wairua Papers (private collection); *Nga Kaupapa i Whakaotia e te Hui i tu ki te Kauhanganui i te 26 o nga ra o Hune 1948*, Hamilton, n.d. [1948?].
89. Adams, *Fatal Necessity*, p.222.
90. Robert FitzRoy, *Remarks on New Zealand*, London, 1846, pp.45, 60.
91. FitzRoy to Stanley, 25 May 1844, GBPP, 1845 (247), p.13; cf. Clarke Report, GBPP, 1842 (569), p.94, where Clarke had reassured Maori that prisons were to protect Maori from 'bad' Pakeha.
92. See *Southern Cross*, 4 May 1844, for comment.
93. William Martin, *Ko Nga Tikanga a te Pakeha*, Auckland, 1845; FitzRoy to Earl Grey, 20 March 1847, GBPP, 1847 [837], p.74.
94. Clarke to Earl Grey, 30 March 1846, in Grey to Stanley, 12 June 1846, GBPP, 1847 [837], p.17.

CHAPTER 6: CHALLENGES TO
SOVEREIGNTY AND THE TREATY
1. Clarke Report, 1 July 1845, in FitzRoy to Stanley, 17 September 1845, GBPP, 1846 (337), p.132.
2. H. Williams to Busby, 20 April 1842, in Hugh Carleton, *The Life of Henry Williams*, Auckland, 1874, vol.2, pp.xxi–xxii.
3. *NZ Government Gazette*, 3 November 1841; and 26 January 1842 where it was withdrawn; Peter Adams, *Fatal Necessity*, Auckland, 1977. p.201; Carleton, *Henry Williams*, vol.2, pp.66–67. For contemporary observations on the need for restrictions, see Clarke Report, GBPP, 1842 (569), p.98; Chapman Journal, vol.1, pp.176,208–9, and Morgan Journal, vol.1, p.141, AUL.
4. Carleton, *Henry Williams*, vol.2, pp.xx–xxi, 41.
5. The most notable cases were those of Edward Meurant and a Mr Marshall.
6. Ashworth Journal, 28 January 1844, MS 1841–45P, ATL; Chapman Journal, 14 December 1845, and vol.1, p.438, (1852), AUL.
7. E.g. *The Journal of Ensign Best, 1837–1842*, ed. N. Taylor, Wellington, 1966, Appendix 14.
8. For a full discussion of this see. R. Parsonson, 'He Whenua Te Utu (The Payment will be land)', PhD thesis, Canterbury (1978), Part 2, Ch.7.

9. Buller Journal, 19 November 1840, q MS [1838–44], ATL; Register, MA-2, 42/98, NA.
10. H.T. Kemp to Clarke, 10 February 1843, Report, Appendix 4, p.125, GBPP, 1844 (556); also Godfrey to Col. Sec., 10 February 1843, in FitzRoy to Stanley, 18 December 1844, GBPP, 1845 (369), p.73; Shortland to Stanley, 18 January 1845, GBPP, 1845 (108), p.7, where Shortland expressed his concern about Maori reluctance to sell.
11. E.g. Clarke Report in Hobson to Russell, 13 November 1841, GBPP, 1842 (569), p.172.
12. Cit. FitzRoy to Stanley, 25 May 1844, GBPP, 1845 (247), p.14.
13. Robert FitzRoy, *Remarks on New Zealand*, London, 1846, pp.29–30.
14. Letter of Police Magistrate, 14 September 1841, in Hobson to Russell, 13 November 1841, GBPP, 1842 (569), p.173.
15. See *Journal of Ensign Best*, p.243, where Best commented on this.
16. *Wellington Spectator*, 10 July 1844, cit. R.A.A. Sherrin and J.H. Wallace, *Early History of New Zealand*, ed. T.W. Leys, Auckland, 1890, p.690.
17. E.g. Hobson to Russell, 13 November 1841 and encls., GBPP, 1842 (569), p.170; Buller Journal, 24 January 1840, q MS [1838–44], ATL; FitzRoy, *Remarks on New Zealand*, p.17.
18. See Ian Wards, *The Shadow of the Land*, Wellington, 1968, pp.74–78, 88–89.
19. Clarke Jnr to Clarke Snr, 29 June 1844, in FitzRoy to Stanley, 18 December 1844, GBPP, 1845 (369), p.73.
20. George Clarke [Jun.], *Notes on early life in New Zealand*, Hobart, 1903, p.62.
21. Cit. Richmond to FitzRoy, 23 May 1844, in FitzRoy to Stanley, 10 December 1844, GBPP, 1845 (369), p.60, and for the deed of sale and map, see pp.54–56.
22. J. Rutherford, *Hone Heke's Rebellion, 1844–46*, Auckland, 1947; Wards, *Shadow of the Land*, Ch.4. Various printings of British parliamentary papers carried reports of the war: GBPP, 1845 (131), (517-II), and 1846 (337), (448), (690).
23. FitzRoy to Stanley, 14 September 1844, GBPP, 1845 (247), p.138; FitzRoy to Stanley, 29 September 1844, GBPP, 1845 (369), p.11; Clarke to Col.Sec., 1 January 1845 in FitzRoy to Stanley, 24 February 1845, GBPP, 1846 (377), p.8; Hone Kingi and Noa Kiroa to Governor, 24 February 1844, Register, MA-2, NA.
24. Carleton, *Henry Williams*, vol.2, p.269.
25. Heke to the Governor, 2 December 1845, encl. in Grey to Stanley, 9 February 1846 (690), p.11, and also Heke to FitzRoy, 19 July 1845, in FitzRoy to Stanley, 25 October 1845, p.148.
26. Brown Journal, 8 March 1845, AUL.
27. After 1840, Heke often stayed at Te Tii, on the Paihia side of the Waitangi River mouth where he had a village: W. Colenso, *Fifty Years Ago in New Zealand*, Napier, 1888, p.39.
28. See T. Lindsay Buick, *New Zealand's First*

War, Wellington, 1926, pp.2 (fn.4), 133–4; *Southern Cross*, 25 January 1845.
29. See above, p.21. *Maori Messenger*, February 1858, p.5; Nene, Hohaia Waikato, Rapata Tahua and others to the Governor, 22 July [1844?], MA 24/21, 44/168, NA; *The Founding of New Zealand : The Journals of Felton Mathew and his wife*, ed. J. Rutherford, Auckland, 1840, p.98.
30. Extract from Protector of Aborigines, Bay of Islands, to Hobbs, 6 December 1844, in Hobbs Diaries, 15 January 1845, MS 144, AML.
31. Brown Journal, 11 March 1845, AUL; Nene and other chiefs to the Governor, 22 July [1844?], MA 24/21, 44/168, and Hira Pure to the Governor, September 1844, Register, MA–2, 44/251, NA.
32. H.F. McKillop, *Reminiscences of Twelve Months' Service in New Zealand*, London, 1849, pp.24ff.; Clarke to Col. Sec., 1 January 1845, in FitzRoy to Stanley, 24 February 1845, GBPP. 1846 (337), p.10; *The New Zealand Journal 1842–44, (of John B. Williams)*, ed. R.W. Kenny, Salem, [Mass.], 1956.
33. W.D. Westervelt, *Hawaiian Historical Legends*, 3rd ed., New York, 1926, Ch.21; C. Haldane, *Tempest over Tahiti*, London, 1963, esp. Chs.8–16; C. Newbury, 'Resistance and Collaboration in French Polynesia: The Tahitian War: 1844–47', *JPS*, LXXXII, 1 (1973), pp.5–27.
34. *Southern Cross*, 13 April 1844. Pacific news appeared regularly in the New Zealand press. In 1843–44 there were numerous reports including news of a large meeting in Sydney which intended to petition the imperial government over Tahitian affairs.
35. Waimate Meeting, September 1844, MS 430, AML; *Southern Cross*, 7 September 1844; FitzRoy to Stanley, 16 September 1844, GBPP, 1845 (247), p.140. FitzRoy feared the activity of other nations in the Pacific, especially France and the United States; see *The New Zealand Journal*, pp. 15ff., for United States commercial interests in Fiji.
36. FitzRoy to Heke, 5 October 1844, in FitzRoy to Stanley, 19 October 1844, GBPP, 1845 (369), p.37.
37. Williams to E.G. Marsh, 9 September 1846, in Carleton, *Henry Williams*, vol.2, pp.142–3.
38. Cit. R.M. Ross, 'Te Tiriti o Waitangi, texts and translations', *NZJH*, VI, 2 (1972), pp.152–3; Carleton, *Henry Williams*, vol.2, p.142.
39. Williams to Selwyn, 20 February 1845, in Carleton, *Henry Williams*, vol.2, pp.88–89.
40. R. Burrows, *Extracts from a Diary kept during Heke's War in the North in 1845*, Auckland, 1886, pp.9–10; Carleton, *Henry Williams*, vol.2, pp.xlii, xlix.
41. *New-Zealander*, 20 December 1845, noted the *Maori Messenger's* argument.
42. Letter of 7 November 1844, MA–4/58, NA. The printing is no.114 in Herbert W. Williams, *A Bibliography of Printed Maori to 1900 and supplement*, Wellington, 1975 (reprint).

43. Clarke to Col. Sec., 1 July 1845 in FitzRoy to Stanley, 17 September 1845, GBPP, 1846 (337), p.131.
44. Carleton, *Henry Williams*, vol.2, pp.200–201.
45. E.g. Busby to Hope, 17 January 1845, GBPP, 1845 (108), p.15.
46. *New-Zealander*, 26 July, 2, 9, 16, 30 August, 6, 13, 27 December 1845; Selwyn letter, November 1845, G 19/1, NA.
47. Kawiti to FitzRoy, 7 October 1845, in FitzRoy to Stanley, 25 October 1845, GBPP, 1846 (337), p.148; Burrows, *Extracts from a Diary*, p.49; Brown Journal, 30 April 1845, AUL.
48. Clarke to Col. Sec., 30 September 1844, in FitzRoy to Stanley, 19 October 1844, GBPP, 1845 (369), p.31; Waimate Meeting, September 1844, MS 430, AML.
49. Clarke to Col. Sec., 1 July 1845, in FitzRoy to Stanley, 17 September 1845, GBPP, 1846 (337), p.132.
50. Te Rauparaha to Te Wherowhero [n.d.], in FitzRoy to Stanley, 11 September 1845, GBPP, 1846 (337), p.128; Tawhiao to Native Minister, 17 May 1886, AJHR, 1886, G-14, p.2.
51. Brown Journal, 29 April 1845, AUL; FitzRoy, *Remarks*, p.52; *Southern Cross*, 5 April 1845; Buller Journal, 5 August 1844, q MS [1838–44], ATL.
52. E.g. *Southern Cross*, 12 August 1843, which noted that Waikato Maori had adopted European clothing, lifestyle and food in the previous two years.
53. *New-Zealander*, 28 March 1845; Meurant Journal, 18 [?] 1845, MS 205, AML.
54. Chapman Journal, 24–27 March 1845, 'Memoranda', and Chapman to CMS 25 September 1845, AUL.
55. McLean Report, 11 July 1845, in FitzRoy to Stanley, 13 September 1845, GBPP, 1846 (337), p.130.
56. Brown Journal, 22–23 November 1845, AUL; McLean Report, 11 July 1845, in FitzRoy to Stanley, 13 September 1845, GBPP, 1846 (337), p.130.
57. See above p.14; Meurant Diary, 18 [?] 1845, MS 205, AML; and *New-Zealander*, 5 July 1845.
58. Grey to Stanley, 14 December 1845, GBPP, 1846 (690), p.3; Grey's interview with northern chiefs encl. in Grey to Stanley, 10 December 1845, GBPP, 1846 (712), p.13; Grey to Gladstone, 19 September 1846, GBPP, 1847 (763), p.60; *New-Zealander*, 3 May 1848.
59. F. Keene, (ed.), *Richard Davis, 1790–1863: By this we conquer*, Whangarei, 1974, pp.101–2.
60. *Southern Cross*, 26 February, 18,25 March, 8 April, 28 June 1848; *New-Zealander*, 28 June 1848; and see below, Chs.9,10.
61. Heke to the Queen of England, 10 July 1849, in Grey to Earl Grey, 28 July, 1849, GBPP, 1850 [1280], p.16.
62. Heke to FitzRoy, in Grey to Stanley, 4 February 1846, GBPP, 1846 (690), p.8; Patten to Grey, 8 March 1846 in Grey to Stanley, 27

April 1846, GBPP, 1847 [763], p.12; for the reerecting of the flag, see below, p.147.

63. Earl Grey to Governor Grey, 23 December 1846 and encls., GBPP, 1847 [763], pp.64ff. The dispatch sparked off a lengthy correspondence, printed in parliamentary papers of 1847–48, 1849.

64. Cit. A.H. McLintock, *Crown Colony Government in New Zealand*, Wellington, 1958, p.288.

65. *New-Zealander*, 18 June 1847.

66. Carleton, *Henry Williams*, vol.2, p.147; *Southern Cross*, 7 August 1847.

67. *New-Zealander*, 3 July and 10, 14, 16 July 1847; *Southern Cross*, 10 July 1847.

68. Petition encl. in Grey to Earl Grey, 9 March 1848, GBPP, 1847–48 [1002], pp.79–80; *Southern Cross*, 3 February 1849. See *Southern Cross*, 6 November 1847, which reported a rumour that Maori had been offered assistance from American whalers and a French man of war in the event of an uprising against the government.

69. J. Rutherford, *Sir George Grey K.C.B. 1812–1898: A Study in Colonial Government*, London, 1961, pp.166–72; Grey to Earl Grey, 3 September 1847, GBPP, 1847–48 [899], p.21; Grey to Earl Grey, 15 May 1848, GBPP, 1849 [1120], p.22.

70. Selwyn to Earl Grey, 1 July 1847, encl. in Grey to Earl Grey, 7 July 1847, GBPP, 1847–48 [892], p.81.

71. Maunsell to Grey, 18 October 1847, encl. in Grey to Earl Grey, 26 October 1847, GBPP, 1847–48 [1002], p.8; H. Williams to Grey, 1 December 1847, encl. in Grey to Earl Grey, 22 March 1848, GBPP, 1849 [1120]. The letter was published in the *New-Zealander*, 1 January 1848. Hadfield to Williams, 14 August 1847, Williams Letters, MS 72c, AML; W. Lawry letter, 16 March 1848, in L.A. Chamerovzow, *The New Zealand Question and the Rights of Aborigines*, London, 1848, p.417; Hobbs to Martin, 22 October 1847, in William Martin, *England and the New Zealanders*, Auckland, 1847, pp.73–74; G. Brazendale, 'John Whiteley, land, sovereignty and the Anglo-Maori wars', MA thesis, Auckland (1976), pp.25ff.

72. Morgan Journal, 5 August 1847, AUL; Carleton, *Henry Williams*, vol.2, pp.168–9; Sotheby to Maxwell, 31 August 1847, in Grey to Earl Grey, 3 September 1847, GBPP, 1847–48 [899], pp.21ff.

73. Te Wherowhero and other chiefs to the Queen, 8 November 1847, in Grey to Earl Grey, 13 November 1847, GBPP, 1847–48 [1002], p.15; *Southern Cross*, 10 July 1847, and 4 March 1848, concerning a proposal to send a deputation to the Queen.

74. Earl Grey to Grey, 3 May 1848, GBPP, 1847–48 [1002], p.144; Morgan Journal, 23 November 1848, AUL.

75. Earl Grey to Grey, 27 July 1848, GBPP, 1847–48 [1002], p.179.

76. GBPD, 1847–48, vol.95, 13 December 1847, vol.96, 9,14 February 1848, and vol.97, 29 February 1848; Selwyn to Gladstone, various letters from 1845 to 1848, Gladstone

Papers, 44299, ff.1–196, British Museum Library.

77. *Correspondence between the Wesleyan Missionary Committee and Earl Grey on the apprehended infringement of the Treaty of Waitangi*, [London], 1848; Earl Grey to Grey, 3 May and 10 May 1848, and encls., GBPP 1847–48 [1002], pp.144ff. A New Zealand branch of the APS, formed in 1842, considered drawing up a 'peace address' in Maori, but no record of it has been found: *Southern Cross*, 25 September 1847.

78. Grey to Earl Grey, 15 May 1848, GBPP, 1849 [1120]; Rutherford, *Sir George Grey*, pp.165–66, 172ff.

79. H.W. Tucker, *Memoir of the Life and Episcopate of George Augustus Selwyn*, London, 1879, vol.1, p.272. Selwyn to Coleridge, 4 September 1848; cf. Mrs Mary Martin to Mrs Owen, December 1848, which gives a different view. Owen Papers, 33954, f.48, British Museum Library.

80. WMS to Earl Grey, 23 February 1848, and Merrivale to Beecham, 13 April 1848, in Earl Grey to Grey, 3 May 1848, GBPP, 1847–48 [1002], p.144.

81. William Martin, *England and the New Zealanders*, Auckland, 1847. See Tucker, *Life of Selwyn*, p.274, where Selwyn to Coleridge, 7 October 1848, notes that Martin's pamphlet had been given to Major Richmond, Mr Justice Chapman, Hadfield, Rev. G.A. Kissling and Governor Grey.

82. *The Times*, 28, 29 December 1846, 9 January, 3 July, 15 December 1847. For press comment on *The Times*, see *Southern Cross*, 28 April 1849.

83. *New-Zealander*, 16 June and 19 June 1847, which notes that Tahiti news had arrived by the schooner *Columbine*. The first group of 'Fencibles' (retired soldiers who were to form defensive settlements on Auckland's outskirts), arrived at Auckland, 5 August 1847. Further groups arrived on 8, 10 October and 26 November 1847, 23 January, 15 May 1848, and in 1849 and 1852.

84. Rutherford, *Sir George Grey*, pp.130ff.

85. Grey to Earl Grey, 5 July 1847, and encl., GBPP, 1847–48 [892], p.64, *New-Zealander*, 29 May, 12 June 1847.

86. Martin to Grey, 20 October 1848, in Grey to Earl Grey, 28 October 1848, GBPP, 1849 [1120], p.52; Martin, *England and the New Zealanders*, p.29.

87. Chamerovzow, *The New Zealand Question*, Appendix, p.49, and p.7.

88. G. Brazendale, 'John Whiteley, land, sovereignty and the Anglo-Maori Wars', MA thesis, Auckland (1976), pp.27ff.

89. Russell to Hobson, 9 December 1840, GBPP, 1840 (311), p.27; and see above, pp.111; Stanley to Grey, 13 June 1845, GBPP, 1846 (337), p.70.

90. Report from the Select Committee on New Zealand, GBPP, 1844 (556), p.5.

91. Williams, *Bibliography of Printed Maori*, no.114.

92. See above, p.103.

93. E.g. Charles Wilkes, *Narrative of the*

United States Exploring Expedition, London, 1845, vol.1, pp.474–6; Hobbs Diaries, March 1842, MS 144, AML.
94. Maori Messenger, February 1842; and see above, p.121.
95. E.g. New-Zealander, 10 July 1847.
96. Martin to Grey, 20 October 1848, GBPP, 1849 [1120], p.55, said he had regularly been questioned by Maori about the safety of their lands and that he had 'always given one answer: the words of the first Governor were the words of the Queen, they will never be broken'.
97. E.g. Maori Messenger, January and February 1844; FitzRoy to Ngati Whatua, 9 March 1844, GBPP, 1845 (131), p.40.
98. E.g. Ngati Raukawa, Ngati Toa and others to the Queen, 5 May 1849, encl. in Grey to Earl Grey, 3 August 1849, GBPP, 1850 [1280], p.18; Morgan Letters and Journals, 1850 Report, AUL, notes a gift of four from Rangiaohia Maori, accompanied by a letter, subsequently published in the Maori Messenger, 1850: 'We trust in you, on account of your letter [to Te Wherowhero] saying that the lands should not be taken away from us, but that the treaty of Waitangi should be scrupulously observed.'
99. New-Zealander, 1, 18 September 1847, 10 July 1850.
100. Ibid., 25 October 1843; Southern Cross, 17 February 1849; T.H. FitzGerald to the Superintendent, Wellington, 1 July 1847, in Grey to Earl Grey, 31 July 1847, GBPP, 1847–48 [899], p.4.
101. Southern Cross, 28 October 1843.
102. New-Zealander, 15 April 1848.
103. Southern Cross, 12 August, 28 October 1843; return of flour mills in Grey to Earl Grey, 22 August 1849; and Morgan to Grey, 20 November 1849, in Grey to Earl Grey, 1 December 1849, GBPP, 1850 [1280], pp.24,106; Morgan Letters and Journals, 1850 Report, AUL.
104. Eyre to Grey, 26 August 1847, in Grey to Earl Grey, 3 September 1847, GBPP, 1847–48 [899], p.18.
105. E.g. New-Zealander, 30 January 1847, 27 May 1848, 26 May 1849.
106. Auckland Times, 15 September 1842.
107. E.g. Bay of Islands Observer, 30 June 1842; New-Zealander, 28 February, 4 July 1846; Southern Cross, 31 August, 4, 11 September 1849.
108. Maori Messenger, 22 November 1849, describes the Auckland hostel, called Waipawa, sited at Mechanics Bay (now Stanley Street) Auckland.
109. New-Zealander, 10 July 1847, 19, 25 March 1848; Southern Cross, 27 January 1849.
110. E.g. Chapman to CMS, January 1844 and 'Memoranda', 9 February 1845, Chapman Letters and Journals, AUL.
111. Ngapora to Grey, 19 February 1848, in Grey to Earl Grey, 3 April 1848, GBPP, 1849 [1120], p.18; McLintock, Crown Colony Government, pp.393–5. Similar comments had been made a few years earlier by Selwyn and Clarke: Clarke to Col. Sec., 1 January 1845 in

FitzRoy to Stanley, 24 February 1845, GBPP, 1846 (337), pp.10–12.
112. Southern Cross, 19 April, 16 July 1850.
113. Maori Messenger, 19 January 1849. The colonial press often discussed amalgamation, advancing various schemes for Maori 'advancement'.

CHAPTER 7: A MATTER OF MANA
1. Maori Messenger, 3 December 1853. The idea was repeated in other issues, e.g. 1 February 1855.
2. W. Swainson, New Zealand : Lectures on the Colonization of New Zealand, London, 1856, pp.8–10.
3. Domett's speech to the Legislative Council of New Munster, NZ Spectator, 2 August 1851.
4. J.C. Richmond to J.M. Richmond, 13 August 1851, The Richmond-Atkinson Papers ed. G.H. Scholefield, Wellington, 1960, vol.1, p.103.
5. GBPD, 1852, 122, p.46; see also GBPD, 1852, 121, pp.102–36, 922–82, and 122, pp.17–66.
6. A.H. McLintock, Crown Colony Government in New Zealand, Wellington, 1958, pp.344–5.
7. GBPD, 1852, 122, p.1135. Sir Edward Buxton of the Aborigines Protection Society was an exception.
8. W.L. Renwick, 'Self-government and protection: A study of Stephen's two cardinal points of policy in their bearing upon constitutional development in New Zealand in the years 1837–1867', MA thesis, Victoria University of Wellington (1962), pp.154ff.; New Zealand Government Bill, a reprint from Aborigines' Friend, IV (June/July 1852).
9. Aborigines' Friend, II, April 1850, pp.410–12.
10. Correspondence between the Wesleyan Missionary Committee and Sir James Pakington ..., London, 1852.
11. Aborigines' Friend, IV, nos. I & II, April, May 1852, p.55.
12. A.F. Madden, 'The Attitudes of the Evangelicals to the Empire and Imperial Problems', D Phil. thesis, Oxford (1950), p.614.
13. P. Knaplund, Gladstone and Britain's Imperial Policy, London, 1927, pp.40–70, in particular; GBPD, 1852, 121, pp.951ff.; C.C. Eldridge, 'The Colonial Policy of the Fifth Duke of Newcastle', D Phil. thesis, Nottingham (1966), pp.72–74; Gladstone to Selwyn, 20 September 1860, Gladstone Papers, 44531, f.48, British Museum Library.
14. W.L. Renwick, 'Self-government and protection', MA thesis, Victoria University of Wellington (1962), Chs.4,5, discuss this and subsequent points in detail. The Maori Messenger, 1 January 1855, p.28, printed an elementary explanation of the constitution.
15. Apart from individual correspondence with the governor evidence was collected by a Board of Native Affairs, 1856. G 51, NA, has a series of reports and submissions.
16. Maori Messenger, I, no.7, July 1855,

pp.11–12, 18–20, 29–31, and III, no.4, 30 April 1857.

17. Ibid., I, no.6, 1 July 1855; Mathias Tiramorehu on behalf of Ngai Tahu, 23 September 1857, and Mantell to Ngai Tahu, 16 September 1858, Mantell Papers, MS Papers 83, ff.166, 166a, ATL.

18. Chapman Diary, 1852, pp.434–5, AUL. Chapman is conveying the meaning in this quote; the literal translation of 'to tatou' is 'ours' in the inclusive sense, i.e. both Maori and Pakeha, whereas 'to matou' is 'ours' in the exclusive sense, in this case meaning a queen for the Pakeha and not for the Maori.

19. *Maori Messenger*, I, no.8, 1 November 1855, p.45.

20. Ibid., III, no.4, 30 April 1857, pp.4–5.

21. For various analyses of the movement, see Alan Ward, *A Show of Justice: Racial 'amalgamation' in nineteenth century New Zealand*, Auckland, 1973, especially Chs.7, 8; B.J. Dalton, *War and Politics in New Zealand, 1855–1870*, Sydney, 1967, Ch.3; Keith Sinclair, *The Origins of the Maori Wars*, 2nd ed. Wellington, 1961, Ch.6; M.P.K. Sorrenson, 'The Maori King Movement, 1858–1885', *Studies of a Small Democracy*, ed. Robert Chapman and Keith Sinclair, Auckland, 1963, pp.33–55; and for contemporary accounts, J. Gorst, *The Maori King*, London, 1864; and T. Buddle, *The Maori King Movement in New Zealand*, Auckland, 1860.

22. The 'King Maker', Wiremu Tamihana Tarapipipi Te Waharoa, is sometimes spelt with an 'e' in Tamehana, but a letter in his own hand indicates that he spelt his name Tamihana (Thompson): Wiremu Tamihana to Morgan, 14 January 1860, IA 1860/678, NA.

23. For a King movement statement on the major steps leading to the movement's formation, see *Te Hokioi*, 15 June 1862, p.3. See J. Grace, *Tuwharetoa: The History of the Maori People of the Taupo district*, Wellington, 1959, Ch.57, for a Ngati Tuwharetoa view of the meeting and for the role of missionary Thomas Grace in the proceedings. For another Ngati Tuwharetoa explanation, see Tureiti Te Heuheu's evidence in AJHR, 1898, I–3A, pp.26, 30. According to *Te Hokioi*, it was Te Moananui from Hawke's Bay who suggested the name 'king' since it would distinguish the bearer from among the many rangatira; this was at the final meeting at Ngaruawahia.

24. D. Stafford, *Te Arawa: A history of the Arawa people*, Wellington, 1967, pp.347–8; Grace, *Tuwharetoa*, p.450, notes the Arawa stand at the Paetai meeting; and see above, p.141.

25. Sinclair, *Origins of the Maori Wars*, p.75.

26. Ward, *Show of Justice*, pp.101, 123. Ashwell to CMS, 1 May 1861, Ashwell Letters and Journals, pp.377–8, AUL, has a diagram which represents something akin to this.

27. Sinclair, *Origins of the Maori Wars*, p.69.

28. Ward, *Show of Justice*, pp.100–101.

29. J. Cowan, *The New Zealand Wars: A history of the Maori campaigns and the pioneering period*, Wellington, 1922–23, vol.1, pp.147–8;

Buddle, *Maori King Movement*, p.8. See also, Stafford, *Te Arawa*, p.348.

30. Buddle, *Maori King Movement*, pp.17–18; Gorst, *Maori King*, p.8.

31. Browne's attitude to the King is discussed by Ward, *Show of Justice*, pp.104, 121–22, 124.

32. Responsibility for the Waitara outbreak has been assessed elsewhere; e.g. Sinclair, *Origins of the Maori Wars*, Ch.12; Dalton, *War and Politics*, pp.93–107.

33. For a record of the conference see 'Kohimarama Conference', AJHR, 1860, E-9; and Register of Proceedings of conference of Native chiefs at Kohimarama, MA 23/10, NA. A list of chiefs is given in AJHR, 1860, E-9, pp.4,25; on the opening day 112 chiefs were present, but a further 40 arrived later. The proceedings of the conference were also printed in English and Maori by the *Maori Messenger*, 1860, nos.13–18, edited by Walter Buller, secretary of the conference. The record in the first two references is in English only.

34. At about the same time Browne was sounding out other opinions: Memo to ministers, 21 April 1860, McLean Papers, MS Papers 32, f.10; and Browne to Selwyn, Martin and Swainson, [n.d.], but reply acknowledged, 6 June 1860, G36/3, pp.240, 253, NA.

35. For a detailed assessment of this subject see Claudia Orange, 'The Covenant of Kohimarama: A ratification of the Treaty of Waitangi', *NZJH*, XIV, 1 (1980), pp.61–82. The Kohimarama site is now known as Mission Bay.

36. 'Kohimarama Conference', AJHR, 1860, E-9, pp.4–5.

37. *Maori Messenger*, 24 July 1860, p.17, 26 July 1860, p.32, 27 July 1860, p.43.

38. *Maori Messenger*, 27 July 1860, p.44, 10 July 1860, p.15, and 13 July, p.41.

39. See *Maori Messenger*, 11 July 1860, pp.18ff., for examples of Ngapuhi attitudes.

40. Ibid., 3 August 1860, p.71. In early 1858, Maihi Paraone Kawiti, son of Heke's ally, Kawiti, together with a group of northern Maori selected on the basis of their opposition to the government in the 1840s war, re-erected the flagstaff. Nene had erected a flagstaff some years before but the forces occupying Kororareka at the time had insisted that he site it on the beachfront. In 1858 a piece of land for a township was also offered to the government. Kawiti appears to have taken an oath of allegiance, receiving in return the rongomai seal which is held in trust at Waitangi. M.P. Kawiti to Grey, 15 November 1861, *Maori Messenger*, II, 2, 15 January 1862.

41. Ibid., 13 July 1860, p.38.

42. Ibid., 13,26 July 1860.

43. Ibid., pp.32, 35, 36.

44. AJHR, 1860, E-9, p.24.

45. E.g. Register of proceedings at Kohimarama, MA 23/10, NA. The report printed in AJHR, 1860, does not indicate this. See also Sinclair, *Origins of the Maori Wars*, p.231. A European present at the conference observed that only one-third of the chiefs supported the resolution endorsing government policy in Taranaki.

46. The absence of these two tribal groupings was noted by the *Maori Messenger*. Ngati Tuwharetoa and Tuhoe also appear to have had no representatives present. Sewell Journal, 15 July 1860, MS 459, AML, notes the late invitations to Waikato.

47. William Martin, *The Taranaki Question*, Auckland, 1860, pp.117–18; and see NZPD, 1860, pp.249ff.

48. The relevant issues of *Maori Messenger* were bound, together with letters from various chiefs and tribal groups. Chiefs had an opportunity of checking their speeches before the conference ended to ensure accuracy, that is, in the Maori language; the English translation did not always convey the same meaning. For a list of the recipients see MA 24/16, NA. The governor's opening speech was also printed and distributed at the conference: 'Ko ta te Kawana Korero', NZM 315, APL.

49. Kohimarama Conference, AJHR, 1860, E-9, pp.21, 25; Browne to General Assemby, 7 August 1860, enclosing conference request of 3 August 1860, LE 1/1860/100, NA.

50. For further discussion on mana, see Claudia Orange, 'The Covenant of Kohimarama: A ratification of the Treaty of Waitangi', *NZJH*, XIV, 1 (1980), pp.74–76.

51. Cf. *Maori Messenger*, 10 July and 26 July 1860, and the Maori text of the treaty in Appendix 2.

52. *Maori Messenger*, 10 July 1860, pp.5–16, 13 July, 26 July, pp.36–37; cf. the Maori text with the English.

53. Sewell Journal, vol.1, pp.313–4, MS 459, AML; for the measures, see Dalton, *War and Politics*, pp.61, 76–81.

54. A draft of the Bill dated July 1859 can be found in Stafford Papers, MS Papers 28, f.2, ATL.

55. Dalton, *War and Politics*, pp.91, 119–21, 141–2.

56. J. FitzGerald, 'Memorandum relating to the conduct of Native Affairs in New Zealand as affected by a Bill now before Parliament', Newcastle Papers, no.11,078, Nottingham University Library. Colonists had voiced similar fears about Kohimarama-style conferences: see NZPD, 1858–60, pp.347–8.

57. GBPD, 1860, 160, pp.1317ff., and 1639.

58. Martin to McLean, 22, 29 November 1860; McLean to Browne, 1 December 1860, and a first draft, 8 November 1860; also a May letter [1860?]: McLean Papers, MS Papers 32, f.449, and for May letter, f.9, ATL; Browne to Bell and Browne to McLean, 30 November 1860, G 36/3, NA. McLean was opposed to responsibility for Maori affairs passing to the General Assembly. With regard to the proposed council, he stated that it would be ineffective unless given administrative powers, a budget of £35,000 p.a., and a representation of leading chiefs who would sit in council.

59. NZPD, 1858–60, pp.260, 323, 326.

60. Ibid., pp.239–40.

61. Ibid., p.361.

62. Ibid., pp.358ff.

63. Ibid., pp.349–50.

64. NZPD, 1858–60, p.501; W. Fox, *The Six Colonies of New Zealand*, London, 1851. The particular section of the work was not specified; it was possibly pp.98–108, on waste lands.

65. J. Martineau, *The Life of Henry Pelham, Fifth Duke of Newcastle, 1811–1864*, London, 1908, p.322, notes correspondence between Newcastle and George Grey, 5 June 1861. See also Chichester Fortescue to Earl Grey, 8 November 1860, (referring to correspondence of E. Grey to Gore Browne, 31 October 1860), Earl Grey papers, 180/11, Durham University Library.

66. O. Hadfield, *Recent Outbreak at Taranaki*, [Otaki?] 1860; O. Hadfield, *One of England's Little Wars*, Otaki, 1860. Hadfield produced two further pieces: *A Sequel to 'One of England's Little Wars'*, London, 1861, and *The Second Year of One of England's Little Wars*, London, 1861.

67. 'Remarks on an act', Newcastle Papers, no.11093b, Nottingham University Library; NZPD, 1858–60, p.479.

68. E.g. *Occasional Papers: The Treaty of Waitangi and its Interpreters*, 1 July 1861, [Melanesian Press] Auckland; *New Zealand Memorial to the Secretary of State for Colonies together with a Memorandum on New Zealand Affairs*, London, 1861. This originated with the CMS, signed by the Earl of Chichester, President, 4 January 1861.

69. E.g. Newcastle to Browne, 27 May 1861, in Martineau, *Life of Henry Pelham*, p.320; officials noted that the Wesleyans did not participate in criticisms of the government in the same way.

70. The book was reprinted twice in London and there was at least one more New Zealand edition in 1861. See also *Appendix to the Journals of the House of Lords*, 30 May 1864 when Martin's paper was tabled.

71. Martin, *Taranaki Question*, pp.9–10.

72. Ibid., p.82.

73. [F.D. Bell, F. Whitaker, T. Gore Browne], *Notes on Sir William Martin's Pamphlet entitled The Taranaki Question*, Auckland, 1861. The joint authors did not claim responsibility for the work which was usually attributed to C.W. Richmond. The work first appeared in 1860 and was revised for publication.

74. Justice Johnson, *Notes on Maori Matters*, [Auckland], July 1860.

75. Sewell Journal, vol.1, p.218, MS 459, AML.

76. [C.O. Torlesse], *The New Zealand War*, Christchurch, 1860; W. Fox, *The War in New Zealand*, London, 1860.

77. J. Busby, *Remarks upon a Pamphlet entitled 'The Taranaki Question, by Sir William Martin'*, Auckland, 1860. Busby, for a time, had his own paper, *The Aucklander*.

78. Busby, *Remarks upon a Pamphlet*, p.5.

79. G. Clarke [Sen.], *Remarks upon a pamphlet by James Busby*, Auckland, 1861, (reprint Auckland, 1923), p.3.

80. From Te Puhipi [Busby] to the Kaumatua of the Maori nation, 22 June 1860, *Maori Messenger*, VII, 11,30 June 1860.
81. E.g. NZPD, 1858–60, pp.184, 194, 206; *New-Zealander*, 18 July 1860, p.3; *Southern Cross*, 3 July 1860, 21 August 1860.
82. E.g. Te Rangikaheke to Ngati Whakaue chiefs, 3 December 1855, discussed in Ward, *Show of Justice*, pp.95–96.
83. *Maori Messenger*, VII, no.5, March 1860, p.8.
84. Declaration by the Governor to the natives assembled at Ngaruawahia, 21 May 1861, in AJHR, 1861, E–lb, pp.11–12; NZPD, 1861–63, p.23.
85. *Maori Messenger*, 15 March 1861.
86. AJHR, 1861, Elb, pp.13–17.
87. Dalton, *War and Politics*, pp.135,145; NZPD, 1861–63, pp.10,40,143,314,365–6.
88. Grey to Newcastle, 30 November 1861, AJHR, 1862, Sec. II no.14, cit. Dalton, *War and Politics*. p.145. Browne had held out some hope of Maori self-government but only when British 'supremacy' had been established. See *Maori Messenger*, 15 August 1861, p.2, where a memo from Browne to the General Assembly is published.

CHAPTER 8: A WAR OF SOVEREIGNTY
1. *The Times*, 16 December 1864.
2. NZPD, 1861–63, pp.67,94.
3. Ibid., p.127.
4. Sewell Journal, 24 February 1861, MS 459, AML.
5. Mrs Martin to Mrs Owen, 17 October 1861, Owen Papers, 39954, f.400, British Museum Library.
6. *The Journal of Henry Sewell, 1853–57*, ed. W.D. McIntyre, Christchurch, 1980, vol.2, pp.314–5.
7. Sewell Journal, 5 May 1861, MS 459, AML.
8. NZPD, 1861–63, pp.103ff.
9. Ibid., pp.120–21; and see above, p.152 for Fox's change of tactics on the treaty.
10. New Zealand's acceptance of full responsibility for Maori affairs has been a debatable point with historians, e.g. B.J. Dalton, *War and Politics in New Zealand 1855–1870*, Sydney, 1967, references listed under (control of) Native Affairs; W.L. Renwick, 'Self-government and protection', MA thesis, Victoria University of Wellington (1962), pp.15–73, 431–4; W. Fox in *Wellington Independent*, 7 January 1865, noted in Sewell Journal, vol.2, p.47, MS 459, AML, NZPD, 1861–63, p.763; for the policies of Newcastle and Cardwell: Colin Eldridge, 'The Colonial Policy of the 5th Duke of Newcastle, 1859–64', PhD thesis, Nottingham (1966) and 210–39; G. Sellers. 'Edward Cardwell at the Colonial Office, 1864–66: Some aspects of his policy and ideas', B Litt. thesis, Oxford (1958).
11. Dalton, *War and Politics*, p.22; Newcastle Papers, no.11,753, Nottingham University; J. Martineau, *The Life of Henry Pelham Fifth Duke of Newcastle, 1811–1864*, London, 1908, p.319.

12. Keith Sinclair, *The Origins of the Maori Wars*, 2nd ed., Wellington, 1961, p.238; Alan Ward, *A Show of Justice : Racial 'amalgamation' in nineteenth century New Zealand*, Auckland, 1973, pp.130–31.
13. Sewell Journal, entries for October-December 1861, MS 459, AML. His assessment of Grey, rapidly arrived at, was of a man unfit for the task at hand, having no set opinion or policy, 'essentially an egotist, sees and judges everything only in reference to himself'.
14. Sinclair, *Origins of the Maori Wars*, pp.237–44; Sewell Journal, 20 October 1861, MS 459, AML; Fox to Mantell, 2 November 1861, Mantell Papers, MS Papers 83, f.281, ATL; for a comprehensive assessment, Ward, *Show of Justice*, Ch.9; *Maori Messenger*, 16 December 1861 and 13 March 1862, where Grey's policy and the 'new Institutions' were explained for Maori readers. The section that follows is based on these sources, in particular Ward.
15. Ward, *Show of Justice*, Ch.9, fn.2, differentiates between the government-sponsored Runanga and the Maori traditional runanga, which often co-existed, by using a capital in the former, a precedent followed in this discussion. For Sewell's criticism, see Sewell Journal, 25 October 1861, MS 459, AML.
16. Ward, *Show of Justice*, pp.125, 147–50.
17. Native Lands Act, 1862.
18. *NZ Herald*, 23 March 1881.
19. NZPD, 1861–63, pp.608–25, 627–38.
20. Ibid., p.633; Sewell Journal, 17 August 1862, MS 459, AML.
21. Newcastle to Grey, 5 June 1861, cit. F.D. Bell, NZPD, 1861–63, p.610.
22. Sewell Journal, 6, 9 September 1862, MS 459, AML.
23. Ibid., 3 September 1862. For the following discussion on government policy leading to war, the sources are Sinclair, *Origins of the Maori Wars*, Ch.16, and Ward, *Show of Justice*, Ch.10.
24. The Kingite paper, *Te Hokioi*, 10 February 1863, reported the meeting. Kingites had agreed on various points of policy at a meeting at Peria the previous October. See also *Te Hokioi*, 10 November 1862; and Morgan Journal, 4 September 1861, AUL, where he refutes any suggestion that Kingites plead treaty rights.
25. *Te Hokioi*, 26 April 1863.
26. Halse to Bell, from Mangere, 23 May 1863, Mantell Papers, MS Papers 83, f.218, ATL.
27. Ashwell Letters and Journals, 26 November 1863, AUL; *Te Hokioi*, 24 March 1863.
28. Proclamation to chiefs of Waikato, 11 July 1863, *NZ Gazette*, 15 July 1863; and see M.P.K. Sorrenson, 'Maori and Pakeha', *The Oxford History of New Zealand*, ed, W.H. Oliver with B.R. Williams, Oxford and Wellington, 1981, p.182, where this is discussed.
29. For the best recent study see James Belich, *The New Zealand Wars and the Victorian Interpretation of Racial Conflict*, Auckland, 1986.

30. P. Clark, *'Hauhau': The Pai Marire search for Maori identity*, Auckland, 1975.

31. Sewell Journal, 9 August 1863, subsequent entries for that year, and see also September 1862, MS 459, AUL, where Sewell notes the absence of an Attorney-General in the ministry.

32. Sewell Journal, 17 November 1863; and see Sinclair, *Origins of the Maori Wars*, pp.256–7 and fn.24 for comments on Auckland speculators in the government.

33. See NZPD, 1861–63, pp.782–90, 869–74, for the debates on the New Zealand Settlements Act, pp.791–800, 855–60, for the Suppression of Rebellion Act, and pp.846–905, where the debates on the Loan Act are scattered through the session.

34. Sewell Journal, 17 November 1863, MS 459, AML.

35. NZPD, 1861–63, p.782.

36. Dr Pollen, who had witnessed the treaty signing on 6 February 1840, opposed the Act but voted in favour of it.

37. NZPD, 1861–63, pp.783–9.

38. Cit. Swainson, NZPD, 1861–63, p.870.

39. The experts cited were Blackstone's *Commentaries*, and Phillimore and Woolmer, the two legal experts who had presented opinions on behalf of the APS in the 1840s debate; see p.130 above.

40. NZPD, 1861–63, p.869.

41. Sewell Journal, 19 November 1863, MS 459, AML.

42. H. Sewell, *The New Zealand Native Rebellion. Letter to Lord Lyttelton*, Auckland, 1864.

43. Ibid., pp.5, 9, 40–41, deal with the following argument although the entire work is an exposition of the theme.

44. Sewell Journal, 27 November 1863, MS 459, AML, discusses this fully.

45. Sewell, *New Zealand Native Rebellion*, pp.40ff. in particular for the following discussion. Sewell had previously expressed the opinion that New Zealand was a 'colony of occupation' notwithstanding the treaty. See NZPD, 1860, p.477.

46. Sewell Journal, 8,17 November 1863, MS 459, AML.

47. Dalton, *War and Politics*, pp.195–6; G. Sellers, 'Edward Cardwell at the Colonial Office, 1864–66', B Litt. thesis, Oxford (1958), pp.177–88. The Crown had the prerogative of disallowing New Zealand legislation within two years of its receipt by the Secretary of State, whether assented to by the governor or not.

48. *NZ Gazette*, 17 December 1864; Dalton, *War and Politics*, pp.188–216.

49. Sorrenson, 'Maori and Pakeha', *Oxford History*, pp.185–6.

50. Dalton, *War and Politics*, pp.195ff.; Sewell Journal, 27 November 1863, MS 459, AML, discusses the problem. Sewell looked to two ruling decisions, Cherokee Nation against the State of Georgia and Worcester and the State of Georgia, with which the dicta of esteemed American lawyers like Story were in accord. The cases were heard in the 1830s. Sewell likened Chief Judge Marshall's language to the

New Zealand problem with the Maori, that is, that the indigenous race was a 'domestic dependent people', rather than a foreign nation, that they were not independent and yet still entitled to rights of self–government. See p.95 above where the cases are also noted. The tendency to seek precedents from elsewhere was also evident in the issue of compensation for plunder, e.g. Bell to Domett, [?] May 1863, in Mantell papers, MS Papers 83, f.218, ATL, which looked to the American experience; and in the confiscation issue, where Stafford, as early as 1861, noted the allocation of land for compensation purposes at the Cape Colony: NZPD, 1861–63, p.71.

51. Jeanine Williams, *Frederick Weld: A Political Biography*, Auckland, 1983, Ch.6; Sewell Journal, 21 November 1864, MS 459, AML.

52. NZPD, 1861–63, pp.925–6.

53. Williams, *Frederick Weld*, Ch.6.

54. NZPD, 1864–66, p.47.

55. New Zealand Settlements Amendment Act, 1864; New Zealand Settlements Amendment Act, 1865.

56. NZPD, 1864–66, pp.154.

57. Sewell Journal, MS 459, AML, entries in mid–1865.

58. Ward, *Show of Justice*, p.178.

59. Dalton, *War and Politics*, p.208; 'Petition of Auckland Provincial Council to the Queen, 31 December 1864', Gladstone Papers, 44798, British Museum Library; Sewell Journal, 20 December 1864, MS 459, AML. For a dissenting opinion on shifting the capital: John Hobbs to Grey, 9 December 1864, 64/2713, NA.

60. Sewell Journal, 29 January 1865, MS 459, AML.

61. Ibid., 8, 19 January 1865, describes the Waikato meetings and approaches to the government.

62. NZPD, 1864–66, pp.621–5; Ward, *Show of Justice*, pp.189–90.

63. 'Copy of the Treaty of Waitangi ... and Mr Baker's annotations thereon', AJLC, 1869, pp.67–78. The list of chiefs was subsequently used by T. Lindsay Buick, *The Treaty of Waitangi*, 3rd ed., New Plymouth, 1936, pp.256–67, thus perpetuating various errors.

64. Notes on the treaty, [n.d. 1865?], Mantell Papers, MS Papers 83, f.129, ATL, suggest that the treaty would be made a 'nudum pactum'. D. Walker, *The Oxford Companion to Law*, Oxford, 1980, p.894, defines nudum pactum: 'In the Roman law, an informal bargain not amounting to a contract and not the basis for an action ... The term is sometimes used in common law in the quite different sense of an agreement lacking consideration and on which accordingly, unless made under seal, no action will lie; hence the maxim ex nudo pacto non oritur actio.'

65. NZPD, 1864–66, pp.197–8; Ward, *Show of Justice*, p.183.

66. 'Return to an order of the House, 1 August 1865', Le 1/1865/139, 3 August 1865, NA.

67. NZPD, 1864–66, pp.292–3; JHR, 11 August 1865, no.14 The question of an 'improper construction' being put on the treaty and the point of variance in Maori understanding had been raised in the General Assembly previously, but had not been pressed. Sewell had recommended postponement, NZPD, 1855, pp.524–5.

68. Ward, *Show of Justice*, pp.192–3.

69. For the resolutions and debate, see NZPD, 1862, pp.483ff., 510ff.

70. NZPD, 1865, pp.321–2, 325.

71. FitzGerald to J.C. Richmond, 25 August 1865, in *The Richmond–Atkinson Papers*, ed. G.H. Scholefield, Wellington, 1960, vol.2, pp.178–9.

72. NZPD, 1864–66, pp.17, 254–5; Sewell Journal, December 1864, MS 459, AML; Sewell, *New Zealand Native Rebellion*, p.46.

73. Ward, *Show of Justice*, pp.188–9; Sewell Journal, 20 August 1865, MS 459, AML; NZPD, 1865, pp.342ff.

74. See NZPD, 1864–66, pp.263–4, for Sewell's explanations.

75. NZPD, 1864–66, pp.259–63, 274, 346–51; Ward, *Show of Justice*, pp.187–8.

76. NZPD, 1864–66, p.337.

77. Sewell Journal, 20 August 1865, MS 459, AML; NZPD, 1864–66, p.348; Ward, *Show of Justice*, p.184.

78. See NZPD, 1864–66, p.325, for Fitz-Gerald's introduction of the Bill.

79. Ward, *Show of Justice*, pp.180–87; Martin to Native Minister, 18 July 1865, and Notes, AJHR, 1866, A-1, pp.74–85; Martin to Mantell, 21 July 1865, Mantell Papers, MS Papers 83, f.348, ATL.

80. NZPD, 1864–66, p.629.

81. NZPD, 1864–66, pp.370–71.

82. M.P.K. Sorrenson, 'Land purchase methods and their effect on Maori population 1865–1901', JPS, LXV, 3 (1956), pp.183–99; NZPD, 1864–66, p.205.

83. The 1865 petition was printed in The *Press*, 7 July 1865, with an accompanying editorial.

84. NZPD, 1864–66, pp.279–81, 293–8, 303; Ward, *Show of Justice*, pp.190, 334 fn.56. For Tamihana's submissions before a House committee, see Le 1/1866/11, NA.

85. Williams, *Frederick Weld*, Ch.6.

86. Dalton, *War and Politics*, p.239.

87. Bowen to Gladstone, 4 November 1880, Gladstone Papers, 44466, British Museum Library.

88. Ward, *Show of Justice*, Chs.15, 16; Diary notes 1871, in Diaries, Box VI, and (on Maori status) see Maning to McLean, 20 May 1870, McLean Papers, MS Papers 32, f.311, ATL.

89. G. Hensley, 'The Withdrawal of the British troops from New Zealand, 1864–1870 : A study in imperial relations', MA thesis, University of NZ, Canterbury (1957).

90. 'Copy of the Treaty of Waitangi ... and Mr Baker's annotations thereon', AJLC, 1869, pp.67–78. The treaty, 'English version', had been printed in 1840 in the British parliamentary papers. For the mining and foreshore issue, see a report, AJHR, 1869, F-7; also NZPD, 1869, 27 July, and 5 August; and JLC, 1869, 27 July and 5 August.

91. AJLC, 1869, p.67; see Appendix 5.

92. Thomas Edward Young had been employed as a translator in the Native Department since 1 March 1863 when he was sixteen. On such an important translation it is unlikely that his work evaded careful scrutiny by other staff.

93. Ward, *Show of Justice*, pp.228–9, where he notes that the sentence was 'hanging, drawing and quartering, the only penalty applicable according to the then state of the law of treason, before it was hastily amended'.

94. E.g. GBPD, 173, 26 April 1864. The British periodical press also published numerous articles on colonial events, sometimes indicating their relationship to the treaty; e.g. the *Saturday Review* ran a series of articles written by Lord Cecil (later the Marquis of Salisbury) who had experienced New Zealand first-hand, staying in the country for six months in the early 1850s. Many of these publications found their way to New Zealand readers. In the *Saturday Review*, XIII, p.72, 18 January 1862, Cecil referred to colonies such as New Zealand, as 'spendthrift' children who 'sponged shamelessly' on Britain.

95. [Aborigines Protection Society], *The New Zealand Government and the Maori War of 1863–64*, London, 1864.

96. E.g. Morrison to Colonial Secretary, 19 October 1865, with newspaper enclosures, IA 65/3568, NA. Other material is filed in IA 65/1192, 65/3568, 65/2897 and 65/436, NA.

CHAPTER 9: THE QUEST FOR LOST RIGHTS

1. Eric Ramsden, *Busby of Waitangi*, Wellington, 1942, pp.342–66; 'Petition ... of Early Settlers of New Zealand', AJHR, 1875 , J-1.

2. NZPD, 1858–60, p.477; J. Williams, 'Settler Society', *The Oxford History of New Zealand*, ed. W.H. Oliver with B.R. Williams, Oxford and Wellington, 1981, p.117; D. Ian Pool, *The Maori Population of New Zealand 1769–1971*, Auckland, 1971, p.237; M.P.K. Sorrenson, 'Colonial Rule and Local Response: Maori Responses to European Domination in New Zealand since 1860', *The Journal of Imperial and Commonwealth History*, IV, 2 (1976), p.128.

3. M.P.K. Sorrenson, 'The Purchase of Maori Lands, 1865–1892', MA thesis, University of NZ, (Auckland 1955), pp.33, 124.

4. For files on the Princes Street Reserve, see MA 13/68, NA; G.W. Rusden, *Aureretanga: Groans of the Maoris*, London, 1888, pp.67–84; Alan Ward, *A Show of Justice: Racial 'amalgamation' in nineteenth century New Zealand*, Auckland, 1973, pp.215–16, 251–2. Problems relating to government shortcomings were revealed in court action: e.g. Regina v. Fitzherbert, noted in Hugh Carleton, *The Life of Henry Williams*, Auckland, 1874, vol.1, p.242 and note; Mantell to Minister of Native Affairs, 20 August 1873, enclosing the Judgement of Court of Appeal in case of Regina v. Fitzherbert, AJHR, 1873. G-2c. Another question of trust, but of a different kind, was involved in Mangakahia v. New Zealand Tim-

ber Co. Ltd. (1881-82), *NZLR*, 2 SC 345.
5. 1877 3 NZ Jur R (NS) SC 72. The Wi
Parata case had come up first as a petition to
the General Assembly, reported on in AJHR,
1876, I-4, p.1, by the Native Affairs Committee chaired by John Bryce.
6. Ward, *Show of Justice*, p.340, fn.5, notes
that McLean, who took office as Native
Minister soon after the 1869 judgement,
thought it unjust, but was persuaded by Fox
to accept it. There is extensive material on the
Rangitikei-Manawatu case in MA 13/69-76,
NA. The land had been excluded from the
workings of the 1865 Native Lands Act.
7. T.C. Williams, *The Manawatu Purchase completed, the Treaty of Waitangi broken*, London,
1868. See also AJHR, 1874, A-1, no.12, where
an address to Gladstone from T.C. Williams
concerning the injustice done Ngati Raukawa
was forwarded to Kimberley by Ferguson, 30
September 1873.
8. Such fishing rights were used to substanti-
ate claims to land before the Native Land
Court. There are many examples of early recognition of fishing rights. Clarke noted feasts
in the Thames-Waikato where rights of prop-
rietorship in 'eel preserves' were settled:
GBPP, 1842 (569), p.96; 1846 (337), p.135.
9. GBPP, 1845 (369), p.98; Harry Evison,
Ngai Tahu Land Rights, Christchurch, 1986,
pp.22-32. See also Ward, *Show of Justice*,
p.258.
10. Internal Affairs files show the growing interest in harbour development from the late
1850s: IA 1858/713, 1860/2181, 1861/166,
1862/1570, 1864/1468, also G 36/3, NA. Before the abolition of provinces, a number of
provincial enactments intruded on Maori
rights, e.g., the Auckland Harbour Board Act,
1871, but the General Assembly passed a Harbours Act in 1878 that applied throughout the
colony.
11. MA 13/97, NA, covers the Lake case.
It was also reported upon in AJHR, 1891,
Sess.II, G-4.
12. E.g. IA 63/449, 63/530, 64/1856, NA;
Maori Messenger, 16 December 1861, p.19.
There were various acts, e.g., The Salmon and
Trout Act, 1867, The Protection of Animals
Act, 1867, The Oyster Fisheries Act, 1866,
and amendments, and the Fish Protection Act,
1877, and amendments.
13. 'Opinion of the Attorney General ...',
AJLC, 1872, I no.1.
14. Report ... on the Thames Sea Beach Bill,
AJHR, 1869, F-7; JHR, 1869, 18 August, no.2
(3 + 4), 24 August, no.3 (4 + 5) no.6, and 27
August, no.2.
15. See Ward, *Show of Justice*, p.342, fn.2, and
the Shortland Beach Act 1869. In an earlier
decision, on the Kawau Copper Mines, the
Court had given the same ruling.
16. The Fish Protection Act, 1877.
17. See the Highway Boards Empowering
Act, 1871, and the Native Districts Road
Board Act, 1871. For complaints, see e.g.
Mackay to Native Minister, 18 June 1875;
memo from Undersecretary to Native Minis-

ter, 21 June 1875, AJHR, 1875, G-10, nos.1,2.
For Bowen's tour, see AJHR, 1872, F-3A.
18. A provincial act in the 1860s had been
disallowed. See Ward, *Show of Justice*, pp.169,
231. The Bay of Islands Settlement Act, 1858,
had also allowed for the taking of land.
19. This is examined by A. Parsonson, 'Te
Mana o te Kingitanga Maori: A study of
Waikato-Maniapoto relations during the
struggle for the King Country, 1878-1884',
MA thesis, Canterbury (1975).
20. E.g. Bishop to Native Department,
AJHR, 1884, Sess.II, G-1, no.2.
21. Evidence ... of Wi Tako and others, 15
July 1870, in 'Report ... on the petition',
AJHR, 1870, F. no.7.
22. For an excellent, brief evaluation of
McLean in the post-war period, see Ward,
Show of Justice, p.257.
23. At Rotorua, e.g. the large house,
Tamatekapua, was opened in the early 1870s;
the Queen and the laws were said to be the
ridge-pole of the house, an expression of unity
and loyalty, AJHR, 1872, F, no.5.
24. Woon to Native Minister, 23 April 1872,
AJHR, 1872, F-3A, no.1; Brabant to Native
Minister, 25 May 1874, AJHR, 1874, G-2,
no.8; Ward, *Show of Justice*, p.272; Brabant to
Native Department, 15 May 1880, AJHR,
1880, G-4, no.8; Locke to Native Minister, 4
July 1872, AJHR, 1872, F-3A, no.36; Maunsell
to Native Minister, 23 April 1880, AJHR,
1880, G-4, no.15.
25. S.M. Cole, 'The Hawke's Bay Repudiation Movement', MA thesis, Massey (1977).
26. Cit. Ward, *Show of Justice*, p.273.
27. E.g. 'Petition of Henare Matua', AJLC,
1873, no.22.
28. Rangitakaiwaho and others to the General
Assembly, AJHR, 1876, J-6; see also Renata
Kawepo, Piripi Ropata and others to the
House of Representatives, AJHR, 1877, J-1.
29. *Te Wananga*, 22 January 1876, pp.37-39.
30. Ward, *Show of Justice*, p.173.
31. Tamihana Te Rauparaha to Fox and
McLean, 20 July 1869, and Tuhaere to
McLean, 13 December 1869, AJHR, 1870, A-
21, nos. 1 and 31. Other chiefs were involved
too, e.g. Matene Te Whiwhi and Hone Mohi
Tawhai. They had all been participants in a
large meeting of the King movement at
Tokangamutu where they had hoped to en-
gineer a reconciliation of King and government.
32. E.g. Report on the petition of Wi Hakiro
and others, 26 July 1876, AJHR, 1876, I-4,
p.3. Petitions of Te Ara, Katene and others,
AJHR, 1878, I-3, p.5, nos.55 and 150.
33. Evidence ... on the petition of Wi Tako
and others, 15 July 1870, in 'Report ... on the
petition', AJHR, 1870, F. no.7.
34. E.g. McLean to Tirarau, 15 November
1869, and Tirarau and Aperahama Taonui to
McLean, 2 December 1869, AJHR, 1870, A-
21, nos.26 and 27.
35. Correspondence between Maning and
McLean in early 1870, McLean Papers, MS
Papers 32, ATL, seems to indicate this. See

also Ward, *Show of Justice*, p.247; a Council Bill in the early 1870s was defeated.

36. Minutes of conference proceedings, MA 23/12, NA; and 'Paora Tuhaere's Parliament at Orakei', AJHR, 1879, Sess. II, G-8. There had been two earlier conferences at Kaipara: Nga Runanga i Aotea (1884–86), NZ MS 718, APL.

37. AJHR, 1879, Sess.II, G-8, p.8.

38. See AJHR, 1879, Sess.II, G-8, p.16, however, where an Arawa dated his commitment from the 1860 Kohimarama conference. There is a memorial at ohinemutu, Rotorua, which records Arawa participation at Kohimarama.

39. AJHR, 1879, Sess.II, G-8,e.g. pp.16–18.

40. Ibid., p.13.

41. R.C.J. Stone, 'The Maori Lands Question and the Fall of the Grey Government, 1879', *NZJH*, I, 1 (1967), pp.51–74.

42. The minutes of the 1880 conference can be found in MA 23/12, NA. The conferences and their resolutions were also reported in *NZ Herald*, 20, 22, 26 March 1880, and 12, 14, 21, 22, 23 March 1881.

43. AJHR, 1879, Sess.II, G-8, p.28.

44. Ibid., p.24.

45. See R.G. Scott, *Ask that mountain : The story of Parihaka*, Auckland, 1975.

46. Ward, *Show of Justice*, pp.281–3.

47. In pre-European times, the land where Te Tii is situated had been occupied by Te Kemara who is said to have had a pa there called Matai-whetu. At some stage, the land was purchased by Henry Williams and various Europeans lived on it. In the land title investigations following 1840, Henry Williams vested the land in the Maori [Ngatirahiri?] for their use and enjoyment. The block is also known as Tahunanui.

48. AJHR, 1875, G-1, no.4. Te Tai Hakuene was connected to the Waitangi area through his marriage to the daughter of Te Kemara of Waitangi.

49. 'Meeting at the Treaty of Waitangi House, Ngapuhi, 1875', *Pukapuka-Tauira*, Auckland, 1922–23, pp.14–18, for this and following paragraphs.

50. Taonui letters (Maori), 1863–82, (Private), and e.g. Tirarau and Taonui to McLean, 2 December 1869, AJHR, 1870, A-21, no.27.

51. *Visit of His Excellency the Governor to the North, 1876*, (reprint from *The Daily Southern Cross)*, Auckland, 1876.

52. Petition of Hare Hongi Hika and others, AJHR, 1878, I-3, no.139.

53. Williams to Native Department, 7 May 1880, AJHR, 1880, G-4, no.4. According to Taonui, the idea of searching into the treaty had arisen first at a tea party at Hare Hongi's house in 1873. Hare was a grandson of Hongi Hika.

54. *NZ Herald*, 27 August 1880. The monument, made by Messrs Buchanan of Auckland, had a foundation of blocks of Sydney freestone; the monument itself was of Oamaru stone. It is possible that the monument was erected on approximately the spot where the Confederation flag of 1834–35 stood. See a reference, made by Riwi of Whangarei, that might relate to this: *NZ Herald*, 25 March 1881, p.6.

55. Von Sturmer to Native Department, 7 May 1880, AJHR, 1880 G-4, no.3. For an assessment, see 'Report of the Commission ... Native Land Laws', AJHR, 1891, Sess. II, G-1.

56. MA 13/80, NA, has various letters on file: see also a petition from Kawiti and others against the Native Lands Acts: AJHR, 1876, I-4, p.27.

57. E.g. 'Visit of the Governor to the North', AJHR, 1870, A-7, p.7.

58. G.W. Rusden, *History of New Zealand*, London, 1883, vol.3, pp.301–3.

59. Von Sturmer to Native Department, 7 May 1880, AJHR, 1880, G-4, no.3.

60. *He Panui Tenei*, in MA 24/20, NA. The committee was chaired by H.K. Taiaroa, MLC, the secretary was Wi Parata, members were Wi Tako Ngatata, MLC, Mokena Kohere, MLC, Henare Tomoana, MHR, H.K. Tawhiti, MHR, M.P. Kawiti, Keepa Te Rangihiwinui (Major Kemp) and Peeti Te Aweawe.

61. Clendon to Native Minister, 23 May 1881, AJHR, G-8, no.4; *NZ Herald*, 24, 25, 26 March 1881; *Northern Luminary*, 12 February, 5, 12, 19, 26 March, 2, 23 April 1881. Reports relating to the meeting can be found in the above, but no record was kept by the government as with the Ngati Whatua meetings. Another useful source has been manuscripts in private possession, many in the Maori language, especially an outline headed 'Taonui's wishes, March 23, 1881', Wairua Papers.

62. 'Te Puaretanga o te Tiriti o Waitangi, 23 Maehe 1881', Wairua Papers.

63. J.M. Henderson, *Ratana: The Man, the Church, the Political Movement*, Wellington, 1963, p.12, cites Taonui as saying in 1863: 'E nga rangatira o Ngapuhi whakarongo mai ki ahau. Kaua te Tiriti o Waitangi e uhia ki te kara o Ingarangi, engari me uhi ano ki te kahu Maori, ki te kahu ake o tenei motu.' ('O chiefs of the Ngapuhi, listen to me; let not the Treaty of Waitangi be covered by the flag but let it be enshrined in a cloak of this land.')

64. Taonui to Kawiti, 28 October 1878 in Taonui Letters, 1863–82. Taonui had been particularly annoyed by S. 147 in the Harbours Act of 1878 that asserted rights over the foreshore and effectively disregarded Maori claims.

65. *Northern Luminary*, 23 April 1881.

66. Woon to Native Department, 22 May 1880, AJHR, 1880, G-4, no.17.

67. *Northern Luminary*, 26 March 1881. Beneath the Union Jack flew a blue ensign with the word 'Waima' inscribed on it and three stars.

68. Ibid.; *NZ Herald*, 24 March, p.5.

69. J.K. Chapman, *The Career of Arthur Hamilton Gordon; First Lord Stanmore, 1829–1912*, Toronto, 1964, Ch.6

70. 'Te Puaretanga', Wairua Papers. The reading was II Corinthians, Ch.3, v.6.

71. The stone was finally unveiled though the date is unsure. In March 1884 there were complaints to the governor that the unveiling had not taken place: Kawiti, Kira and Hare Hongi to Governor, 6 March 1884, G 49/20, NA.
72. Mair to Native Department, 20 May 1880, AJHR, 1880, G-4a.
73. This assessment is made by P.J. McRae, 'Participation: Native Committees (1883) and Papatupu Block Committees (1900) in Tai Tokerau', MA thesis, Auckland (1982), by Ward, *Show of Justice*, p.290, and has been confirmed by further research of committee material: MA 23/13, NA.
74. 'Report of the Commission ... Native Land Laws', AJHR, 1891, Sess.II, G-1, p.XVI.
75. Chapman, *Career of Arthur Hamilton Gordon*, Ch.6, has been referred to for the following points.
76. Ibid., p.235.
77. Gordon to Mantell, 6 September 1883, Mantell Papers, MS Papers 83, f.287, ATL.
78. Notes by William Fox [1881?], G 49/20, NA.

CHAPTER 10: A STRUGGLE FOR AUTONOMY
1. Taiwhanga to Native Minister, 4 May 1881, MA 13/80, NA. Alan Ward, *A Show of Justice: Racial 'amalgamation' in nineteenth century New Zealand*, Auckland, 1973, pp.290–91; and see MA 23/1, NA, for correspondence concerning Taiwhanga.
2. Meeting at the Treaty of Waitangi House, 1875, in *Pukapuka Tauira*, Auckland, 1922–23, p.15; Petition of Hirini Taiwhanga, AJHR, 1878, I-3, no.138; Minutes of Orakei conference, 1880 and 1881, MA 23/12, NA, for various references; Maning to Lewis, n.d. [September 1882?], New Zealand Land Court Papers, NZ MS 68, APL.
3. *Aborigines' Friend*, New Series, no.14, October 1882, p.511; AJHR, 1883, A-6, pp.1–3; Maning to Lewis, n.d. [September 1882?], NZ Native Land Court Papers, NZ MS 68, APL; Clendon to Native Department, 31 May 1882, MA 23/1, NA.
4. The petition and related correspondence are printed in AJHR 1883, A-6 and in GBPP 1882 [3382], p.287.
5. Correspondence on the Maori visit in Aborigines Protection Society Papers, G 98, 99, Rhodes House Library; *Aborigines' Friend*, October 1882, pp.505–19.
6. See minutes on APS for Kimberley, 6 July, 24 July, 1 August, 14 August 1882, CO 209/241; Agent-General to Colonial Secretary, 28 July 1882, IA 1, 82/4154, NA; Report in AJHR, 1883, A-6, pp.3–4. The section that follows is based on the report.
7. Weale to Chesson, n.d. [August?] 1882; Gorst to Chesson, 15 July 1882, APS Papers, G 98,99. *Aborigines' Friend*, New Series, no.14, October 1882, p.507, notes that Gorst presented the petition on 3 August 1882.
8. Cropper and others to Kimberley, 2 August 1882, GBPP, 1883 [3689]; copy of a scheme addressed 'To the chiefs of the Native Race in New Zealand', Tait Papers, Lambeth Palace Library; also 'Maori Lands and Perpetual Annuities Association (Limited)', AJHR, 1884, Sess.I, G-2. For a later version, see 'Proposals of Mr Sydney David Taiwhanga, M.H.R., for the Colonization and Settlement of Maori Lands', Wellington, 1888; Hone Mohi Tawhai to Native Minister, 10 January 1883, MA 23/1, NA, notes this.
9. *Aborigines' Friend*, New Series, no.14, October 1882, pp.509–13; various letters on file in APS Papers, G-98, 99; Weale to Chesson, 16 August 1882, APS Papers, Rhodes House Library.
10. Reports can be found in MA 23/1, NA; see Maning to Lewis, n.d. [September 1882?], NZ Native Land Court Papers, NZ MS 68, APL; and Maning to Webster, 3 September 1882, Maning Letters, NZ MS, APL.
11. For memo and the following document discussed, see AJHR, 1883, A-6.
12. Ibid., p.6.
13. Gordon to Mantell, 10,14 June 1882, Mantell Papers, MS Papers 83, f.287, ATL. Efforts to have it made public finally met with success. See Rusden to Hicks Beach, 7 July 1882, Hicks Beach to Rusden, 12 November 1882, Gorst to Rusden, 20,27,30 July 1882, Rusden Papers, Micro MS 758 ATL.
14. The speech and discussions were reported in the Institute's publication, *The Colonies and India*, 26 January, 2 February 1883, encl. in Bell to Premier, 9 February 1883, MA 23/1, 83/102, NA; Weale to Chesson, 29 January 1883, APS Papers.
15. H.M. Tawhai to Native Minister, 10 January 1883, MA 23/1, 83/204, NA. Taiwhanga to Chesson, 29 December 1882, APS Papers; 'Printed material relating to the English visit', Tait Papers, Lambeth Palace.
16. Clendon to Native Office, Auckland, 23 September 1882, MA 23/1, NA; Taiwhanga to Chesson, 29 December 1882, Weale to Chesson, 4 June 1884, APS Papers: H.M. Tawhai to Native Minister, 10 January 1883, MA 23/1, 83/204, NA. 'Ko te Pitihana a nga Iwi o Niu Tireni ki Ingarangi, 7 April 1883', Grey Papers, no.667a, APL.
17. Clendon report, 23 May 1881, AJHR, 1881, G-8, no.4.
18. Taiwhanga to Weale, November 1882, APS Papers; Clendon to Native Department, 31 March 1884, MA 23/1, 84/1271, and 13 April 1884, MA 23/1, 84/1198, NA; copies of *NZ Times* filed MA 23/1, 82/1654, are most critical of Taiwhanga. For a more favourable view, Weale to Chesson, 2 October 1883, 15 March 1884, APS Papers.
19. Chesson to Weale, 19 February 1883, APS Papers; printed Maori text of the petition in Greenway to Lewis, 5 December 1883, MA 23/1, 83/3793, NA, together with two different translations of it. A copy in longhand and in English can also be found in APS Papers, but there is no record of how it came to be there nor why it should have been dated 7 April 1884, whereas the copy in the Grey Papers is dated 7 April 1883.

20. Maori MHRs to the Aborigines Protection Society, 16 July 1883 (and related correspondence), APS Papers, and GBPP, 1884–85 [c.4413]. See also *Transactions of the Aborigines Protection Society, 1883–89*, March 1884.

21. A. Parsonson, 'Te Mana o te Kingitanga Maori: A Study of Waikato-Maniapoto relations during the struggle for the King Country 1878–1884', MA thesis, Canterbury (1975). Files in MA 23/4, NA, trace the government's efforts from around 1870 to break down King movement resistance.

22. Parsonson, 'Te Mana o te Kingitanga Maori', pp.169–81; and records in MA 23/4, NA.

23. *Aborigines' Friend*, December 1884, and Memorial and related correspondence, GBPP, 1884–85 [c.4413] and [c.4492]. Parsonson, 'Te Mana o te Kingitanga Maori', pp.174,181 discusses the memorial. Tawhiao to Chesson, 22 March 1884, APS Papers, indicates that the draft memorial was written in NZ not England.

24. Derby to Jervois, 9 August 1884, GBPP, 1884–85 [c.4413].

25. E.g. Bell to Undersecretary of State for Colonies, 9 April 1884, CO 209/244/5975.

26. Correspondence on the King's visit, CO 209/243 and CO 209/244. See also telegram on file, rec'd 27 May 1884 from NZ government, CO 209/244/11376; and note in Meade memo, 15 August 1884, CO 209/244/13887.

27. Herbert to Derby, 18 July 1884, CO 209/244/12242; Fuller to Derby, 16 July 1884, Herbert to Derby, 17 July 1884, Derby minute, 19 July 1884, CO 209/244/12118.

28. Report of the interview, *Aborigines' Friend*, December 1884.

29. Bell to Fuller, 15 July 1884, CO 209/244/12118.

30. The Cetawayo affair had been reported in the NZ press before the King's trip; the similarity in the African and NZ situations had not gone unnoticed in government circles. For a full account of Cetawayo, see J.G. Guy, *The Destruction of the Zulu Kingdom: the Civil War in Zululand, 1879–1884*, London, 1979.

31. Tawhiao and chiefs to Derby, 13 August 1884, and Herbert memo, 16 August 1884, CO 209/244/13887. Derby was given fresh information about land court operations in the Waikato-Maniapoto district that exemplified Maori grievances.

32. 'Farewell to the Maori chiefs'. *Aborigines' Friend*, December 1884.

33. Letters between Te Wheoro and Chesson, latter half of 1884, APS Papers; Bell to Herbert, 20 August 1884, encl. in Bell to Premier, 20 August 1884, no.383, PM 5/2, NA.

34. Te Wheoro to Chesson, 28 January, 28 March 1885, and Tangata to Weale, 24 January 1885, APS Papers; Te Wheoro to Gorst, 23 March 1885, GBPP, 1884–85 [c.4492].

35. 'Notes of Native Meetings', AJHR, 1885 G-1; also Te Wheoro to Gorst, 27 March 1885, GBPP, 1884–85 [c.4492].

36. Notes of a meeting between Ballance and Wanganui Natives, 7 January 1885, in 'Notes of Native Meetings', AJHR, 1885, G-1, p.5,

also Notes of a meeting at Whatiwhatihoe, 6 February 1885.

37. Stout memorandum, 12 March 1885, encl. in Jervois to Derby, 28 March 1885, GBPP, 1884–85 [c.4413].

38. Report in *Aborigines' Friend*, November 1885, pp.250–52; Derby to Jervois, 23 June, GBPP, 1884–85 [c.4492]; Colonial Office minutes and draft letter, 10, 15, 24 June 1885, CO 209/245/9171.

39. Bell to Fuller, 23 June 1885, CO 209/245/9171.

40. Te Wheoro to Chesson, 8 October, 26 November 1885, APS Papers.

41. R. Walker, 'Korero: The never-open door', *NZ Listener*, 7 May 1983, p.58.

42. Ballance to Katene, 2 February 1885 (printed letter in Maori), APS Papers.

43. Taiwhanga to Chesson, 30 July, 26 November 1883; 19 February, 30 October 1884, APS Papers.

44. Bishop to Native Department, 12 May 1884, AJHR, 1884, Sess.II, G-1, no.2; Treaty of Waitangi Minute Books, Department of Maori Affairs, Whangarei.

45. P.J. McRae, 'Participation: Native Committees (1883) and Papatupu Block Committees (1900) in Tai Tokerau', MA thesis, Auckland (1981); 'Ko te Pitihana a Nga Iwi o Niu Tireni Ki Ingarangi, 7 April 1883', section 4, Grey Papers, no.667a, APL.

46. Taiwhanga to Chesson, 31 March 1885, APS Papers.

47. *Northern Luminary*, 12 May 1885; also Greenway to Native Department, 16 April 1885, AJHR, 1885, G-2, p.5.

48. Description of the meeting, Taumarere, 5 May 1885, Taonui Letters, Private Collection. The pact was recognised with various gifts from Kawiti.

49. Wilkinson to Native Department, 25 May 1886, AJHR, 1886, G-1, no.5; Correspondence between Tawhiao and the Native Minister on a Maori Council, May/June 1886, AJHR, 1886, G-14.

50. Apart from several letters to the APS, there was a petition from Tawhiao to Gorst, and a letter from Rewi Maniapoto seeking an answer to the 1884 appeal. Gorst to Chesson, 11 February 1886, Holland to APS, 26 May 1887, and other correspondence between the Colonial Office and APS in 'Correspondence', 1886, 1887, 1888, APS Papers.

51. Copy of Ballance memorandum, 25 March 1887, encl. in Jervois to Holland, 5 April 1887, APS Papers. The King was seeking an English-appointed commissioner to investigate the Kawhia problem where Maori had been destroying harbour buoys to obstruct government forcibly reopening Kawhia harbour. See also Ward, *Show of Justice*, p.287.

52. Tawhiao to Ballance, 17 May 1886, AJHR, 1886, G-14.

53. John A. Williams, *Politics of the New Zealand Maori*, Auckland, 1969, pp.44–47. The constitution is printed in *Speeches and Documents on New Zealand History*, ed. W.D. McIntyre and W.J. Gardner, Oxford, 1971, p.165.

54. See this discussion dated 19 April in *Te Paki o Matariki*, 2 June 1894.
55. Ward to Native Department, 14 April 1884, AJHR, 1884, Sess. II. G-1; 'Native Meeting, Taupo', 7 September 1885, called by Ropiha and Turoa to report on their English trip, AJHR, 1886, G-3; 'Native Meeting at Hastings', 2 January 1886, AJHR, 1886, G-2.
56. 'Native Meeting at Hastings', AJHR, 1886, G-2.
57. E.g. Ward, *Show of Justice*, p.296–7; also letter dated 15 March 1887 in Grey letter collection D 20 (1), APL; Native Lands Commission, AJHR, 1891, G-1, p.xvi.
58. Ballance memorandum, 25 March 1887, encl. in Jervois to Holland, 5 April 1887, APS Papers; 'Native Meeting at Hastings', AJHR, 1886, G-2, p.18.
59. 'Nga Runanga i Aotea' (Shelly Beach, Kaipara), 1885 [?], 1886, NZ MS 718, APL; Von Sturmer to Native Department, 20 April 1885, AJHR, 1885, G-2, no.2.
60. 'Native Views on Native Land Legislation', AJHR, 1888, Sess.II, G-7.
61. E.g. Tawhai to Native Minister, 5 December 1883, MA 23/4, and Tawhai to Lewis, 27 September 1883, G 49/31, NA.
62. 'Notes on a meeting at Putiki-Wharenui, Wanganui', dated 10 May 1888, Tuhaere to Tawhiao, 8 May 1888, Tawhiao to Tuhaere, 17 May 1888, Wairua Papers (private); *Wanganui Herald*, 9 May 1888.
63. Copy in Treaty of Waitangi minutes, 1888 meeting, Wairua Papers (private).
64. 'Notes on Native meeting at Wanganui', Wairua Papers; *Wanganui Herald*, 9 May 1888.
65. *Te Huihuinga o etahi o nga rangatira o te motu nei ki Kohimarama, 1889*, p.1.
66. E.g. Tuhaere (and others) to the House of Representatives, 20 August 1888; a petition to the Queen from the chiefs of New Zealand; letter to the Governor (from the chiefs), 15 August 1888; 'Panuitanga' (committee election for the north), 28 May 1888. All documents in Maori and in Wairua Papers.
67. Tuhaere to the House of Representatives, 20 August 1888, Wairua Papers.
68. Petition to the Queen, n.d. [1888?]; chiefs to the Governor, 15 August 1888, Wairua Papers.
69. 'I meatia tenei ki te Tiriti o Waitangi', dated 14 March 1889, Wairua Papers.
70. *Te Huihuinga ... o nga rangatira*, Orakei, 28 March 1889, p.6; Williams, *Politics of the New Zealand Maori*, p.60, states that by 1898 some 37,000 Maori had adhered to the agreement, a figure that seems too large in view of the total Maori population of some 45,000.
71. *NZ Herald*, 28, 29, 30 March 1889; *Auckland Star*, 26, 27, 28, 29 March, 1 April 1889. *The Star* reports were published in pamphlet form, see fn.65 above. The meeting made it clear that it was in the tradition of the 1860 Kohimarama conference and referred to the 1889 agreement of union as a 'covenant'.
72. E.g. R. Pharazyn, 'Two letters from the *Evening Press*, January 3 and January 12, 1892', (reprint), 1892.
73. 'Te Huihuinga ... o nga rangatira', p.1. At

their 1888 meeting, the south had created a model for Kotahitanga, a carved figure incorporating the breaking of a bundle of sticks. Tuhaere had suggested that the figure be sent throughout the country right to the north but the figure had not arrived; this created doubts about the south's attitudes to the rest of the movement.
74. M.P. Kawiti to Tuhaere, 20 March 1889, in *Te Huihuinga ... o nga rangatira*, p.2.
75. 'Meeting at Omanaia, 15–17 May 1890', and 'Notes of Ohaewai meeting, 22 June 1889', Wairua Papers.
76. Various letters in Taonui Letters (private); also Tawhai to Te Haara, August 1881, Wairua Papers.
77. 'Omanaia, 3 Maehe 1880', Wairua Papers: fragments of notes on the setting up of a stone at Omanaia in memory of Penetana Papahurihia, the Hokianga prophet of earlier years. Certain men, chosen to read from the Bible, had some significance in the subsequent Treaty of Waitangi movement: Heta Te Haara, Raniera Wharerau, Te Tane Haratua, Hone Mohi Tawhai, Hone Te Ra Ngapua. Taonui, Penetana's successor, often referred to seeing the future in the stars and made allusions to other phenomena that are obscure and puzzling.
78. *Northern Advocate*, 22 April 1891; *Nga Korero o te hui o te Whakakotahitanga i tu ki te Tiriti o Waitangi, April 14, 1892*, Auckland, [1892?]; *NZ Herald*, 21, 23, 28 April 1892; *Northern Advocate*, 23 April 1892.
79. There had been another meeting at Waima, December 1891, to organise the 1892 Waitangi meeting, and Wanganui had met at Parekino in January 1892; Williams, *Politics of the New Zealand Maori*, pp.51–52.
80. *Paremata Maori o Niu Tireni*, Otaki, 1892.
81. *Marsden Times and Whangarei County Gazette*, 4 May 1892, gave the tribal representatives at Waitangi and outlined the organisation decided upon there. Williams, *Politics of the New Zealand Maori*, p.53, varies slightly from the above.

CHAPTER 11: A RESIDUE OF GUILT: 1890–1987

1. Michael King, 'Between two worlds', *The Oxford History of New Zealand*, ed. W.H. Oliver with B.R. Williams, Wellington and Oxford, 1981, p.300.
2. John A. Williams, *Politics of the New Zealand Maori*, Auckland, 1969, pp.55, 61–63.
3. AJHR, 1893, J-1; AJLC, 1893, no.6; AJHR, 1891, G-1; Williams, *Politics*, Ch.8, and pp.108–11, 147.
4. Cit. Williams, *Politics*, p.137. The flag was given in 1834, not 1836.
5. Ibid., pp.139–40; 'Taingakawa petition', MA 24/8, NA; J. Binney, et al., *Mihaia: The Prophet Rua Kenana and his community at Maungapohatu*, Wellington, 1979, pp.39–40, 42.
6. Michael King, *Te Puea: A Biography*, Auckland, 1977, pp.74–75; G. Scholefield, 'Maori Sovereignty: The Deputation to London', *United Empire*, V, n.s., (1914), pp.584–7; Williams, *Politics*, p.140. When Tawhiao

died in 1894 he was succeeded by Mahuta and then Te Rata.

7. Williams, *Politics*, pp.150–54; G.V. Butterworth, 'The Politics of Adaptation: The career of Sir Apirana Ngata 1874–1928', MA thesis, Victoria (1969); King, *Te Puea*, pp.263–64.
8. A. Ngata, *Te Tiriti o Waitangi: He Whakamarama*, Hastings, 1922.
9. See above p.83.
10. Williams, *Politics*, p.155; Ngata, *Te Tiriti o Waitangi*, pp.11, 18.
11. A. Ngata, *The Treaty of Waitangi: An explanation*, trans. M.R. Jones, Wellington, 1963.
12. *Ko te tiriti i tuhia ki Waitangi 1840*, Auckland, 1922.
13. *Ko te pukapuka a te Wherowhero Potatau ki a te Kuini, me te whakahoki mai o te Kuini ki a ia*, Auckland, 1922; see above, p.128, where this is discussed.
14. Earl Grey to Governor Grey, 3 May 1848, in *Ko te pukapuka a te Wherowhero*, p.1.
15. *Pukapuka Tauira*, Auckland, 1922–23.
16. Ngata, *The Treaty of Waitangi*, p.2.
17. 'Maori claims to certain North Island Lakes', *Te Wananga*, I, 2 (December 1929), pp.128–40; *NZ Herald*, 29 March 1922, p.6; F.A. Bennett, *Te keehi a te Arawa mo nga moana, me te whawhai mo te mana o te tiriti o Waitangi*, Rotorua, 1912.
18. Petitions in AJHR, 1887, I-2, nos.28, 29, from Wanganui, and JHR, 1916, no.132, from North Auckland, all relating to tidal waters; Ngai Tahu petition, G 49/31, NA; Clendon to Native Department, 27 April 1885, AJHR, 1885, G-2, no.5; Greenway to Native Department, 16 April 1885, AJHR, 1885, G-2, no.4; H.F. von Haast, 'The Treaty of Waitangi: Its consideration by the courts', *NZLJ*, X, 2 (6 February 1934), p.21; Jones memo, 7 July, [1920s?] MA 28, 4/5, NA; AJHR, 1887, I-2, no.140, and 1891, Sess.II, G-4; 'Taupo waters fishing rights, 1924–1929', special file 137, MA 31/23, NA; see also Report of the Waitangi Tribunal ... in relation to fishing grounds in the Waitara district', March 1983, section 4.8, where rights are mentioned in Lakes Rotokakahi, Rotoaira, Horowhenua and Forsyth.
19. *NZ Herald*, 30 March 1922, p.6; Kay Boese, *Tides of History*, Whangarei, 1977, pp.128–31.
20. R. Ngatata Love, 'Policies of frustration: the growth of Maori politics: The Ratana/Labour era', PhD thesis, Victoria (1977), p.530; *NZ Herald*, 30 March 1922, p.6.
21. The sections on Ratana and Labour that follow are based on Love, 'Policies of frustration'; J.M. Henderson, *Ratana. The Man, the Church, The Political Movement*, 2nd ed., Wellington, 1972; Claudia Orange, 'A kind of equality: Labour and the Maori people 1935–1949', MA thesis, Auckland (1977), Ch.2.
22. Love, 'Policies of frustration', pp.230–36, and 529–34 for the petition.
23. NZPD, 1932, pp.120–22; Love, 'Policies of frustration', pp.277–8, 541–6; Henderson, *Ratana*, p.88.

24. Orange, 'A kind of equality', Ch.2, and pp.230–31.
25. R. Mawhete, *Maori Rights under 'The Constitution Act 1852': review*, Palmerston North, 1925.
26. Vernon H. Reed, *The Gift of Waitangi*, Wellington, 1957, Chs.1 and 2; also 'Waitangi', G-48, W4, NA.
27. Reed, *Gift of Waitangi*, pp.32–33.
28. T. Lindsay Buick, *Waitangi, Ninety-four Years After*, New Plymouth, 1934.
29. King, *Te Puea*, pp.80–81; Reed, *Gift of Waitangi*, Ch.8; *NZ Herald*, 30 March 1922, p.6; Agnes Busby to Bledisloe, 21 February 1935, 'Waitangi', G-48, W4, NA.
30. Buick, *Waitangi*, pp.90–91.
31. Buick, *Waitangi*, does not mention the flag at all, but *Auckland Star*, 31 January 1934, shows photos of the flags to be flown – the Union Jack and the 1834 flag.
32. Reed, *Gift of Waitangi*, Ch.10; various correspondence including C. Leys to Bledisloe, 8 June 1834, G-48, W4, NA.
33. See above, p.174.
34. *Auckland Star*, 8, 17 February 1926; *NZ Herald*, 5 June 1950.
35. Reed, *Gift of Waitangi*, Ch.14; *NZ Herald*, 7 February 1940.
36. E.g. *Taranaki Daily News*, 5 February 1940; *Northern Advocate*, 5, 6 February 1940; various reports in 'The Treaty of Waitangi' (press clippings), ATL.
37. AJHR, 1928, G-7.
38. King, *Te Puea*, pp.204–5; Reed, *Gift of Waitangi*, pp.92–93; *NZ Herald*, 3 February 1940; *Dominion*, 22 April 1940, 'Miscellaneous', MA 24/28, NA; Hampson Papers, MS Papers 1472, ATL.
39. Cit. King, *Te Puea*, p.205.
40. *NZ Herald*, 23 May 1939, 7 February 1940.
41. Cit. King, *Te Puea*, pp.207.
42. Orange, 'A kind of equality', Ch.4.
43. Henderson, *Ratana*, p.89.
44. Love, 'Policies of frustration', pp.441–86 for the following section.
45. Reed, *Gift of Waitangi*, Ch.8.
46. Ibid., pp.104–5, 114–17.
47. *Northern Advocate*, 6, 17 October 1953; correspondence in MA 28/12, NA.
48. 'Royal Tour: Waikato Visit', MA 28/12, f.31/5, NA.
49. Cit. Reed, *Gift of Waitangi*, p.116.
50. 'Signposts of the Future', 6 February 1959, *Lord Cobham's Speeches*, ed. O.S. Hintz, Auckland, 1962, pp.99–101; *NZ Herald*, 8 February 1960.
51. H.K. Ngata, 'The Treaty of Waitangi and land: Parts of the current law in contravention of the treaty', *The Treaty of Waitangi: Its origins and significance*, Wellington, 1972, pp.49–57.
52. J.K. Hunn, *Report on the Department of Maori Affairs*, Wellington, 1961.
53. *NZ Herald*, 26 January 1968.
54. Koro Dewes, 'Waitangi Day 1968; Some food for thought', *Comment*, XXXV, (June 1968), pp.12–14.
55. *NZ Herald*, 2 February 1968.
56. Dewes, 'Waitangi Day 1968', *Comment*,

XXXV, (June 1968); P.W. Hohepa. 'Waitangi: A Promise or a Betrayal', *Occasional Papers in Race Relations*, no.2, Wellington, 1971.
57. *NZ Herald*, 8 February 1971.
58. D.V. Jones, *Licence for Empire: Colonialism by Treaty in Early America*, Chicago, 1982; W.R. Jacobs, *Dispossessing the American Indian: Indians and Whites on the Colonial Frontier*, New York, 1972; R.W. Johnson, 'Indians and Equal Protection', *Washington Law Review*, LIV, 3 (1979), pp.587–631.
59. 1956: Inspector of Fisheries v. Weepu, *NZLR* 920; 1962: re Bed of Wanganui River, *NZLR* 600 623; 1963: re 90 Mile Beach, *NZLR* 461.
60. Donna Awatere, 'Maori Sovereignty', *Broadsheet*, Auckland, June 1982–February 1983 (a series subsequently published in revised form as *Maori Sovereignty*, Auckland, 1984).
61. 'Submission from the New Zealand Maori Council, 5 October 1971, to the Minister of Maori Affairs and the Minister of Justice, on the Treaty of Waitangi and parts of the current statutory law in contravention thereof', (t.s.), p.6; and 'Submissions to the Select Committee, Human Rights Commission Bill', jointly prepared by the New Zealand Maori Council and the Maori Women's Welfare League [1976?], (t.s.).
62. R.M. Ross, 'Te Tiriti o Waitangi: texts and translations', *NZJH*, Vl,2 (1972), pp.129–57; E.J. Haughey, 'Maori claims to lakes, river beds and the foreshore', *NZULR*, II, (1966), pp.29–42; F.M. Auburn, 'Te Tiriti o Waitangi (The Treaty of Waitangi in New Zealand Law)', *NZULR*, IV (1971), pp.309–11; A.P. Molloy, 'The Non-Treaty of Waitangi', *NZLJ*, IX, (1971), pp.193–7; W.A. McKean, 'The Treaty of Waitangi Revisited', *W.P. Morrell: A Tribute*, ed. G.A. Wood and P.S. O'Connor, Dunedin, 1973, pp.237–249; Betty Carter, 'The Incorporation of the Treaty of Waitangi into Municipal Law', *AULR*, IV, 1 (1980), pp.1–18; J.D. Sutton, 'The Treaty of Waitangi today', *VUWLR*,XI, 1 (1981), pp.17–40; F. Hackshaw, 'The Recognition of Native Customary Land Rights at Common Law', LL B thesis, Auckland (1984); P. McHugh, 'The legal status of Maori fishing rights in tidal waters', *VUWLR*, XIV (1984), p.247; P. McHugh, 'Aboriginal title in N.Z. Courts', *Canterbury Law Review*, II (1984), p.235; P. McHugh, 'Maori fishing rights and the North American Indian', unpublished article, 1984.
63. New Zealand Day Act 1973; *NZ Herald*, 7 February 1973; *Auckland Star*, 13 February 1973.
64. E.g. 'Who stole Waitangi Day?', *Thursday*, Auckland, 31 January 1974, pp.26–29.
65. *Auckland Star*, 21 October 1976, p.14.
66. K. Holyoake, 'Waitangi Day', printed speech, 6 February 1979.
67. Minister of Maori Affairs, Ben Couch, Speech Notes for Waitangi Day, 6 February

1980, (t.s.); Minister of Lands, J. Elworthy, cit. *Auckland Star*, 8 February 1982; and for comment on 'one people' theme: S.M. Mead, 'Maori-Pakeha Relationships: An obstacle race', *Turnbull Winter Lectures*, Wellington, 1982.
68. *New Hope for our society*, (Catholic Commission for Evangelisation, Justice and Development), 1984; *What happened at Waitangi Day, 1984*, (National Council of Churches), 1984; *The Treaty of Waitangi: Discussion Paper*, (Treaty of Waitangi Commission, Anglican Church), 1985.
69. *NZ Herald*, 22 March 1983.
70. Cit. Rusden, *History of New Zealand*, vol.3, p.485.
71. Eruera Stirling and Ann Salmond, *Eruera : The Teachings of a Maori Elder*, Wellington, 1980, p.225; *NZ Herald*, 19 January 1983, sec.2, p.1.
72. E.g. *NZ Herald*, 21 January 1980; *Auckland Star*, 5 January 1980.
73. *Auckland Star*, 8 February 1982.
74. *Auckland Star*, 12 February, 16 July 1982; *NZ Herald*, 27 February 1982.
75. 'Leave the Treaty Alone', *NZ Herald*, 28 October 1983; *Te Hikoi Ki Waitangi*, Auckland, 1984.
76. *Treaty of Waitangi Hui*, Whangarei, 1985.
77. 'Report . . . in relation to fishing grounds in the Waitara district', March 1983; 'Finding . . . on the Kaituna claim', November 1984; 'Finding . . . on the Manukau claim', July 1985; (all Waitangi Tribunal).
78. 'Finding . . . relating to Te Reo Maori', April 1986.
79. *NZ Herald*, February 1986, Sec.1, pp.1, 3.
80. *NZ Herald*, 24 October 1986, Sec.1 p.3. and 5 February 1987, Sec.1, p.1.
81. *Puao-Te-Ata-Tu (day break)*, Wellington, p.14.
82. E.g. Whatarangi Winiata, 'Good Morning New Zealand', National Radio, 3 February 1987; Claudia Orange, 'An Exercise in Maori Autonomy: The Rise and Demise of the Maori War Effort Organization', *NZJH*, XXI, 1 (1987), p.156.
83. Judgment of Williamson J. 19 August 1986; heard in the Christchurch Registry of the High Court of NZ; *NZ Herald*, 22 August 1986, Sec.1, p.10.
84. *NZ Herald*, 22 August, 1986, Sec.1, p.2.
85. For a review of the tribunal's work, see M.P.K. Sorrenson, 'Towards a Radical Reinterpretation of New Zealand History: The Role of the Waitangi Tribunal', *NZJH*, XXI, 1(1987), pp.173–88.
86. *Dominion*, 5 May 1987, p.2.
87. E.g. In April 1987 'Project Waitangi' was launched with the support of the Governor-General, Sir Paul Reeves. In an effort to better educate the public about the treaty, the project's research group put together study material, mounted a publicity campaign and sponsored lectures and other informative events throughout the country.

BIBLIOGRAPHY

I PRIVATE AND OFFICIAL PAPERS

1. *Alexander Turnbull Library, Wellington*

Ashworth, Edward. Journals, 1841–45. MS 1841–45P.
Bell, Francis Dillon. Letters, 1859–66. MS Papers 693.
Best, Elsdon. Papers, 1869–1930. MS Papers 72.
Buick, Thomas Lindsay. Papers, 1900–1938. MS Papers 58.
Buller, James. A continuation of the journal of James Buller. q MS [1838–44].
Busby, James. Dispatches from the British Resident in New Zealand, 1833–39. q MS 1833–39.
Colenso, William. 'Memoranda of the arrival of Lieut. Govr. Hobson in New Zealand 1840'. MS Papers 1611.
Colenso, William. Papers. MS Col 1833–63.
FitzGerald, James Edward. Papers, 1839–1895. MS Papers 64.
Hadfield, Octavius. Papers, 1833–1902. q MS 1833–1902.
Hamlin, James. Journal, 1826–1837. q MS Ham 1826–37.
Hampson, Martin Hayward. Papers, 1940–41. MS Papers 1472.
Hobson, William. Papers, 1833–1846. MS Papers 46.
Hobson, William. Letters, 1841–42. MS Papers 813.
Hobson, William. Records, 1840. MS Papers 2227.
Ironside, Samuel. Diary, 1839–43. Micro MS 474.
McDonnell, Alexander Francis. Papers, 1845–1938. MS Papers 151.
McLean, Donald. Papers, 1832–1927. MS Papers 32.
Mair Family. Papers, 1839–1940. MS Papers 93.
Mantell, Walter Baldock Durrant. Papers, 1842–95. MS Papers 83.
Marsden Family. Papers, 1802–94. MS Papers 453.
Official Correspondence relating to the signing of the Treaty of Waitangi, 1840. q MS 1840.
Orton, Joseph. Journal, 1840. Micro MS 90.
Rusden, George William. Papers, 1860–95. Micro MS 758.
Stafford, Edward. Papers. MS Papers 28.
Weld, Frederick Aloysius. Correspondence, 1846–91. q MS 1846–99.
Williams, Edward Marsh. Journal of a voyage to the Northern and Southern Islands of New Zealand in H.M.S. *Herald*, 1840. MS 1840.
Woon, William. Journal, 1830–59. q MS 1830–59.

2. *Auckland Institute and Museum Library*

Busby, James. Letters and Papers. MS 46.
Colenso, William. Day and Waste Book. MS 76.
Hobbs, John. Diaries, 1823–60. MS 144.
Hobson, William. Letters. MS 802.
Jenkins, William. Diary, 1863–64. MS 155.
Meurant, Edward. Diary. MS 205.
Sewell, Henry. Journal. MS 459.
Taylor, Richard. Journal, 1833–73. MS 302.
Visit of His Excellency the Governor to the North, 1876. MS 561.
Waimate Meeting, 1844. MS 430.
Whiteley, John. Journal, 1832–63, MS 331.
Williams, Henry. Letters, 1822–1850. MS 72c.

3. *Auckland Public Library*

Clendon, James Reddy. Journal and Papers, 1839–72. MS 476.
Declaration of Independence, 28 October 1835 (Maori text), G NZM 21a.
Fairburn, Edwin, 'Maharatanga', NZ MS 91.
Fedarb, James. Diary, 1839–52. NZ MS 375.
Johnson, John. Journal, 1840. NZ MS 27.
Ko ta te Kawana korero ki nga Rangatira Maori i huihui ki Waitemata i te 10 o nga ra o Hurae, 1860. NZM.
Ko te Pitihana a Nga Iwi o Niu Tireni ki Ingarani, (7 April 1883). G NZM.
Mathew, Felton. Papers, 1840–48. NZ MS 78–89.
New Zealand Native Land Court. Papers. NZ MS 68.
Nga Runanga: Aotea (1884–86). NZ MS 718.

4. Auckland University Library

Ashwell, Benjamin Y. Letters and Journals, 1834–69.
Brown, Alfred N. Journal, 1835–50.
Chapman, Thomas. Letters and Journals, 1830–69.
Church Missionary Society Archives (microfilm).
Kemp, James. Journal, 1832–52.
Lee, John R. Historical Maps of the Bay of Islands.
Morgan, John. Letters and Journals, 1833–65.
Puckey, William G. Letters and Journals, 1831–68.

5. British Library, London

Gladstone Papers. Addit. MSS 44118, ff.172–3, ff.199–207; 44137, ff.228–385; 44263, ff.147–50; 44299, ff.1–196; 44321, ff.124–41; 44403, ff.110–11; 44531, ff.10,25,48,77; 44532, ff.37,50,54,148; 44533, f.79; 44534, f.70; 44535, f.48; 44466; 44798.
Owen, R. Correspondence. Addit. MSS 39954.
Peel Papers. Addit. MSS 40453, 40600.

6. Durham University Library

The Third Earl Grey Papers. Correspondence on New Zealand.

7. Hawke's Bay Museum, Napier

Colenso, William. Journal, 1839–40.
Colenso, William. Notebook, 1840.

8. Lambeth Palace Library, London

Tait Papers. 'Printed material relating to the English Visit', 1882/17.

9. National Archives, Wellington

British Resident Papers, 1832–40.
Governor New Zealand.
Internal Affairs Department (previously Colonial Secretary's Department).
Legislative Department.
Maori Affairs Department (previously Native Department).

10. Nottingham University: Department of Manuscripts

The fifth Duke of Newcastle. Papers. MS 9600–10, 11073, 11077–101, 11076, 11753.

11. Public Record Office, London

Colonial Office. Original Correspondence of the Secretary of State for Colonies, and Governors' dispatches, 1837–51 and various years thereafter.

12. Queen's College, Oxford

Derby Papers. Correspondence and official papers : items on NZ.

13. Rhodes House Library, Oxford

Aborigines' Protection Society. Papers. G98, 99.

14. Held privately

Mawhete, Rangi. Papers.
Taonui, Aperahama. Letters, 1863–82.
Wairua, Peta. Papers.

II PUBLISHED DOCUMENTS AND OFFICIAL PUBLICATIONS

Appendices to the Journals of the House of Representatives, NZ, 1858–1980, and various years.
Appendices to the Journals of the Legislative Council, NZ, 1858–1900, and various years.
Journals of the House of Representatives, NZ.
Journals of the Legislative Council, NZ.
Historical Records of Australia, Sydney, 1923, vols.16, 17.

Bibliography

Historical Records of New Zealand, 2 vols., ed. R. McNab, Wellington, 1914.
New Zealand Government Gazette (various).
New Zealand Parliamentary Debates, 1854–70, and various years.
Parliamentary Debates, Great Britain, 1840–70, 1885.
Parliamentary Papers, Great Britain. (Papers relating to NZ) 1836–86.

III NEWSPAPERS AND PERIODICALS

Aborigines' Friend or Colonial Intelligencer, 1847–71.
Maori Messenger, Te Karere Maori, 1842–63.
New Zealand Herald and Auckland Gazette, 1841–42.
New–Zealander, 1845–66.
Southern Cross, 1843–45, 1847–60.
Te Hokioi, 1861–63.
Te Paki o te Matariki, 1891–1902.
Te Pihoihoi Mokemoke, 1863.
Te Wananga, 1874–76.
The Times, 1840, 1843–48, 1860–67.
Waka Maori, 1873–77
Newspaper clippings in Auckland Public Library files and in a series, 'New Zealand Scrap Books', 1929–75.

IV BOOKS, ARTICLES AND PAMPHLETS

Aborigines' Protection Society, *Annual Reports*, London, 1838–46.
——, *Extracts from the Papers and Proceedings of the Society*, London, May 1839–September 1841.
——, *The New Zealand Government and the Native War of 1863–64, with especial reference to the confiscation of Native Lands, and the colonial ministry's defence of their war policy*, London, 1864.
——, *The New Zealand War of 1860*, London, 1861.
——, *Transactions of the Aborigines' Protection Society*, London, 1878–82, 1883–89.
Adams, Peter, *Fatal Necessity: British Intervention in New Zealand, 1830–47*, Auckland, 1977.
Alexandrowicz, C.H., *An Introduction to the History of the Law of Nations in the East Indies (16th, 17th, 18th centuries)*, Oxford, 1967.
——, *The European–African Confrontation: A Study in Treatymaking*, Leiden, 1973.
Andaya, L.Y., 'Treaty Conceptions and Misconceptions: A Case Study from South Sulawesi', Bijdragen, *Tot de Taal-, land-en volkenkunde*, Deel 134, 2e en 3e aflevering, The Hague, 1978.
Anglican Treaty of Waitangi Commission. *The Treaty of Waitangi: a discussion paper*, [Wellington?] 1985.
Auburn, F.M., 'Te Tiriti o Waitangi', *NZULR*, IV (1971), pp.309–11.
Awatere, Donna, 'Maori Sovereignty', *Broadsheet*, Auckland, June 1982–February 1983.
——, 'Maori Sovereignty', *Broadsheet*, Auckland, 1984.
Bagnall, A.G. and Petersen, G.C., *William Colenso, printer, missionary, botanist, explorer, politician; his life and journeys*, Wellington, 1948.
[Bell, F.D., Whitaker, F. and Gore Browne, T.], *Notes on Sir William Martin's Pamphlet entitled The Taranaki Question*, Auckland, 1861.
Belich, James, *The New Zealand Wars, and the Victorian Interpretation of Racial Conflict*, Auckland, 1986.
Bennett, F.A., *Te Keehi a te Arawa mo nga moana, me te whaiwhai mo te mana o te tiriti o Waitangi*, Rotorua, 1912.
Best, A.D.W., *The Journal of Ensign Best, 1837–1842*, ed. Nancy Taylor, Wellington, 1966.
Binney, Judith, 'Christianity and the Maoris to 1840; a Comment', *NZJH*, III, 2 (1969), pp.143–65.
Boese, Kay, *Tides of History*, Whangarei, 1977.
Bowden, Ross, 'Tapu and Mana : ritual authority and political power in traditional Maori society', *The Journal of Pacific History*, XIV, 1 (1979), pp.50–61.
Bright, John, *Handbook for Emigrants and others*, London, 1841
Brown, William, *New Zealand and its Aborigines*, London, 1845.
Buddle, Thomas, *The Maori King Movement*, Auckland, 1860.
Buick, T. Lindsay, *New Zealand's First War; or the rebellion of Hone Heke*, Wellington, 1926.
——, *Waitangi: Ninety-Four Years After*, New Plymouth, 1934.
——, *The Treaty of Waitangi; or How New Zealand became a British Colony*, 3rd ed., New Plymouth, 1936 (Capper reprint 1976).
Bunbury, Thomas, *Reminiscences of a Veteran*, 3 vols., London, 1861.
Busby, James, *Authentic Information relative to New South Wales and New Zealand*, London, 1832.
——, *Our Colonial Empire and the case of New Zealand*, London, 1866.
——, *Remarks upon a Pamphlet entitled 'The Taranaki Question, by Sir William Martin'*, Auckland, 1860.
Carleton, Hugh, *The Life of Henry Williams, Archdeacon of Waimate*, 2 vols., Auckland, 1874.
Carter, Betty, 'The Incorporation of the Treaty of Waitangi into Municipal Law', *AULR*, IV, 1 (1980), pp.1–18.

Bibliography

Catholic Commission for Evangelisation, Justice and Development, *New Hope for our Society*, Wellington, 1984.

Chamerovzow, L.A., *The New Zealand Question and the Rights of Aborigines*, London, 1848.

Clarke, George [Sen.], *Remarks upon a pamphlet by James Busby ... on The Taranaki Question, and the Treaty of Waitangi, by Sir William Martin*, Auckland, 1861 (reprint, Auckland, 1923).

Clarke, George [Jun.], *Notes on early life in New Zealand*, Hobart, 1903.

Coleman, J. Noble, *A Memoir of the Rev. Richard Davis*, London, 1865.

Colenso, William, *Fifty Years Ago in New Zealand*, Napier, 1888.

——, *The Authentic and Genuine History of the Signing of the Treaty of Waitangi*, Wellington, 1890 (Capper reprint, 1971).

Cruden, Alexander, *Complete Concordance to the Old and New Testaments with notes and biblical proper names*, revised ed., London, 1954.

Cruise, Richard A., *Journal of a Ten Months' Residence in New Zealand*, 2nd ed., London, 1824 (Capper reprint, 1974).

Curtin, Philip D., ed., *Imperialism*, New York, 1971.

Dalton, B.J., *War and Politics in New Zealand 1855–1870*, Sydney, 1967.

Dewes, Koro, 'Waitangi Day 1968: Some Food for Thought', *Comment*, no.35, (June 1968), pp.12–14.

Earle, Augustus, *A Narrative of a Nine Months' Residence in New Zealand: Journal of a residence in Tristan da Cunha*, London, 1832, ed. E.H. McCormick, Oxford, 1966.

Eldridge, Colin C., *Victorian Imperialism*, London, 1978.

Evison, Harry C, *Ngai Tahu Land Rights and the Crown Pastoral Lease Lands in the South Island*, Christchurch, 1986.

Facsimiles of the Declaration of Independence and the Treaty of Waitangi, Wellington, 1877 (reprint Government Printer, 1976).

FitzRoy, Robert, *Remarks on New Zealand*, London, 1846.

FitzRoy, Robert, [P. Parker King and Charles Darwin], *Narrative of the Surveying Voyages of His Majesty's Ships Adventure and Beagle, between the years 1826 and 1836*, 3 vols., London, 1839.

Fox, W., *A Chapter in the history of New Zealand : The Treaty of Waitangi*, London, 1883.

Gorst, J.E., *The Maori King*, London, 1864, ed. Keith Sinclair, London, 1959.

Hadfield, Octavius, *One of England's Little Wars*, Otaki, 1860.

——, *Recent Outbreak at Taranaki, New Zealand*, [Otaki?], 1860.

——, *A Sequel to 'One of England's Little Wars'*, London, 1861.

——, *The Second Year of One of England's Little Wars*, London, 1861.

Hall, T.D.H., *Captain Joseph Nias and the Treaty of Waitangi: A vindication*, Wellington, 1938.

Hardy, Charles, *Te Tiriti o Waitangi: He Karo Whakaora mo nga tangata Maori*, (A defence for the Maori people), Auckland, 1887.

Haughey, E.J., 'Maori Claims to the Lakes, River Beds and the Foreshore', *NZULR*, 2 (1966), pp.29–42.

Henderson, J. McLeod, *Ratana. The Man, the Church, the Political Movement*, Wellington, 1963.

Hinsley, F.H., *Sovereignty*, London, 1966.

Hohepa, P.W., 'Waitangi: A Promise or a Betrayal', *Occasional Papers in Race Relations*, no.2, Wellington, 1971.

Jacobs, Wilbur, R., *Dispossessing the American Indian. Indians and Whites on the Colonial Frontier*, New York, 1972.

Johnson, Ralph W. and E. Susan Crystal, 'Indians and Equal Protection', *Washington Law Review*, LIV, 3 (1979), pp.587–631.

Johnston, M. Justice, *Notes on Maori Matters*, Auckland, 1860.

Jones, D.V., *Licence for Empire: Colonialism by Treaty in Early America*, Chicago, 1982.

Keene, Florence, (ed.), *By this we conquer: Richard Davis, 1790–1863*, Whangarei, 1974.

Keith, K.J., 'International Law and New Zealand Municipal Law', *The A.G. Davis Essays in Law*, ed. J.F. Northey, London, 1965, pp.130–48.

Kemp, Henry Tacy, *Revised narrative of incidents and events in the early colonizing history of New Zealand, from 1840 to 1880*, Auckland, 1901.

King, Michael, 'Some attitudes to Maori Documents', *Tihe Mauri Ora*, ed. Michael King, Wellington, 1978.

Ko te pukapuka a te Wherowhero Potatau ki a te Kuini, me te whakahoki mai o te Kuini ki a ia, Auckland, 1922.

Ko te Pukapuka o te Tiriti o Kohimarama, Orakei, Auckland, 1889.

Ko te tiriti i tuhia ki Waitangi 1840, Auckland, 1922.

Ko te Tiriti o Waitangi: He Karo Whakaora o nga tangata Maori, Auckland, 1922.

Lindley, M.F., *The Acquisition and Government of Backward Territory in International Law*, London, 1926.

McHugh, Paul, 'Aboriginal title in N.Z. Courts', *Canterbury Law Review*, II (1984), p.235.

——, 'The legal status of Maori fishing rights in tidal waters', *Victoria University of Wellington Law Review*, XIV (1984), p.247.

McKean, W.A., ed., *Essays on Race Relations and the Law in New Zealand*, Wellington, 1971.

——, 'The Treaty of Waitangi Revisited', *W.P. Morrell: A Tribute*, ed. G.A. Wood and P.S. O'Connor, Dunedin, 1973, pp.237–49.

Bibliography

McKenzie, D.F., *Oral culture literacy and print in early New Zealand: The Treaty of Waitangi*, Wellington, 1985.

McLintock, A.H., *Crown Colony Government in New Zealand*, Wellington, 1958.

McNab, Robert, *The Old Whaling Days: A History of Southern New Zealand from 1830–1840*, Christchurch, 1913.

'Maori Claims to Certain North Island Lakes', *Te Wananga*, I, 2 (December 1929).

Markham, Edward, *New Zealand or recollections of it*, ed. E.H. McCormick, Wellington, 1963.

Marsden, Samuel, *The Letters and Journals of Samuel Marsden, 1765–1838*, ed. J.R. Elder, Dunedin, 1932.

Marshall, William Barrett, *A Personal Narrative of Two Visits to New Zealand in His Majesty's Ship Alligator, A.D. 1834*, London, 1836.

Martin, William, *Ko nga Tikanga a te Pakeha*, Auckland, 1845.

——, *England and the New Zealanders*, Auckland, 1847.

——, *The Taranaki Question*, Auckland, 1860.

Mathew, Felton, *The Founding of New Zealand: The Journals of Felton Mathew and his wife, 1840–1847*, ed. J. Rutherford, Auckland, 1840.

Mawhete, Rangi, *The Maori Rights under 'The Constitution Act, 1852': A Review*, Palmerston North, [1925?].

Mead, S.M., 'Maori–Pakeha Relationships: An Obstacle Race', *Turnbull Winter Lectures*, Wellington, 1982.

Meath, Earl of, 'A Maori Meeting', *Nineteenth Century*, XXXI, (May 1892), pp.778–86.

Mellor, George R., *British Imperial Trusteeship 1783–1850*, London, 1951.

Miller, John, *Early Victorian New Zealand*, London, 1958.

Molloy, A.P., 'The Non-Treaty of Waitangi', *NZLJ*, no.9, (May 1971), pp.193–7.

National Council of Churches (Church and Society Commission), *What happened at Waitangi in 1983*, Auckland 1983.

——, *Waitangi, 1984 – a turning point?*, Auckland, 1984.

——, *The Pakeha and the Treaty: Signposts*, Auckland, 1986.

Native Meetings at Wellington, 1896, Wellington, 1896.

Nga Korero o te hui i tu ki te Kuiti, Otorohanga, 1916.

Notes of Meetings, Wellington, 1900.

Newbury, Colin, 'Resistance and Collaboration in French Polynesia: The Tahitian War: 1844–7', *JPS*, LXXXII, 1 (1973), pp.5–27.

Nga Kaupapa i whakaotia e te hui i tu ki te Kauhanganui i te 26 o nga ra o Hune 1948, Hamilton, [1948?].

Nga Korero o te Hui o te Whakakotahitanga i tu ki te Tiriti o Waitangi, Aperira 14, 1892, Auckland, 1892.

Ngata, Apirana, *The Treaty of Waitangi: An explanation*, trans. M.R. Jones, Wellington, 1963.

——, *Te Tiriti o Waitangi: He Whakamarama*, Hastings, 1922.

Nicholas, John Liddiard, *Narrative of a Voyage to New Zealand*, 2 vols., London, 1817.

Oliver, W.H. with B.R. Williams, eds., *The Oxford History of New Zealand*, Oxford and Wellington, 1981.

Orange, Claudia, 'The Covenant of Kohimarama: A ratification of the Treaty of Waitangi', *NZJH*, XIV, 1 (1980), pp.61–82.

——, 'An Exercise in Maori Autonomy: The Rise and Demise of the Maori War Effort Organisation', *NZJH*, XXI, 1(1987) pp.156–72.

Owens, J.M.R, 'Christianity and the Maori to 1840', *NZJH*, II, 1 (1968), pp.18–40.

——, 'The Treaty of Waitangi', *Wesley Historical Society Journal* (NZ), no.49, 1986, pp.17–40.

Paremata Maori o Nui Tireni, Auckland, 1895.

Paremata Maori o Niu Tireni, Otaki, 1892.

Parsonson, A.R., 'The Expansion of a Competitive Society : A Study in Nineteenth-Century Maori History', *NZJH*, XIV, 1 (1980), pp.45–60.

Pharazyn, Robert, 'Two Letters from the *Evening Press*, January 3 and 12, 1892', (reprint), 1892.

Polack, J.S., *New Zealand : Being a narrative of travels and adventures during a residence in that country between the years 1831 and 1837*, 2 vols., London, 1837.

Pompallier, J.B.F., *Early History of the Catholic Church in Oceania*, Auckland, 1888.

Pukapuka–Tauira, Auckland, 1922–23, (reprint from *Te Manukura*).

Ramsden, Eric, *Busby of Waitangi, H. M.'s Resident at New Zealand 1833–40*, Wellington, 1942.

Reed, Vernon, H., *The Gift of Waitangi*, Wellington, 1957.

Ritchie, James, *One Nation or Two?*, Wellington, 1971.

Ross, J.O., 'Busby and the Declaration of Independence', *NZJH*, XIV, 1 (1980), pp.83–89.

Ross, R.M., 'Te Tiriti o Waitangi: texts and translations', *NZJH*, VI, 2 (1972), pp.129–57.

Rough, D., 'Early Days of Auckland', reprint from *New Zealand Herald*, January 11–25, 1896.

Runanga o Waitangi, Ngaruawahia, 1984.

Rusden, G.W., *Aureretanga: Groans of the Maoris*, London, 1888.

Rutherford, James, *Hone Heke's rebellion, 1844–1846: An episode in the establishment of British rule in New Zealand*, Auckland, 1947.

——, *The Treaty of Waitangi and the Acquisition of British Sovereignty in New Zealand*, Auckland, 1949.

——, *Sir George Grey K.C.B. 1812–1898: A Study in Colonial Government*, London, 1961.

Scholefield, Guy H., 'Maori Sovereignty: The Deputation to London', *United Empire*, V, new series, (1914), pp.584–7.

——, *Captain William Hobson, first governor of New Zealand*, London, 1934.
Scholefield, Guy H., (ed.), *The Richmond—Atkinson Papers*, 2 vols., Wellington, 1960.
Sewell, Henry, *The New Zealand Native Rebellion: Letter to Lord Lyttelton*, Auckland, 1864 (Hocken reprint 1974).
——, *The Journal of Henry Sewell*, 1853–7, 2 vols., ed. W. David McIntyre, Christchurch, 1980.
Sinclair, Keith, *The Origins of the Maori Wars*, 2nd ed., Wellington, 1961.
Sorrenson, M.P.K., 'Land Purchase Methods and their Effect on Maori Population', 1865–1901, *JPS*, LXV, 3 (1956), pp.183–99.
——, 'Colonial Rule and Local Response: Maori Responses to European Domination in New Zealand since 1860', *The Journal of Imperial and Commonwealth History*, IV, 2 (1976), pp.127–37.
Speeches by the Premier, The Rt. Hon. R.J. Seddon, and Rangatiras or Chiefs of the Maori Race, Wellington, 1897.
Sutton, J.D., 'The Treaty of Waitangi today', *Victoria University of Wellington Law Review*, XI, 1 (1981), pp.17–40.
Sweetman, Edward, *The Unsigned New Zealand Treaty*, Melbourne, 1939.
Taiwhanga, Sydney David, *Proposals of Mr Sydney David Taiwhanga, M.H.R., for the Colonization and Settlement of Maori Lands*, Wellington, 1888.
Tapp, E.J., *Early New Zealand: A dependency of New South Wales, 1788–1841*, Melbourne, 1958.
Te Hikoi ki Waitangi, 1984, Auckland, 1984.
Te Huihuinga o etahi o nga rangatira o te motu nei ki Kohimarama, 1889, [Auckland], 1889.
Te Huihuinga ki Waharoa, April 7, 1910, Hamilton, 1910.
Te Huihuinga ki Te Au-o-Waikato, September 13, 1910, Hamilton, 1910.
Te Hui ki Parawera, Morrinsville, 1916.
'The Ngaitahu Trust Board', *Te Wananga*, I, 1 (September 1929), pp.31–32.
The Treaty of Waitangi and its interpreters, 1 July 1861, Occasional Papers, Auckland, 1861.
The Treaty of Waitangi: Its origins and significance, Wellington, 1972.
Treaty of Waitangi Hui, Whangarei, 1985.
Von Haast, H.F., 'The Treaty of Waitangi: Its Consideration by the Courts', *NZLJ*, X, 2 (1934), pp.20–21.
——, 'The Effects of the Treaty of Waitangi on Subsequent Legislation', *NZLJ*, X, 2 (1934), pp.13–15,25–27.
Waitangi Action Committee, *Remember Waitangi*, Auckland, 1982.
Wake, C.H., 'George Clarke and the Government of the Maoris, 1840–45', *Historical Studies, Australia and New Zealand*, X, 39 (1962), pp.339–56.
Ward, Alan, *A Show of Justice: Racial 'amalgamation' in nineteenth century New Zealand*, Auckland, 1973.
Ward, John, *British Policy in the South Pacific* (1786–1893), Sydney, 1948.
——, *Empire in the Antipodes: The British in Australasia, 1840–1860*, London, 1966.
Wards, Ian, *The Shadow of the Land*, Wellington, 1968.
Wesleyan Missionary Committee, *Correspondence between the Wesleyan Missionary Committee and Earl Grey on the apprehended infringement of the Treaty of Waitangi*, [London], 1848.
——, *Correspondence between the Wesleyan Missionary Committee and Sir James Pakington*, London, 1852.
'Who stole Waitangi Day?', *Thursday*, Auckland, 31 January 1974, pp.26–29.
Wilkes, Charles, *Narrative of the United States Exploring Expedition During the Years 1838–1842*, 2 vols., London, 1845.
Williams, E. Trevor, 'The Treaty of Waitangi', *History*, new series, XXV, 99 (1940), pp.237–51.
——, 'James Stephen and British Intervention in New Zealand', *Journal of Modern History*, XIII, 1 (1941), pp.19–35.
Williams, Henry, *The Early Journals of Henry Williams, 1826–40*, Ed. L.M. Rogers, Christchurch, 1961.
Williams, Herbert W., *A Bibliography of Printed Maori to 1900 and supplement*, Wellington, 1975, (reprint).
Williams, John A., *Politics of the New Zealand Maori: Protest and Co-operation, 1891–1909*, Auckland, 1969.
Williams, Jeanine, *Frederick Weld: A Political Biography*, Auckland, 1983.
Williams, T.C., *The Manawatu Purchase completed, the Treaty of Waitangi broken*, London, 1868.
Williams, William and Jane, *Turanga Journals, 1840–1850*, ed. Frances Porter, Wellington, 1974.
Wright, Harrison M., *New Zealand, 1769–1840: Early years of Western contact*, Cambridge, (Mass.), 1959.
Yate, William, *An Account of New Zealand and of the Formation and Progress of the Church Missionary Society's Mission in the Northern Island*, 2nd ed., London, 1835.

V(a) UNPUBLISHED THESES, RESEARCH ESSAYS

Brookfield, F.M., 'The Constitution in 1985: The Search for Legitimacy', unpublished paper, September 1985.
Brazendale, G., 'John Whiteley, land, sovereignty and the Anglo-Maori wars', MA, Auckland (1976).
Cairns, H.A.C., 'Race and cultural attitudes of the British precursors of Imperialism in Central Africa, 1840–90', D Phil., Oxford (1962).
Cole, S., 'The Hawke's Bay repudiation movement', MA, Massey (1977).
Eldridge, Colin C., 'The Colonial Policy of the 5th Duke of Newcastle, 1859–64', PhD, Nottingham (1966).
Hackshaw, F., 'The Recognition of Native Customary Land Rights at Common Law', LL D thesis (Auckland), 1984.

Bibliography

Lange, S.M., 'Baron Charles de Thierry: Utopian coloniser', MA, Auckland (1976).
Love, R. Ngatata, 'Policies of frustration: the growth of Maori politics: The Ratana–Labour Era', PhD, Victoria University of Wellington (1977).
McRae, P.J., 'Participation: Native Committees (1883) and Papatupu Block Committees (1900) in Tai Tokerau', MA, Auckland (1981).
Madden, A. F., 'The Attitudes of the Evangelicals to the Empire and Imperial Problems', D Phil., Oxford (1950).
Molloy, J.S., 'The era of civilization: British policy for the Indians of Canada, 1830–1860', D Phil., Oxford (1978).
Orange, Claudia, 'A kind of equality: Labour and the Maori people 1935–1949', MA, Auckland (1977).
Orange, Claudia. 'The Treaty of Waitangi: A study of its making, interpretation and role in New Zealand History', PhD, Auckland (1984).
Owens, J.M.R., 'The Wesleyan Mission to New Zealand 1819–40', PhD, Victoria University of Wellington (1969).
Parsonson, A., 'Te Mana o te Kingitanga Maori: A study of Waikato–Maniapoto relations during the struggle for the King Country 1878–1884', MA, Canterbury (1975).
Parsonson, Ann R., 'He Whenua Te Utu (The Payment will be land)', PhD, Canterbury (1978).
Renwick, W.L., 'Self-government and protection: A study of Stephen's two cardinal points of policy in their bearing upon constitutional development in New Zealand in the years 1837–1867', MA, Victoria University of Wellington (1962).
Sellers, G.J., 'Edward Cardwell at the Colonial Office, 1864–66: Some aspects of his policy and ideas', B Litt., Oxford (1958).
Shawcross, K., 'Maoris of the Bay of Islands 1769–1840: A study of changing Maori responses to European Contact', MA, Auckland (1967).
Sinclair, K., 'The Aborigines' Protection Society and New Zealand: A Study in Nineteenth Century Opinion', MA, University of NZ, Auckland (1946).
Turner, Phillip, 'The Politics of Neutrality: The Catholic Mission and the Maori 1838–1870', MA, Auckland (1986).
Wigglesworth, R.P., 'The New Zealand Timber and Flax Trade 1769–1840', Massey (1981).
Williams, David, 'The use of law in the process of colonisation: An historical and comparative study of Tanzania and New Zealand', PhD, Dar es Salaam (1984).

V(b)   UNPUBLISHED PAPERS

Barber, L. 'The Return of the King', Radio NZ Concert Programme, 9 July 1981. (t.s.)
Couch, Ben. Speech notes for Waitangi Day, 6 February 1980. (t.s.)
Holyoake, Keith. 'Waitangi Day 1979'. (Printed address)
Department of Justice. Interdepartmental Committee on Maori Fishing Rights : First Report, November 1985.
McHugh, Paul. 'Maori fishing rights and the North American Indian', unpublished paper, 1984.
New Zealand Maori Council. Submission, 5 October 1971, to the Minister of Maori Affairs and the Minister of Justice on the Treaty of Waitangi and parts of the current statutory law in contravention thereof. (t.s.)
New Zealand Maori Council and New Zealand Maori Women's Welfare League. Submission to the Select Committee, Human Rights Commission Bill [1976?]. (t.s.)
Waitangi Tribunal. 'Report . . . in relation to fishing grounds in the Waitara district', March 1983.
Waitangi Tribunal. 'Finding . . . on the Kaituna claim', November 1984.
Waitangi Tribunal. 'Finding . . . on the Manukau claim', July 1985.
Waitangi Tribunal. 'Finding . . . relating to Te Reo Maori', April 1986.

INDEX

Note: *passim* = scattered throughout the pages indicated.
 et passim = explanatory first reference or references on pages indicated, and scattered throughout
  the pages thereafter.

Index

Index